CHINESE ECONOMIC STATECRAFT

CHINESE ECONOMIC STATECRAFT

Commercial Actors, Grand Strategy, and State Control

William J. Norris

CORNELL UNIVERSITY PRESS   ITHACA AND LONDON

First published 2016 by Cornell University Press

Printed in the United States of America

Library of Congress Cataloging-in-Publication Data

Names: Norris, William J. (Economist), author.
Title: Chinese economic statecraft : commercial actors, grand strategy, and state
    control / William J. Norris.
Description: Ithaca ; London : Cornell University Press, 2016. | ©2016 |
    Includes bibliographical references and index.
Identifiers: LCCN 2015037800 | ISBN 9780801454493 (cloth : alk. paper)
Subjects: LCSH: China—Economic policy—2000– | China—Economic
    conditions—2000– | China—Economic relations—Taiwan.
Classification: LCC HC427.95 .N67 2016 | DDC 330.951—dc23
LC record available at http://lccn.loc.gov/2015037800

Cornell University Press strives to use environmentally responsible suppliers and materials to the fullest extent possible in the publishing of its books. Such materials include vegetable-based, low-VOC inks and acid-free papers that are recycled, totally chlorine-free, or partly composed of nonwood fibers. For further informa- tion, visit our website at www.cornellpress.cornell.edu.

Cloth printing   10 9 8 7 6 5 4 3 2 1

For Lima

Contents

Acknowledgments

When writing a book, one incurs a good deal of debt: intellectual, personal, and professional. The scale of this debt leaves in doubt whether it can ever be fully repaid. Much like the debt held by special-purpose municipal trust vehicles in China following the 2008 financial crisis, providers of this assistance might have to content themselves with a fractional repayment. Although inadequate to wholly repay the principal, these acknowledgments seek to cover at least some of the interest.

A number of colleagues and institutions were instrumental both in facilitating the Chinese fieldwork as well as providing helpful feedback on the manuscript. The Scowcroft Institute of International Affairs generously funded an Ansary Conference on Chinese Economic Statecraft, which brought together leading scholars on the subject to closely read the manuscript. Particular thanks go to Thomas Moore, Norrin Ripsman, and the other workshop participants for their detailed comments on the manuscript. This finished product's design, architecture, and content owes a good deal to their efforts. I have also been fortunate to be surrounded by terrific colleagues at the Bush School of Government and Public Service, who often acted as a valuable sounding board. In addition to constructive marginalia and productive whiteboard sessions with individual colleagues across Texas A&M University, the biweekly convening of the "Writers' Bloc" of Bush School junior faculty provided a collegial small group setting in which to further refine this work. My work has also been inspired by the A&M students' sense of service and their dedication to helping others. Nowhere do I see that more directly than in the Bush School classrooms, where I am honored to teach and mentor members of the next generation of national servants. Several of these, like Kevin Allshouse and Eric Gomez, were research assistants for portions of this work. Of course, I will always be deeply indebted to my own mentors at MIT. This project was originally inspired by my work with Dick Samuels, Barry Posen, Taylor Fravel, Ed Steinfeld, and Ken Oye there. My time in Cambridge (especially with MIT's Security Studies Program and the MIT Security Studies Work in Progress Group) helped incubate many of the theoretical ideas that would eventually find their way into this book. Early conversations and input from David Baldwin, Joe Fewsmith, Jonathan Kirshner, Joe Nye, and Bob Ross proved particularly helpful. My time with the Princeton-Harvard China and the World Program provided the opportunity to write the initial draft of the book manuscript. Special thanks belong to Tom Christensen and Iain Johnston for leading that effort to foster a new generation of emerging China scholars committed to bridging the academic stovepipes between China studies and the field of international relations. Theirs is important work that produces cross-fertilized insights for both subfields. The early versions of the manuscript benefited immensely from comments by Scott Kastner, Yu Zheng, Todd Hall, and other participants in the China and the World Program. I also received helpful comments from Kyle Jaros, Jeehye Kim, Sun Taiyi, and other members of the Cambridge China Politics Research Workshop at the Fairbank Center of Harvard University, an inspiring collection of the next generation of China scholars committed to conducting rigorous fieldwork in China. The Fairbank Center at Harvard has proven to be an inexhaustible source of mentorship, materials, training, and feedback for my work in many guises. In particular, the Fung Library (and its most valuable resource, Nancy Hearst) deserves special appreciation. A good deal of the book's fieldwork was generously supported by a World Politics and Statecraft Fellowship I received from the Smith Richardson Foundation. The Bradley Fellowship also facilitated a significant portion of the Taiwan fieldwork for this book. I am deeply grateful to both. In addition to these above-named individuals and institutions, I am also thankful for the assistance of several others whose resources, time, information, contacts, services, skills, and knowledge helped make this project possible. Unfortunately, sensitivities surrounding their contributions require that they remain anonymous. Also falling in the realm of anonymous gratitude were the constructive and thoughtful external reviews of the manuscript elicited by Cornell University Press.

Roger Haydon, Emily Powers, Ange Romeo-Hall, Drew Bryan (who deserves special recognition for his tireless attention to detail and patient copyediting), and the entire acquisition, editorial, and production team at Cornell University Press have been terrific partners. From the very beginning, I have been deeply impressed with their professionalism and dedication. Institutions such as this sustain the academy with their irreplaceable contributions to knowledge. Roger, in particular, deserves much gratitude for his helpful stewardship of this manuscript and its jejune, first-time author through the labyrinthine academic publishing process. One could not hope for a more expert (or better-spirited) Sherpa for this journey.

Finally, I would like to thank my family. Without their loving support, this work would not have been possible. In particular, my wife, Jen, has graciously endured extended trips abroad, weekends at the office, three household relocations, working vacations, and countless other selfless sacrifices for the sake of these pages. I am deeply appreciative for all that she does and I love her dearly.

CHINESE ECONOMIC STATECRAFT

OIL, IRON, MANGOES, AND CASH

"It can be a plot for a novel."

This was how the man responsible for China's largest overseas purchase of stock described the events surrounding the Aluminum Corporation of China (Chinalco)'s "Midnight Raid," a successful, after-market-hours acquisition of 9 percent of Rio Tinto's stock on the London Stock Exchange. The operation was conducted in January 2008 to block the consolidation of global iron ore supplies, which would have left 70 percent of one of China's most strategic imports in the hands of two foreign suppliers. Such an outcome was unacceptable to the Chinese government, and it acted deftly through commercial actors to stop it. Yet in Sudan, similar Chinese commercial actors repeatedly acted in ways that directly undercut the government's efforts to present China as a responsible stakeholder. Chinese national oil companies had taken the initiative to venture abroad in the 1990s. By the early 2000s in Sudan, they were providing foreign investment to a despotic regime, and Chinese economic actors supplied the regime with weapons that were used to carry out atrocities. At the same time, Beijing was expending considerable diplomatic capital to convince the international community that a "rising China" was a responsible state. Both cases centered on Chinese state-owned enterprises (SOEs) in extractive resources. Both firms were top Chinese companies venturing abroad in highly consolidated industries. But in one case, China was able to wield its economic power to advance its strategic interests, while in the other the SOE actively undermined China's diplomatic efforts. Why the variation?

These diverging outcomes are not limited to China's state-owned enterprises. On several occasions, Beijing has tried to lean on private Taiwanese investors in mainland China in order to limit the electoral success of proindependence candidates on Taiwan. These efforts have had the opposite effect; in both the 2000 and 2004 national elections such activity galvanized domestic support for proindependence sentiment on Taiwan. Observers might conclude that toying with economics is not an effective tool (perhaps even counterproductive) for influencing the independence issue on Taiwan. Yet since at least 2008, China's economic statecraft has significantly reduced the friction across the Taiwan Strait. Taiwanese independence has been largely eclipsed as an electoral issue. For the foreseeable future, de jure independence for Taiwan is off the table, and no proindependence candidate seems electable in Taiwan. Recent candidates from the DPP (the party traditionally in favor of independence) have gone to great lengths to reassure voters that they would not pursue independence. This outcome is largely the result of increasing economic ties between Taiwan and mainland China, ties the initial rationale of which was to generate this precise result. But once again, we are faced with a perplexing outcome: why was mainland China unable to use economic statecraft to limit support for Taiwanese independence in the early 2000s but had marginalized the independence issue only a few years later? In both instances, Beijing was working through private (not state-owned) enterprises; China's economic statecraft is not limited to the realm of state-owned firms. Also, in both cases, the commercial actors were Taiwanese (as opposed to mainland) firms, illustrating that Beijing's use of economic power is not confined to Chinese companies venturing abroad. The two cases have opposite outcomes but share many features in common: same geography, same strategic context, same historical context, same firm nationality, same private sector orientation, and same political leanings (i.e., sympathetic toward Taiwanese independence). Despite these similarities the outcomes were different. Why?

Why is China sometimes able to marshal its economic power for strategic objectives and sometimes not? How should policy makers and analysts understand these dynamics? Current discussions of China's economic statecraft have largely been framed in terms of whether China has been or will be able to use economic power to achieve its strategic objectives.[1] Much of this work tends to argue one of two positions. One position is that China's growing economic clout and the dominant role of the state in occupying the "commanding heights" of the domestic economic landscape suggest that China is indeed an emerging, mercantilist juggernaut of twenty-first-century economic statecraft. The other view is that the growing complexity and modernization that has underpinned China's economic liberalization carries intrinsically limiting constraints on any meaningful coordination of China's economic power. The Chinese state is simply too weak to effectively direct and control its growing economic clout.

I suggest that the empirical reality encompasses both sides of this debate. At times, China seems incapable of marshaling its economic power to achieve strategic objectives. At others, China's economic activity has advanced the nation's foreign policy goals. A complex reality characterizes China's strategic use of economics to pursue its national objectives, and framing the issue as an either-or question does not capture the rich variation found in recent history. Rather than argue that China is or is not able to employ economic means in pursuit of national objectives, I ask what the conditions are under which China is more successful or less successful in its pursuit of economic statecraft. One of my central findings is that economic actors play a pivotal role in both successful and unsuccessful episodes of Chinese economic statecraft. As we shall see, China's ability to direct the activities of these economic actors is essential for economic statecraft.

Security analysts have focused intently on developing our understanding of the military dimensions of grand strategy: the manner in which force is applied, conditions under which military power is most effective, its limitations, etc. But we do not understand the economic elements of national power to the same degree. This state of affairs persists even though militarized conflict is actually quite a rare event in the international system. In the day-to-day conduct of international affairs, states more frequently rely on diplomatic and economic levers of national power rather than military tools to pursue their objectives. How should we understand the relationships among grand strategy, security, international economic activity, and the commercial actors that conduct those interactions?

In this book, I explore how China uses economics as a tool of national power in the twenty-first century. I am hesitant to generalize beyond China, although many of the conceptual frameworks should be able to apply to other states' strategic use of economic power as well. For example, the rise of the BRIC nations (Brazil, Russia, India, and China), with their legacies of mixed domestic political economies, prompts several interesting questions regarding the manner and limitations of using economic power to achieve strategic and security goals. I address these broader questions through the lens of China.

Although I focus on China's ability to control the behavior of commercial actors, my overall purpose is to take a close look at Chinese economic statecraft to see what it is, how it works, and why it is more or less effective. Economic statecraft can be broadly understood as state manipulation of international economic activities for strategic purposes.[2] To do this effectively, states must first be able to control the behavior of commercial actors that conduct the vast majority of international economic activity. This prerequisite is often overlooked in studies of economic statecraft. I explore economic statecraft in the context of contemporary Chinese grand strategy to show how China uses firms to pursue its strategic goals and to show when the Chinese state can and cannot control the behavior of commercial actors. That knowledge, in turn, enhances our understanding of how states in general use economic tools to advance national power.

So how much do we know about Chinese economic statecraft? Although there is a general understanding that Chinese economic statecraft is an important phenomenon, we still know very little. The current discussions tend to polarize. For example, a widely held assumption about China's growing economic power holds that because China is a communist country in which the state has direct ownership of a significant portion of the productive economic assets, naturally the state can direct this economic capacity to strategically advance political, rather than purely commercial, goals.[3] According to this perspective, rising China is an economic juggernaut[4] and there is no need to problematize the issue of state control because state control of economic actors is a given in a communist nation. Indeed, there is something appealing about this logic that resonates with preconceptions of a Cold War–style command economy. The reality on the ground, however, suggests that such state control may not be unwavering. Indeed, the empirical reality of China's partial reforms has generated considerable leeway for some economic actors that, at times, propels them along a trajectory at odds with the state's objectives.

Thus, at the opposite extreme from the "economic juggernaut" perspective, we find the notion that modern China is such a complex entity that any semblance of a grand strategy is impossible; the state is simply never able to marshal its economic power in a strategic way.[5] Again, the evidence suggests a more nuanced approach may be warranted. The reality in today's China is that sometimes the state is able to direct the behavior of economic actors and thus shape the associated security externalities; on other occasions, the state is unable to control them. We need a theory of Chinese economic statecraft that accounts for this empirical complexity.

Economics and Grand Strategy

Despite a long-standing recognition of the organic relationship between economics and national security, the study of the economic aspects of grand strategy remains underdeveloped. Relatively little work has focused on the microfoundations of precisely *how* states might mobilize their economic interaction to further security goals. Specifically, the field suffers from too little research on the economic mechanisms states use to pursue their grand strategy under conditions of modern globalization.[6] As a result, contemporary analyses of grand strategy remain incomplete. One reason for this underdevelopment may be found in a division between security studies and international political economy. As a result of these disciplinary barriers, we are left with incomplete treatments both of the economic elements of grand strategy and of the strategic aspects of economic interaction. Security studies often concern themselves almost exclusively with military matters and pay little attention to the economic dimensions of grand strategy.[7] Yet economic tools may also be used to achieve strategic national objectives.

Indeed, as China pursues a "peaceful development" (formerly "peaceful rise")[8] grand strategy, economic power promises to be a more and more attractive alternative to military force. In addition, China's experience using economics to improve relations with many of its neighbors suggests that this economically oriented "peaceful development" approach produces favorable results. In contrast, China's occasional attempts to take a more "assertive" position that relies on militarized tools of national power have proved counterproductive for China's efforts to reassure the international community. The aggressive challenge to the USNS *Impeccable*, submarine patrols that violate Japan's territorial waters, and escalating territorial disputes in the South and East China Seas are recent examples of China's use of military tools that have stoked regional fears about growing Chinese power. Ultimately, such behavior provided a regional context that supported the American "rebalance" to Asia. Military power can thus be strategically counterproductive for China. At the same time, China's economic success enables it to use economic rather than military tools to pursue its national interests. This book links China's domestic political economy with China's use of economic power as a foreign policy tool.

China's Economic Statecraft

Surprisingly little work has been done to develop a systematic account of Chinese economic statecraft. China's rise has attracted considerable attention, and some of this work has recognized the increasingly sophisticated nature of China's foreign policy, but we do not yet understand the economic dimension of China's foreign policy. A small but growing body of literature focuses on China's use of economics in its foreign policy; that is the good news. The bad news is that while these works do occasionally recognize the salience of state-firm interactions, they still lack a robust way to generalize these dynamics. They mirror the shortcomings of the general literature on economic statecraft in international relations, namely an undertheorized role for commercial actors and their relationship to the strategic goals of the nation-state.

Works on China's economic statecraft can be categorized into two types. The first starts from the perspective of China's grand strategy. For example, Russell Ong has highlighted the influential role economics plays in China's grand strategy.[9] Although Ong notes the centrality of economics, he also calls for deeper analysis of the largely unexplored economic dimension of grand strategy. David Lampton's *The Three Faces of Chinese Power* also calls attention not only to China's growing military capabilities but also to China's growing "soft power."[10] He parses China's power into its coercive, remunerative, and ideational elements. I build on these descriptive concepts by dissecting the business-government dynamics that underpin these strategic effects. In an insightful treatment, Phillip Saunders highlights the main motivations behind China's international activism.[11] Saunders neatly lays out the strategic rationale for China's foreign policy actions, and economics features prominently in his analysis. Like many authors, Saunders struggles to accommodate the complex mixture of multiple actors and interests that pervade China's attempts to use commercial activity as part of its grand strategy.[12] We do not yet have a comprehensive framework that reflects China's domestic political economic dynamics and their strategic international effects.

Rather than starting from the top and moving down, examining China's grand strategy and highlighting economic aspects, a second approach looks explicitly at China's economic behavior to better understand the grand strategic implications or consequences of economic interaction. Although this bottom-up approach holds out the possibility of a more fine-grained examination of the mechanisms of economic statecraft, it still lacks a capacious framework for analyzing actual practice. For example, Adam Segal has argued that China is making increasing use of economic statecraft in its pursuit of foreign policy objectives.[13] Segal and Scott Kastner have done commendable work examining whether China's use of economics has translated into strategic results.[14] But asking whether China's economic power is resulting in increased influence leads to frustratingly inconclusive findings. Both authors conclude that China's growing economic clout sometimes can be leveraged for political objectives and sometimes not. I build upon their work by asking not *whether* China's economic power is used strategically, but rather *under what circumstances* it can be used effectively. China's sophisticated use of economics in its foreign policy is still a fairly recent phenomenon, and scholars are only beginning to explore the strategic implications of China's economic power.[15] I build upon this emerging work to understand China's strategic use of economics.

This endeavor differs from earlier work in its emphasis on state control as an often overlooked prerequisite for economic statecraft. State-centric analyses of economic statecraft tend to treat the state as a unitary actor that can control its international economic behavior. By relaxing this assumption, I discover interesting variation around the state's ability to control the commercial actors responsible for actually conducting international economic activities. I offer an explanation, derived from the economics literature on principal-agent challenges, of why the Chinese state can or cannot control the behavior of commercial actors.

Layout of the Book

We start with a discussion of economics and its relationship to national security before introducing a general theory of economic statecraft. The key lies in the ability to control and direct this increasingly unwieldy economic tool of influence. To explain variation in state control, five factors are examined that reflect the business-government conditions under which states will be able to control commercial actors (and thus direct their activities to generate the desired strategic effects). These determinants of whether a state will be able to mobilize and direct its economic power are (1) compatibility of goals between the state and the commercial actors that carry on the economic activity of the state, (2) commercial market structure, (3) unity of the state, (4) the reporting relationship between the commercial firm(s) and the state, and (5) relative distribution of resources between the state and commercial actor(s).

Given the centrality of state-business relations in this account of economic statecraft and given the country's growing stature in world affairs, China is an especially attractive test bed. Chapter 3 examines the role of economics in China's grand strategy. Chinese economic statecraft provides useful variation across cases to illustrate and test the general theory. The data for these cases are drawn from more than two years of field research in China and Taiwan, involving interviews with current and former central and local government officials, politicians, academics, bankers, journalists, advisors, lawyers, and businessmen, as well as examinations of available primary materials in Chinese and secondary sources in both English and Chinese. Whenever possible, official documents and publications were used. When interviewing, multiple sources, independent confirmation, and triangulation (in which various interviewees are asked to describe the same events) were used. This work enabled me to reconstruct the intricacies of (attempted) economic statecraft. Paired comparisons help to hold background conditions constant while allowing the key variables to fluctuate. The empirical chapters describe in detail some of the most significant episodes in the contemporary Chinese strategic use of economics.

Chapters 4 and 5 focus on China's global search for strategic raw materials. China's search for oil comes to mind when one considers the role of the state in Chinese commercial endeavors abroad. Contrary to some popular conceptions, however, when Chinese oil companies embarked on their "going out" strategy, they caused strategic difficulties for the state. That difficulty is then juxtaposed with the state's success in directing commercial actions to help prevent the upstream concentration of another strategic resource: iron ore. Chapter 5 examines China's largest overseas stock market investment, its 2008 purchase on the open market of 9 percent of Rio Tinto's stock. Examining China's efforts to work through commercial actors to secure access to strategic resources, chapters 4 and 5 highlight the business-government dynamics responsible for determining when the state has been effective and when commercial actors have damaged national interests.

We then turn our attention to Taiwan, one of China's top strategic priorities. This section goes beyond state-owned enterprises to include the wholly private actors that conduct the majority of cross-strait business. Chapter 6 examines mainland China's fruitless efforts to lean on Taiwanese firms conducting business in the mainland, and specifically Beijing's use of coercive leverage against prominent Taiwanese corporations with mainland operations in order to influence the outcome of Taiwan's presidential elections. In that instance, divisions between central and local government undermined the mainland's ability to control commercial actors. The use of economic statecraft in this phase of the cross-strait relationship contrasts with the mainland's current and more successful use of economics to achieve its objectives. Chapter 7 shows how mainland authorities worked together with Taiwan's opposition parties, providing economic concessions to the support base of President Chen Shui-bian as part of a successful electoral effort to mitigate Taiwan's appetite for independence.

Last, we examine China's sovereign wealth funds, specifically China's propensity to use overseas direct investment as a tool of economic statecraft. As China continues to liberalize its economy, traditional avenues of direct state control seem likely to weaken. China's massive, state-controlled finance entities, however, seem well-placed to continue exerting state influence over strategic commercial conduct. Two of these government financial entities are juxtaposed to understand the institutional dynamics that make the State Administration for Foreign Exchange (SAFE) an effective tool of economic statecraft, whereas the National Social Security Fund (NSSF) has little potential as an instrument of national power. Understanding this variation provides insight into the conditions under which Chinese state capital can be used to pursue political (rather than commercial) objectives. Finally, chapter 10 evaluates a case of contemporary strategic concern: the China Investment Corporation (CIC). Earlier chapters develop different aspects of the theory; chapter 10 walks the reader through an application that evaluates the CIC's potential as an instrument of Chinese economic statecraft. The evidence suggests that the CIC will function on a largely commercial basis (albeit "with Chinese characteristics").

Scholars have struggled to accommodate the role of multinational corporations in international relations. Most work on economic statecraft fails to explain exactly how states exercise their economic power. In particular, efforts to study the national use of economic tools of power have failed to consider the more or less independent commercial actors that characterize modern interstate economic interaction. The next chapter specifies how economic interaction may be used to generate security consequences. Firms, not states, conduct the vast majority of transnational economic activity, and I suggest that if states wish to use economics to pursue strategic objectives, they must resolve a series of principal-agent issues inherent in the practice of economic statecraft.

Part I

ON ECONOMIC STATECRAFT

1

WHAT IS ECONOMIC STATECRAFT?

How should we think about this phenomenon called economic statecraft? How do we know economic statecraft when we see it, and how does it differ from "normal" commerce? Before going further, let us define a few key terms and elaborate on some of the concepts used throughout this book. We will begin by challenging a common misunderstanding in the field of international relations: that states conduct economic relations with each other. Although states may be uniquely responsible for writing the "rules of the road" or acting as referees in the international game of modern global economics, they are not the primary players on the field.

International economic activity (trade, investment, etc.) is actually conducted by commercial actors, not by states. *Commercial actors* are defined as those entities that actually carry out international economic transactions. Examples of these activities include buying and selling of commodities, making investments, selling products, building factories, purchasing assets, and employing workers. They are often (but not always) multinational corporations.[1] Scholars engage in an intellectual shorthand when they refer to international economic relations between *states*. Generally speaking, this state-based orientation is a perfectly appropriate point of reference from which to analyze international affairs. When applied to questions of economic statecraft, however, it blinds us to some very important dynamics. That commercial actors, rather than states per se, conduct the majority of international economic activity is an empirical reality that has not been appropriately incorporated into a theory of economic statecraft. Understanding how states use economics to pursue their strategic objectives requires that we first focus more explicitly on the role of commercial actors, the entities that actually conduct the vast majority of international economic transactions.

The topic of civil-military relations provides an illustrative, epistemological parallel. Much of the civil-military relations literature problematizes the issue of state control of military power. This approach allows analysts to explore and understand important dynamics in the relationship between a nation's military forces and its political leadership. At the heart of this type of inquiry lies what is essentially a principal-agent problem: how can a nation's political leadership maintain control and be able to productively direct its military forces? Although analysts will often talk about "nations" exercising military might, technically speaking, armies, navies, and other services are actually responsible for conducting military operations. These military actors are beholden (to varying degrees) to a state's political leadership. The intellectual challenge that the civil-military literature explores is *how* such control is (or is not) practiced. Indeed, analyzing the nature of exactly how states marshal, control, direct, and apply such military power has yielded interesting insights about doctrine, command and control, organizational culture, and national military effectiveness, to name but a few.

Just as states must rely on militaries to exercise national military power, so too must modern states rely on commercial actors to exercise national *economic* power. In both instances, states find themselves facing principal-agent challenges. That is, the state must work through agents with the specialized capacity to actually conduct the activity that will lead to the desired national political outcome. This principal-agent relationship introduces a host of challenges and complications into the international application of both military and economic power. For example, how does the principal ensure that the agent acts in the principal's best interests if the agent's goals are not identical to the principal's? How can the principal monitor the agent's behavior and credibly enforce compliance if the principal lacks adequate information or other resources? Such challenges must be overcome if the state hopes to deftly wield these forms of national power. We will return to this principal-agent framework in more detail in the next chapter. For now, we simply note the existence of a principal-agent dynamic inherent in the national exercise of both military and economic power. Just as the civil-military literature studies the components and particular dynamics of the state-military relationship, so too do we need to focus on business-government dynamics when analyzing economic power and its relation to national security.

An Issue of Externalities

The relationship between economics and national security is best thought of as one of externalities, a concept borrowed from the field of economics. It captures the notion that a given transaction may produce effects that are not fully internalized among the parties that are directly conducting the transaction. This book uses the term *security externalities* to denote such security effects.

Two caveats are in order. First, economic activity can also generate nonsecurity externalities. For instance, economic tools of national power can be used to pursue strictly economic objectives. Economic interaction may also easily generate environmental externalities. In this book, though, we are primarily concerned with the strategic, political, and security consequences that result from various economic interactions. As a result, the scope of inquiry is narrowed to focus on security externalities. Second, of course not all security externalities result solely from economic activity. There may be security externalities that stem from social changes, environmental activities, demographic trends, or any number of factors. This book, however, will be limited to those security externalities resulting from economic activity. Thus, the term "security externalities" is used to denote the security consequences arising as a by-product of economic interaction.

Joanne Gowa and Edward Mansfield wrote a seminal article on the security externalities arising from trade,[2] although it should be noted that they use the term to describe one particular type of security externality, that of the efficiency benefits stemming from Ricardian gains. Such bolstering is undoubtedly an important security externality, but I would suggest that it is only one particular type of security externality. One can imagine a range of various types of security externalities, each with a distinct causal relationship between the specific economic activity and the security consequences stemming from that activity. Some examples of types of security externalities arising from economic interaction include sensitive technology transfer, loss of strategic industries, concentrated supply or demand dependence (in areas of trade, investment, and monetary relations), the forging of common interests resulting from currency unions, joint ventures, macroeconomic coordination, or even simple trade complementarity.

States are, to varying degrees, aware of these security externalities, and some externalities may be beneficial while others may be detrimental. Whether or not states or firms are conscious of these security externalities does not—strictly speaking—matter. Whether these security effects are intended or not also does not matter in terms of the security consequences of the economic interaction.[3] Neither intentionality nor awareness changes the fact that a particular pattern of economic activity results in security effects for states. Intentionality does, however, play a role when it comes to the concept of economic statecraft.

Defining Economic Statecraft

Economic statecraft is defined as the state's intentional manipulation of economic interaction to capitalize on, reinforce, or reduce the associated strategic externalities. Because the externalities are generated by commercial actors that are subject to incentive structures that are at least partly determined by states, states can seek to influence the behavior of commercial actors in an effort to achieve the state's strategic objectives. Such manipulation occurs through a range of state policy tools including sanctions, taxation, embargoes, trade agreements, asset freezing, engagement policies, currency manipulation, subsidies, tariffs, trade agreements, etc. It ought to be noted that economic statecraft is analytically distinct from the security externalities themselves. Security externalities may be (inadvertently) generated by commercial actors engaging in various types of economic interaction simply for their narrow commercial reasons. For example, security externalities like the transfer of sensitive dual-use technology may simply result from the autonomous activities of commercial actors pursuing profits (without any direction by the state). Economic statecraft, however, is the intentional attempt of the state to incentivize commercial actors to act in a manner that generates security externalities that are conducive to the state's strategic interests. To extend our example, if the state passed legislation requiring dual-use technology transfer as a prerequisite for awarding a lucrative government purchase contract, that would constitute economic statecraft. Economic statecraft thus requires an element of a state's intentionality (i.e., a deliberate manipulation of commercial actors' incentives).[4] It ought to be noted that these incentives can be used to both encourage and discourage particular commercial actor behavior.

Given that the vast majority of international economic activity is actually carried out by commercial actors, an appropriate theory of economic statecraft ought to feature an explicit role for these commercial actors. Yet all too often commercial actors are missing in the international relations literature. Because commercial actors' agency is generally absent from studies in international relations, the literature effectively assumes away the fundamental challenge for states seeking to wield economic tools of national power, namely whether or not the state can get the commercial actors to behave in a manner that produces the strategic effects the state seeks. As a result, the field continues to struggle with understanding the specific microfoundations of economic statecraft as it is actually practiced in grand strategy. This study seeks to address that gap.

To do so, I focus on the element of state control, whether the state can control or direct the behavior of the economic actors that are conducting the international economic activity. This is an important (and often overlooked) prerequisite for states to be able to conduct effective economic statecraft. Rather than assume that states can perfectly direct their economic power, I introduce an explicit role for the agency of commercial actors vis-à-vis the state. In particular, this approach focuses on the state's ability to control or direct the behavior of commercial actors so as to generate security externalities. In fact, the distinction between security externalities and economic statecraft discussed above turns on this issue of state control. Because this approach to economic statecraft is a novel one, we should be explicit about how this definition of *economic statecraft* and this larger conceptualization of the relationship between economics and national security extends some of the existing work that has been done on the topic of economic statecraft.

International Relations and the Study of Economic Statecraft

David Baldwin's *Economic Statecraft* is one of the field's best efforts to understand the wide range of economic tools states could call upon to achieve their national interests.[5] Much of the subsequent work in political science focused almost exclusively on sanctions and the coercive elements of economic statecraft. Such a conceptualization represents an overly narrow approach to the rich array of phenomena encompassed by the term *economic statecraft*.[6] Baldwin's work attempts to systematically catalogue and evaluate the various types of economic statecraft states can use to achieve their strategic objectives. By calling attention to the political rather than economic effects of using economic tools, he sought to challenge the view that economic statecraft is not an effective tool of international relations. The early chapters wrestle with the conceptual elements of how to analyze economic statecraft, while the later chapters discuss particular cases of economic statecraft. This work is often cited as the seminal modern text on economic statecraft, and it still provides a useful reference for students seeking to understand the economic tools of international power.

Baldwin focuses his scholarship on the phenomenon of "economic statecraft," which he defines as "influence attempts relying primarily on resources that have a reasonable semblance of a market price in terms of money."[7] Essentially, Baldwin's definition begins by saying that *statecraft* defines the range of tools, policies, etc. a state has at its disposal to pursue its interests in the international system.[8] This definition is straightforward. He goes on to define *economic* as those transactions, goods, etc. that can be measured and priced in terms of money.[9] This logic leads Baldwin to conclude that *economic statecraft* defines the activities, policies, etc. of a state that rely on resources that have a price tag. The purpose in constructing such a definition seems to have been to emphasize that the term "economic" merely defines the means employed (rather than the end-state goals that are sought, which may be purely political).[10] At the time of his writing thirty years ago, it was important to make this case. Although defining *economic statecraft* in this way is not incorrect—and in the practice of international relations, states do frequently seek to achieve noneconomic ends by using economic means—today we are in a position to advance our understanding of economic statecraft beyond the basic claim that economic means can be used to pursue political ends. It would be interesting if we could say something about exactly how states use such tools. What is different about state use of economic tools as opposed to other means of international influence, and what are their limits? In what manner, exactly, do state applications of economic instruments produce the strategic consequences states seek? These are the questions that drive this book. The section above offered a new, more specific, analytically precise definition of *economic statecraft* that moves beyond Baldwin's "intentionally broad" definition in favor of an understanding of *economic statecraft* that frames the strategic outcomes as security externalities that result from the economic activities of commercial actors. Defining *economic statecraft* in this way will allow us to be more precise about the conditions under which and the manner in which states seek to use economic interaction to promote their strategic goals. This definition provides a useful foundation for understanding how states *actually mobilize* and use their economic power to achieve their strategic objectives.

Of course Baldwin's is not the only seminal work on this important topic. There is a long history of scholarly efforts to examine how states could use their economic relations to pursue security goals. In fact, unlike much of the more recent scholarship on the topic, many of these earliest works were empirically driven analyses that paid considerable attention to understanding the role of commercial actors in states' foreign policy. Eugene Staley premised his 1935 work *War and the Private Investor* on the notion that the economic behavior of private-sector actors cannot be fully understood without also considering the political and military contexts that frequently influenced ultimate economic outcomes.[11] His work drove home the importance of considering the commercial actors when examining how states wield their international economic power. In particular, Staley's framing of his cases reflected the heart of the business-government challenge inherent in economic statecraft: namely whether the commercial actor or the state is ultimately driving the strategic outcome. One of the best-known classics is Albert Hirschman's study of Germany's trade relations with its weaker eastern European neighbors.[12] Hirschman depicted the German state policies designed to establish, deepen, and exploit eastern European states' asymmetric structural economic dependence on Germany before World War II. By the time Hirschman wrote his well-known book, Herbert Feis had already discussed how pre–World War I powers used investment and finance to facilitate their own security policies.[13] Each of these works helped to frame how states could use various types of economic interaction to pursue their strategic goals.

Although some of these early works in the field of economics and security examined ways states may seek to further their strategic goals through private-sector or quasi-private-sector actors,[14] most of this literature was largely framed in mercantilistic terms that do not account for the complex relations between the state and the firm in a more modern, liberalized economic context. Although the broad general concepts pertaining to the role of the state in managing its economic affairs still provide insightful conceptual leverage, much of the specific empirical relevance of these early works are naturally limited in a contemporary twenty-first-century context.

Later works did seek to explore how states could use economic power to achieve their interests in a more modern, globalized, and interdependent environment. Authors in this spirit include Klaus Knorr, Robert Gilpin, Robert O. Keohane, and Joseph S. Nye, whose work on the nature and exercise of modern transnational economic power was both insightful and path breaking.[15] Knorr's work carried E. H. Carr's initial insight—that economic power and military power are merely two sides of the same coin—into a more modern multinational context. Knorr sought to provide a theoretical framework for understanding how modern states use economic tools in international relations. He applied economic concepts and principles to parse out the nature of economic power.[16] In many respects, this book is an extension of Knorr's efforts to analyze the economic dimensions of the strategic international power dynamics between states in the international system.

While Knorr's work is an important contribution, he focused on the macrolevel strategic aspects of economic power: "Our focus on government policy excludes from major consideration those kinds of international relations that occur between private groups and individuals across national boundaries."[17] As a result, he was not able to fully explore the tactical dimensions of the actual exercise of economic power. One area lacking in Knorr's work is the role of commercial actors.[18] Even though "many of these interactions are fostered by governments (e.g., international trade conducted by private business), and their regulation often raises issues of foreign policy," Knorr was not able to go into any significant level of detail regarding the operational role of commercial actors in the exercise of economic statecraft.[19] By developing a commercial-actor-based approach to economic power, I extend some of Knorr's principles and examine how they actually play out in modern practice.

Other important authors that contributed to the development of this economic power literature, while providing important theoretical insights, likewise tended to lose sight of the commercial actors. Susan Strange made a significant contribution with her depiction of the structural dimension of economic power.[20] Although mainly concerned with national macroeconomic goals, Richard Cooper was among the first to elucidate the constraining nature of modern interdependence on states' use of economic tools to achieve their objectives in the international system.[21] Because this interdependence is often not symmetric, it is possible that greater interconnectedness may increase opportunities for using economic tools of national power. Keohane and Nye explicitly sought to examine the various ways in which states were made vulnerable to economic pressures from other states in this interdependent world.[22] Their notions of asymmetry and dependence exploitation inform many of the concepts and ideas put forward in this book. Although these works blazed important new paths in the study of international economic power, they often sacrificed specificity in their efforts to build a general theoretical foundation for the exercise of economic power. These works tended to focus almost exclusively on the state and drifted away from the commercial-actor-driven approach that characterized the earlier generation of scholarship (e.g., Staley). In so doing, they drifted further and further away from an analytical framework that integrated commercial actors into a larger strategic understanding of economic statecraft.

One notable exception is Robert Gilpin's *US Power and the Multinational Corporation*. Gilpin argued that multinational corporations thrive because the international system's hegemon creates and maintains an international environment in which private-sector actors can succeed.[23] At the abstract level, Gilpin's work seeks to directly account for the role of commercial actors in international strategic relations. Gilpin, however, was mainly motivated by the desire to explain the long-term rise and decline of hegemons in the international system. The field is still lacking a middle-range theory that bridges the levels of abstract theory and the more concrete applications of exactly *how* commercial actors do the strategic bidding of the hegemon.

Although Gilpin's work is largely compatible with the theory put forward in this book, there are inevitably some areas of friction: Gilpin's book emphasized the unique role of the hegemon in the international system and the benefits accruing to the *hegemon*'s multinational corporations (MNCs). This perspective stands in contrast to my work, which argues that *any* state is more or less theoretically capable of using commercial actors to further its national strategic interests. Moreover, there does not seem to be any a priori reason to assume that the MNCs of nonhegemonic states would not also accrue benefits in a modern, liberalized global regime (e.g., World Trade Organization). Gilpin's work raises many additional questions about which corporations can benefit from state action and about the processes through which a strategic alignment of interests between the commercial actors and the state actually take place? Gilpin's work was an important step forward in considering the interrelationship of modern multinational corporations and US national interests. His book frames a discussion of how the behavior of MNCs served that interest. As with Knorr, my work builds on elements of Gilpin's theoretical foundation and examines the resulting theory in the empirical context of contemporary Chinese interests.

Many of the other works in the literature on globalization that did seek to explore the role of commercial actors have tended to overstate the autonomy of multinational corporations and the erosion of the nation-state as the dominant actor in international relations.[24] This book's empirical research suggests that even if the direct, classical mercantilist power of the state to dictate policy to its private sector actors has diminished under a more liberalized system, sufficient power remains for the state to influence and generate incentives for the private sector to behave in ways that are conducive to state interests. Although many of the exaggerated claims of a "vanishing state"[25] have since been largely corrected,[26] the field has yet to develop a theory that would connect the microlevel behavior of commercial actors who possess some degree of autonomous agency to the macrolevel strategic outcome of how modern sovereign states actually mobilize their economic interaction to further national security goals. It is not enough to simply "bring the state back in" to our analyses; as scholars, we should also illuminate *how* states interact with commercial actors in a strategic context. Without doing this, the literature on economics and security will continue to lack an integrated theory that links microeconomic, firm-level behavior with the grand strategy of states.

So if the English-language literature does not get economic statecraft quite right, perhaps Chinese-language sources do a better job. After all, if China is a productive case setting in which to study the phenomenon, it seems reasonable that Chinese scholars of international relations may offer a more sophisticated theoretical treatment of how states exercise their international economic power. Alas, a survey of Chinese-language scholarship on economic statecraft indicates that it is prone to many of the same shortcomings as the English-language literature. Perhaps this is not so surprising. A good deal of the leading Chinese scholarship on international relations reflects a strong influence from Western international relations theory.[27] In fact, most Chinese-language work in international relations is derivative of Western international relations; many of the leading Chinese scholars were trained in American doctoral programs, many of the theoretical assumptions stem from Western international relations theory, and basic lines of reasoning often parallel those found in Western scholarship. It should not be surprising, then, to discover that Chinese-language work that has been done at the intersection of economics and security maps neatly onto the English language scholarship and suffers from many of the same shortcomings.

So, how does Chinese scholarship treat the subject? Broadly speaking, Chinese scholars think about the relationship between economics and security in two ways. The first is internally focused and is distinguished by its emphasis on China's vulnerability. This category includes works that view economic performance as one of the linchpins of regime legitimacy. According to this line of reasoning, ongoing economic development serves to help secure and legitimize the governing regime. This conception of economics is closely tied to stability (*wending*). Stability is both domestically oriented—to directly limit sources of threat to the regime—and internationally oriented—to provide an international environment that is conducive to China's continued economic growth.[28] Continued economic growth provides an ongoing reaffirmation of the Chinese Communist

Party's (CCP) ruling mandate by underscoring the CCP's ability to deliver economic growth to the society. The body of literature addressing statist industrial policy and the planning elements of China's economy can both be grouped into this domestically focused category dealing with economics and security.[29] Works pertaining to energy security and resource strategy are also a part of the Chinese literature on economics and security that falls into this vulnerability category.[30] To the extent that China depends on imported raw materials, there are some who worry about the security vulnerabilities of dependence.[31]

The second category of Chinese works on economics and security examine the instrumental use of economics. This body of work is more focused on how economics can be used to generate effects on others. Growing economic clout plays a key role in enabling China's national power (usually discussed as a component of China's "comprehensive national power"). Like many states, China seeks to employ all elements of national power (including economic tools) to pursue its priorities in the international system.[32] One way for China to pursue this is by building regional economic relationships and structures that facilitate Sino-centric regional economic integration.[33] Increasingly dense economic interaction between China and Central Asia, or between China and Southeast Asia, helps align the incentives facing smaller states on China's periphery by linking regional economic success to China's own economic growth. China's growth has been predicated on continued reform and opening up that has emphasized deep economic ties to the rest of the global economy.[34] Even as the official term of art in China has shifted from a discussion of China's "peaceful rise" toward China's "peaceful development," "harmonious society/world," and now more recently "the China Dream," "New Silk Road Economic Belt," and "the 21st Century Maritime Silk Road," economics continues to play a prominent role in furthering Chinese foreign policy.

This last aspect of the Chinese literature on the relationship between economics and China's grand strategy is the area most closely related to this project. While the literature—like its English-language counterpart—still lacks a theory that links the behavior of commercial actors to the grand strategy of the state, this literature has produced several useful concepts that my work will seek to build upon. Perhaps the concept that is most germane to this area of research is *jingji waijiao* (economic diplomacy).[35] Chinese scholars use the term *jingji waijiao* in two ways.[36] In the first sense, *jingji waijiao* is used to identify diplomatic efforts designed to advance economic goals.[37] The other use of the term (and more interesting for our purposes) is the instrumental use of economic means to achieve national strategic objectives.[38] This use of the term is similar to the English-language literature's discussion of how states go about exercising their international economic power.[39] This phenomenon is an important area of

international relations that deserves better understanding.[40] The Chinese literature on this topic, however, is even less theoretically developed than its English
equivalent.[41] In addition to the methodological, evidentiary, argumentation, and
research design challenges that bedevil a significant number of Chinese-language
publications, perhaps not surprisingly, this literature also suffers from many of
the same gaps found in the English-language treatment of economic statecraft.
Virtually all the Chinese literature on the subject examines the state as the unit of
analysis; notably absent is an adequate, theoretically informed accommodation
of commercial actors. Like their Western counterparts, these efforts to explore
the intersection of economics and security often fail to adequately incorporate
the role of commercial actors in economic statecraft. For the most part, Chinese
works at the intersection of economics and security tend to focus on the state as
the unit of analysis and make the same basic error found in many Western works
on economic statecraft. Again, commercial actors, not states, are responsible for
conducting the majority of international economic interaction, and a suitable
theory of economic statecraft ought to accommodate this reality.

This book argues that by ignoring the agency of commercial actors vis-à-vis
the state, we have been overlooking important variation in the state's ability to
control the behavior of the economic actors that are primarily responsible for
conducting international economic activities. Scholars are thus omitting a critical prerequisite that is necessary for a state to use its economic power effectively,
namely, the ability of the state to control commercial actors. State control of
commercial actors ultimately lies at the heart of economic statecraft. For this
reason, state control is the dependent variable of this study. So what exactly is
state control and how would we know it when we see it?

State Control of Commercial Actors

State control is the critical linchpin for understanding where the rubber meets
the road in the study of economic statecraft. To dissect precisely how modern
states wield economic tools of national power, one ought to examine this nexus
between the state and commercial actors. Developing a better understanding of
state control is critical for understanding how the economic elements of grand
strategy actually work in practice.

So what exactly is state control? I use the term *state control* to indicate when
the state is able to control or direct the behavior of economic actors, typically
through the state's shaping of the economic actors' incentive structure. The concept of *state control* posits that the state and the economic actor each have a set
of preferences. Sometimes these align and sometimes they diverge. State control

can be detected by observing whether a given economic entity does what the state wants it to do. State control is most easily observed under conditions when the preferences of the state are diametrically opposed to those of the economic actor. Under such conditions, the state preferences and those of the economic actor can be brought into stark relief, thus affording the analyst a clearer view. State control is likely occurring in such a case when the economic actor's self-interest would suggest one course of action but the actor takes a different course.

When thinking about state control it may be helpful to focus on three units of analysis: the state, the commercial actor(s), and the relationship between the two. Each of these units of analysis can be independently described. The presence or absence of state control in any given instance is going to be a function of the characteristics of the state, the characteristics of the economic actor(s), and the characteristics of the relationship between them. The next chapter will delve into more detail on precisely what these characteristics are and how this causality works, but for now it is sufficient to focus only on whether the state can or cannot control the behavior of commercial actors in a given case. The outcome of state control is a function of these three types of characteristics as represented by the simple diagram in figure 1.1.

The state, commercial actors, and the relationship between them constitute the three units of analysis where one can look to explain when the state can and when it cannot control the behavior of economic entities.[42]

The dependent variable (DV) of this study is whether the state succeeds or fails to control, direct, or otherwise use commercial actors in the state's pursuit of its strategic goals. This is called "control" for short. The cases are coded for

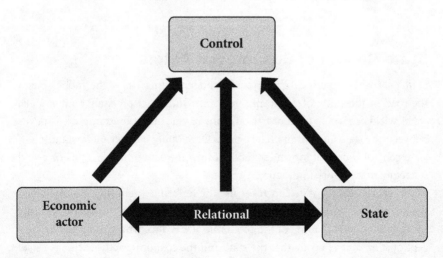

FIGURE 1.1   Drivers of state control

whether or not the state was able to use commercial actors to pursue its strategic objectives. Using fine-grained analysis and process tracing of detailed case studies, one can examine the nature of the economic actor–state interaction in a given case-specific context. In practical terms, this allows one to observe evidence of whether or not the commercial actors do what China wants done strategically vis-à-vis a given foreign policy issue area. Coding for the dependent variable in the cases requires an examination of what China's particular goals are in a given case context and comparing these objectives with what commercial actors actually did in that case. Changes in the DV are often evidenced by the observable actions of the economic actor. This sort of case-specific comparison will demonstrate whether the state was or was not able to control the commercial actor(s). So the dependent variable of the book's cases is control, whether the state succeeds or fails to manipulate, control, direct, or otherwise use commercial actors in the state's pursuit of its strategic goals. The values for this DV range from high levels of control to an absence of state control. While in reality state control varies continuously along this spectrum, to keep the theory manageable I operationalize the coding as a discrete binomial variable: either the state does or does not control the commercial actors. That said, the narrative tries to provide a sense of the relative levels of state control when making comparisons across the book's empirical cases.

In the context of a mixed regime like China's in which the state tends to own the largest firms across most strategic industries, one might expect that the issue of state control of the economic actors may not be an interesting variable (after all, variables need to vary). Indeed, when it comes to the existing literature in security studies, the state's ability to control economic actors is generally taken for granted; if the state owns an economic actor, then surely it can control the behavior of that actor. But as the literature on principal-agent problems suggests, the Chinese case is more complicated than this simple assertion suggests. Although state ownership might make it easier to control a commercial actor ceteris paribus, it by no means ensures state control. This book explores how and why the state is sometimes able to control or direct the behavior of economic actors, while under other conditions the state finds itself unable to exercise control.

The empirical analysis focuses on this issue of state control of commercial actors. As mentioned earlier, control is a critical necessary condition for successful economic statecraft. Despite its significance, this element of economic statecraft is something the literature tends to omit. Although *control* is an important prerequisite, it ought not to be conflated with successful outcomes of economic statecraft. Economic statecraft can succeed or fail for a wide variety of reasons, and these factors have often been a subject in the field's existing scholarship on economic statecraft. A main contribution of this book is to highlight and develop a better understanding of how states (specifically China) harness and use their economic power; for that to occur, state control of the commercial actors that conduct international economic relations is critical. The next chapter develops a theory of Chinese economic statecraft focusing on the conditions that enable state control of commercial actors. Such control is important because it provides the state with a means to direct the security externalities that result from various types of economic interaction.

In summary, the book is situated in a long tradition of scholarly work that has sought to understand how states use economic power. Inspired by the early twentieth-century classical realists who emphasized the importance of both national strategic goals *and* the role of commercial actors in pursuing those goals, this book seeks to address a number of gaps in the literature.[43] This work seeks to extend and tactically operationalize some of the earlier work done on the nature of economic power and how states *actually mobilize* commercial actors to pursue national strategic interests in a contemporary context. Specifically, this work answers the following questions: In what manner do states seek to use economic interaction to further their larger strategic goals? What is the role of commercial actors in states' strategic efforts to wield economic power? Why do these efforts succeed or fail? What factors facilitate or hinder state control of commercial actors?

Much of the literature dealing with the use of economics to pursue strategic goals tends to take a state-centric approach. By focusing predominantly on states as the unit of analysis, these perspectives give relatively little consideration to a rigorous treatment of the role of commercial actors, the agents *actually* responsible for conducting most of the economic activities of the modern state.[44] Because economic actors conduct the majority of interstate economic activity, the state's ability to control and direct their behavior is an important prerequisite for effective economic statecraft. As demonstrated by the empirical work in this book, the behavior of these commercial actors plays a crucial role in determining economic interaction and, ultimately, how states may or may not use that economic interaction to pursue their strategic interests. The book adopts a framework that facilitates a meaningful exploration of the business-government dynamics that are so important for understanding how states use economic interaction to further their strategic interests.

This book seeks to make two specific contributions to the existing body of scholarship on economic statecraft. First, it seeks to call attention to the undertheorized role of economic actors in the study of economic statecraft. In particular, a state's control of these economic actors constitutes an important and overlooked prerequisite for economic statecraft. By not explicitly addressing the issue of agency for commercial actors in security studies, much of the existing work on economic statecraft simply assumes that the state can control international economic activity.[45] This book relaxes that assumption and explores exactly when states can (or cannot) be expected to be able to control the behavior of commercial actors. The resulting analysis suggests that the field ought to more explicitly integrate business-government relations into its study of economic statecraft. Second, this book argues that state control of commercial actors is not automatic. It is also not impossible. Thus there is a need to understand when it is likely to happen and when not. Specifying the causality behind this variation is the primary focus of the next chapter.

The framework for thinking about the relationship between the economic activities of commercial actors and the security of a nation-state presented in this chapter raises the question of how a state goes about harnessing these dynamics for strategic ends. What are the factors that enable a state to effectively control or direct the behavior of commercial actors such that their activities generate the types of security externalities that are conducive to national strategic objectives? This causal logic lies at the heart of economic statecraft. Commercial actors, acting on their own interests, engage in various forms of cross-border economic interaction. This interaction often generates security externalities. States can create incentives for commercial actors to behave in ways that encourage the creation of security externalities that are consistent with a state's strategic interests. In this way, states can manipulate these externalities by structuring the incentives of the commercial actors involved. Such manipulation is defined as economic statecraft.

Thus, to understand economic statecraft, one must take a closer look at *how* the state manipulates economic interaction, more precisely, how the state controls the commercial actors responsible for conducting the economic interaction that produces these strategic effects. The next chapter presents a theory designed to explain the conditions that are likely to lead to state control. The goal is to provide a more precise understanding of how states use economics to pursue their grand strategic objectives. The resulting theory provides an account of how aggregate economic agents' microlevel incentives and consequent behavior generate national security outcomes at the macrolevel of China's grand strategy.

2

THE CHALLENGE OF STATE CONTROL

Understanding business-government dynamics is the key to understanding how states engage in economic statecraft. In particular, it is important to note that commercial actors have agency and they seek to maximize their own interests. That said, states can play an important role by influencing the commercial actors' incentive structure. States, especially powerful ones with good enforcement and monitoring capabilities, can make it painful for firms to behave in certain ways. States can also make it attractive for firms to behave in certain ways. Ultimately, however, it is still firms that are engaging in the day-to-day economic transactions across borders. The conceptual framework presented in the previous chapter calls attention to the need to disaggregate these important business-government dynamics when studying economic statecraft. The behavior of economic actors often generates security externalities that states care about. States need to be able to control or direct the behavior of economic actors in order to channel these security externalities. Such manipulation constitutes economic statecraft.

Thus for states to be able to harness their economic power, states must first be able to control or direct the economic behavior of commercial actors. To conduct economic statecraft, the government must be able to incentivize commercial actors to behave in a manner that is conducive to producing security externalities that are in line with the state's strategic interests.[1] Being able to control the behavior of commercial actors is critical for states to engage in economic statecraft. The central challenge in understanding economic statecraft is knowing when a state can or cannot control the behavior of economic actors.

This puzzle provides the primary empirical anchor for this study: sometimes the state is able to exercise control over economic actors, and at other times the state seems unable to effectively control their behavior. How can we account for this variation? This chapter offers a theory that explains such control. This theory identifies the conditions under which the state is likely to be able to control the behavior of commercial actors. Recall that the previous chapter identified the dependent variable of this study as "state control," the ability of the state to control or direct the behavior of commercial actors. By controlling commercial actors, states can manipulate the security externalities that result from international economic interactions, thus engaging in economic statecraft. So what factors determine when the state is able to exercise such control?

I have identified five salient factors that determine when a state will be more able to control commercial actors. My inspiration for understanding how the state can direct its economic interaction comes from the principal-agent literature in economics. Principal-agent theory offers a useful conceptual framework for unpacking the dynamics governing the interaction of the state and the private sector. Bates Gill and James Reilly have also suggested the appropriateness of using a principal-agent approach to understanding the challenges China faces in managing its corporate actors in the African context.[2] They use a principal-agent framework to argue that management challenges are difficult and likely to preclude effective coordination from Beijing. Much of the work on China's economic statecraft exhibits a similar either/or perspective. I employ principal-agent theory to go beyond the question of *whether* the principal can coordinate the agent(s) to focus on identifying the *conditions under which* the state can control commercial actors. The theory presented in this chapter identifies the salient conditions that enable state management of commercial actors. Using principal-agent concepts in this way provides the theoretical bedrock for the five factors discussed below.

The Independent Variables and Their Causal Logics

Five factors are responsible for determining whether the state is able to control the commercial actor(s). First is the number of commercial actors in the market. If there are too many agents, the principal will have a hard time controlling them, and if there are only one or two, these commercial actors may be powerful enough to resist government efforts to control their behavior. The ideal market structure is an oligopolistic one in which there are not so many players that the state cannot monitor and enforce effectively, but not so concentrated that the state has no alternatives. Second is the degree to which the government is acting with one voice. To the extent the government itself is divided, it will be more difficult to exercise control over commercial actors. In addition to these two characteristics of the state and the commercial actors, there are three aspects of the nature of the relationship between the state and commercial actors that also influence whether or not a state will be able to control the behavior of commercial firms. First among these is whether the goals of the commercial agent conflict with the goals of the state. One must also consider the nature of the reporting relationship between the government and the commercial actor. If the commercial actor is directly owned, financed, or managed by the government, it should be easier for the government to direct the behavior of the firm. Finally, there is the question of the relative resource endowments between the principal and the agent; if the commercial actor has considerably more resources than the government, it will be that much more difficult for the government to exercise control. Together, these five factors determine whether the government will be more likely or less likely able to control the behavior of commercial actors. As mentioned above, these five factors can be grouped into those primarily having to do with

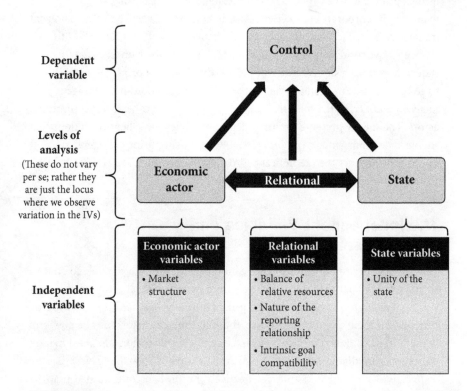

FIGURE 2.1   The independent variables

the commercial actor side of the business-government interaction, those that are characteristics of the state, and those that capture elements of the relationship between the state and the economic actors. This conceptual organization can be mapped onto the simple diagram introduced earlier, as figure 2.1 shows.

By examining the characteristics of the state, the commercial actors, and their relationship in any given case, this theoretical framework can provide a useful heuristic that indicates whether the state will be more able or less able to control the commercial actors.[3] Let us now take a closer look at the variables of this study and the moving parts of the theory.

What is the causal logic connecting each of these to outcomes on the dependent variable? How should we think about the range of values that these variables can take on? These questions can be addressed most efficiently by the following two decision trees linking values on the independent variables to outcomes in the dependent variable.

Sequencing the Independent Variables

The two diagrams below (figures 2.2 and 2.3) reflect the possible outcomes across these five factors. Each of the five factors can be grouped onto the decision tree in a way that specifies how these IVs interact with each other and, ultimately, result in outcome values for the dependent variable of state control.

We will begin by examining the fundamental factor of state unity—whether the state is acting as a unified, rational actor in any particular, case-specific empirical context. All states suffer from varying degrees of intrastate division. To the extent the state is divided about its desired goals, the national interest, or riven over more parochial subnational conflicting interests, it will be significantly harder for a state to effectively control the behavior of economic actors. Indeed, as will become more evident in the empirical portions of the book, state unity is a critically important condition that enables state control. Without effective unity of the state, the "state" finds it difficult to agree upon and define its strategic goals, let alone be able to effectively coordinate commercial actors. Although all states suffer from varying degrees of contention over what the "national interest" may be, consensus over the general direction or goals of the state may vary from one domestic political context to the next. Such variation may be a function of the international threat environment the state finds itself in, diverse ideological perspectives, domestic politics, special interests, or any number of drivers. Although questions of how the national interest is defined constitutes a potentially fruitful field of inquiry in the study of grand strategy, it must largely fall outside the scope of this book. Suffice it to say that the degree to which a state

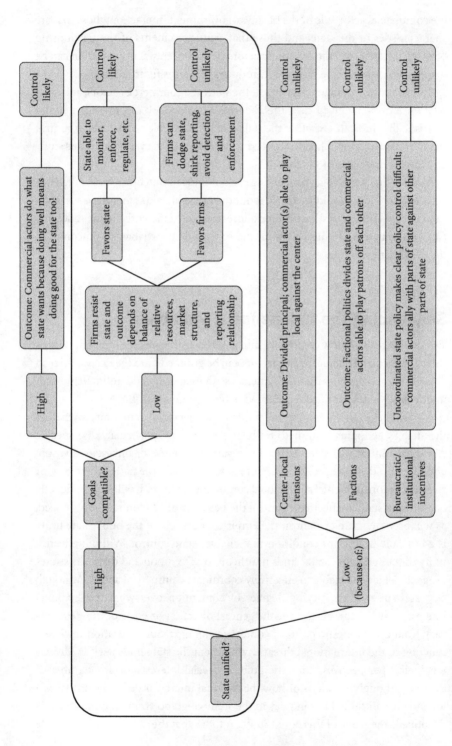

FIGURE 2.2 Economic statecraft decision tree (state characteristics)

acts in a unified manner can vary by context, over time, and from one state to the next. If a given state cannot achieve some minimal consensus over what its strategic objectives are (at least in that particular case context), it is highly unlikely that that state would be able to effectively marshal economic actors to pursue its national interests. As a result, state unity holds a special place among the factors accounting for when state control is likely. Without state unity, it is nearly impossible for the state to exercise control over commercial actors.

In situations where there may be multiple, competing, and conflicting bureaucratic authorities, or in situations in which the state is internally divided among competing factions or groups, it will be more difficult to direct and control commercial actors. For instance, when the central state must also contend with provincial and municipal authorities, it may be more difficult to use commercial actors to pursue national strategic goals. Likewise, when the central state is sharply divided by contending ministries or political factions, we can expect commercial actors to be more easily able to play one set of interests off the other, thus weakening any coherent attempt on the part of the state to control the commercial actors. The values for this factor range from a highly unified state to a deeply divided state. Such divisions typically occur in three realms: across various institutional divides (I call these "interbureaucratic" divisions), for example, the Ministry of Finance versus the National Development and Reform Council; across various levels of government (called "decentralized" divisions), for example, the central government versus a provincial government; and across ideological or patronage factions (factional divisions), for example, rival senior patrons within the Politburo.

The second consideration is how divergent the goals of the commercial actors are from the goals of the state. In any given episode, the goals of the commercial actor(s) may be more or less compatible with the goals of the state. If the basic objectives of the commercial actors are closely compatible with the basic goals of the state, one would expect to observe less friction. In such cases, the goals that the commercial actors seek (e.g., profit, market expansion, securing access to basic inputs, improved productivity, etc.) do not necessarily conflict with the goals of the state. This facilitates the ability of the state to achieve its objectives because motivating the commercial actor to pursue goals that are complementary to what it would like to do anyway is fairly easy. In some extreme instances, goals of the economic actors may actually be enhanced by the state's achieving its goals. But at the simplest level, the key variation that matters in terms of affecting the outcome is whether the goals of the state and the goals of the commercial actor are in conflict or not. Some indicators to look at when assessing the intrinsic compatibility of the goals include whether the commercial actor's goals are defined by the state, the degree to which the commercial actor is driven by purely profit motives, and whether the goals of the state and the goals of the commercial actor can both be successfully realized (as opposed to being mutually exclusive). To the degree the state's goals are compatible with those of the commercial actors, the state will find it easier to control or direct commercial actors in its pursuit of strategic national objectives.

Based on the discussion up to this point, we can begin to gain some insight into when the state is likely able to control commercial actors and direct their behavior. The pathway of greatest theoretical interest to be explored in more detail is when the state is unified but its goals are at odds with those of the commercial actors.[4] This pathway has been highlighted in the diagram above. Under those circumstances, the variables of market structure, reporting relationship, and the balance of relative resources are likely to play a key role in determining the outcome. Once we know something about the unity of the state and the ex ante compatibility of the goals, we can explore these other three variables to gain some purchase on whether the state would be able to overcome the principal-agent challenges inherent in state control.

The Facilitators of State Control

The first of these factors to consider is the number of agents that would have to be coordinated by the principal. If a market in a particular industry or sector is highly fragmented and made up of many firms (a "competitive" market structure), it may be more difficult for a state to control the numerous commercial actors. Monitoring, coordinating, and enforcing compliance all become more challenging as the number of commercial actors increases. Conversely, a highly concentrated market with a few large firms may more easily be directed by the state. A monopolistic or duopolistic market structure, however, tends to produce large, powerful firms with significant autonomy that are likely to enjoy relative bargaining power vis-à-vis the government. Important firms with considerable influence are more easily able to resist state attempts to direct commercial actors.[5] The state's ability to control commercial actors is most likely in an oligopolistic market structure.[6] Such a market is concentrated enough that the firms are easy to monitor, punish, and reward, but not so concentrated that commercial actors can gain leverage vis-à-vis the state.

The nature of the reporting relationship between the state and the commercial actors is another important factor influencing the likelihood of state control. This relationship generally consists of three attributes: the nature of the ownership arrangements, the management arrangements, and the financing structure. The more direct any of these relationships are between the government and the commercial actors, the easier it will be for the state to exercise control over the commercial actor. For example, in situations of direct state ownership, one would expect higher levels of control. Similarly, a firm whose managers are directly appointed by the government will be more easily controlled than a firm whose managers are elected by private shareholders. Likewise, a firm that relies significantly upon state sources for its financing is more likely to respect the wishes of the government than one that raises money from capital markets and is beholden to private shareholders. The values on this dimension range from a direct, tight relationship that is closely monitored ("direct") to a more distant, arms-length regulatory relationship ("indirect") to being completely independent of any governmental reporting. In situations of direct state ownership, state-appointed managers, or state funding, higher levels of state control would be expected.

Finally, the balance of material resources available to either the state or the commercial actors will play an important role in determining whether or not the state will be able to control the behavior of the commercial actor. The relative resource endowments between the state and the commercial actors reflects the relative institutional capabilities each side enjoys vis-à-vis the other. If the state is well-endowed with a considerable budget, large staff of experienced professionals, and a track record of active direction of a sector's commercial activities, one would expect control of commercial actors to be more likely. The more advanced the state's organizational capacity to monitor, enforce, and regulate commercial actors, the more likely that challenges in exercising economic statecraft will be overcome. Significant bureaucratic and organizational capacity, such as leadership, resources, experience, scale, talent, etc., enables states to overcome problems of information and incentive structure that typically plague business-government coordination efforts. Likewise, if the commercial actor is comparatively well-resourced with a deep pool of knowledge and significant financial resources, it should be easier for the commercial actor to exercise its autonomy from a more poorly resourced government entity.

A second decision tree diagram may be useful in helping to understand how these three factors relate to one another (figure 2.3). The three possible market structure conditions introduced earlier can be used to organize this discussion. Oligopolistic conditions seem to be the most conducive to state control of commercial actors. If the market structure is concentrated or competitive, we can expect that state control will not be easy, although it is not impossible to observe control under these circumstances.

In a highly concentrated market, there are a few large firms with powerful domestic political equities. Would the state have what it needs vis-à-vis these powerful economic actors to ensure that the state is able to get them to do what it

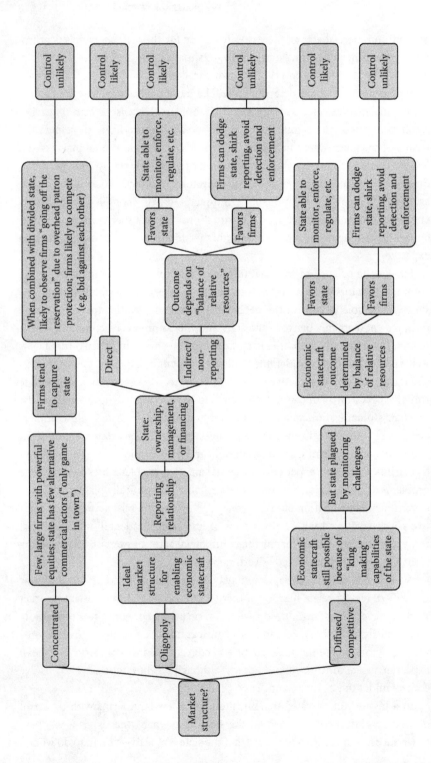

FIGURE 2.3 Economic statecraft decision tree (economic actor characteristics)

wants? Under a concentrated market structure, the balance of relative resources would only rarely be in the state's favor, for several reasons. Dominant firms tend to enjoy large budgets, and the personnel of large monopolies often outnumber those on the side of the state regulator. Under conditions of a concentrated market, much of the technical expertise is resident within the firm, and the state frequently struggles to maintain familiarity with the state of the art. This is particularly true in highly technical areas. The result is that the state often lacks adequate capacity to monitor the behavior of the dominant commercial actors in that space. In such circumstances, it is not unusual for these dominant firms to "capture" parts of the state even when the statutory reporting relationship is a direct one. While it is still better for the state to have direct reporting authority over the commercial actor, under concentrated market structure conditions, the statutory nature of the reporting relationship is actually less important than some may think. This is true partly because the state has no real alternative agents through which to conduct its economic statecraft. In a concentrated industry—for example, the petroleum industry—that is dominated by one or two colluding firms, the state has no alternative but to rely on these firms to carry out its energy security objectives (for example, seeking equity oil abroad). Moreover, in a setting like China's, a good deal of the subject matter expertise and information resides with the economic actor(s) in such industries, thus further limiting the state's position. For all these reasons, we would expect that the balance of relative resources would usually favor the firm rather than the state under highly concentrated market conditions. A highly concentrated market condition does not make state control impossible, but we should expect that it would be quite difficult. The state would have to be acting in a unified manner and, ideally, the goals would be mutually compatible. Even then, the state's control would be tenuous as the state would likely have few possible alternative agents, so its ability to play one firm off another would be limited.

If the market structure is a highly diffuse one in which many firms are competing with each other, the principal-agent literature tells us that the state is likely to have a difficult time monitoring and enforcing compliance across such an unwieldy number of firms. Under such conditions, the nature of the reporting relationship can rarely be classified as "direct," making state control of the economic actors more difficult. Direct state ownership, management, and financing are not typically found under highly competitive market structures given the numbers of economic actors involved. This suggests that the balance of resources may determine whether the state can control the behavior of economic actors under these conditions. When the balance of resources favors the state, the state can more effectively monitor and track the multiple economic actors. In addition, the state can play the role of "king maker" by discriminating against some commercial actors and favoring others. In highly competitive environments, such good graces of the state can translate into decisive commercial competitive advantages.

The most ideal market structure for state control seems to be an oligopolistic market structure. Under these conditions, there are not so many economic actors that the state cannot monitor all of them, yet there are also not so few that the state has no opportunity to play one off the other to advance the state's own interests. In addition to an oligopolistic market structure, direct reporting relationships to the state and a relative balance of resources that favors the state all facilitate state control over commercial actors. In aggregate, then, analysts and policy makers can examine the ex ante characteristics of the state as well as the commercial actors involved in any given episode of (potential) economic statecraft. By focusing on these relational attributes, one can develop a sense of how easily a state will be able to control the behavior of commercial actors.

Case Selection

The critical factor motivating the case selection is to understand why, in certain instances, the state is able to control the behavior of commercial actors. In each of the three areas of China's foreign policy I have selected for study (China's sovereign investment, China's extractive resources strategy, and China's cross-strait economic interaction), economics serves as a critical tool of China's statecraft. Moreover, these cases include elements of both success and failure. Examining both types of results provides better insight into the conditions under which the state can and cannot control the commercial actor(s). Comparable cases with differing outcomes have been selected in order to study what factors may be driving the observed results.

As mentioned earlier, state unity and goal compatibility are distinctive independent variables. These two variables share existential qualities that can be used to provide a source of methodological leverage for the research design. It is difficult for the state to control commercial actors if the state itself is divided. Such factional bureaucratic or regional divisions can prevent consistent articulation of the state's strategic interest. A divided state is also likely to have a difficult time implementing a strategically consistent vision, thus providing commercial actors with ample opportunities to play one portion of the state off another. Goal compatibility is important because compatible objectives make it much easier for the state to "control" the commercial actor. One should not be surprised to find that it is relatively easy for the state to get the economic actor to do what the actor would want to do anyway. Indeed, under conditions of high compatibility, the state may not even need to be actively manipulating the commercial actors at all. It can simply sit back and enjoy the benefits of the security externalities that are generated. Such cases are extreme-value cases that, while they tend to be overdetermined, provide a helpful illustration of the theory's posited causality. This circumstance is quite different from a situation in which the state must actively force the commercial actor to engage in activity that runs counter to the commercial actor's own interests. Such cases are more interesting from a theory-building perspective because these conditions make for an interesting dynamic in which a state's ability to control is reduced to the economic actors' capacity to resist. These cases are classic principal-agent challenges. To understand the outcomes of these kinds of cases, we ought to look at the balance of relative resources between the state and the commercial actors, the nature of the reporting relationship between the state in the commercial actors, and the market structure and competitive dynamics that the commercial actors face. Ideally, cases in which the state acted in a fairly unified manner and the wishes of the state are diametrically opposed to the commercial incentives provide productive circumstances for surfacing the other factors that enable state control. Under such conditions we should be more likely to find interesting variation in the state's ability to control or direct the behavior of economic actors.

We can take advantage of these variables' domain-defining properties to map out the universe of possible cases. This might be most easily done with a

		Goal compatibility	
		Low	**High**
State unity	**High**	**Principal-agent cases** Outcome becomes a classic principal-agent challenge (need to look at: balance of relative resources, market structure, and reporting relationship)	**Overdetermined cases of state control**
	Low	**Cases in which control is unlikely**	**Incidental cases** Security externalities may be generated (but unlikely as a result of economic statecraft)

FIGURE 2.4 Types of cases

two-by-two chart that categorizes the various types of cases that may exist (figure 2.4). In the cases that follow, we will examine multiple instances of strategic interaction between commercial actors and the Chinese state across each of these four quadrants.

From the point of view of developing the theory, the most interesting quadrant may be the upper left: when the state is unified and firms have differing objectives. Under these circumstances, the outcome is least known and will require state manipulation to produce effective strategic results. As implied by the decision trees, once we know something about the unity of the state and the ex ante compatibility of the goals, we can explore the other three variables to gain some insight on whether the state would be able to overcome the principal-agent challenges inherent in state control.

The Cases

One of the key aspects of useful case analysis is comparability. Cases being compared to each other ought to be similar enough to hold confounding factors as fixed as possible while allowing variables of interest to fluctuate. One way to do this is to draw cases from roughly the same time period. This book also uses a nested case design that compares two or more episodes taken from a similar strategic context of Chinese economic statecraft. In some of these episodes, the state was able to control the behavior of commercial actors, while in other comparable instances the state was not able to do so. Understanding the differences that drove these divergent results helps to shed light on the factors determining when a state is or is not able to control commercial actors.

The first set of cases looks at SOEs (state-owned enterprises) in China's resource extraction sector and their investments abroad. The first case, appropriately enough, examines China National Petroleum Corporation's initial foray abroad, the origins of China's "going out" strategy. This is a useful case with which to begin because it depicts how the government was initially unable to control the commercial actor but later was able to re-establish its control over the commercial actor. This provides nice within-case variation on the key dependent variable. The analysis of the case unpacks the factors leading to this change. The Chinalco case offers an interesting counterpoint to the state's difficulty in controlling CNPC. In the case of Chinalco, the state was able to work through pliant commercial actors to establish a blocking position that prevented a major upstream consolidation of China's imported iron ore supply, which would have been a strategic liability for Beijing. Whereas the state struggled to control commercial actor behavior in Sudan, Chinalco's efforts to thwart BHP-Billiton's bid for Rio Tinto afford a close look at the state's efforts to orchestrate a successful strategic outcome. The cross-strait trade between mainland China and Taiwan provides another empirical context to study the operative business-government dynamics, but this time the commercial actors are not large Chinese SOEs, but instead are public and private Taiwanese companies. Although mainland operations feature prominently for such firms, the Beijing authorities have little direct, statutory reporting power over these commercial actors. Once again, we compare two cases in this context: one in which the state was able to exercise control over the commercial actors and another in which the state was unable to do so. Finally, we examine a set of cases drawn from the realm of China's state finance. In this context, we explore the factors that enable state control and (importantly from a policy prescription perspective) those conditions that make state control less likely. One case examines how the State Administration of Foreign Exchange (SAFE) can be used as a tool of foreign policy. On the other end of the spectrum lies the National Social Security Fund (NSSF), a state finance entity that has been institutionally designed to limit its utility as a tool of economic statecraft. The final case turns to the China Investment Corporation (CIC). Like the CNPC case, the CIC case involves an initial period in which the state was unable to exercise control. This was followed by a consolidation of state power and subsequent state control. Drawing on the NSSF example, the CIC case also includes a brief discussion of the future trajectory of China's state finance. Although all three of the empirical contexts provide fertile ground for economic statecraft, the cases demonstrate that state control is not a foreordained result. As will be discussed in more detail in the conclusion, the research suggests ways that China can reassure its international partners and transparently limit its ability to strategically control commercial actors. Naturally, in developing a theoretical foundation for better understanding exactly how states can wield their economic power, this research also implies ways that China might enhance its ability to control commercial actors and thus facilitate its economic statecraft as well.

These cases can be usefully mapped onto the simple two-by-two chart presented earlier (as shown in figure 2.5). In some instances, state control comes relatively easily. When the state is unified and its goals naturally fit with those of the commercial actors, control comes cheaply for the state. These circumstances were exhibited by the later portions of the CNPC case as well as the Chinalco and SAFE cases. As the goals of the state and the commercial actors diverge, state control of the commercial actors becomes more elusive. The relatively autonomous mandates and institutional structures of the NSSF and the later the CIC both exhibit conditions that make their use as instruments of economic statecraft less likely. But even fully independent economic actors can function as effective agents of economic statecraft, as we observe in the case of the Taiwanese

Goal compatibility		
	Low (divergent goals)	**High (convergent goals)**
State unity — **High (unified)**	**"Challenges"** *Control possible* • Control determined by market structure, relative resources, and reporting relationship Cases: o Taiwan Fruit = control (unified state; balance of resources) o NSSF = control unlikely (reporting relationship: weak bureaucratic unity and outsourcing; relative resources) o Late CIC = control unlikely (reporting relationship: weak bureaucratic unity and some outsourcing; relative resources)	**"Cheap control"** *Control is easy* • Economic actors want what the state wants; unsurprising to observe control under these conditions Cases: o Late CNPC = control (unified state; reporting relationship) o Chinalco = control (oligopoly; convergent goals) o SAFE in Costa Rica = control (oligopoly; reporting relationship)
State unity — **Low (divided)**	**"Cacophony"** *Control and economic statecraft unlikely* • No real statecraft (although can still have uncontrolled/poorly directed security externalities) Cases: o Leaning on Taishang (center-province divisions) o Early CIC (ideologically/factionally divided state)	**"Capture"** *Economic actor (rather than state) control* • Firms often able to capture portions of the state to maximize firm welfare Cases: o Early CNPC in Sudan (bureaucratically divided state; concentrated market; relative resources) o Early cross-strait economic ties (diffuse market structure; monitoring and enforcement problems)

FIGURE 2.5   Cases and state control

fruit farmers. If the state is divided and the goals are divergent, state control (and effective use of commercial actors for economic statecraft) is unlikely. Such conditions were observed in the early days of the CIC and in the case of the mainland's efforts to lean on prominent Taiwanese firms conducting economic activities in China. In some instances, not only might state control be difficult, but firms can even capture portions of a divided state. This is especially likely in cases when the firms possess disproportionate resources (a condition present during the early portion of the CNPC case) and when the state is divided bureaucratically or along center-local lines (as was the case with early Taiwanese investment in the mainland when local municipalities keen on economic reform were highly dependent on Taiwanese capital and know-how).

By examining this chart, we can observe how the set of cases in this book aggregately provide helpful coverage across the range of possible outcomes for the dependent variable. Although each case has its own intrinsic significance as an important example of how economics and security intersect in Chinese grand strategy, taken together the cases allow for productive preliminary testing and refining of the theory. For example, one key characteristic of China's political economy is the degree of state penetration into economic activities. China has a history of a planned economy with institutions by which the state sought to control the productive economic capacity of the commercial actors. Taken together, the three empirical contexts examined in this book provide fundamental variation along the axis of the business-government relationship. The commercial actors in the raw materials context are mainly large SOEs, while the commercial actors in the Taiwan context are private-sector Taiwanese firms (i.e., quite distant from the authorities in Beijing). In the case of China's sovereign wealth funds, the commercial actors are actually extensions of the state itself. The cases examined in this book have been selected to collectively provide a range of legal relations between the state and the economic actors. As a group, these three different empirical contexts provide fundamental cross-case variation along the dimension of the basic statutory relationship between the government and these commercial actors.

As a starting point, one might assume that the legal relationship between the state and a given economic actor is the most important (or only) consideration when determining whether the state will be able to control the behavior of that commercial actor. Many assume that because China is ostensibly communist, surely the state can exercise powerful control over commercial actors. Particularly, given that China's largest multinational corporations are state-owned enterprises, one might expect that the state has little difficulty directing or controlling the behavior of China's commercial actors. As these cases demonstrate, however, even among Chinese state-owned enterprises, there are instances in which the state is not able to control the behavior of commercial actors. The case selection of this book provides significant variation along this dimension of the statutory reporting relationship between the state and firms. Although state ownership may be an important factor, successfully controlling the behavior of commercial actors is a bit more complicated. Indeed, all else being equal, state-owned, -managed, and -financed entities should be more easily controlled than if the distance between the state and the economic actor were greater. As the cases in this book show, however, this is not the only factor determining whether or not the state can control the behavior of economic actors. In each of the three clusters of cases, there are instances of both successful and unsuccessful efforts to control commercial actors.

In addition to the comparative elements of the case selection strategy, the cases examined in the following chapters have merit in their own right as intrinsically important cases to understand: The Chinalco bid for Rio Tinto was the largest overseas open market equity investment by a Chinese company; the issue of Taiwanese independence features as one of the most likely sparks that may ignite great power conflict in East Asia; China's sovereign wealth funds conjure the specter of massive sums of state-owned capital flowing abroad, triggering fears of foreign ownership and manipulation of strategic assets. Finally, the selection of these three areas of Chinese economic statecraft illustrates each of the three forms of economic interaction: trade, in the case of Taiwan; investment, in the resource extraction case cluster; and monetary tools of economic statecraft in the case cluster of China's sovereign wealth funds. This variation is useful to demonstrate how economic statecraft may operate via all three forms of cross-border economic interaction.

This chapter and the last put forward two important concepts that offer analytic leverage for how we study economic statecraft. First, economic statecraft is properly understood in the context of security externalities. Certain types of economic interactions carry significant strategic implications, which manifest themselves in the form of security externalities. The behavior of commercial actors generates various patterns of economic interaction that can carry strategically significant consequences for state security. States often take an active interest in these security consequences. When states seek to deliberately manipulate the behavior of the commercial actors responsible for conducting international economic activity (and its associated security externalities), they are engaging in economic statecraft.

The state's ability to exercise sufficient control over the conduct of its economic interaction has not received adequate attention in the literature and thus provides the focal point for this book's empirical research. Precisely how states go about manipulating their economic interaction requires the state to work with, encourage, restrain, or otherwise direct and control the commercial actors that are ultimately responsible for conducting that economic interaction. Of course, such efforts to control are bound to face challenges. These challenges are a function of a given state's business-government dynamics.[7]

Second, states must resolve a series of business-government coordination challenges if they are to be effective at mobilizing and directing their economic power. Specifically, five independent variables determine whether a state will be able to mobilize and direct its economic power toward strategic goals: (1) the unity of the state, (2) the intrinsic compatibility between the goals of the state and the goals of the commercial actors that carry on the economic activity, (3) the commercial market structure, (4) the nature of the reporting relationship between the commercial firm(s) and the state, and (5) the relative distribution of resources between the state and the commercial actor(s). Each of these factors has a hypothesized relationship to the ability of the state to control or direct the behavior of commercial actors.

The empirical chapters that follow provide detailed illustrations of specific episodes of Chinese business-government relations during the foundational period of contemporary Chinese economic statecraft. Although the time range of specific cases varies, China's "economic gunpowder" has grown considerably since China's accession to the World Trade Organization. China possesses the world's second largest economy and its economic might is considerable. Today China is still learning how to wield its economic power. Indeed, China continues to discover the limits of economic levers of national power. The cases examined in this book are primarily drawn from this formative phase of contemporary Chinese economic statecraft, when the state has been experimenting and drawing lessons related to the application, limits, and usefulness of China's economic dimensions of national power. Studying such cases can be useful not only as a testing ground for the theory presented in this chapter, but can also provide the reader with an empirical sense of China's formative experiences regarding its use of economic statecraft. In the chapters that follow, this theoretical framework is applied to understand and evaluate particular foundational episodes of China's contemporary economic statecraft. But before delving down into the weeds, we will first take a step back to examine the strategic role that economics plays in Chinese grand strategy.

3

ECONOMICS AND CHINA'S GRAND STRATEGY

This chapter examines the evolving role of economics in China's grand strategy as it rises to great power status in the international system. A good deal of China's post-1978 foreign policy has been focused on facilitating China's economic development and enabling China's economic progress. With China's economic success has come greater economic clout in the international system. Increasingly, China finds itself in a position in which it may be able to leverage its growing economic power to achieve foreign policy objectives. Rather than dedicating its foreign policy toward furthering economic ends (which had been the general pattern of the relationship between economics and foreign policy during most of the post-Mao period), China is entering a phase in which it has the luxury of leveraging its growing economic clout to further its foreign policy goals. This shift is an evolutionary one that seems to have begun to manifest itself just before the 2008 financial crisis. The empirical chapters that follow are all taken from this foundational period of contemporary Chinese economic statecraft. Many of the cases date from just before the 2008 financial crisis, when China first began to experiment with leveraging its growing economic power to pursue strategic objectives. The 2008 financial crisis seems to have confirmed a domestic narrative in China about China's rising power and the relative decline of a more liberalized economic model that advocates a smaller role for active state involvement. This short-lived triumphalism not only resulted in greater pressure to mobilize China's economic power, but it also seems to have coincided with a harder-line diplomatic approach that did not shy away from using military power to pursue China's strategic objectives in the international system. Although a military-power-oriented, "tougher" China seems to have spurred regional balancing efforts on the part of China's concerned neighbors, China's "softer" economic power has proven to be a fairly effective (and diplomatically acceptable) channel for China's strategic influence.[1] A close exploration of the foundational experiences of the mid-2000s will yield greater insight into the capabilities and limitations of this economic tool of national power for China going forward. One of the central questions behind this study is precisely how China may or may not be able to mobilize its economic power to realize strategic objectives. As discussed in the cases that follow, one of the keys to successful Chinese economic statecraft is the ability of the state to control the behavior of commercial actors. But first, this chapter provides a contextualization for the rest of the study, namely, offering the reader a broad picture of how economics relates to China's grand strategy.

This chapter begins with a brief discussion of grand strategy as an analytical concept in international relations. The chapter then examines China as a strategic actor and takes a look at the evolving role of economics in China's contemporary grand strategy and at Deng Xiaoping's reassessment and strategic reorientation of China toward economic development. The chapter illustrates how much of China's modern foreign policy has been designed to serve the requirements of economic development and the international integration of a rising China. As China gains more and more "economic gunpowder," however, we are beginning to observe economic tools being used to pursue foreign policy goals. This book is about understanding how, when, and why such strategies work.

Grand Strategy and China

Among the China-watching community there is a difference of opinion regarding the extent to which China possesses a coherent grand strategy. One of the most fundamental questions currently debated by China watchers today is whether or not China actually has a grand strategy that guides China's strategic thinking in its foreign and security policy making. On this topic, intelligent, reasonable, and knowledgeable China hands often disagree.[2] When these arguments are examined more closely, however, most of the debate is at its core an epistemic discussion about whether or not *any* state has a grand strategy and how coherently any state can pursue its national interests. Such positions often argue that states are not unitary actors and are too prone to domestic schisms that effectively prevent any coherent rational pursuit of national interest (or in the extreme, even prevent a meaningful consensus of what those national interests are). Although frequently framed as Chinese exceptionalism, similar debates can apply equally well to discussions of Russian, Indian, Japanese, European, and even American debates over grand strategy. While this is an interesting academic exercise, these issues of whether states have a grand strategy will not be engaged in this work. My analysis of China's economic power assumes that China, like other nations, has a grand strategy. My research suggests that China is not much different from most other countries when it comes to questions of having a coherent grand strategy. In China, as is the case with most other nations, domestic political decision making involves multiple actors, many of which are frequently motivated by their own narrow interests. The result of this domestic political tug-of-war is often a seemingly incongruous pattern of foreign policy behavior on the part of China.[3]

Before delving more deeply into the domestic political forces that shape China's grand strategy, it would be helpful to clarify precisely what grand strategy is. Essentially, a nation's grand strategy provides the strategic guidance that drives its foreign policy behavior. In this section, I provide a general background context of China's grand strategy. This preliminary step is useful because China's case-specific, tactical goals articulated in the empirical chapters that follow are best understood in the context of this larger strategic logic.

To do this, I begin by specifying some of the assumptions I make. These assumptions underpin my understanding of grand strategy as an analytical concept as well as my understanding of China's grand strategy as a particular instance of a national grand strategy. Such assumptions carry important implications for analyzing China's behavior in international affairs. Although these assumptions are not too far removed from the mainstream of the American China-watching academic community, it may be helpful to make these assumptions explicit and transparent at the outset. Readers pressed for time or who are already familiar with Chinese strategic studies may wish to skip forward to the discussion of economics and its role in China's grand strategy found later in this chapter.

Grand Strategy As an Analytical Concept

Like many works in security studies, this research makes several important assumptions about grand strategy. In this section I try to make those assumptions as explicit as possible while recognizing that an exhaustive discussion of grand strategy is not the central focus of this research.

My work is rooted in the intellectual tradition of classical realist international relations scholars. I therefore share several of their assumptions regarding the centrality of international anarchy, the essentially competitive nature of international politics, the importance of power, and the pursuit of national interests, etc.[4] In particular, I assume that countries are relatively rational actors that seek to pursue their national interests in the international system according to their capabilities. Their grand strategy can be thought of as a "means-ends chain" as Barry Posen first described:

> A grand strategy is a political-military, means-ends chain, a state's theory about how it can best "cause" security for itself. Ideally, it includes an explanation of why the theory is expected to work. A grand strategy must identify likely threats to the state's security and it must devise political, economic, military, and other remedies for those threats. Priorities must be established among both threats and remedies because given an anarchical international environment, the number of possible threats is great, and given the inescapable limits of a national economy, resources are scarce. . . . Of course, grand strategies are almost never stated in such rigorous form, but the analyst may be guided by this conceptualization in his attempt to ferret out the grand strategy of the state.[5]

Avery Goldstein similarly defines grand strategy as "the distinctive combination of military, political, and *economic* means by which a state seeks to ensure its national interests."[6] As Posen's and Goldstein's definitions suggest, national interests tend to lie at the heart of grand strategy. States have a grand strategy that is based on their understanding of their national interests, and states seek to pursue these interests according to the ordering of their preferences given the international systemic constraints states face. [7] Moreover, grand strategy tends to provide a rough ordering of state preferences (given the scarcity of national resources for pursuing these preferences). This is the second assumption about grand strategy that I make: grand strategies include an ordering of preferences. For example, states are willing to make trade-offs when goals conflict or when the means for achieving goals are limited. Such trade-offs are based on a set of relative priorities for the state.

Given the varying levels of permissiveness in the international environment and the varying levels of relative limitations of a state's capabilities, states will try to maximally pursue their preferences in the international environment. This is the third assumption about grand strategy that I make in my analysis. A state with greater capabilities will be able to pursue secondary and even tertiary interests, while some states with limited international power will have difficulty even pursuing minimal core national interests. In the same way, an international environment in which other states are supportive of a state's national goals makes pursuit of those goals easier.

In sum, a nation's grand strategy is a rational strategic logic that identifies national objectives and designs policies to best achieve those objectives given the international environment and the capabilities that the state is able to bring to bear. A key aspect of a nation's grand strategy is the domestic political filter that must interpret both the international system and the nation's own interests and capabilities. This implies that some understanding of a nation's domestic politics is required to accurately study its grand strategy. These domestic political conditions play a key role in determining how nations perceive and interpret their international situations. To better understand the process of Chinese grand strategy making, we ought to begin by laying out a few observations about how the domestic political system works in China. To that end, we now turn from a general discussion of grand strategy to a specific examination of the conditions influencing China's grand strategy.

China As a Strategic Actor

I make four major assumptions about China and how it behaves. First, the Chinese Communist Party (CCP) is in control of the government and the sinews of state power in the People's Republic of China (PRC). This is an important fact that most China scholars simply take for granted, but individuals that are not as familiar with China's history might not appreciate the extent to which this reality distinguishes Chinese domestic politics from many other states' domestic political environments.[8] In China's case, the CCP defines China's national interests and implements China's grand strategy. This imparts a few important idiosyncrasies to China's grand strategy.[9] The definition of China's interests today and for the foreseeable future is dominated by the the CCP.[10] In other words, the senior leadership of the CCP determines China's national interests. In defining these interests, the interests of the state are often conflated with the interests of the party itself.[11] This type of blurring has given rise to the use of the term "party-state" to describe the modern Chinese polity.[12] As a result, China's national interests are more often than not the CCP's preferences projected as China's *national* interests. This dynamic serves to magnify the second assumption I make about China.

Factions matter. Many national policy outcomes are the product of domestic political forces within China. This is the second important assumption I make about Chinese foreign policy. This domestic political competition takes two forms. The first is ideologically based division. Such ideological cleavages often manifest themselves as competing personalistic factions that tend to share common ideological perspectives, backgrounds, and values (such as the Shanghai Clique, the Communist Youth League faction, or "Princelings"). I distinguish between such ideological sources of domestic political friction and what I call "bureaucratic" struggles for power and influence, which often stem from an institutional rivalry (for example the Ministry of Finance versus the National Development and Reform Commission in the struggle over economic reform). Such bureaucratic frictions are often of the "where you stand depends on where you sit" variety.[13] In practice, ideological differences may map onto bureaucratic competitions. For example, the Shanghai Clique may be disproportionately represented in the Ministry of Finance or the Communist Youth League faction may dominate the Ministry of Industry and Information Technology. That is to say, ideological factional power may be reflected in and supplemented by institutional bureaucratic dynamics. Analytically, however, the two constitute conceptually distinct sources of domestic political forces shaping China's grand strategy. That these forces influence China's definition and pursuit of its national interests is the second assumption I make.

For most decisions, the general secretary must now consult and forge consensus among the senior leadership and the key players. The composition of who is precisely involved in any given consultation may vary by issue area, by nature of a given crisis, or by period in time. Key players are generally (but not only) the heads of the various *xitong* (organizational/institutional verticals within the Chinese political system). The people sitting at the top of the pinnacles of the various power bases within Chinese domestic politics constitute an important elite with whom the general secretary must work.[14] Membership in this highly personalistic group is dynamic and fluctuates over time as personal equities rise and fall. The interests of these players are also not static, although certain general outlooks and positions exhibit patterns that suggest rough tendencies or patterns of alignments. These alignments, however, are almost always characterized by pragmatic pursuits of narrow self-interests and power maximization. Regardless of the specific motivations, the resulting Chinese foreign policy behavior is often characterized by seeming incoherence, inconsistencies, or vacillations in China's "strategic" behavior as a nation-state in international relations.

Although factions are an important consideration in a discussion of China's grand strategy, I also assume that this factor operates with an important caveat. The party is hierarchically organized, with the general secretary perched squarely on top of the hierarchy. Although power has become less centralized than it was under Mao and even under Deng, ultimate authority still rests at the top. As needed and when he feels it is appropriate, the general secretary of the Communist Party will weigh in on decisions that may be otherwise subject to domestic factional pulling and tugging. In these instances the general secretary is the final arbiter. Once the general secretary gives orders, factions salute and do their job with only minimal passive resistance at the margins.[15] The logic of such behavior is not difficult to grasp. Too much passive resistance on the part of an individual, faction, or bureaucratic entity can attract undesired attention from more powerful entities within a strongly hierarchical system. The result can be marginalization, isolation, purging, or even outright elimination.

Partly because of this hierarchical domestic dynamic, it is reasonably safe to assume that China by and large behaves like a unitary rational actor on matters of strategic concern in the international environment. That is to say, China generally engages in the rational pursuit of its objectives as a singular entity on the international stage. This common assumption in much of the international relations work on grand strategy is valid in China's case because the general secretary ultimately has a firm grip on the party and the party ultimately has a firm grip on the political governance structures of China.[16] I also recognize, however, that many of the salient domestic political features that distinguish China as a unique actor in the international arena suggest that this assumption of unity deserves to be explored more deeply. For this reason, I explicitly allow it to vary in my model.

The fourth aspect of the Chinese political system that influences China's grand strategy is the growing complexity of China's governance system and what I call the "tyranny of time." Operating in an increasingly complicated world where information flows rapidly has necessitated devolution of decision making to lower levels of the hierarchy. Although the general secretary is the most senior position in the political apparatus and is vested with the ultimate authority within the Chinese system, he or she must still confront the reality that there are still only twenty-four hours in every day of every one of the Politburo members' lives. The same holds true for the members of the Standing Committee. Indeed, the same fundamental constraint applies to Xi Jinping and Li Keqiang, just as it did to Hu Jintao, Wen Jiabao, Jiang Zemin, Zhu Rongji, Deng Xiaoping, and Mao Zedong before them. This human limitation is the main reason that these paramount leaders (indeed all heads of state) must to some degree rely on a bureaucratic supporting infrastructure to help make decisions and lead the complex administrative apparatus that governs China. This reality has been the case since imperial times when China first developed path-breaking innovations of civil administration. China's growing complexity prompted Hu Jintao to further institutionalize a subsidiary decision-making model in the Communist Party context. To help manage workloads, the centralized system is forced to resolve most issues as low down on the chain of command as possible. If a solution cannot be worked out there, the system tends to elevate the issue to a higher level of authority that may be better positioned to hammer out a compromise. Of course, many of the well-studied bureaucratic patterns of shirking and passive resistance can be applied to the Chinese case. Indeed, these can generate considerable resistance even to the point of occasionally derailing implementation. But, given the hierarchical nature of Chinese politics, if such resistance is detected, the resisting organizations or individuals run the risk of crossing the intentions of more senior leadership. Such behavior could prove extremely costly for future promotion or could entail other sorts of penalties. In the Chinese system, higher-ranking authorities are often in a position to make life difficult for lower levels, and there is not much institutional defense provided to shelter lower-level dissent. Thus, in aggregate, the result is a strong incentive structure prompting compliance on a given issue area once a higher-level authority has weighed in on a particular issue. That said, some allowance for decentralization ought to be included in a comprehensive treatment of China's grand strategy.

In summary, my paradigmatic perspective may be most closely identified with a classical realist set of assumptions. With regard to China and Chinese grand strategy, I assume that the Communist Party defines China's national interests and the party-state implements China's grand strategy. The general secretary occupies the apex of political authority within this system. This would suggest that China acts (for the most part) like any other unitary, rational actor in pursuing its national goals in the international system. This authority, however, is checked by factionalism and divisions within the party as well as by the "tyranny of time" and the growing complexity of Chinese politics. Such factionalism and decentralization has a limit given the hierarchy of domestic politics and the relative power of the central leadership. As a result, our treatment of China's grand strategy ought to allow for some flexibility in the traditional realist assumption of state unity that is commonly found in studies of grand strategy.

As with my assumptions about grand strategy, many of these assumptions about China and its grand strategy are topics of intense debate in the China field today. I do not pretend to adequately engage in these debates here, but good scholarship should lay bare its important analytical assumptions as explicitly as possible. I do not think that any of these assumptions are far removed from mainstream security studies or from the current conventional wisdom regarding international relations and China. I merely wish to make these assumptions explicit before delving into case discussions that operate under these assumptions.

Chinese Grand Strategy and Policy Making

So in what manner does the party actually define China's interests and how is such a "grand strategy" actually implemented in China? The system takes its broad cues from concepts and ideas emanating from the very top of the party structure. The general secretary issues top-level strategic principles (many of these are made public when formally addressing the National People's Congress or presenting "work reports" or other formal pronouncements and speeches). These can be vague and tend to change in subtle ways over time, changes that are often detected through nuanced changes in rhetoric. This high-level guidance serves as the rough equivalent to the ideas and principles found in the national security strategy of the United States. Such guidance tends to offer little in the way of specifics, but instead highlights general national interests and assumptions about causal logics and suggests particular priorities (often without really prioritizing them) of the current leadership or in the current period of time. These statements tend to be full of platitudes, slogans, catchphrases, and generalities, but they offer important atmospheric guidance to the lower levels of the Chinese decision-making and implementation apparatus. Although we know very little in the open source literature on the details of senior Chinese decision making, there does seem to be some evidence suggesting that clauses in some of the official state and party documents have been subject to hotly contested debates within the most senior circles of the Communist Party. The reason key players may be expending political capital to influence the content and tone of these pronouncements might be because these preambular, general assessments of China's international strategic environment provide an important signaling function to the rest of the chain of command.[17]

This top-level guidance (slogans, policies, catchphrases) is then interpreted by lower levels of the governance apparatus in China. Examples of such guidance include the theme of stability as a guiding priority for the Hu and Wen administration, "Peaceful Rise," "Win-Win Diplomacy," "Scientific Development," and "Harmonious Society." Already in the Xi Jinping era, we have seen evidence of an active discussion and recapitulation of Xi's "China Dream" motif. Xi has also floated the concept of "New Style Great Power Relations" as a framework for US-China relations. Each of these phrases represents a recurrent theme in various aspects of China's domestic and foreign policy. This kind of high-level guidance, in turn, shapes the implementation and policies pursued by the specific *xitong*, which translate these general guiding principles into more specific policies and national strategies along their specific avenues of government. This process represents one channel through which the more parochial substate interests influence and gain access to shaping the larger strategic outlook of "China" as an actor on the international stage.

Of course, substate actors may be prone to interpreting the top-level guidance to maximize their own more narrow bureaucratic/institutional, factional, or ideological interests. This "interpretative leeway" can result in various substate actors working at cross-purposes or can generate friction within the system over which elements of a national policy deserve greater priority. Furthermore, this contestation is merely that portion of the friction that takes place at the *national* level within China. Such institutional frictions can also be found at the provincial, county, and municipal levels of government, where national bureaucracies are often replicated at a more regional scale.[18]

This process then produces issue area and topic-specific strategies and results in the particular policies that are implemented (often by the relevant substate organizational actors). The resulting international behavior that we observe is what "China" does on a given issue or topic. If that issue or topic is controversial enough, important enough, or carries enough international attention to warrant the senior decision makers' focus, than we can expect "China's" behavior to be relatively consistent and tightly managed to reflect the preferences of the top echelons of the senior decision makers in the party. If, however, the issue is seen as merely "business as usual" or clearly within the purviews of one or more delegated authorities on a given issue or topic (e.g., an ASAT test or J-20 test flight), then the outside world has relatively little assurance that the behavior of "China" in that instance accurately reflects the coordinated preferences of China's leadership.

In analyzing China's behavior, what we often perceive as "China's" actions are in fact the result of substate actors making decisions that produce observable "Chinese" behaviors on the international scene that generate controversy for China (such as refusing to allow the USS *Kitty Hawk* to make a Hong Kong port call for Thanksgiving in 2007). Such actions may not only accidentally run counter to the intent of the senior leadership, they may be deliberately designed to undermine that policy as various factions within the Chinese political system vie for influence.

I have observed a pattern in Chinese senior decision making of senior leadership engaging in *ex post* damage control when the lower echelons within the Chinese system have engaged in activities that threaten to undermine China's larger strategic interests. This damage control often comes across as an effort "to get out in front" of an issue. This crisis-management mentality was reflected domestically in the regime's response to issues surrounding school construction quality after the 2008 Sichuan earthquake. It was also present in the quality control scandals involving Melamine-tainted milk, lead paint in children's toys, and dumplings that were being exported to Japan.

Just because the top must rely on the lower levels to interpret and implement senior-level guidance does not mean that China lacks a grand strategy. Rather, the more important a given issue area is to China's top leadership, the more attention and focus the top leadership will give to addressing that issue. The top leadership likewise tends to provide more specific guidance and play a more direct role in implementing policies deemed "too important" to rely on lower level interpretation and implementation.[19] If it could, the top leadership would guide and implement *everything*—perfectly, all of the time—but alas, it recognizes and understands the material limits it faces in light of the growing complexity and the increasing velocity of information in the system it manages.

Being pragmatic, the top leadership recognizes the need to focus its time and resources on only the most important matters.

This notion of "importance" is determined by several attributes. First is the extent to which a given issue threatens the survival of the party. For example, questions of internal unrest such as that caused by ethnic tensions, unemployment, or popular protests pose particular threats to the regime. Likewise, questions related to Taiwan and China's territorial integrity also rank highly. Economic performance and stability feature prominently as well. Of course, the priorities of the leadership figures and the institutional interests of the senior leadership circles also serve to delineate importance. For example, inequality, interior provincial development, and indigenous innovation were all priorities of Hu/Wen administration, while maritime territorial disputes, an anticorruption campaign, and possibly legal and economic reform have emerged early on as priorities for Xi Jinping's leadership. Another feature that demands senior leadership attention is the propensity for a given issue to generate international controversy for China. For example, SARS, the aircraft carrier program, and China's involvement in Sudan all eventually required senior leadership attention given the international fallout.

So if China (like other complicated, modern nation-states) has a grand strategy and a process for fleshing out and implementing a strategic vision, then what is China's grand strategy and how does economics relate to it?

China's Strategic Logic and National Objectives

This book seeks to build on the growing body of work that looks at China's grand strategy and to extend this literature by elaborating on the role played by economics—both as an end to legitimize the regime and as a means to achieve the state's strategic interests. This element, the strategic use of economics, constitutes the central phenomenon under examination here. Exactly how does the Chinese state (or any state for that matter) *actually exercise* its international economic power? This section identifies China's national priorities and the strategic logic underpinning the economic aspects of China's grand strategy, and then explores the economic dimensions of China's grand strategy. I begin by laying out the rough outlines of a hierarchy of national interests that guide contemporary Chinese grand strategy.

A number of prominent works have identified regime stability as the overarching goal of China.[20] To realists, such self-preservation logic strikes a familiar chord: if an entity ceases to exist, all other preferences are moot. Because of the Communist Party's unique relationship to the state in the case of China, maintaining the CCP's control of China is the single most important national interest.[21] Maintaining the CCP's control of China, in turn, rests on legitimacy. Since the Reform and Opening Up Period began in 1978, the CCP's basis for domestic legitimacy has shifted away from revolutionary Maoism toward economically oriented pragmatism. Economic growth has come to replace communist ideology as the chief legitimizing dynamic underpinning the CCP's popular credibility.[22] Economic growth provides China's population with a rising standard of living. Today the CCP maintains its mandate to rule partly by virtue of being able to provide the sort of economic growth that has characterized the past thirty years. As that growth has slowed, there has been a resurgence of Chinese nationalism. To the extent that the party will seek to substitute nationalism in place of economic growth in its legitimating narrative, the region could be headed for some turbulence.[23]

Having secured the regime domestically, China, like other states in the international system, naturally seeks to maximize its ability to shape its international environment to the extent it is capable. Internationally, China's engagement with the world economy provides significant benefits in the form of inexpensive labor and access to a large potential market, making China an attractive partner. Both of these enhance the regime's legitimacy while demonstrating to China's international partners the benefits of China's growing stature.[24] Xi Jinping's "Silk Road Economic Belt" and his "21st Century Maritime Silk Road" provide the most recent instantiations of this regional strategic economic logic. In particular, "the new security diplomacy seeks to counter, co-opt, or circumvent what it [China] perceives as excessive American influence around the Chinese periphery, while avoiding overt confrontation with the United States, all with the aim of shaping its own security environment."[25] By proactively shaping its international environment, China can create conditions that are conducive to realizing its national interests. Although I believe that China is still actively engaged in determining what type of international power it will become, for the time being it seeks to maintain as unconstrained an environment as possible, providing China with a maximally permissive atmosphere in which it can exercise its growing power. Figuring out what to do with its eventual power may be deferred until some future time. For now, the objective is to enable China to rise unfettered and to prevent the constraint of its future exercise of power. One of the most important elements of this strategy is how the United States responds to China's rise. Specifically, it is important for China to avoid the formation of a potential balancing coalition of states that are opposed to China's growing power.[26] Medeiros (like Goldstein) also highlights China's desire to reassure its neighbors and prevent a balancing coalition that could check China's growing power (what he calls a "counter containment" objective).[27] Goldstein traces the origins of this strategic objective to 1996, when Chinese senior leadership re-evaluated the utility of China's use of force and embarked on a new path of regional and global reassurance.[28] Goldstein notes that from approximately 1996, a rough consensus on China's grand strategy has emerged among China's leadership:

> The grand strategy aims to engineer China's rise to great power status within the constraints of a unipolar international system that the United States dominates. It is designed to sustain the conditions necessary for continuing China's program of economic and military modernization as well as to minimize the risk that others, most importantly the peerless United States, will view the ongoing increase in China's capabilities as an unacceptably dangerous threat that must be parried or perhaps even forestalled. China's grand strategy, in short, aims to increase the country's international clout without triggering a counterbalancing reaction.[29]

This goal of avoiding a balancing coalition and reassuring other powers in the region (and globally) is often the driving force behind much of China's regional engagement and multilateral efforts. "This effort aims to create linkages that make China an indispensible, or at least very attractive, actor on whose interests the system's key actors are reluctant to trample."[30] China is also looking to establish and solidify its reputation as a responsible power in the international system as part of its effort to reassure other states that a more powerful China need not be feared.[31] Economic tools provide a critical channel for China to pursue these strategic reassurance goals.

Another important goal for China with strong economic characteristics is "*diversifying its access to energy and other natural resources.*"[32] The logic behind this objective is that China relies heavily on imported inputs for its growing economy.[33] At the same time, it recognizes that such reliance makes China vulnerable in a system whose stability is provided by the dominant United States.[34] In an effort to minimize China's exposure to any one source of natural resources, China has actively sought to diversify its sourcing.[35] The first set of cases that follow in the next two chapters are based on China's efforts to secure its access to these kinds of strategic raw materials. Such unfettered access is a critical enabler of China's continued economic growth. To pursue these critical raw materials, China has relied primarily on its massive state-owned enterprises (SOEs). This first set of cases examines the extent to which the state has (or has not) been able to control these economic actors. By looking closely at specific episodes of Chinese SOE efforts to secure access to strategic raw materials, we can get a better sense of how the exact mechanisms of state control operate.

Finally, Chinese foreign policy has long been motivated by the desire to limit the amount of "international space" that is afforded to Taiwan. This dates back to the earliest foreign policies of the PRC and continues to be an important driver of China's strategic interests. Taiwan and other issues of territorial integrity tend to be sensitive subjects. This is partly a function of history. China views its history as one of dynastic cycles.[36] Proximate causes of dynastic decline can range from corruption and poor administration to conquest by an outside power. One of the historic signals of a weak regime is the loss of peripheral territory deemed to be part of the empire. The CCP views Taiwan's incorporation/reintegration to the mainland as "unfinished business" going back to the battlefield defeat of the Nationalists in the Chinese Civil War. Because regime preservation is such an important goal and territorial integrity is understood to be a harbinger of regime decline, issues like Taiwan strike a sensitive chord for the CCP.[37] As a result, China has frequently sought to curtail Taiwan's international recognition as an independent entity and to limit Taiwan's participation and voice on the international stage. Economic tools of statecraft have been important elements of the mainland's Taiwan strategy. In later chapters, we will also analyze China's use of economic statecraft in the Taiwan context. Specific cases from the cross-strait relationship will be dissected to better understand exactly how the mainland has strategically used (or sought to use) economics to curtail Taiwan's moves toward independence.

Thus, from these broad goals, a rough hierarchy of China's national interests begins to emerge. The most important national interest is to preserve the PRC.[38] First and foremost is maintaining the party's grasp on power in China. This means China's grand strategy focuses a good deal of attention on threats to the party's grip on power. Perhaps it should come as no surprise then that the leadership has such a strong preference for stability and conservatism. This stability is both domestically oriented—to directly limit sources of threat to the regime—and internationally directed—to seek an international environment that is conducive to China's continued economic growth.[39] Economic growth is deemed to be critical in enabling China to complete its rise to great power status. In addition, economic growth provides an ongoing reaffirmation of the CCP's ruling mandate by underscoring the CCP's ability to deliver economic growth. Mutually beneficial economic interaction is also used to reassure other states in the system that China's rising power need not be cause for alarm. In many instances, increasing economic interaction both allays fears of a rising China while providing China with the economic interaction that further augments its influence and power capabilities. Diversification of these sources offers China less concentrated reliance and thus less vulnerability to potential disruption (which would undermine the economic foundations upon which so much of China's national interests rest).

Beyond securing the regime's stability, China seeks to shape its international strategic environment in a way that maximizes China's national interests.[40] In particular, China seeks to ensure that the United States is prevented from checking China's efforts to modernize and enhance its power. A common approach has been to use multilateral institutions to further China's national interests in a relatively nonthreatening manner. In addition, increasingly dense regional and global economic interaction promises to reinforce the atmosphere of international partnership and cooperation that provides China with a peaceful international security environment. Stability in China's security environment allows for the continued global economic interaction that fuels China's rising capabilities. Finally, China seeks to limit the possibility that its claims to Taiwan are undermined.

Now that we have laid out the general outlines of China's national interests and the strategic logic behind its grand strategy, let us now turn to a more detailed exploration of the explicitly economic dimensions of China's grand strategy.

Centrality of Economics to China's Grand Strategy

Economic growth is an important objective sought by the regime, both as a good in its own right and as one of the key means through which the party maintains its grasp on power. The party—and by extension China's grand strategy—is keenly focused on threats to the regime's grip on power. Many of these threats are domestic in origin. As a result, a considerable amount of Chinese leadership attention is devoted to addressing potential threats to the CCP that stem from domestic causes such as unemployment, inequality, corruption, ethnic unrest, etc. Good economic performance provides revenues that allow the state to defuse many of these potentially destabilizing social dynamics. Central funds can be used to subsidize SOE employment, redistribute wealth to poorer regions, and fund preferential treatment for restive ethnic minorities, to name a few.

Not only is economic growth good for the party's legitimacy, but economic growth has also been fueling China's rise to great power status. Since the beginning of the Reform and Opening Up period in 1978, China's economy has grown at an annual rate of more than 9 percent.[41] Continued economic development over the next ten to fifteen years will be needed to solidify China's rise in the international system.[42] This strategy of relying on international links to facilitate China's economic growth is not all that new. Since the Reform and Opening Up era began almost forty years ago, China has pursued an economic development model that emphasized unleashing China's economic potential. The Chinese economy has used an export-oriented growth model that relied on greater and greater integration into the global economy. Such relations have helped fuel China's rise to great power status as this model has delivered near double-digit annual growth for the past thirty years. This is a fairly constant theme underpinning much of mainstream contemporary Chinese grand strategy and Chinese-language scholarship on economic statecraft. To the extent that this line of thinking directly addresses strategic security concerns, it is usually through the notion that beneficial international engagement helps to fuel China's growing military might.[43] Such works often emphasize the need for China to maintain an international environment that is conducive to further economic growth.[44] Authors in this vein often advocate for further opening up and liberalization of the Chinese economy because this represents the most efficient path to achieving even greater economic results.[45] Many of these works grow out of Deng Xiaoping's initial strategic logic of focusing on economic liberalization as a way to increase China's power, and they frequently continue to invoke Deng's strategic thinking that placed economic development at the center of China's grand strategy.[46]

The central role of economics in China's contemporary grand strategy can be traced to the very foundations of China's economic success. Since Deng first set China on a course of modernization, there has been an intimate connection between China's economic success and a liberalization of China's domestic political economy. As soon as rural farmers were permitted to keep some of their surplus production, productivity improved. This same basic capitalist ethos was eventually extended more broadly into a wider range of economic activity in China. As the government retreated from China's domestic economy, it freed productive forces that unleashed years of rapid growth. This initial productivity increase was impressive, but it was to receive an exponential lift in the 1980s as China began to open itself up to the world. Early efforts to encourage foreign investment and attract managerial expertise provided key inputs that helped to jump-start the Chinese economic growth miracle. With the advent of Special Economic Zones (SEZs), China positioned itself to leverage in the wider international economic system its key factor: relatively inexpensive labor. One of the most important drivers of China's economic success was (and continues to be) China's coastal provinces, where these SEZs were originally located. These local economies are heavily oriented toward export industries. Much of China's economic success stems from its export-oriented growth model in which semifinished goods and raw materials are imported into China, processed and assembled, and then re-exported into global supply chains. China's export-oriented industries, in turn, act as engines of growth for the rest of China's economy. The export-oriented portion of China's economy contributes both directly to GDP (via net exports) and indirectly through employment and by acting as an economic catalyst in coastal municipalities (by spurring technology corridors, tax revenue, upstream suppliers, and ancillary businesses). China's foreign-invested, export-oriented enterprises account for roughly 40 percent of China's growth.[47] This export-oriented economic activity spurs additional domestic economic growth in China in areas such as wages remitted by migrant workers back to families in the countryside, technology transfer, investments in human capital, the increased value of coastal real estate, entrepreneurial spin-offs, peripheral supporting industries that grow up to supply the export-oriented industries, and reinvestment. All this activity relies on China's ties to the international economy.

China's Links to the Global Economy

China's contemporary grand strategy is embedded within a strategic environment epitomized by the links between China's domestic political economy (particularly its Reform and Opening Up efforts) and the larger international economic system. Beginning with the creation of Special Economic Zones, China's considerable economic success has been dependent upon its integration with the world economy. China's model of economic development entails deep ties to the globalizing world economy. To help enable China's economic success, a good deal of Chinese foreign policy has been oriented toward establishing China's permanent access to the international economic system. For example, throughout the 1990s much of China's US diplomacy was focused on securing most-favored-nation (MFN) status and gaining access to the World Trade Organization (WTO). China continues to expend much diplomatic energy on securing favorable political relationships and reliable supplies of raw materials from around the world. But China depends on global economic integration not only for secure supply but for secure demand as well. At the macro level, China relies on international demand that ultimately consumes most of China's exports. China's economic logic and strategy effectively seeks to tap into an external global aggregate demand. China acts as the workshop to the world in order to generate the supply to meet this global demand.

China's foreign policy and diplomatic efforts since Reform and Opening Up have been largely successful. China today enjoys deep ties to the international economic order. It has moved from an insulated, relatively autarkic communist model to become a fairly well-integrated critical node in the post–Cold War global economic system. This integration has played a vital role in facilitating China's economic success of the past thirty-five years. China recently surpassed the United States to become the world's largest trading nation (total imports and exports), and it has grown to become the world's second largest economy on the strength of these global economic ties.

But China's strategic use of employing its foreign policy to advance its economic interests is only one side of the economics and grand strategy coin. As mentioned in chapter 1, Chinese scholars use the term *jingji waijiao* (economic diplomacy) in two ways. One meaning is used to denote the diplomatic activity concerned with securing economic objectives, such as China's membership in the WTO and other international economic organizations. This can be thought of as using diplomatic means to realize economic results, the diplomatic logic underpinning the strategy discussed above. The other use of the term entails employing economic tools to pursue foreign policy goals. Studying this strategic use of economics is the primary focus of this study.

One of the mechanisms through which the state might seek to leverage its economic power is its sovereign wealth funds. As a consequence of China's export-oriented development model and its fixed exchange rate, China has accumulated massive foreign exchange reserves. China's sovereign wealth funds are economic actors created to allocate some of these reserves. In the final set of cases in this book, I examine the extent to which China's sovereign wealth funds lend themselves to being used as instruments of China's economic statecraft. Given China's current economic growth model, China's foreign exchange reserves seem likely to continue to accumulate. Because China's sovereign wealth funds function as an outlet for that state capital, it is important to understand whether and how these entities may be used as tools of China's economic statecraft.

Although some strains of liberalism might suggest that China's expansive international economic links will constrain China's foreign policy actions, these economic relationships have also provided new levers of national power for China. The realist tradition in international relations theory suggests that China's economic ties can also be employed as tools of statecraft. As China's economic clout has grown, it is increasingly finding itself able to leverage its economic power to pursue its foreign policy goals.[48] This represents a reversal of the past, in which China's foreign policy was seen as primarily designed to facilitate China's economic goals.[49] China's growing economic stature has enabled it to shift from a grand strategy that merely sought to enable its economic goals to one that can begin to leverage its growing economic power to achieve foreign policy goals that previously may have been out of reach. This new stage in the relationship between economics and China's grand strategy has not yet received adequate scholarly attention.[50] So how should we understand this sort of strategic use of economics? As discussed earlier, the key to understanding China's economic statecraft lies in being able to control and direct this unwieldy tool of influence.

The Utility of Economic Statecraft for China

Before delving into the specific cases, it makes sense to ask just how useful are economic tools of national power for pursuing China's grand strategy? For a variety of reasons, economic tools of national power are a particularly attractive lever for China to use to realize its foreign policy strategic objectives. Diplomatically, the distribution of power in the international system is concentrated in the United States. This unipolar distribution of power fundamentally constrains China's diplomatic options.[51] Military tools of national power are also still too limited for China to employ them as effective tools of statecraft. First, the United States has considerably more military power projection capabilities than does China. Although China has embarked on a lengthy process of military modernization, it is not yet mature, and China's military forces exhibit state-of-the-art technologies in only a few limited areas.[52] Second, China's application of military might as a tool of national power tends to frighten China's regional neighbors. Such actions spark fears of a revisionist China that threatens regional stability, and the result might be regional balancing behavior. Finally, exercising military force runs the risk of isolating China from the international community (a lesson drawn from the post-Tiananmen sanctions). Such a marginalization would threaten to derail China's main economic modernization objective. In addition, military force poses the risk of running afoul of international law. China has worked hard to signal its willingness to abide by international law in many arenas. Applying raw military power risks destabilizing the multilateral institutions China has joined and transgressing their associated norms.

At the same time that these traditional levers of hard power are unattractive for China, the potential utility of economic power for China is considerable. First, its exercise need not be as obvious, threatening, nor as dislocating as military or even diplomatic power can sometimes be. Economic tools of national power are generally less disruptive than military force and can be more nuanced than diplomatic power. Exercising economic power also provides states with a degree of ambiguity or plausible deniability that official diplomatic channels cannot.

Second, relying on economic power helps limit the domestic bureaucratic influence of military-related political interests. By relying on economic power, China is able to strengthen the domestic political clout of economic-oriented parts of the government, institutions, and individuals.

Third, economic power offers the possibility of attracting partners with a win-win mentality. International economic ties have been used to assuage regional concerns over a growing China. This was particularly true during the period from roughly 2001 through 2007. China's "win-win" diplomacy was successful in engaging Southeast Asia and demonstrating to nations like South Korea how China's growing economy can also be a boon for China's regional partners. This strategy illustrated how a rising China need not necessarily only be cause for concern; it can also present an opportunity in the form of a regional economic growth engine to which local economies may hitch their wagons. These elements of China's grand strategy demonstrate that others can benefit handsomely from China's rise if nations are willing to partner with China.

Fourth, economic tools of national power hold out the possibility that China can realize its economic growth objectives while at the same time pursuing its foreign policy goals (to the extent the two are complementary). In this way, economic statecraft offers the possibility of killing two birds with one stone. A fifth reason that economic power is attractive is that China is gaining more and more economic gunpowder as its economy expands and matures. Over time, China's economic power should be a growing asset in China's national power tool kit. Finally, although economic power is often difficult for states to use (and China has had its share of frustration trying to employ economic power), China has also shown that it can be fairly adroit at using economic statecraft. Perhaps we should not be surprised to find that China has been adept in pursuing its foreign policy goals via economic means. China's economic success and its unique mixed economy gives it the unusual combination of both clout and the ability to wield that clout to pursue strategic objectives. China's ability to direct its "private-ish" sector toward strategic ends is much greater than in other, more liberal economies.

As part of its rising great power strategy, China has explicitly sought to develop and incorporate economics into its grand strategy.[53] While continuing economic growth has replaced Maoist ideology as a legitimating trestle for the regime, this is only the most obvious way in which economics has played an important role in rising China's grand strategy. China has sought to utilize economic tools of national power in a variety of other ways as well.

Examples of China's Economic Statecraft

China is a rising power that is increasingly using its economic clout. These applications of economic power can take many forms, such as when China sought to coerce or punish target states. China attempted to retaliate against France for selling arms to Taiwan and for its positions on the Dalai Lama and the Tibet issue in 2009. China subjected Philippine bananas to more stringent inspections and testing following heightened tensions related to the two nations' conflicting territorial claims and the heated standoff at Scarborough Shoal in the spring of 2012. China has threatened to retaliate (unsuccessfully) against proindependence Taiwanese investors in mainland China. China also apparently cut off the pipeline supplying North Korea with most of its oil to "encourage" the north to return to diplomatic talks on its nuclear program.[54] Similar allegations have surfaced with regard to Japan and Mongolia. In the wake of Japan's 2010 arrest of a Chinese fishing captain for ramming a Japanese coast guard cutter near the disputed Senkaku/Diaoyu Islands, China's exports of rare earth metals to Japan, critical for its electronic industry, were curtailed. At the time of the curtailment, China produced almost all the world's supply of rare earths. Although further research into this episode suggests that the cutoff was largely coincidental and part of a planned reduction in China's rare earth exports, the timing of the policy's implementation was unfortunate. Japan (and a good deal of the rest of the world) perceived that China was seeking to send a message to Japan that it was highly dependent on the concentrated Chinese source of rare earth metals supply.

In addition to such coercive uses of economic statecraft, China's international economic interaction has also been a source of strategic transfer. Instead of employing eighteenth- or nineteenth-century tactics of outright military conquest to secure China's access to strategic materials, China has been able to rely on its increasing integration into the global economy to more efficiently secure vital resources. For example, Chinese economic activities in the Russian Far East show how such economic mechanisms can make outright military conquest largely redundant. China's acquisitions and investments abroad have ensured its flows of oil, iron, coal, gas, minerals, and other basic inputs for its economy. China's growing integration in global production chains has also facilitated China's acquisition of dual-use technologies, processes, technical know-how, materials, and capabilities. Such transfers have contributed both to China's military modernization as well as to China's broader science and technology development. Lax intellectual property rights enforcement and outright economic espionage has enabled Chinese firms to "indigenize" state-of-the-art ideas, methods, and materials from abroad. In addition, there have even been explicit attempts to require that multinational companies transfer technology as a requirement for operating in or gaining access to the Chinese market.[55] These efforts are designed to move the Chinese economy up the value chain. Foreign private-sector business success is critically dependent on Chinese government support and local partner cooperation in China to an extent that is uniquely Chinese. China's perceived selective targeting of dominant foreign companies under China's antimonopoly law provides more proof that staying in the government's good graces is essential for commercial success in China.[56] Given the potential for the Chinese market, there is no shortage of foreign enterprises willing to comply with burdensome policies and to endure poorly protected intellectual property rights. As a result, efforts to encourage technology transfer have generated some tactical success for China even as such efforts may be doing long-term damage to China's reputation.

Another way China has leveraged its economic relations is via free trade arrangements. Deborah Brautigam and Xiaoyang Tang have shown the strategic value of free trade zones for China.[57] Beneficial trade and investment relations and free trade agreements have helped solidify and reinforce amicable political and strategic relations with nations that have traditionally been wary of a powerful China. Cold War US allies like Japan, Taiwan, and Korea were traditionally hostile (or at least cool) toward China for most of the twentieth century, but improving economic links have helped thaw these political relations or at least acted as a fire-break on tensions and have generally provided a more receptive strategic context for twenty-first-century regional rapprochement.[58] Economic ties have also served to bind peripheral regions like Xinjiang, Mongolia, and Central Asia more closely to the Chinese economic growth engine. China's economically oriented vision for the development direction of the Shanghai Cooperation Organization (SCO) also plays to China's strength. An economically oriented (as opposed to a militarily oriented) SCO would favor China's strong suit (more so than Russia's). The SCO can thus also provide a multilateral vehicle for projecting China's economic influence into Central Asia. If the SCO proves to be an unsuitable multilateral vehicle, Xi Jinping has displayed a willingness to act more bilaterally, even if in an aggregate fashion, with his New Silk Road Economic Belt initiative.

These are just a few examples of the various ways China (and other states) can use economics as a tool of national power. Scholars interested in how grand strategy is actually pursued in practice ought to focus more closely on how states like China use economic tools of national power to realize their strategic objectives. In the chapters that follow, we will look at how the Chinese state can (and cannot) control economics and what conditions facilitate the effective use of economic interaction to achieve Chinese foreign policy objectives.

As discussed in this chapter, contemporary Chinese grand strategy seeks to use economics as an important instrument of national power. Military tools have proven counterproductive for China to realize its grand strategic goals because they prompt regional balancing, arms racing, fears of a revisionist China, etc. At the same time, China's economic success—largely on the back of deepening international economic activity—has enabled China to begin using economics to achieve its national strategic objectives. This book helps to shed light on the use of economic tools of national power to facilitate China's grand strategy. To meaningfully engage in an empirical study of precisely how economic statecraft works, one must focus the analytical lens at a minute level of detail to uncover the mechanisms by which China is (or is not) able to control commercial actors. The next few chapters examine specific cases in which China sought to achieve national strategic objectives via commercial actors. Through detailed case analysis, we can begin to develop a better understanding of the factors that enable the state to control or direct the behavior of commercial actors.

Part II

SECURING STRATEGIC RAW MATERIALS

In part 2 of the book I examine two cases taken from China's extractive resources industry, a sector that many countries (including China) consider to be strategically vital. The first case discusses the China National Petroleum Corporation (CNPC) and its activities in Sudan. This case is a useful illustration of how a lack of state control (a negative value on the dependent variable) can produce strategic consequences for China. The second case provides a useful point of comparison. In studying the details of the attempted Chinalco–Rio Tinto merger (2007–2009), one can observe an instance of state control over the behavior of the corporate actors (a positive value on the dependent variable). The juxtaposition of the Chinalco case with the CNPC case allows us to identify the factors that account for the different outcomes we observe in each case.

To explore exactly how the state utilizes economic statecraft in the context of strategic resources, this part of the book focuses on China's efforts to secure oil and iron, two critical raw inputs for China. State planners have identified petroleum as one of the most important (if not the most important) strategic resource that must be secured.[1] The government's efforts in this area involve the creation and subsequent "going out" of the Chinese national oil corporations (NOCs). These corporations were among the earliest Chinese commercial actors to venture abroad. Chapter 4 highlights these efforts with a particular focus on the China National Petroleum Corporation (CNPC) and its activities in Sudan. This case is a useful illustration of how a lack of state control can produce strategic consequences for China. The case is also useful from a theory-building and testing perspective in that it demonstrates how changes in values on the independent variables generate the expected corresponding effects on the dependent variable (state control). For instance, the state is not acting as a unified actor in the early portion of the CNPC case, and we observe the expected inability to control the commercial actor. Another key factor in this case is the balance of relative resources, which favors the firm. In fact, all the indicators except for the reporting relationship variable suggest it would be difficult for the state to control the firm in this episode. In fact, because this first set of cases all deal with state-owned enterprises in the resource extraction sector, this variable remains relatively fixed in favor of state control across these cases. All the cases in this part of the book involve commercial actors that are state-owned enterprises with direct reporting relationships to the state. These important features provide a useful basis for comparison. Between the early CNPC minicase and the later CNPC minicase, we observe only the state unity independent variable changing direction. In the CNPC case, once the state was able to "unify," it was able to re-establish control over the commercial actor. Such within-case variation is methodologically useful because it enables us to hold many other potentially confounding factors constant. For instance, leadership personalities, company culture, geographic locations, regime type, internal corporate structure, ownership, etc., all remain unchanged in the comparison of the early and late CNPC episodes. This allows us to isolate the explanatory power of the change in the state unity independent variable.

Chapter 5 revolves around a case that provides a useful point of comparison. In studying the details of the attempted Chinalco–Rio Tinto merger, one can observe an instance of state control over the behavior of the Chinese corporate actors. The juxtaposition of the Chinalco case with the CNPC case also serves a useful theory-building function by allowing us to identify the factors that account for the different outcomes we observe in each case. In making this cross-case comparison, we again attempt to hold as many potentially background conditions constant to enable productive observation of variation across the independent variables.

So how does China secure access to what it views as strategic raw materials? The Chinese government has relied on a strategy that seeks to create internationally competitive corporations over which the state seeks to maintain control. This strategy looks to reap the benefits of commercialization (e.g., efficiency, productivity, innovation, economic strength, etc.) without losing the stability and sense of security that comes from state control.[2] The results are massive state-owned enterprises with elements of partial privatization. Although many of these firms are no longer fully under state control, in some instances China is still able to direct their behavior. On other occasions, the firms—rather than the state—seem to be running the show. The two CNPC minicases and the Chinalco case provide some empirical insight into the factors that determine when the state can or cannot control such firms.

4

"GOING OUT" AND CHINA'S SEARCH FOR ENERGY SECURITY

This chapter focuses on the challenge of state control with regard to the China National Petroleum Corporation (CNPC). As the Chinese oil sector has matured, there has been a general trend of creating a more and more commercially driven set of corporate energy actors. This dynamic has introduced the predictable principal-agent challenges for state control in a sector deemed to be a strategic national interest. This chapter briefly examines this evolution and the initial CNPC forays abroad. In particular, CNPC's activities in Africa generated unwelcome consequences for the state, but the Chinese state was able to eventually regain control over this commercial actor. The story of how the state was initially unable to control the commercial actor (referred to as the "early CNPC" minicase) and later was able to reassert its control ("late CNPC") constitutes an empirical illustration of some of the moving parts of the theory presented earlier.

The values on the independent variables suggest that control should have been difficult in this case. In the early portion of this case, the state was divided along bureaucratic lines. The goals of CNPC did not really take China's larger diplomatic priorities into consideration. The oil industry was highly concentrated and the balance of relative resources favored the firm. The only factor whose value suggested state control may have been possible was the reporting relationship. CNPC was a state-owned, state-operated, and state-financed enterprise. This alone proved insufficient for the state to establish control over the early CNPC activities in Sudan.

Methodologically, the juxtaposition of the early and late CNPC cases allows us to hold many of the independent variables fixed: CNPC was still a state-owned enterprise in the late case, much of the expertise continued to reside with the firm rather than with the state, the industry was still highly concentrated, and the firm's profit motive continued to exert a powerful influence. The state, however, was able to act in a more unified manner in the late CNPC case context, a shift that enabled the state to reassert its control over CNPC. This outcome attests to the importance of the Unity of State variable.

This chapter begins with background information regarding the Chinese state and its relationship to the oil industry before describing the CNPC's early efforts to venture abroad. The Sudan episode is described, and the latter portion of the chapter explicitly draws on the variables presented earlier to understand how the state reasserted control over the commercial actor.

China's Security and Strategic Resources

The discussion of China's grand strategy in the previous chapter noted the importance of regime stability. Continued economic growth in a relatively benign international environment has been a critical component of this regime stability. China today defines its strategic security interests in terms of maintaining the Communist Party's control of government. Keeping the regime in power is at the core of many of China's strategic interests. Maintaining the party's legitimacy requires continued economic growth.[1] Economic growth, in turn, needs raw inputs,[2] especially energy inputs. "The legitimacy of the CPC's political system is based on its ability to sustain economic growth in the postmillennial era—one that is hampered by a long-term decline in domestic oil production."[3] This declining production is coupled with a monumental surge in Chinese demand for energy.[4] Much of this energy need is met with coal, which is viewed as being more reliable given China's huge domestic deposits of it. But coal cannot supply all of China's energy needs. Much of the rest of China's energy comes from oil, and more and more of this oil is imported from abroad. Thus China's strategic interests are intimately connected to its ability to secure raw materials.[5]

A Brief History of China's Oil Sector

The evolution of China's oil industry has been a process of creating distance between the state and the commercial agents that make up China's oil sector today. The development of China's oil sector has been marked by three major periods. In the early days of the People's Republic of China (PRC), oil exploration and production were fully concentrated on China's domestic territory. China was not yet industrialized and oil production was conducted via localized, mass-mobilization programs. These efforts (when successful) produced many fragmented provincial or even township-level petroleum enterprises. These integrated oil entities (called petroleum administrative bureaus) lacked economies of scale and often included exploration, drilling, and refining operations (such as they were). These localized efforts were eventually organized into the Ministry of Petroleum Industry (MPI), which owned, managed, and operated all the petroleum production capacity of China.[6] China's petroleum activities were conducted according to the government's economic planning. The oil sector was a fully government-controlled entity and there were no significant issues concerning the state's ability to control the commercial activities in this sector. Under communism, the commercial actors *were* the state. The bigger problem was the host of economic inefficiencies, underinvestment, and long-term decline of productivity that frequently plagues state economic planning efforts.[7] For example, the sector suffered from underinvestment, which often resulted in low yields from oil fields. Investment levels were suboptimal because oil producers had no incentive to invest because oil prices were so low. Oil prices in the plan were kept low because of fears of inflation and a general desire to stimulate economic growth.

In the second phase of China's oil industry, efforts were made to liberalize China's oil sector. In 1981, China introduced a two-tiered pricing system under which the MPI was obligated to supply the central government with a specific, contracted amount of oil. Any oil that was produced in excess of this contracted amount could then be sold directly into the domestic Chinese market at prices above those stipulated in the plan. Excess oil could also be sold on the international market (to buy technology, equipment, data, etc. for its operations). This was designed to create pricing incentives to increase oil production. MPI, in turn, subcontracted production agreements with local petroleum administration bureaus (the local, integrated petroleum operations mentioned above). Any oil the petroleum administration bureaus produced over contract could, in turn, also be sold directly into the market at above-plan prices. Again, as was the case with MPI's obligation, the individual petroleum administration bureaus were allowed to keep the resulting revenues.

In addition to these basic pricing reforms, China's oil industry was reorganized in the 1980s. Up until that point, the Ministry of Petroleum Industry (or one of its predecessor ministries) controlled the exploration, production, and refinery assets of China.[8] These government ministries were also responsible for the administration, oversight, and planning of China's petroleum industry. In 1982, MPI's offshore upstream oil assets and offshore exploration and production assets were reorganized into the China National Offshore Oil Corporation (CNOOC). CNOOC continued to be wholly owned by and still reported to MPI. The new corporate structure, however, was designed to improve the productivity of China's oil assets and to begin to split off the government's regulatory and administrative roles from its commercial activities. The reforms also allowed CNOOC to engage in cooperation with foreign oil companies as part of an effort to enhance CNOOC's offshore drilling technology. The head of CNOOC maintained his vice ministerial rank. In 1983, the refining and petrochemical operations of MPI were combined with the chemical operations of the Ministry of Chemical Industry and the synthetic fiber manufacturing assets of the Ministry of Textile Industry to create the China Petroleum and Chemical Corporation (Sinopec).[9] Like CNOOC, the head of Sinopec maintained his bureaucratic rank (in this case, minister). With Sinopec focused on owning and operating China's downstream refining assets, and CNOOC owning and operating China's offshore upstream production assets, MPI was left with China's natural gas and onshore, upstream oil production and exploration assets. These assets were grouped into the China National Petroleum Corporation (CNPC) in 1988. Interestingly, CNPC also inherited all of MPI's administrative functions, including product quality standards and environmental regulation.[10] The head of CNPC also retained his ministerial rank. CNPC and Sinopec eventually consolidated and rolled up the numerous local and provincial production and refining entities to create national oil majors. When the reorganization dust had settled, China was left with CNOOC, which controlled China's offshore, upstream production assets; Sinopec, which was primarily focused on refining assets; and CNPC, which encompassed the rest of China's petroleum industry (primarily onshore, upstream production assets). All three state-owned corporations reported directly to the State Council.

In 1994, the system was further liberalized and the central government did away with plan contracts. Instead, in-plan pricing was integrated with the prevailing above-plan pricing. Although the government still controlled pricing closely, this was a meaningful step toward liberalization. Also in 1994, all state-owned enterprises (SOEs) (including those in the oil industry) were officially permitted to keep profits. This was an important step in China's reform efforts and injected a considerable degree of commercialization into SOE operations. By 1998, Chinese oil companies were permitted to use marker pricing, which tied Chinese pump prices to world crude prices. This pricing reform allowed China's domestic prices to more accurately reflect world energy prices, but the pricing still did not really connect to China's domestic market demand. Eventually, the oil companies were permitted to adjust prices within 5 percent then 8 percent ranges, but the state continued to keep tight reins on petroleum pricing given its inflationary potential.

The reforms of China's oil sector mirror the larger Chinese economic reforms of the 1980s and 1990s: a pattern of gradual liberalization and reform of the

Chinese economy and a move toward a more commercial orientation. Although these reforms were initially designed to improve the productivity of China's oil production efforts, they would also sow the seeds of the commercialization of China's oil industry. This commercialization would eventually make it difficult for the state to maintain control over the behavior of its commercial actors.[11] "Indeed, the more China liberalizes, the less easy it is to control private businesses domestically, let alone in far-off Africa."[12] As its commercial actors took on more and more active roles internationally, China would find that their activities often had strategic consequences for the state.

By 1998, China's oil sector had entered the third phase of its evolution. As China was increasingly becoming integrated into the global economy, it became evident that China's partially liberalized oil sector was not sustainable. The new oil companies lacked integrated petroleum operations, which exposed them to significant shocks from price volatility. In other words, by concentrating a company only on upstream production and exploration assets, that company would be heavily exposed to the price of oil. Such companies would have a difficult time absorbing price volatility; when the price of oil was high it would reap windfall profits, but when the price was low it would suffer significant shortfalls. The same logic punished or rewarded companies focused exclusively on downstream refining, processing, and distribution. If the price of oil was high, a refining operation would suffer losses. When oil was cheap, a refinery was poised to make significant profits. To help smooth out some of this instability and to prepare China's national oil companies (NOCs) for the global competition that they would face once China entered the WTO, the State Council swapped some of CNPC's (upstream) and Sinopec's (downstream) assets with each other. This was done roughly on the basis of geography, giving CNPC assets concentrated in the North and Sinopec's in the South. This move gave both major players upstream and downstream assets in their portfolio. The State Council also gave the companies trading rights that enabled them to engage in the international trading of petroleum and petroleum products. This wave of reorganization also took the corporations out of their administrative and regulatory roles, moving those to a relatively weak State Petroleum and Chemical Industry Bureau (under the State Economic and Trade Commission).[13]

The final move toward commercialization occurred with the public listings of the crown jewel assets of each of these NOCs. The central government sought not only to conduct public offerings of China's NOCs in order to tap international capital markets, but also to expose these firms to market pressures, shareholder obligations, and even corporate governance as a way to improve their international competiveness. When these firms were listed, however, the government structured the offerings so that the state would be assured of retaining control of the parent company. The assets that were attractive to the markets were placed into new shell companies that would trade on the exchanges. For CNPC, its assets were placed in PetroChina, which was listed in April 2000, with the state retaining 90 percent ownership of the company. Sinopec was listed in October 2000, with the state retaining 77 percent ownership. CNOOC was listed in February 2001, with the state retaining 71 percent ownership. Creating these publicly traded companies was another important step toward reform and liberalization. These moves were designed to improve the NOCs' efficiency and create more effective commercial tools for China to procure oil.[14] This commercialization, however (in particular the growing gap between the state and the commercial firms), laid the groundwork for future challenges for state control that characterize the business-government relationship today.[15]

For example, the reorganization of the MPI created many of the large asymmetries that can be observed along the Relative Resources dimension of business-government relations in the petroleum sector. In the wake of the transition, virtually all of the government's institutional knowledge and resources related to the petroleum sector, as well as the state's expert personnel and even regulatory budgets, moved over to take up residence within the new oil corporations that were formed. The new companies inherited their predecessors' bureaucratic rank, administrative functions, personnel, and the institutional memory of the state ministries. This left few resources in government. Regulatory agencies were understaffed and operated with large gaps in industry knowledge, expertise, and appropriate personnel.[16]

In addition, the balance of human capital resources suggested that state control of these commercial actors would not be easy. For example, during the reorganization process, the ministerial leadership transitioned right over into the leadership posts of the new NOCs. Wang Tao, then the minister of MPI, went on to become the head of CNPC. His deputy, Zhou Yongkang, became vice president of CNPC.[17] Chen Tonghai went from being the deputy director of the State Planning Commission to becoming the deputy general manager of Sinopec in the 1998 reshuffle. He would be promoted to director and vice chairman in 2000 and became chairman of Sinopec in 2006. Sheng Huaren was formerly the director of the Planning Bureau of the Ministry of Chemical Industry before eventually becoming the head of Sinopec. Qin Wencai was formerly vice minister of the MPI before becoming president of CNOOC. When these leaders transitioned to these new corporations they also brought over their bureaucratic ranks. Given the relatively lower-ranking supervisory and administrative bodies that later were created to oversee China's petroleum industry, the disparities in bureaucratic rank between the regulators and the regulated further complicated state efforts to control these commercial actors. Finally, although these high-powered leaders at the helm of China's NOCs made state control over the commercial actors difficult, it did provide for a certain amount of trust between them and the CCP leadership because the leaders of the state personally knew and had worked with many of the leaders of these commercial actors.

These reforms empowered commercial actors to take the lead in China's efforts to secure its access to petroleum. Although the reforms helped address inefficiencies in China's petroleum management system, they also set the stage for commercial actors to pursue their own interests, even if that sometimes undermined other national priorities. The issue of China's state control over its petroleum firms featured prominently once these firms began taking on more active roles as international actors. Their involvement on the international stage is the subject of the next section.

China's NOCs "Go Out"

Current efforts on the part of some of China's largest and most successful corporations to expand operations internationally are part of China's *zouchuqu* strategy.[18] This case is about the origins of this multinationalization strategy. Interestingly, in the oil sector, forays into the international marketplace were initially led not by the state but rather by the commercial actors. The state eventually justified the strategy ex post facto and encouraged other strategic sectors to similarly engage in the global market as a way to enhance China's international competitiveness. In the oil industry, going abroad was driven by inefficiencies at home and production declines in China's domestic petroleum resources. As outlined above, the state first created corporations from the government ministries as a way of addressing inefficiencies in China's domestic oil industry. Possessing technical expertise that the state lacked (after most of the state's expertise went over to the commercial actors as discussed above), the NOCs recognized, before the state did, that demand from China's booming economy was going to outpace China's domestic supply and would force China to look abroad to find alternative sources of petroleum to make up the difference. The impetus to go abroad was thus driven by the commercial actors, and their moves were initially made without prior government approval.[19]

State enthusiasm for expanding China's access to oil grew over time. Initially, the government only officially supported the NOCs' efforts to develop China's domestic western oil fields in 1991, making this a part of the Eighth Five-Year Plan. Noticeably, the government did not a give similar endorsement to the NOCs' efforts to develop *international* sources of oil until the end of 1993, when the state officially embraced the "going out" policy. The NOCs' strategy of going out to find oil was further supported by Premier Li Peng in 1997, and state support built momentum when Jiang Zemin embraced China's need for oil as a matter of strategic importance in October 2000.[20] The "going out" strategy was endorsed and extended to other strategic sectors in the Tenth Five-Year Plan. The state had shifted from passive endorsement to proactive measures to support and encourage going out. By 2001, the state had established four prerequisites for obtaining government financial support for going out and China's oil companies have not looked back.[21]

Although the initial moves abroad in the oil sector were led by the CNPC, it was not until the government officially sanctioned and endorsed this strategy that China's NOCs began to make major moves internationally. That the firms first moved to venture abroad indicates that much of the human capital, talent, and technical expertise of the industry resided within the NOCs. That these initial moves were circumscribed until the state leadership provided its full endorsement of this strategic direction, however, shows that the strategic guidance for China's petroleum policy continues to emanate from the central government authorities. In large matters, the state still calls the shots. But, as discussed in more detail below, effective use of this power requires the attention of the highest echelons within the Communist Party to overcome any lower-level divisions within the state. In the absence of such centralized leadership, institutionally powerful commercial actors will take the opportunity to act on their own interests. CNPC's initial moves internationally (without state endorsement) serve to illustrate this dynamic.

CNPC's ventures abroad began tentatively. Beginning with an April 1991 agreement to cooperate with Alberta in exploring oil sands deposits, CNPC launched its international efforts on its own initiative. The first major oil field development rights were acquired in Thailand in March 1993 and the first equity stake was in an oil field in Alberta in July 1993 for $5 million. In October of that year, CNPC won a $25 million bid to enhance oil recovery in Peru. These initial moves abroad were driven largely by the more attractive commercial opportunities to be found overseas as opposed to China's own aging domestic oil fields. These initial efforts were fairly small, however, because CNPC was forced to deal with many layers of regulatory red tape to secure approvals for any international investment.[22] As China's energy shortfall became more apparent throughout the 1990s, government support for the NOCs' international activities grew. As the state got behind the "going out" strategy, barriers to international investments gave way to subsidies and inducements. As NOCs sought a larger presence overseas, they felt that much of the low-hanging fruit had already been claimed by the large multinational companies. As a result, China had little choice but to seek out untapped opportunities in countries whose petroleum resources were otherwise shunned for one reason or another.[23] Such logic led Chinese NOCs to work with unsavory regimes where reserves were still available.[24]

Sudan

One of the most notorious destinations to which CNPC ventured was Sudan, where China's presence would result in considerable damage to China's international reputation. In the 1990s, Sudan found a willing partner in China at a time when Western governments were applying pressure on the regime in Khartoum for its support of terrorism. Beginning in 1995, CNPC purchased Chevron's concession in West Kordofan and expanded its role in Sudan when it won an international bid in November 1996. A Canadian firm (Arakis) sold off its stake in three prospecting blocks. CNPC partnered with Malaysia's Petronnas, another Canadian firm (Talisman Energy, that had taken over Arakis), and Sudan's Sudapet to create the Greater Nile Petroleum Operating Company (GNPOC), in which CNPC took a 40 percent stake. Although it seems that China's initial involvement in Sudan was driven by CNPC's desire to secure access to international sources of oil, the Chinese government's amoral policies of noninterference in domestic affairs and its willingness to engage countries with little regard to their human rights records set up Beijing for diplomatic failure. Sinopec and CNPC have both remained actively engaged in developing Sudan's oil resources.[25] By 2008, China was importing around 60 percent of Sudan's oil output and had invested approximately US$4 billion.[26] These activities in Sudan provided critical support to the Sudanese government.[27]

Perhaps even more unsettling was China's complicity in providing arms and military assistance to regimes like Sudan's that engage in substantial human rights violations against their people. China transferred helicopters, strike fighters, trucks, and small arms to Sudan, and many of these arms made their way to Darfur, fueling the conflict there.[28] In addition, the Sudanese government apparently used military force to clear populations from the oil fields that China was interested in exploiting.[29] China's search for oil in Sudan entangled it in a web of ties between China's oil extraction efforts, arms, and human rights concerns.[30] Such ties created a caustic combination for China.

China's provision of military aid was not limited to Sudan, or even to Africa. China had also come under fire for providing military support to Zimbabwe and Congo, and China was also a key source of military assistance to the military junta that ran Myanmar (where China had a number of natural gas interests as well as strategic interests in using Myanmar as a possible energy transportation route to circumvent the Malacca Straits) and Nepal.

The Consequences of "Going Out"

The activities of China's companies generated considerable diplomatic embarrassment for China.[31] China's inability (or unwillingness) to rein in its commercial actors brought it under significant international pressure, which undermined some of China's larger strategic objectives. Three major criticisms have been leveled at China for its involvement in Sudan. First, international activists have pressured most international investors to divest from Sudan because such investments help fund the regime's suppressive and genocidal activities. China, however, stood by its NOCs' decisions not to withdraw from Sudan and had, for a long time, insisted on upholding its commitment to national sovereignty and noninterference in Sudan's domestic affairs. Second, human rights organizations documented that Chinese arms helped fuel the ongoing conflict. Allegations included transfer of aircraft and small arms that were used on civilian populations in Darfur.[32] Third, critics attacked China for doing nothing to stop the genocide. Under the principle of sovereignty and noninterference, China was not only avoiding condemnation of the Khartoum regime, but China also actively blocked attempts by the United Nations and the international community to put an end to the killing in Darfur. This caused some to question China's commitment to international norms and undermined the claim that a rising China would integrate well into the international system. The ostensibly commercial activity of China's NOCs was generating negative blowback for the state. The NOCs "going out" strategy and the freedom that the commercial actors enjoyed combined to create a situation in which commercial actors were empowered to engage in activities that generated negative strategic consequences for the Chinese state. China's international reputation was significantly damaged by its involvement in Sudan.

To address these concerns, Beijing took a number of steps to repair its international image. First, it launched a substantial public relations campaign to improve public perceptions of Beijing's engagement with Africa. At the 2006 Forum on China-Africa Cooperation, it signed the "Beijing Declaration," which "calls for halting the illegal production, circulation, and trafficking of small arms and light weapons to Africa."[33] Beijing also shifted from its stance of initially opposing the UN peacekeeping force for Darfur that was proposed to augment the weak African Union force.[34] In February 2007, during Hu Jintao's trip to Sudan, China pushed President Bashir to accept the hybrid AU/UN peacekeeping force. In addition, China began pushing Sudan's government toward a more positive policy by playing a more active role in mediation and more openly criticizing the Sudanese government.[35] Finally, many observers began highlighting that China's significant resource demand was good for the economies of Africa.[36] Chinese demand was, indeed, a particularly important driver behind the surge in African exports,[37] and African economies grew considerably on the back of this international demand for raw materials, the vast majority of which were (not surprisingly) oil exports.[38]

Although China made some progress on addressing the concerns stemming from its commercial actors' involvement in Sudan, China's search for oil drew it into other prickly situations as well. Indeed, Sudan was not the only place the activities of aggressive commercial actors in the oil industry created strategic headaches for Beijing. The presence of Chinese NOCs in dangerous areas naturally also opened up the possibility of threats to Chinese workers being kidnapped, attacked, or killed. Darfurian rebels targeted Chinese citizens as part of a strategy to prevent CNPC and Sinopec from operating (and thus indirectly—or directly—supporting the Sudanese government). Employing a similar logic, separatist rebels of the Ogaden National Liberation Front killed nine Chinese workers in Ethiopia in April 2007.[39] In January 2007, five Chinese workers were kidnapped by rebels belonging to the Movement for the Emancipation of the Niger Delta (MEND). This followed a deterioration of security in the Niger River Delta, where 90 percent of Nigeria's oil is produced. Following Hu Jintao's April 2006 visit and pledge to invest $4 billion in Nigeria, MEND warned Chinese companies to leave the delta or risk being targeted. Nigeria turned to China for coastal patrol boats and other military supplies to help secure the region, and China obliged despite the reputation of Nigeria's armed forced for corruption, unprofessionalism, and human rights abuses. "China's reason for supplying Nigeria's military, however dysfunctional, with armament is very pragmatic: China needs Nigeria's oil."[40] Such security considerations will likely continue to surround the work of China's oil companies as they engage in unstable regions of the world.

The state has come under fire as Chinese NOCs have become more and more involved with problematic regimes in places like Iran, Burma, and Angola. In the early part of the 2000s, Angola accounted for roughly half of the Chinese crude oil that was coming from Africa. Sinopec invested $3.5 billion in partnership with the Angolan national oil firm, Sonangol, to pump oil from Angola's auctioned offshore blocks. In addition, Sinopec pledged to build a $3 billion refinery in Angola.[41] Some have suspected that much of this partnership grew out of a controversial $2 billion aid package that China's Export-Import Bank provided to Angola.[42] Angola had been close to signing an IMF-provided aid package that would have required considerable transparency and disclosure requirements, but once Angola discovered it had a much more forgiving source of financing in the Export-Import Bank, it pulled out of the IMF negotiations. Angola is a corrupt state, and China's no-strings-attached engagement policies undercut Western efforts to improve governance or impose any sort of transparency on the Angolan regime. Such activities also served to undermine Chinese claims of being a responsible stakeholder.

The problems that the activities of the commercial actors generated for the central government bedeviled other extractive industries as well. China was actively involved in Zambia's copper mining industry, but poor working conditions and safety concerns resulted in anti-Chinese sentiment there. In April 2005, an explosion at the Beijing General Research Institute of Mining and Metallurgy explosives factory near the Chambishi copper mine killed more than fifty Zambian workers.[43] The blast seems to have been the result of unsafe working conditions, and Chinese management was blamed. The runner-up populist presidential candidate in Zambia's 2006 election campaigned on a platform of "kicking out the Chinese," who he argued were exploiting Zambia's resources in a neocolonial fashion.[44] During Hu Jintao's 2007 trip to Africa, plans to have Hu inaugurate the Chambishi Special Economic Zone had to be cancelled because of fears of anti-Chinese protests there. In March 2008, workers building a copper smelter at the Chambishi Mine attacked Chinese management when wage negotiations stalled. Such anti-Chinese sentiment undermined larger Chinese strategic objectives of reassurance and acting as a responsible stakeholder in international affairs. Eventually, the Chinese state sought to rein in the commercial actors and limit their ability to generate counterproductive results for China.

Tools of State Control

Recognizing that the activities of commercial actors were creating problems for China, the Chinese authorities sought to re-establish control over the international activities of its commercial actors in the extractive resources sector. These efforts were primarily concentrated in two of the independent variables: Balance of Relative Resources (particularly along the human capital and finance/budget dimensions) and Unity of the State. First, China strengthened bureaucratic control over the commercial actors by reorganizing the state monitoring, enforcement, and compliance capabilities. With a particular focus on the State Assets Supervision and Administration Commission (SASAC), the state's administrative body for oversight and supervision of SOEs, China sought to strengthen the supervision and bureaucratic control of all SOEs (including the CNPC).[45] In addition, Chinese policy makers became concerned that limited oversight of commercial actors endangered China's longer-term interests in Africa. In August 2006, the Chinese Ministry of Commerce (MofCOM) reasserted its own leadership over China's international commercial activities with a set of policy guidelines that sought "to strengthen regulations in order to avoid conflicts . . . in order to protect the national interest."[46] The state also had a powerful tool at its disposal in the form of China's Communist Party. Specifically, the CCP's promotional career advancement structure provides central authorities with veto points on the careers of rising stars within the party, many of whom often spend time running one of China's prestigious SOEs on their way to the top. China's NOCs are among the elite SOEs for up-and-coming stars of the Communist Party to lead. This creates a strong incentive for the leadership of China's NOCs to toe the party line and avoid acting against the wishes of the state. Finally, as discussed in more detail in the CDB/Chinalco case in the next chapter, the central government took on a more active role coordinating major overseas acquisitions.[47]

Second, the central authorities increased their budgetary control over the commercial actors. As "going out" gathered steam, state-provided financing became a new source of leverage over increasingly commercially oriented actors. Although many of China's largest firms had undergone public offerings, China's equity markets are still thin, and most major corporate financing (particularly in the extractive resources sector) is done using debt issuances. Because the state still exercises a good deal of control over China's banking system, this proved to be another good source of leverage for the state to exercise control over the commercial actors. The general pattern seemed to include a high-level state visit from Hu Jintao, Wen Jiabao, or one of the other senior leaders in China, supported by the Chinese Ministry of Foreign Affairs (MoFA) and MofCom. Deals were struck and signed during such visits.[48] China's "deal sweeteners" would often include arms and military assistance as well as high-profile construction projects (new stadiums, ports, government office buildings, transportation infrastructure, etc.).[49] This activity would often be underwritten at concessionary rates by state financial institutions. These deals were then implemented by the National Development and Reform Commission (NDRC) and specific companies that would be involved in the ongoing investment. At several points in this process, the state would be able to exert influence to help shape the nature and content of how China's commercial actors engage with the world.

A good example of this type of behavior can be found in China's Export-Import Bank and its influence in providing state control over Chinese corporations' engagement in Africa. The basic model is to provide below-market rates on credit and loans to Chinese investment projects that have been struck with the host government. Part of the terms for these projects is that the work then needs to be awarded to Chinese firms, mainly SOE construction and engineering firms. This arrangement has the added benefit for China of keeping surplus labor gainfully employed building infrastructure in Africa. Of course, this infrastructure also helps the recipient countries, particularly in their efforts to bring raw resources to market.[50] Finally, such sweetheart deals also obviously help secure Chinese NOCs' favorable treatment from host governments with regard to new oil assets/deals. Such practices thus enable China's growing influence. At the same time, the state explicitly controls the Export-Import Bank (which is legally mandated to fulfill China's political goals) and is thus able to assert control over a good deal of China's strategic investments in resource-producing states.

Another example of how the state is able to use finance to exert control over efforts to secure strategic resources is what has become known as the "Angola Model." This approach uses oil reserves (or some other valuable, generally extractive, resource) as the collateral and medium for loan repayment. In this scheme, loans are granted and repaid on the basis of future oil output. For example, a loan would be structured to be repaid over twenty years by delivering twenty thousand barrels of oil per month. The Export-Import Bank acts as the broker facilitating this deal by providing credits to the Chinese construction company and to the Chinese refinery. Interestingly, these deals do not seem to be designed to ensure against price risk, but rather against supply risk, because the contracts were for *quantities* of oil (or whatever other resource is used as collateral). If prices of the underlying commodity fluctuate, the term of the loan that changes is merely the length of the payback period. The effect of this sort of structure is to ensure against supply risk, because price risk is effectively transposed into a potentially shorter payment time horizon.[51] During the global financial crisis in 2008, worldwide demand for oil dropped considerably as national economies slowed (and anticipated slowing further). This provided cash-rich Chinese NOCs and banks with good opportunities to acquire natural resource assets at fire-sale prices, and China took advantage of the opportunity to secure additional sources of raw material, particularly oil.[52]

The third factor contributing to the Chinese state's ability to reassert control over commercial actors was a periodic unification of the state. Although China is often beset by multiple forces that create a divided state, when the senior leadership focuses on a particular issue area, it is able to provide effective state unity. One indicator of such attention was the frequent official state visits China's Politburo paid to Africa.[53] Such attention is necessary to overcome the various other divergent forces that serve to weaken the ability of the state to control commercial actors. The presence of top-level guidance (for as long as it can be sustained) tends to overcome divisions within the Chinese state. The resulting unified state is more effectively able to issue orders, monitor compliance, and enforce penalties on the commercial actors for noncompliance. As mentioned earlier, this unifying quality is limited by the finite capacity of the senior leadership, both in terms of demands on their time and level of their engagement on what can be technical issue areas. Although China's government system supports such powerful, centralized authority, the reality of governing modern China physically limits the volume of activity the senior leaders can engage in. Many issues never make it to the highest levels of government. In practice, other factors can easily divide the state and prevent it from effectively controlling the behavior of China's commercial actors.

Evaluating China's Efforts to Secure Strategic Materials

Have China's efforts to secure access to strategic raw materials worked? Narrowly speaking, yes. Through its commercial actors, China has been able to gain access to a considerable amount of oil and other raw materials and has been able to meet increases in Chinese demand with little disruption. But, as illustrated by several cases discussed briefly above, the government's lack of control over its commercial firms has also generated strategic problems for China.

China's strategy for securing resources has relied on the international invest-ments, acquisitions, and partnerships of its leading corporate actors. Although many of these firms were formally parts of government ministries or closely managed state-owned enterprises under the planned economy, China's interna-tional corporate expansion followed closely on the heels of the more general eco-nomic liberalization and reforms in China's domestic economy that took place in the 1980s and 1990s. These reforms unleashed considerable economic growth, which in turn drove China's demand for raw materials. As China became more and more integrated into the global economy, this demand increased further. At the same time, the state increasingly relied on commercial actors (over which it held less and less control) to satisfy one of China's strategic priorities.

As these firms took on a greater commercial orientation, the state found it increasingly difficult to control their activities.[54] China found it difficult to coor-dinate across MoFA, MofCom, and the NOCs. Successful imposition of state con-trol often required direct State Council involvement, but at the very top of the Communist Party, elites tend to be overtasked. Given the scarce time of China's top leaders (like national leaders in most great powers), issues only get escalated to that level when they have reached a crisis threshold.[55] For instance, Jiang Zemin only focused national attention on China's petroleum strategy once China was under pressure of a fuel shortage. Thus, in practice, institutional bureaucracies, ideological factions, patronage loyalties, tensions between the central government and local governments, and other dynamics can often divide the state and under-mine its ability to effectively control its commercial actors. These divisions within the state allow commercial actors to pursue their own best interests, often without regard to larger national strategic interests. In the case of China's search for oil, the goals of the commercial firms mirrored those of the state with regard to securing raw materials, but the corporate pursuit of those objectives has also frequently involved actions that worked against China's other, nonenergy strategic interests. Corporate involvement in Sudan and elsewhere undermined Chinese efforts to demonstrate its role as a responsible stakeholder in the international system. The next section examines the drivers behind state control of its commercial actors in the context of China's international resource extraction efforts.

Explaining Government Control (or Lack Thereof)

This examination of China's efforts to go out in search of petroleum has suggested mixed results when it comes to China's ability to control its commercial actors. There have been times when the firms seem to be leading the way and other times when the state seems to be directing the behavior of firms. This section sheds some light on the factors accounting for when the state is able to control its commercial actors and when it is less able to do so.

There are two main reasons for the state's inability to control the NOCs. First, the state has often been beset by bureaucratic struggles for influence among the many competing centers of power (e.g., NDRC, MofCOM, MoFA, as well as the numerous, relatively weak successor regulatory bodies for the petroleum industry). Second, the relative distribution of resources was highly skewed in favor of the commercial actors. From the theoretical point of view, these values across the Unity of State and Relative Resources IVs seem to account for the state's inability to control the commercial actors.

These dynamics have characterized much of the business-government relations during China's "going out" strategy. As mentioned above, however, the state did reassert its power to guide its commercial actors. Three factors in particular seemed to be key in enabling the state to reassert its control over the commercial actors in the oil industry. First was the unification of the state that occurred when China's senior leadership weighed in on a particular issue. Second was the use of financial purse strings to coordinate a more organized "going out" strategy. By leveraging the state-dominated banking sector to provide commercially irresistible terms of financing, the state ensured that projects would be undertaken on its terms. Third, administrative reforms helped consolidate the approval authorities of the state over the firms.

Drawing on the theoretical framework presented earlier helps to disaggregate the factors accounting for the (in)ability of the Chinese state to control the commercial actors in this context. In terms of the Goals IV, the state and firms share largely complementary goals regarding securing access to petroleum. But the behavior of the firms often creates blowback for the state, which frequently undermines other national strategic priorities beyond resource extraction. In many instances, the Unity of the State IV was divided primarily along bureaucratic lines, although when the state did exert control over the commercial actors, it was often because the state was able to act in a unified manner, generally under the leadership of senior national figures. The Market Fragmentation IV was highly concentrated, with only three significant commercial firms controlling nearly 100 percent of China's oil industry. This gave these firms considerable power vis-à-vis the state. In addition, perhaps most significantly, the Relative Resources IV was highly skewed in favor of the firms. The vast majority of the

TABLE 4.1 Early CNPC Case Summary Table

	IV CODING	EVIDENCE	DV PREDICTION	DV OUTCOME
Unity of state	Divided	Case exhibits significant bureaucratic rivalries; high party ranking of heads of national oil companies undermines ability of Ministry of Foreign Affairs; factional tensions may have exacerbated friction, although little evidence of center-local divisions in this case	Control unlikely	State was unable to control behavior of commercial actors in this case; firm presence and activities in Sudan undermined China's image internationally
Goals	Somewhat divergent	State wants to promote China's image as a "Responsible Stakeholder"; SOEs are seeking profits and new sources of revenue abroad; although the goals are not necessarily mutually exclusive, there could be friction as the principal and agent do not necessarily have the same priorities	Control unlikely	Commercial actors pursued profits and investment opportunities even at the expense of China's larger strategic concerns about how its growing international presence would be perceived
Market structure	Concentrated	Highly concentrated industry with 3 dominant state-owned firms controlling	Control difficult	State was unable to impose its preferences over the powerful

(Continued)

TABLE 4.1   (Continued)

	IV CODING	EVIDENCE	DV PREDICTION	DV OUTCOME
		relatively noncompetitive segments of the domestic petroleum production chain		commercial actors (who were also endowed with considerable power within the state hierarchy)
Reporting relationship	Direct	State retains significant majority ownership stakes even after IPOs; management is appointed by the state; most financing is from operations or state banks; IPOs do generate some public equity financing, but overall this IV suggests state control	Control likely	Although this IV points in the direction of state control (and indeed, in the later CNPC case, the state does leverage this IV to re-establish control), in the early CNPC case, this factor was not enough to engender state control
Relative resources	Favors commercial actor	Industry knowledge resides almost exclusively with the firms in the petroleum sector; limited government oversight capacity in terms of resources, personnel, and expertise	Control unlikely	State struggles to keep pace with the faster commercial actor in this case; the initiative rests with the commercial actor and state often found itself to be inadequately reactive

government's expertise, industry knowledge, and administrative capabilities resided within CNPC. Because of such asymmetries, the state frequently deferred to the firms. Finally, from the perspective of the Reporting Relationship IV, these firms are all state-controlled enterprises with publicly listed arms. On paper, this reporting relationship would seem to facilitate state control. The senior stature of the NOCs within China's central government bureaucracy, however, often afforded these firms a good deal of bureaucratic weight.

Together, these factors accounted for the business-government dynamics observed in this case. The state's reassertion of control occurred as a result of a

TABLE 4.2 Later CNPC Case Summary Table

	IV CODING	EVIDENCE	DV PREDICTION	DV OUTCOME
Unity of state	Unified	Bureaucratic rivalries trumped by more direct involvement of senior leadership; MofCom took on more active coordinating role	Control likely	State was able to reassert control over behavior of commercial actors; China eventually even helped bring UN peacekeepers to Sudan
Goals	Divergent	State wants to promote China's image as a "Responsible Stakeholder"; SOEs are seeking profits and new sources of revenue abroad; although the goals are not necessarily mutually exclusive, there could be friction as the principal and agent do not necessarily have the same priorities	Control unlikely	Commercial actors pursued profits and investment opportunities even at the expense of China's larger strategic concerns about how its growing international presence would be perceived
Market structure	Concentrated	Highly concentrated industry with dominant state-owned firms controlling relatively noncompetitive segments of the domestic petroleum production chain	Control difficult	Elevation was necessary to impose national preferences over the powerful commercial actors (who were also endowed with considerable power within the state hierarchy)
Reporting relationship	Direct	State retains significant majority ownership stakes even after IPOs; management is appointed by	Control likely	The state leverages its statutory relationship to re-establish control; party promotional apparatus used

(Continued)

TABLE 4.2   (Continued)

	IV CODING	EVIDENCE	DV PREDICTION	DV OUTCOME
		the state; most financing is from operations or state banks; IPOs do generate some public equity financing, but overall this IV suggests state control		to ensure SOE compliance; SOEs more effectively directed via state finance
Relative resources	More balanced (though still favors commercial actors)	Industry knowledge resides almost exclusively with the firms in the petroleum sector; strengthened SASAC supervision of SOEs, party promotion mechanisms leveraged; state finance tilted resources back in favor of the state	Control unlikely	State struggles to keep pace with the faster commercial actor in this case; the initiative rests with the commercial actor and state often found itself to be inadequately reactive, although some improvement along this dimension from the early CNP case, inadequate to shift control outcome by itself

unification of the state as high-level leadership intervened to settle interbureaucratic frictions.

China has identified several raw materials it views as crucial to fueling its continued economic growth. Securing access to these materials is an important strategic priority for China. To secure its access to oil, the most important of these materials, China has implemented a strategy that relies on its national oil companies. For the most part, this strategy has been moderately successful at meeting China's petroleum needs. Although the goals of the commercial actors are complementary to the goals of the state in this sense (broadly speaking, both wish to secure access to petroleum), in implementing the "going out" strategy, Chinese firms have occasionally also undermined China's other national interests. In some instances, the state has been able to rein in the activities of its firms, and in other instances the state seems unable to control its massive multinational resource extraction companies.

Evidence of government control in this case seems to be mixed at best. For the most part, China's NOCs have taken the lead in going out. The NOCs enjoy a disproportionate share of resources compared to the state. The highly concentrated nature of the petroleum sector in China makes it fairly easy to monitor the firms operating in that space. But because there are only a handful of large firms that dominate the sector, market concentration provides these firms with considerable leverage vis-à-vis the state. The state frequently failed to act in a unified manner to exert its control over the firms. The state has shown, however, that it is not completely without the ability to unite under the CCP's central leadership and rein in the activities of the NOCs.[56]

Because the evidence from this case suggests that the state struggled to control its commercial actors in the context of China's NOCs "going out," it would be useful to examine an instance in which the state exercised a fairly high degree of control over its commercial actors. An ideal case would show how the state used commercial actors to achieve a strategic objective. A particularly tough case would be one in which the state sought to have the economic actor engage in behavior that ran counter to its commercial interests. To provide a useful comparison to illustrate the theory, such a case of economic statecraft should also be taken from the extractive resources space. Chapter 5 examines just such a case in which the state played an important role in controlling and directing the behavior of its commercial actors to achieve a national strategic objective in the context of another extractive resource: iron.

5

RIO TINTO AND THE (IN)VISIBLE HAND OF THE STATE

The petroleum sector case highlighted the challenges facing Chinese state efforts to maintain control over its commercial actors as they searched for international supplies of oil. This chapter focuses on a case of China's efforts to secure another strategic resource: iron ore. Iron ore, like oil, is a strategic raw material deemed vital to China's continued economic growth. As is the case with petroleum, China is highly dependent on imports to meet its demand for this raw material. China imported 820 million tons of iron ore in 2013, making it the world's largest importer of iron ore. China's imports of iron ore account for about two-thirds of its total demand and about three-quarters of the total world supply of sea-borne iron ore.[1] China is a huge consumer of iron ore and is highly reliant on international supplies to augment its insufficient domestic production.

To get a better understanding of exactly how the Chinese state is able to work through commercial actors, it is instructive to drill down into a particular episode concerning one of China's largest efforts to secure a strategic resource. This case study will take a closer look at exactly how China's strategic deployment of state capital functions in practice. The uncharacteristically public attempt by Chinalco (underwritten by the China Development Bank) to acquire a large stake in Rio Tinto in 2007/2008 provides a useful window on how the state can successfully orchestrate control over commercial actors to achieve a strategic objective.

In this case, China was able to successfully control the behavior of a commercial actor and, through Chinalco, was able to realize an important strategic objective. This extreme case provides an instructive counterpoint to the variation observed in the CNPC case. All the independent variables indicated that state control would be likely. The goals of the state and the commercial actor were largely compatible. The commercial actor had an opportunity to potentially acquire an important international asset. At the same time, neither Chinalco nor Beijing wanted to see further upstream supplier consolidation. The reporting relationship of Chinalco also favored state control. The high level of senior engagement on this effort ensured that the state would act in a unified manner. Neither the market structure (competitive) nor the balance of relative resources would hamper the state's ability to control the commercial actor.

This chapter begins by providing the context that originally put Rio Tinto in play. How the theory maps onto these events is then discussed. The role of state-provided financing features prominently in this episode, and the remainder of the chapter is spent examining the China Development Bank: its activities, mandate, organization, and financing. This case suggests that the provision of state capital to state-owned enterprises (SOEs) can serve an important enabling and coordinating function for Chinese state control.

On July 12, 2007, the Canadian aluminum producer Alcan—then the world's third largest aluminum producer—announced it was entertaining a friendly takeover bid from Rio Tinto for $38.1 billion. Rio Tinto's bid was in response to an earlier hostile takeover attempt by Alcoa, which valued Alcan at $27 billion. The Rio-Alcan deal was officially completed on October 25, 2007, creating the world's largest aluminum company.[2] Unfortunately for Rio Tinto, the Alcan price tag would quickly become a significant burden as the fallout from the financial crisis depressed commodity prices. Because the offer for Alcan was all cash, Rio Tinto had financed a portion of the deal with debt. When aluminum prices fell along with the precipitous decline in global demand, it seemed that Rio had overreached and had valued Alcan using top-of-market prices. Rio gradually realized that bottom-of-market commodity prices were not going to improve soon enough to enable Rio to make its scheduled debt payments. Specifically, Rio was left with $19 billion in debt payments coming due in the second half of 2009 and early 2010 but no source of cash to cover them. This put Rio Tinto in play.

In November 2007, Australian mining conglomerate BHP Billiton announced an offer to merge with cash-strapped Rio Tinto and absorb Rio's debt. Because the offer was to trade three (later raised to 3.4) BHP shares for every share of Rio, the exact value of the offer fluctuated, but at one time it was as high as $170 billion. Rio Tinto's CEO, Tom Albanese, felt this undervalued Rio's assets and was not enthusiastic about the offer. Most importantly for our purposes, this proposed merger between the world's largest and third largest mining companies would create "an international commodity juggernaut" with considerable pricing power. BHP-Rio would have controlled a third of the world's iron ore, and another 37 percent would be in the hands the Brazilian mining company Companhia Vale do Rio Doce (CVRD). Combined, the two suppliers would control more than 70 percent of the world's seaborne iron ore. Such a concentration was unacceptable for the buyers of iron ore. The largest of those major buyers of iron ore decided to do something about it.

Sometime during December 2007 or January 2008, the Chinese Iron and Steel Association (CISA), led by its executive director Zou Jian, approached the government authorities and made the case that the Rio Tinto–BHP deal would lock up too much of the iron ore pricing power.[3] Something needed to be done. "Concerned about the potential pricing power of a combined company, China's government hastily called meetings with several big state-owned enterprises, say people familiar with the events."[4] The National Development and Reform Commission (NDRC) apparently evaluated various options and the State Council decided to try to establish a blocking stake to the BHP bid.[5] The China Development Bank (CDB) was selected as the source of funds for buying a significant minority stake on the open market via the large state-owned aluminum giant, Chinalco.[6] As a commercial agent, Chinalco had a recent track record of successful international and domestic acquisitions experience that Baosteel and other contenders lacked.[7] Moreover, the move would satisfy both the government's desire to prevent a concentration of supply in a strategic resource and Chinalco's own goals of becoming a diversified multimetal international conglomerate. Chinalco partnered with CDB as the main underwriter and sought advice from Lehman Brothers and China International Capital Corporation (CICC), which was run by the son of former premier Zhu Rongji. Chinalco also formed an acquisition vehicle with Alcoa in a politically savvy move that added a "multinational" element to what might otherwise be viewed as a wholly Chinese operation.[8]

After the markets closed on January 31, 2008, Lehman traders at the London desk bought up as many shares of Rio Tinto as they could find. Xiao Yaqing, general manager of Chinalco, was quoted as saying the events surrounding the surreptitious buy "can be a plot for a novel."[9] Xiao apparently sat by Lehman's London trading desk as the operation unfolded. He was too nervous to eat. By the time the dust settled, Chinalco had spent $14 billion to buy 9 percent of Rio Tinto's total shares in the after-hours market, China's largest overseas equity investment ever. Overnight, Chinalco had become Rio Tinto's biggest shareholder.

Suspiciously, the official Chinese-language Xinhua coverage of the incident included an entire section that dwelt on the strategic rationale of why China's central government was involved and why the government chose Chinalco instead of Baosteel or other steel industry players to conduct this operation.[10] None of this discussion made it into the edited English-language version of the report.[11] This evidence corroborates interviews suggesting that the State Council played an important role in directing the Rio effort, although the Chinese government frequently seeks to minimize international awareness of its hand in such matters.[12]

Chinalco has publicly denied that its intent was to block the BHP bid, but bankers familiar with the operation have said that Chinalco sought to influence the acquisition, especially given the timing of Chinalco's buy.[13] At the time of Chinalco's "midnight ambush," BHP had about one week remaining (February 6) before it had to declare to the British regulatory authorities its intent regarding an acquisition of Rio Tinto. Despite trying to sweeten its offer for Rio by increasing its bid from 3 to 3.4 shares for every share of Rio, BHP-Billiton was not able to match Chinalco's cash offer. In November 2008, BHP formally withdrew its offer to buy Rio, and the value of Rio shares dropped considerably.

Although this outcome was widely viewed as a victory for China, it left Chinalco with an unrealized loss of as much as $10 billion on its 9 percent stake at one point. In addition, Rio still had to find the cash to service the $8.9 billion of debt that was coming due in October 2009. Chinalco signaled that it was still interested in long-term cooperation with Rio, and in December one of Rio's executives expressed an interest in financing from China's banks. He shared this sentiment with his neighbor in Brisbane, Wang Wenfu, head of Chinalco's Australian subsidiary.[14] Chinalco proposed to provide a mixture of $7.2 billion in convertible bonds and a $12.3 billion asset purchase that would provide it with a joint stake in some of Rio Tinto's most valuable copper and iron mines. At the time the offer was made, the terms seemed to offer Rio Tinto a favorable way out of its debt burden, and Rio's management was enthusiastic.[15] The $19.5 billion package was to be China's largest foreign investment ever, surpassing the 2005 proposed $18.5 billion CNOOC deal for Unocal. In February of 2009, the Chinalco deal for Rio Tinto was announced. If it went through, it would raise Chinalco's stake in Rio to 18 percent. In Beijing, Xiao Yaqing was heralded as a hero and awarded a position on China's State Council.[16]

As economic events unfolded in 2009, however, it grew increasingly less likely that the deal would succeed. China's economy was recovering from the recession more quickly than originally expected, and with China's recovery came renewed global demand for commodities. This buoyed commodity asset prices and increasingly made Chinalco's offer appear less and less attractive to Rio Tinto's shareholders.[17] In addition, the Australian government faced mounting pressure domestically to block the "fire sale" of Australia's crown jewels—its mining assets—to China.

Finally, on June 5, 2009, Rio walked away from what had become a moribund $19.5 billion deal. On the back of renewed commodity prices, Rio had decided to issue new shares and partnered with BHP-Billiton to codevelop adjacent mines in Australia and share those costs. These combined efforts would enable Rio to service its debt obligations. Government officials in Beijing were not pleased. In

July, China arrested four members of Rio's negotiating team in China on allegations of spying. The Chinese government contended that they were stealing state secrets regarding the operations of China's steel producers. Among those arrested was Stern Hu, an Australian citizen. The team was negotiating prices for iron ore, and the arrests were widely interpreted at the time as an expression of China's anger at Rio Tinto's walking away from the Chinalco deal.

This case is a useful one because the size of the potential deal meant that it received a considerable amount of public coverage. It also illustrates how interconnected the commercial interests of many of China's leading corporations are with China's national interests. For purposes of testing the theory, the case is useful because we observe CDB being directed by the State Council to underwrite a commercial acquisition that serves China's national interests. Chinalco's own narrow goals were highly conducive to this path of action and played an important facilitating role in enabling it to act as a willing agent.

Essentially this case is the story of commercial actors (Chinalco, backed by CDB financing) being used to pursue a national objective of securing a strategically important resource. This is a case in which China was trying to manage inputs it viewed as critical to its national well-being. In the meetings that preceded Chinalco's initial purchase of the Rio shares in London, we see a coordinated effort on the part of the state to use commercial actors to further China's strategic interests.

To the extent that the strategic consequences of China's outbound capital flows have been addressed in the public and academic debate, the discussion is often framed as a question of whether China's largest companies are scouring the globe looking to do the bidding of China's government or if these commercial actors are simply pursuing their own narrowly commercial interests. Xiao Yaqing's promotion to the State Council illustrates the close personal and institutional ties between China's commercial and governmental leadership that often spark such discussions. "The move by aluminum czar Xiao Yaqing into politics in February raised a critical question about China's state-owned corporate giants as they step onto the global stage: Are they driven by profits, or are they pursuing a nationalist agenda for the Chinese government? A close look at the Rio Tinto deal suggests that the answer is both, as business and politics intertwine for a new breed of globally savvy Chinese executives."[18] I would agree that the answer is often complex and frequently involves a mix of commercial motives as well as national interest.

More importantly, however, is that this is the wrong way to frame the question. A much better way to think about this issue is to ask: Under what circumstances can we expect that the government will be able to pursue its strategic policy objectives by using commercial actors? It should not be a question of "whether," because that is likely to vary from one episode to the next, but rather a question of "why." This is how I have structured the analysis that follows.

Mapping the Theory onto the Chinalco Episode

The goals of Chinalco were to expand internationally, gain access to nonaluminum operations, and further enhance Chinalco's prestige within China's domestic political-economic environment. The goals of CDB were to gain additional international underwriting experience, enhance its international and domestic prestige, deploy recently infused capital from the CIC, and perhaps to assert its ability to act independently of its new CIC owners. The goals of the State Council were to prevent supplier market consolidation that would enhance foreign-controlled iron ore pricing power and would likely result in higher prices, which would jeopardize future economic growth. NDRC shared similar priorities. The goals of the commercial actors and the government were highly compatible and there was little friction. The values on the Goals IV in this case would suggest state control.

Although evidence suggests that both the State Council and NDRC were involved in this case, they seemed to share a common vision to encourage actions designed to secure resources and a desire to coordinate the efforts of various commercial actors. Although there may have been more than one government principal, the evidence suggests that the state acted in a unified manner. The value of the Unity of State IV in this case suggests state control.

Early in the deliberation process, there were several commercial actors that could have played a role in securing Rio Tinto, including Baosteel, Shenhua Coal, and CDB. The presence of these alternative commercial agents provided an incentive to "compete" for the right to represent China's interests abroad. This type of dynamic helped ensure state control because alternative agents were available in the wings should the chosen firm prove unreliable.

Regarding the issue of relative resources, this episode represented uncharted territory for China's international economic activity. This was to be the largest overseas deal ever conducted by China. Therefore there was no true expertise resident in either the commercial or governmental sectors. By virtue of its recent Peru Copper acquisition and its previous familiarity with investing in Australian assets, Chinalco did seem to have some experience that could be leveraged. In addition, CDB's recent support of Barclays' effort to buy ABN Amro and its resulting 3 percent stake in Barclays provided some background experience for CDB to draw on.[19] Both of these suggest that the commercial actors enjoyed a certain amount of resource advantage over the state, but the unknown aspects of the endeavor more than outweighed any real knowledge asymmetry that might embolden the commercial actors to avoid the state's control.

Finally, the status of Chinalco as a SASAC-owned-and-operated SOE and CDB's position as a policy bank meant that the value of the Reporting Relationship IV was strongly skewed toward state control. Given these values across the five IVs in this case, one should not be surprised to find state control over the commercial actors taking place. The causal arrows all pointed toward state control. The state actively supported the commercial agents and encouraged them to change the status quo. This international commercial activity was designed to realize the state's strategic interests, namely the prevention of foreign supplier concentration in a strategic raw material. The Chinese leadership was interested in blocking the BHP bid to take over Rio Tinto, which was realized when BHP withdrew its offer to buy Rio in November 2008. As the situation developed, the possibility arose of not only blocking BHP's bid, but of going one step better and taking advantage of depressed commodity prices to secure an 18 percent ownership stake in Rio, which would have cemented future access to a reliable supply. Although that objective failed to materialize, the case nonetheless still stands as a useful illustration of state control. For purposes of illustrating the theory, the specific outcome of the case (whether Chinalco was successful in acquiring Rio or whether Chinalco's actions merely prevented a consolidation of iron ore supply) matters less than *how* the dynamics between the state and its commercial agents unfolded.

Other Examples of CDB's Activities

The Chinalco-Rio case is just one prominent example of CDB's financing activities in support of the Chinese state's goals, but it is by no means an isolated case. The 2008 financial crisis and subsequent decline in asset prices provided long-term valuation opportunities for investment and acquisition. Concurrently, China's government gave its commercial actors the green light to acquire international holdings. Expressing a recurring motif in the deployment of China's state-owned capital, Charles Tang, head of the Brazil-China Chamber of Commerce and Industry, said, "Brazil needs the liquidity and investment, and China now has the finances to buy resources at a discount."[20] Although he was speaking in the context of CDB's loan to Petrobras, his comment applies more broadly to China's overall extractive resources strategy.

One of the largest deals was a $25 billion long-term loan to Russia's OAO Rosneft (oil producer) and OAO Transneft (pipeline operator),[21] designed to enable Rosneft to recapitalize its relatively undeveloped East Siberian oil fields and build a pipeline to deliver oil to Chinese refineries. CDB was to supply the loan in exchange for fifteen million metric tons of crude oil a year (about 300,000 barrels a day, 10 percent of China's current volume of oil imports) for twenty years.[22] "In 2008, Russia exported 11.64 million tons of crude to China, equivalent to 233,000 barrels a day, down nearly 20% from the previous year."[23] So CDB's deal enabled

China to more than double the oil it was receiving from Russia. This diversifying away from Middle Eastern sources of petroleum (and the concomitant "Malacca Dilemma") was seen as an important national energy security goal. On May 21, 2014, Gazprom and CNPC finally signed a massive $400 billion deal to supply Russian gas to China for the next thirty years.[24] This further solidified the Russian supply of gas to the Chinese market.

Another such deal was the $10 billion financing package that CDB provided to Brazil's state-run oil giant, Petroleo Brasileiro SA (Petrobras) to explore deep-water oil reserves. Petrobras had been receiving pressure from the Brazilian government to increase its countercyclical spending, and CDB was happy to finance its expanded oil exploration.[25] In an ostensibly separate agreement, Petrobras agreed "to sell to China Petroleum and Chemical Corp. 60,000 to 100,000 barrels of heavy crude oil a day, or as much as 5% of total Petrobras production, starting immediately."[26] These announcements at a signing ceremony between Chinese vice president Xi Jinping and Brazilian president Luiz Inacio Lula da Silva also alluded to a possible memorandum of understanding between Petrobras and CNPC to sell China another 60,000 barrels per day. Replicating a tried-and-true strategy, China sought to leverage the synergies between closer economic cooperation on energy and minerals into improved diplomatic relations.

As evidenced by the Chinalco/Rio case and these other big-ticket deals, the Chinese state was using state financing as an effective lever of control to guide, encourage, and influence the international activities of its commercial actors. In the lead-up to Chinalco's investment in Rio Tinto, the Chinese state brought together potential commercial actors, vetted them, and matched the winning Chinalco with state-sponsored financing to complete its "midnight ambush." By underwriting these types of major transactions, the state was able to shape the behavior of firms. To better understand exactly how this mechanism of state power is used, the next few sections examine CDB, its goals, reporting relationships, and financing activities.[27] Such operational details provide insight into exactly *how* the Chinese state is able to exercise effective economic statecraft to achieve national strategic objectives.

The China Development Bank: Origins and Mandate

In 1994 China established three policy banks as part of the plan to transition the "Big Four" national banks to a more commercial footing by hiving off their noncommercial work and moving it to the policy banks.[28] This gradual commercialization of the banking sector was part of the larger economic reform effort designed to modernize China's economic system. These three policy banks were the China Development Bank (CDB), the Export-Import Bank (Ex-Im) and the Agricultural Development Bank of China (ADBC). The mandate of each was slightly different: CDB was designed to finance key domestic infrastructure construction projects and coordinate a scattered national investment loan effort; the Ex-Im Bank was designed to promote the development of foreign trade by providing trade financing; and the ADBC was to provide for capital needs of the government development plans for the rural areas and agricultural sectors.

From the start, CDB was saddled with a large portfolio of nonperforming loans and a legacy of loose lending practices, the product of government-directed lending to otherwise insolvent SOEs. In addition to the expected rent-seeking behavior of such large political institutions, the Chinese Communist Party had a strong incentive to maintain these SOEs on life support because the SOEs substituted for China's underdeveloped social welfare net. Under the centrally planned economy, SOEs often provided health care, pension, education, and other public welfare benefits. Suddenly subjecting these largely inefficient enterprises to market competition would drive many of them out of business, and with them would go important public services. This had the potential to set off considerable popular discontent and generate social instability. As a result, the NDRC and its predecessor planning bureaucracy directed that credits and loans be extended to keep the SOEs afloat. While this kept the SOEs running, it left much of China's banking sector with a growing portfolio of nonperforming loans. As a policy bank carved out of what would become the commercial banks, CDB was left with many commercially unsustainable loans. In addition, CDB continued to operate under the legal mandate of a policy bank, meaning it could expect additional noncommercial tasking in the future.[29]

Since the early 2000s, CDB has aggressively moved away from only underwriting large domestic Chinese infrastructure and development project financing. Although still supportive of state goals, CDB now engages in international activities on a large scale. For example, the previously mentioned Russian and Brazilian oil development deals helped secure long-term supply agreements for China. CDB has also expanded its scope to underwrite international development financing and international corporate expansion and acquisitions on the part of China's leading SOEs. A case in point was the September 9, 2009, announcement that CDB provided a $30 billion loan to CNPC to finance CNPC's planned international acquisitions. As part of the state's "going out" mandate, CDB has supported a number of activities closely tied to both commercial and foreign policy goals.

The China Development Bank: Structure, Financing Sources, and Uses

The China Development Bank is fully owned by the state. While the state may still hold a controlling interest in China's "commercial banks," these entities at least have some portion of their equity publicly traded on market exchanges in Shanghai and Hong Kong, which provides some externally driven commercial motivation, governance, and public oversight. At the time of the Rio deal, CDB was not yet listed on any stock exchanges and had only recently begun issuing public disclosures. Yet by 2008 CDB was already one of the most significant forces in international finance: it had more assets than the World Bank and the Asian Development Bank combined.[30]

"At present, CDB functions much like a domestic version of the World Bank, raising money through bond sales and lending to projects favoured by Communist Party policy."[31] CDB is financed not by deposits, but rather by bond issuances. These bonds are auctioned off to raise capital, which the CDB then uses to underwrite loans and lines of credit to various entities (often at favorable, below-market terms). Over the course of its existence, CDB has issued more than $275 billion in bonds, more than a quarter of all the debt securities outstanding in China's financial markets. CDB has issued more bonds internationally than any other Chinese institution. As part of the recapitalization and reorganization of China's domestic banking sector, CDB was placed in Central Huijin, a holding vehicle directly under the Ministry of Finance. When the CIC was created, the assets of Central Huijin were transferred to the CIC.[32] Thus, today the CDB is now technically a holding of the Ministry of Finance and the CIC via the Central Huijin vehicle. At the end of 2007, the CIC injected $20 billion into the CDB in part to help it prepare for an eventual public listing.[33]

In the aftermath of the 2008 financial crisis, the CDB appears to have become a favored investment financing vehicle for Chinese SOEs looking to make acquisitions abroad. In 2008, CDB reported that it had $64.5 billion in foreign currency loans outstanding, two-thirds of which were directly issued to underwrite Chinese corporate efforts to "go out."[34] By the end of 2012, this had risen to $224.5 billion.[35] Typically, Chinese multinational firms will partner with a state-backed financial entity to underwrite major foreign investments and acquisitions. Sometimes these activities are instigated by the firm and sometimes by the state.[36] In almost every case, such international economic interaction is now closely coordinated by the state (although as we observed in the previous chapter, in the early days of the "going out" policy, SOEs were acting much more independently). The state's reassertion of control over its commercial actors has deftly relied on centralized provision of inexpensive capital. Generally, this domestic coordination process begins early to ensure that attractively priced funds and state support exist before the Chinese firm moves forward with negotiating deals internationally.

One final aspect of CDB's operations that differs from some of China's other state-directed financing vehicles is that it often underwrites specific loans or provides direct financing to Chinese companies for particular purposes. This method of debt financing is different from the investments made by NSSF, the CIC, and SAFE, which generally take the form of equity ownership and provide stakes in specific companies or industries.[37] Of the two means of financing, CDB's project-specific approach provides the financier with more direct tactical discretion, as it can approve or reject activities on a project-by-project basis. Ceteris paribus, project-specific debt financing should provide the lender with more precise leverage than a minority equity stake. Direct equity stakes delegate more of the decision making to a firm's professional managers. That said, the influence of large equity stakeholders, particularly on matters of high-level strategic guidance, should not be underestimated.

The China Development Bank: Analyzing CDB's Activities

Although CDB was in the process of transitioning from a policy lender to a commercial operator on the eve of the financial crisis, this process did not move beyond reorganizing CDB as a corporation. In China, the 2008 financial crisis witnessed liberalization and reform efforts falling out of favor among senior Chinese elites. Reading the political winds, CDB's chairman shelved plans to shift CDB in a commercial direction and instead made the most of the opportunity to act as one of the state's primary financing vehicles to support China's stimulus and strategic funding priorities. If such a transition were to eventually take place, it would have the effect of shifting CDB's operations to a more commercially driven footing and away from today's policy-driven dynamics.

Most of CDB's activities have exhibited significant noncommercial dimensions. During China's domestic lending spree in response to the global financial crisis, CDB enthusiastically embraced government priorities in doling out its support.[38] CDB's international projects have also been in support of the stated policy goals of promoting an outward expansion of China's leading industries. The strategic goals of the state in encouraging these efforts have been to improve the general efficiency of China's largest enterprises (and by extension the efficiency of China's economy) largely by gaining access to the latest technologies and state-of-the-art management practices. The Chinese government has also stated that it views access to reliable supplies of resources like iron ore, petroleum, and copper to be in the national interest.

CDB seems to conduct its financing operations using three general models. The first is direct investments into companies or projects, a straightforward capital infusion in which CDB becomes the purchaser of the equity. Examples of such activities include the aborted effort to provide Citibank with a capital infusion in the midst of the financial crisis (this was stopped by the State Council) and the Barclays equity stake. In a bold move abroad, CDB paid close to $3 billion to buy a 3.1 percent stake in Barclays Bank.[39] Barclays, a British bank, was looking to raise capital to fund its attempted acquisition of the Dutch bank ABN Amro. CDB seized the opportunity to partner with Barclays as a part of an effort to move into international finance and learn from the leading players. CDB hoped to learn more about commodities trading and commodities risk hedging, presumably because these were areas in which CDB anticipated continuing involvement.[40] CDB also acquired the ability to appoint directors to the board of Barclays. Perhaps most significantly, the stake provided CDB with a potential opportunity to invest in a much larger position had Barclays succeeded in acquiring ABN Amro. CDB was prepared to fund much of the acquisition in exchange for a sizeable part of the equity of the combined company. This would have catapulted CDB to the forefront of international banking and would have gone a long way in meeting the government's desire to place its financial industry on a more globally competitive footing. In the end, Barclays did not succeed and CDB's stake in Barclays was limited to 3 percent. Despite losing a considerable sum in this investment, CDB elected to maintain its 3 percent position by exercising its right to purchase additional shares in subsequent offerings.

Although CDB seems to be a willing supporter of state goals when they align closely with its own commercial goals, the state is also able to exercise control over CDB when the commercial goals conflict with state preferences. For example, in early January of 2008 Citigroup was looking for a capital infusion to shore up its balance sheet. CDB had planned to provide $5 billion for a stake in the wounded company. But China's senior leadership was having second thoughts about the severity of the global credit crunch. Although generally supportive of the efforts of Chinese companies snapping up assets abroad when their prices were down, the government had decided that financial companies had become too unstable, and China's previous experience with strategic stakes in Blackstone, Barclays, Morgan Stanley, and Fortis did not provide reassurance. As a result, the State Council tried to stop CDB from investing the $5 billion in Citigroup. In response, a dutiful CDB rebuffed Citigroup's offer. Although the commercial actor, CDB, seemed to want to partner with Citibank, when the state principal indicated it was not in favor of such action, the deal was halted. CDB was forced to forgo its narrow interests of acquiring international banking skills and building up its international partnerships, which would have made it more commercially competitive, in favor of conforming with state preferences to avoid further exposure to the international financial sector. This episode demonstrates the state's ability to control CDB even when commercial forces pulled against state preferences.

The second model of CDB's investments is one in which CDB plays a secondary, enabling role for other companies' activities. In this type of strategic support, CDB provides a line of credit, financing, or other financial assistance to another (almost always Chinese) corporation to allow that entity to undertake some project or conduct some activity the state supports. Based on my research, this seems to be CDB's most common type of operation. Some examples from this period include CDB's provision of $30 billion in financing to CNPC to underwrite CNPC's international acquisitions and CDB's funding of a ten-year debt facility to underwrite Huawei's upgrading of a Polish telecom system.

The third type of operation involves setting up investment funds with specific mandates or missions. These are often considerably smaller and frequently have a regional or sectoral focus. CDB infuses this sort of fund with capital and the fund then looks to invest that capital according to its mandate. Examples of such funds CDB has set up include the Sino-Swiss Partnership Fund, China-Belgium Direct Equity Investment Fund, ASEAN China Investment Fund L.P., Sino-Israel Investment Fund, and the China-Africa Development Fund.

Most of CDB's large-scale international investments have fallen into one of three sectors: finance, extractive industries, and infrastructure. CDB's roots were in domestic infrastructure, and building on this institutional expertise was a logical way to extend CDB's operations internationally. Activities in the financial sector are largely driven by a desire to modernize CDB's own banking operations and risk-management practices. Strategic partnerships with international banking entities provide CDB with access to best practices, technology transfer, and financial product innovation. Another benefit of investment operations in finance is the networking and personal relationship cultivation that are so important for doing successful business in China.[41] China's involvement in extractive industries is largely fueled by its projected needs and a desire to hedge price and supply risk. As discussed earlier, the government was explicitly encouraging large Chinese companies to venture abroad as a way of improving their competitiveness while securing access to raw materials. Extractive sectors also tend to be the least reliant on skilled mergers-and-acquisitions management and execution expertise, because most commodities are fairly easy to value. Extractive companies often retain the "hard value" of their underlying assets regardless of acquisition skill, unlike tertiary industries, which are often reliant on human capital or brand value that might be destroyed by poor merger execution. Finally, because of the "hard value" nature of their assets, extractive sectors tend to be less reliant on intellectual property or other political-legal supporting infrastructure, making such industries particularly resilient in otherwise unstable host nation conditions.

Assessing Evidence from China Development Bank

The Chinalco deal indicates that the State Council was able to "encourage" CDB participation. Evidence from the Chinalco case suggests that as a policy bank, CDB is subject to control by the state.[42] This high degree of control is the result of values on the IVs that make CDB a particularly useful agent for achieving state foreign policy goals. As a policy bank, CDB is unique as a commercial actor whose interests are statutorily constructed to mirror those of the government. This case represents an extreme value on the Goals Compatibility IV. As expected, state control is strong.

In many instances, there is more than one commercial actor available to finance a given international investment. For instance, several entities could have financed the Chinalco deal. China Ex-Im is another policy bank with an explicit international mandate that could provide an alternative source of financing for state-sanctioned international investment activities. To the degree that alternative agents exist for the state to select from, the competitive dynamic in the Market Fragmentation IV suggests that CDB will be more pliable and accommodating to the state's interests. Because there are only three policy banks, the monitoring burden on the part of the state is tolerable. The CDB/Chinalco case represents an instance of oligopolistic market fragmentation and, as hypothesized, results in significant state control.

From the Unity of State IV perspective, CDB's major projects (including the Chinalco case) also result in state control. The State Council exercises supervisory jurisdiction on China's most significant, high-visibility international investment projects. As was the case with state supervision of Chinese oil companies, such high-level attention in the context of the Communist Party's hierarchical structure provides an effective degree of unified state supervision. This unified state element was reflected in the involvement of China's state leadership in aspects of the Chinalco, Petrobras, and Rosneft episodes (all CDB-financed deals).

With regard to the Relative Resource IV, CDB occasionally enjoys some latitude in its activities stemming from its financial expertise and unique foreign partnership relationships that afford it a relative resource advantage. That said, the empirical evidence suggests that any independent agency CDB might enjoy from this asymmetry is generally offset by the confluence of goals and the extreme values on the other IVs that favor state control. Interestingly, the high-profile nature of several of these cases meant that it would have been difficult for CDB to directly undermine the wishes of the State Council. The public nature of some of these cases provided the state with additional monitoring capability.

With respect to the Reporting Relationship IV, almost every dimension indicates that the state is clearly in charge of CDB. CDB is a wholly-owned

TABLE 5.1 Chinalco-CDB Case Summary Table

	IV coding	Evidence	DV prediction	DV outcome
Unity of state	Unified	Both the State Council and the NDRC shared a common vision to encourage actions designed to secure resources and a desire to coordinate the efforts of various commercial actors; little evidence of bureaucratic rivalries; center-local tensions and factional splits did not feature in this case	Control likely	State coordinated effort to use commercial actors to further China's strategic interests
Goals	Convergent	The state sought to prevent upstream supplier concentration that would enhance foreign controlled iron ore pricing power; this fit nicely with the expansion goals of the commercial actors	Control likely	Getting the commercial actors to pursue the state's objectives was fairly easy given that the requested activity fit nicely with Chinalco's ambitions
Market structure	Oligopolistic	At least two other large steel and coal firms and one alternative financing source were potential contenders to act as agents; the presence of these alternatives provided the state with options should Chinalco and CDB prove unwilling or unable to complete the task	Control likely	State's credible ability to leverage alternative commercial actors helped to foster state control in this case
Reporting relationship	Direct	Chinalco was a SASAC-owned and operated SOE; financing for	Control likely	Close coordination between the state and commercial actors

(Continued)

TABLE 5.1   (Continued)

	IV coding	Evidence	DV prediction	DV outcome
		this case came from CDB, a Chinese policy bank; the Reporting Relationship IV was skewed toward state control		
Relative resources	Somewhat favors commercial actor	CDB's experience with project financing and Chinalco's recent streak of international M&A provided some knowledge advantage, but the unknown aspects of this endeavor more than outweighed any temptation to venture far beyond the state's desired objectives	Not a significant factor	Once state provided high-level direction, commercial actors were given discretion to execute operations and commercial activity to pursue Rio Tinto

government entity, financed by the Ministry of Finance and the China Investment Corporation (which, as argued in chapter 10, is itself beholden to the Ministry of Finance), and CDB's management must answer to the State Council. It was created explicitly to implement government policy priorities, and its legal mandate reflects this mission. Again, the value on this IV is extreme, and state control is the result, as the theory would predict.

This cluster of cases examined China's efforts to secure raw materials and highlighted both the government's inability to control commercial actors (early CNPC activities in Sudan) and the government's ability to control commercial actors (the Rio Tinto case and CDB). Specifically, Part II has examined how China secures strategic resources in the form of both petroleum and iron.[43] The Chinese state often seeks to work through commercial actors to secure raw materials it views as strategic. In different times and across different contexts, the state enjoys varying degrees of control over these commercial actors. Rather than arguing that the state is categorically "weak" or "strong," it is more helpful to use a dynamic theoretical framework for understanding the elements of a state's successful use of commercial actors to realize its strategic objectives.

The five factors introduced in chapter 2 account for when the state is able to control its commercial actors in this sector. In the case of China's NOCs, the state was often divided by internal bureaucratic coordination difficulties that undermined the unity of the state. The senior bureaucratic ranking of the NOCs also meant that the reporting relationship between the state and the commercial actors further limited state control. In addition, the relative resources were highly skewed in favor of the commercial actors. As a result, the Chinese state often had a difficult time controlling these commercial actors. In contrast, in the CDB/Chinalco the state was able to control the behavior of its commercial actors. In that case, the extreme values across almost all of the independent variables were skewed in favor of the state. The complementarity of the state's goals and the goals of the commercial actors facilitated state objectives. Also, the reporting relationship was clearly in favor of the state. The CDB/Chinalco case provides a useful illustration of how the Chinese state may successfully use commercial actors to pursue its strategic objectives. The evidence shows CDB being directed by the State Council to underwrite a commercial acquisition that served China's national interests, even if these activities ran counter to the economic actors' own narrow commercial motivations. Essentially, this case is the story of commercial actors (Chinalco, backed by CDB financing) being used to pursue a national objective of securing a strategically important resource.

In part 3, we will turn our discussion toward the strategic use of economics to pursue a very different set of national strategic objectives. That set of cases examines China's economic statecraft in the context of the cross-strait relationship with Taiwan. Whereas the cases discussed in this chapter are cases involving large-scale investments by Chinese SOEs in extractive resources abroad, the Taiwan cases revolve around purely private-sector Taiwanese businesses with few direct ties to Beijing.

Part III
CROSS-STRAIT ECONOMIC STATECRAFT

The two empirical chapters in this section of the book highlight two different strategic economic logics pursued by mainland China as part of its effort to influence Taiwan's propensity toward de jure independence from mainland China. Chapter 6 describes how the mainland first cultivated deepening economic relations with Taiwan, and then sought to exploit what it perceived as Taiwanese investors' increasing economic dependence on mainland China. Chapter 7, on the other hand, describes how the logic behind mainland China's more recent economic statecraft has been quite different: by late 2004, mainland China had shifted its strategic approach to emphasize a causal logic premised on fundamentally transforming the preferences of the target. Rather than relying on coercive leverage, mainland China sought to transform interests by targeting beneficial economic rewards toward strategically significant sectors on Taiwan.

These Taiwan cases are important because they serve to illustrate two very different causal logics of economic statecraft in the same cross-strait setting. Coercive leverage rests on credibly threatening (or in some instances actually implementing) punitive actions against the target, while interest transformation seeks to fundamentally redefine the objectives that the target seeks to achieve. Coercive leverage can be thought of as requiring the target to at least tactically comply with the wishes of the sender, while interest transformation runs much deeper. An interest transformation strategy elementally alters the target's sense of its own preferences so they become more in alignment with the sender's wishes. By employing an interest transformation economic statecraft strategy, Beijing has been able to shape and ultimately redefine the actual strategic preferences of Taiwan.

This section of the book compares these two different economic statecraft strategies in the common context of the cross-strait relationship. Chapter 6 examines China's attempts to coercively leverage Taiwan's growing economic dependence on the mainland. These measures were not only strategically ineffective, but they often were heavy-handed, clumsy, and counterproductive. Efforts to impose Beijing's will led to a nationalist backlash on the part of the Taiwanese electorate. Because this type of economic statecraft strategy is different from the strategic logic highlighted by Beijing's current engagement policies, it is useful to juxtapose this period against the common background conditions of the cross-strait relationship. By holding background conditions relatively constant, it is easier to explore exactly how various forms of economic statecraft work. Chapter 7 examines the foundations of China's interest transformation strategy as well as the specific tactics that characterize the present phase of the cross-strait relationship. Studying both periods also allows for an understanding of how China's economic statecraft strategies have matured and developed over time while holding the overall geographic, cultural, and historical contexts relatively constant. That said, there are key variables whose values do shift between these two cases. In particular, these cases exhibit interesting variation regarding how much the mainland state acts as a unified actor. There are clear center-local divergences in the coercive leverage episodes, while the interest transformation episodes exhibit more mainland state cohesiveness. In addition to theoretically helpful cross-case variation within the context of the cross-strait relationship, these cases provide a useful comparison with the previous empirical section.

Whereas the previous empirical section focused on firms in China's extractive resources industry (arguably "most likely" types of cases for state control because the firms are owned, financed, and managed directly by the state), the following two chapters examine the behavior of completely private-sector actors that are neither managed nor financed by the central authorities in Beijing. In fact, the firms examined in this chapter are not even PRC companies. As a result, they provide a useful cross-case comparison to the large state-owned enterprises that were the subject of chapters 4 and 5. Conventional wisdom might suggest that private economic actors make for unlikely tools of economic statecraft. But as the chapters that follow provocatively suggest, even non-Chinese firms can be effectively used to pursue China's strategic objectives.

The Taiwan context is an important empirical arena for understanding the interplay between economics and strategic considerations.[1] Understanding economic statecraft in the cross-strait environment is critical not only for its own sake as a key strategic dynamic influencing East Asian security, but also as a bellwether of what can (or cannot) be realistically achieved with economic tools of statecraft. Given the significance of the Taiwan relationship, this study is not the first to look at economics and its strategic use across the strait. Scott Kastner has done good work in this area although his focus has largely been on the effects of political conflict on economic ties.[2] Equally—if not more—important are the effects of economic ties on the security relationship between Beijing and Taiwan. Scot Tanner did attempt to examine the ability of Beijing to use its economic power to coerce Taiwan.[3] In what is probably the most comprehensive treatment of the use of economics to coerce Taiwan, Tanner concludes that political factors often complicate the use of economics in the cross-strait relationship. This study largely agrees with Tanner's analysis and seeks to build a more comprehensive framework for thinking about the conditions under which economic statecraft is likely to succeed. Moving beyond idiosyncratic explanations, this study offers a more theoretically grounded treatment of the conditions and business-state relationships that facilitate economic statecraft. Tung Chen-yuan is another scholar who has looked at the issue of strategic economics in a cross-strait context.[4] Tung does seek to introduce a theoretical frame to his analysis, but his cost-benefit approach must ultimately rely on inferred utility functions that are, in reality, quite dynamic and inherently difficult to accurately specify ex ante. Moreover, Tung's empirical focus on sanctions limits the scope of his analysis. My work suggests that sanctions are just one of many mechanisms that states can use in pursuing their strategic objectives. Economic relations can affect strategic security issues in a number of ways, any one or any combination of which may be manipulated to achieve strategic ends.[5] This section of the book is focused on exploring two of these strategic logics, namely coercive leverage and interest transformation, in the cross-strait context.

6

COERCIVE LEVERAGE ACROSS THE TAIWAN STRAIT

Arguably for Beijing, no strategic concern (other than regime survival itself) features more importantly than that of Taiwan, particularly its potential independence. The state's primary objective in its relationship with Taiwan is to prevent de jure moves toward independence. Over the years, mainland China has marshaled all elements of national power—at various times emphasizing some more than others—toward achieving this goal. One of the most prominent features of the China-Taiwan relationship is its significant economic dimension despite a long history of historical rivalry. This chapter explores a particular strategic role for economics in the cross-strait relationship: that of building then applying coercive leverage. The evolution of the cross-strait economic relationship and China's corresponding strategic use of economics can be usefully broken into two phases, each of which highlights a different strategic logic of economic statecraft.[1]

In the early days of the cross-strait economic relationship, China was mainly focused on attracting Taiwanese capital investment and management expertise. Both of these valuable contributions were scarce during the early stages of China's opening up and reform efforts.[2] As China became isolated from the international community in the aftermath of the Tiananmen Square massacre, financial and trade ties to Taiwan continued to be an important source of both financial and human capital for the mainland. As the cross-strait economic interaction expanded and deepened throughout the 1990s, China began to consider the possibility of using this economic interaction as a coercive lever of power. As the economic relationship deepened, Beijing focused its economic statecraft on trying to leverage what it viewed as an increasingly asymmetric relationship. During this period, China emerged from the East Asian financial crisis relatively unscathed and in a much stronger economic position relative to the Southeast Asian economies and a fading Japan. As China entered the World Trade Organization (WTO) and the cross-strait economic interaction was poised to take off, the increasing asymmetry in the relationship made a coercive strategy appear more attractive. But efforts to lean on Taiwanese investors and blunt threats to jeopardize their mainland investments to achieve political goals have been, for the most part, crude and relatively ineffective.

To understand why this coercive approach was ineffective, we can revisit the theory of economic statecraft presented earlier. Values for this case across the five factors presented in chapter 2 suggest that controlling these firms would not be easy. First, the Chinese state in this case was internally divided between the central authorities in Beijing and the local governments on the mainland. Second, there was no natural complementarity between the Chinese state's goals and the goals of the commercial actors. These first two variables suggest an absence of state control, but not all the factors did. For example, many of these firms were substantially larger and more visible than the small- and medium-scale enterprises that had characterized the initial cross-strait economic interactions. This size and visibility should have made it easier (but still far from easy) for the state to monitor their behavior and enforce threats. The reporting relationship between these commercial actors and the mainland state was not conducive to state control. These were private, Taiwanese firms. Their reporting relationship to Beijing was indirect, a regulatory business-government relationship relying primarily on sympathetic, local municipal authorities for enforcement. The balance of relative resources did not play much of a role in these episodes. To the extent that this factor did matter, it seemed to favor local governments and the Taiwanese firms operating there rather than the central authorities in Beijing. Despite this pessimistic coding for this case, mainland China nevertheless felt that a coercive strategy would be an effective mechanism for leveraging China's growing economic clout. As it would turn out, this bellicose approach proved to be counterproductive for Beijing. In defiance of Beijing's wishes, the population on Taiwan rallied to the flag during the 1996, 2000, and 2004 presidential elections.[3]

In the aftermath of the 2004 elections, China revisited its cross-strait economic statecraft strategy. With the consolidation of Hu Jintao's leadership, a strategy emerged that seeks interest transformation that results from ever-deepening economic interaction across the strait. Mainland China's economic statecraft has gotten more sophisticated and now seems capable of generating fifth-column effects that can shape Taiwan's definition of its interests. Such dynamics are explored in the next chapter through a detailed case study of China's elimination of the tariffs on fruit exported to the mainland. Tanner and others have provided in-depth analysis on the coercive approach in China's economic statecraft, but the most effective form of China's economic statecraft may involve strategies that leverage interest transformation types of security externalities.[4] More research ought to be directed toward this type of security externality to better understand how economic interaction fits into the strategic political dynamics of the contemporary cross-strait relationship. As Tanner noted in his research, "Virtually every expert consulted for this [*Chinese Economic Coercion Against Taiwan: A Tricky Weapon to Use*] project agreed that Taiwan businesspeople engaged in commerce with the Mainland—known as *taishang* for short—are the most important conduit through which Beijing hopes to exercise its economic influence."[5] Yet we know very little about *how* such influence actually might happen.[6] To begin to shed some light on this form of economic statecraft, this chapter focuses on the mainland's attempt to use economics coercively. In the next chapter, this strategy is contrasted with an economic statecraft strategy designed to exploit interest transformation. But first we will explore the roots and development of the economic dimension of the cross-strait relationship.

Initiating and Deepening of Cross-Strait Economic Ties (1979–1996)

Initial cross-strait ties were characterized by the mainland's efforts to attract Taiwanese investment, expertise, and trade. At the outset of the cross-strait economic relationship, the mainland was largely reliant on Taiwan. It was not until Beijing's post-Tiananmen isolation had begun to thaw that China felt it could try to employ a coercive leverage strategy. This chapter begins by laying out the foundation of the cross-strait economic interaction, from the initial contact through the 1995–1996 Taiwan Straits Crisis. The discussion begins by briefly highlighting the background conditions that both pulled and pushed Taiwanese capital toward the mainland.

The origins of cross-strait economic statecraft are rooted in three background conditions that laid the foundation for the deep economic interaction across the Taiwan Strait that we observe today. First, domestic developments in China's political economy, namely Deng Xiaoping's Reform and Opening Up policy, created significant "pull" for economic engagement with Taiwan. China's emerging export-oriented development strategy relied heavily on foreign capital. Perhaps more importantly than capital, though, China needed Taiwanese management expertise. This often accompanied foreign investment and was particularly important as

China was emerging from a socialist, planned economic model. Taiwan provided a uniquely "Chinese" source of both of these key inputs for the mainland's developing economy. In addition to recently undergoing a similar transition from a state-dominated economic system to a more liberalized, dynamic economy, Taiwan's early investors brought a unique, efficiency-oriented perspective to the mainland. Moreover, Taiwanese investors were coming from a similar cultural background. Many still had familial ties in the mainland, which could provide valuable networks and sources of partnerships. Building on these elements, the mainland sought to encourage Taiwanese investment. The initial cross-strait ties were driven by these dynamics. After Tiananmen, the mainland was seriously isolated as many countries cut off their economic ties to the repressive regime. Reform efforts ground to a halt. China's economic development needs, however, did not change, even though the political climate had altered considerably. As a result, during the early 1990s when China was diplomatically isolated, it was particularly desperate for foreign capital and quality managerial talent. Taiwanese entrepreneurs stepped into the breach, which led to the first major surge of Taiwanese investment in the mainland. During this period, mainland China came to depend on Taiwanese capital, and this became even more true following Deng Xiaoping's "Southern Tour" in 1992.

Second, rising production costs on Taiwan helped push economic activity toward the mainland. Rising standards of living meant domestic production costs in Taiwan had risen considerably, making the Taiwanese operating environment less internationally competitive. As part of an effort to ferret out new low-cost production centers, Taiwanese businesses began to explore the possibility of transferring some of their production to the mainland. Three domestic conditions in Taiwan encouraged investment in mainland China: First, as capital controls were loosened and wages began to rise concurrent with Taiwanese economic development levels, the private sector increasingly sought out lower-wage labor abroad.[7] In addition, as local communities began to enjoy greater voice and representation under democratization, environmental regulations tightened. This had the effect of increasing the costs for some of the heavier-polluting Taiwanese industries like petrochemical refineries and industrial manufacturing.[8] Finally, there was evidence of a surplus of foreign exchange reserves that had been built up in the late 1980s, which would have found a productive home in capital hungry mainland China of the early 1990s.[9]

These two factors were catalyzed by the third background condition: the liberalization of Taiwan's domestic political economy. Taiwan was in the process of consolidating its own nascent democratization during the late 1980s and early 1990s. During the early portion of this economic relationship, as Taiwan democratized, the KMT (the Guomindang or Nationalist Party of China, usually known by its Wade-Giles romanization, KMT) loosened its dominant grip on

Taiwan's government and economy. As part of the democratization process, the KMT began to divest many of its large, state-owned assets. Although done as part of the larger move from an authoritarian, single-party state to a democratically elected form of government, the divestiture had the effect of privatizing much of Taiwan's economic activity, which meant that the interests of Taiwan's large economic actors would no longer be closely dictated by the centralized government.[10] As would be seen in even more stark relief in later years, the private sector increasingly based its behavior on a set of incentives that did not necessarily take into consideration the goals of the government.[11] Another consequence of Taiwan's democratization was the need for the state (especially the political parties) to curry favor with business interests.[12] Incidentally, this business influence on Taiwan's politics provided the pretext that would later underpin China's attempts to lean on the *taishang* as part of its coercive leverage strategy.

Thus, these three background factors set conditions for the initialization of cross-strait economic interaction. First, Taiwan's democratization led to the liberalization of its state-dominated economic model, which increased the distance between the Taiwanese government and its commercial actors. As these assets were spun off and privatized, Taiwan's commercial actors increasingly responded to commercial incentives rather than governmental direction. Second, the commercial conditions on Taiwan were changing as rising production costs caused firms to seek out new, low-cost production centers. Third, China's Reform and Opening Up effort created substantial demand for foreign capital and expertise. The confluence of these three conditions enabled the start of the cross-strait economic relationship.

How the Mainland Fostered Cross-Strait Economic Ties

Beijing sought to encourage higher levels of economic interaction with Taiwan.[13] Although the specific rationale for how economic ties would serve their interests were not always precisely or consistently articulated, the mainland Chinese leadership generally seemed to agree that it was in Beijing's interests to develop closer economic ties to Taiwan. Specifically, deeper economic ties would not only further the mainland's economic development by providing additional capital and culturally relevant managerial expertise, it was also hoped that deepening economic links would lay the foundation for closer political ties sometime in the future.[14]

China actively began to reach out to attract Taiwanese capital in Deng's 1979 New Year "Message to Taiwan Compatriots." After Taiwanese premier Chiang

Ching-Kuo's 1979 "Three No's" policy (no contact, no negotiation, no compromise) was implemented in response to Deng's message, Taiwanese investors were officially prohibited from directly engaging in economic interaction with the mainland. Despite these prohibitions, limited extralegal economic ties began to form in the early 1980s. These nascent efforts to develop cross-strait economic relations originated with mainland overtures directly to Taiwanese investors.[15] As part of Beijing's export-oriented development strategy, in 1983 the PRC passed the "Guidance on Taiwanese Investments in Special Economic Zones" and related favorable policies. These initial overtures attracted early small business entrepreneurs, who exploited familial and cultural ties in localized and regional investments on the mainland. The scale and scope of these activities, however, remained minimal and levels of investment continued to be generally insignificant.

As the Taiwan government began to allow Taiwanese citizens to visit relatives on the mainland in late 1987, the PRC's State Council took the opportunity to pass Regulations for Encouraging Investment by Taiwan Compatriots (sometimes called the 22 Articles) in July of 1988 to clarify the incentives governing Taiwanese mainland investment.[16] Less than a year later, in May of 1989, Xiamen and Fuzhou (both in Fujian Province, a province with strong historical, cultural, and familial ties to Taiwan) were designated as investment zones for Taiwan firms. T. J. Cheng, in his chapter contribution to *Dangerous Strait*, offers a useful observation that mainland government policy designed to attract Taiwanese investment has had two components: protection of Taiwanese investment and the creation of incentives. These events show that the initial spark of cross-strait economic interaction was largely motivated by changes in the mainland investment environment. These changes were designed to attract Taiwanese investment, which would help bolster the mainland's economic development. This was the dominant strategic priority for China under Deng Xiaoping.

Investment levels remained at insignificant levels, though, until the events of Tiananmen in June of 1989 diplomatically isolated Beijing from the rest of the world community. As part of the sanctions imposed on China in response to its crackdown on student protestors, the Western-based foreign direct investment (FDI) upon which much of China's future development strategy rested was suspended.[17] While most of the world community suspended economic ties to China, entrepreneurial Taiwanese investors leapt at the opportunity to fill the void.[18] By the end of 1989, some 1,600 Taiwan enterprises had invested $1.2 billion, and indirect trade volume in 1990 would grow to $3.5 billion as capital-hungry China took measures to encourage and facilitate Taiwanese investment even further.[19] In March of 1990, Wang Yung-ching, CEO of Formosa Plastics, signed an agreement of intention to move a multibillion-dollar investment to Haichang. Deng Xiaoping ordered "green-light treatment" and priority development for this project in Haichang.[20] Although the plan eventually folded under heavy pressure from Taipei, this effort illustrated a notable shift that began to occur in the early 1990s. Increasingly, larger Taiwanese enterprises were looking to invest in mainland China. The huge growth in economic activity in the run-up to and the aftermath of the Koo-Wang talks illustrates this point.[21] Contracted FDI levels in 1992 and 1993 show a big jump as the Taiwan and PRC governments signaled their official sanctioning of this economic interaction.[22] The lack of an established track record and the absence of or questionable reliability of Chinese economic infrastructure and supporting legal frameworks gave investors some pause.[23] But by 1994, the National People's Congress enacted the Investment Protection Law, whose further codification of private property rights cleared the way for larger, more complex, and more formal investments. This effort, combined with tax incentives and land provisions, was effective in attracting not only small and medium Taiwanese enterprises but increasingly larger Taiwanese corporations.[24]

In summary, the initial development and expansion of cross-strait economic ties was driven by active Chinese government regulations and policies designed to attract Taiwanese capital. The Deng-era reforms and an increased demand for Taiwanese FDI following the events of Tiananmen made the mainland investment climate even more attractive. At the same time, economic changes on Taiwan such as rising textile wages and stricter environmental regulations seemed to add additional force to private-sector assessments of whether or not to invest in mainland China. As evidenced above, cross-strait economic interaction began and then proceeded to rise rapidly during this time.

During the more than fifteen years that Taiwanese investments had been flowing into mainland China, the Chinese had increasingly developed the supporting economic infrastructure. Property rights became increasingly better secured and legal protection was passed to facilitate investment activities.[25] As the mainland investment environment became less risky, larger second-mover investors became active in the mainland. As the asymmetry in the relationship began to shift in the mid-1990s, these *taishang* would be targeted when China shifted its economic statecraft strategy from seeking to merely attract Taiwanese economic interaction to more aggressively seeking to influence the elections in Taiwan by employing the type of coercive leverage discussed below.

The Mainland's Shift to a Coercive Leverage Strategy (1996–Summer 2004)

To pursue its goals of attracting Taiwanese capital, China engaged in a number of policy measures and actions that were designed to attract Taiwanese investors.

While the mainland was working to woo Taiwanese commercial actors, the Taiwanese government was either acquiescent, indifferent, or unable to effectively curtail its own private-sector actors from engaging ever more deeply with the mainland. As Taiwan's economy has developed, it has become more and more dependent on the mainland, but during the initial stages of the relationship, the asymmetry in the relationship largely favored Taiwan. As a result, China went to great lengths during this period to maintain and increase the investment flows from Taiwan. Even in the face of the missile tests in 1995–1996 as the rest of China's cross-strait policy was getting more aggressive, China sought to reassure Taiwanese investors, demonstrating its desire to maintain economic ties even in the face of cross-strait military animosity. As the asymmetry in the economic relationship began to shift in favor of the mainland, the possibility of leveraging Taiwan's economic dependence as a coercive tool began to take on a more prominent role in the mainland's cross-strait economic statecraft strategy.

By the mid-1990s there was a growing realization that the asymmetry in the cross-strait economic relationship was increasingly favoring the mainland. By virtue of its size and rapid pace of development, the mainland was increasingly growing into its natural role as the dominant player in the cross-strait economic relationship. This asymmetry would only increase as China emerged in a stronger relative position following the East Asian financial crisis and the bursting of the Internet bubble in the late 1990s. The level of economic interaction further accelerated when both Taiwan and China entered the WTO in 2001. With this growing realization came the strategic temptation to leverage Taiwan's increasing dependence on the mainland. Mainland China sought to pressure Taiwanese firms that had invested in mainland China in an effort to influence the outcome of presidential elections in Taiwan. Before delving into specific instances of coercive leverage, it is useful to examine the strategic calculus underpinning China's economic statecraft during this phase of the cross-strait relationship.

The Mainland's Strategic Logic

The strategic logic that underpinned mainland China's economic statecraft during this period is not complicated. It is the same basic logic that guides any coercive leverage attempt: economic dependence can be jeopardized, and this ability to threaten generates coercive capabilities. Increasingly during this phase of the cross-strait relationship, the economic dependence of Taiwan, a nation whose economy is based on international trade, began to loom larger and larger. Because Taiwan's international businesses are the commercial actors conducting Taiwan's international commerce, they are a critical element driving Taiwan's economic success. As these firms became more deeply invested in mainland China, their success increasingly depended on the success of their mainland operations. China reasoned that by threatening the ability of these firms to operate in the mainland, it could gain coercive leverage over them. To avoid punishment, China could demand that these firms act in a manner consistent with China's larger strategic interests. This is the basic logic driving Chinese economic statecraft during this phase.

In the mid- to late 1990s, China had reason to believe that a cross-strait strategy of coercive leverage would work. Beijing had employed a similar strategy to derail democratic reforms in Hong Kong.[26] Beijing also thought that its impending entry into the WTO would provide it with additional economic leverage.[27] Finally, China's perception of its coercive military power was also rising during this time. In the early 1990s, China engaged in confrontational behavior in the South China Sea, and in 1995–1996, in response to Lee Tung-hui's provocations, China conducted missile exercises off Taiwan's coast. As China increasingly came to see itself as a rising power in the Asia-Pacific, it is not surprising that China viewed its growing economic clout as yet another instrument of coercive capacity through which it could pursue its strategic objectives. Efforts based on such coercive leverage strategies characterize this case. The episodes that make up this case span the period of cross-strait relations roughly from the 1995–1996 Taiwan Missile Crisis to shortly after the 2004 presidential election in Taiwan. The next two sections will briefly examine the presidential elections of 1996, 2000, and 2004 as three episodes that allow for interesting comparisons of how China's strategic use of economics developed and matured during this time.

China's Coercive Leverage

In the 1996 election, mainland China refrained from using coercive economic leverage against Taiwanese investors per se, even during the 1995–1996 missile crisis, when China was explicitly using coercive military tools of national power to pursue its strategic objectives.[28] The cross-strait economic interaction had been growing rapidly until the mid-1990s regional instability dampened enthusiasm. Even at this low point in cross-strait relations, the mainland went to great pains to reassure Taiwanese investors that their investments would be insulated from broader cross-strait frictions.[29]

Contrary to being coercive, this reassurance was explicitly designed to alleviate any trepidation Taiwanese firms might have had regarding Beijing's intentions. This effort to reassure Taiwanese firms was largely driven by the fact that the mainland still felt dependent upon Taiwanese capital and management expertise for its own economic development.[30] It sought to reassure investors and calm jittery capital markets. During the missile crisis, the mainland sought to restrict its use of coercive power to the military realm in a heavy-handed attempt to intimidate Taiwanese voters and dissuade them from electing Lee Tung-hui as president. The heavy-handed effort backfired and Lee was elected by a wide margin. Following the 1996 election, China sought to apply greater pressure on Taiwan to prevent further moves toward independence.

These efforts eventually manifested themselves in the 2000 White Paper on Taiwan. In this official government document, China went beyond simply trying to prevent Taiwanese moves toward independence. That White Paper menacingly suggested that not only was independence unacceptable, but that eventual reunification could not be delayed indefinitely.[31] Taiwan's insubordination as a renegade province would not be tolerated, and Taiwan was to not only cease its moves toward independence, but should also begin moving toward reunification with the mainland. This represented a fundamental shift in China's official position from one that essentially sought to preserve the status quo toward one that sought to compel reunification.

Although China was determined to apply coercive pressure to prevent further moves toward independence, the modality of China's coercion shifted from the military to the economic realm in the aftermath of the 1995–1996 crisis. This shift was largely driven by the backlash China experienced when it attempted to use military power. For instance, China's aggressive posture in the South China Sea prompted a renewal of ASEAN's ties to the United States and a strengthening of cooperation among Southeast Asian nations largely directed against China. The cross-strait crisis prompted the U.S. Seventh Fleet to intervene in the Taiwan Strait, and the U.S.-Japan Alliance (which had been under re-evaluation in a post–Cold War context) was strengthened, largely driven by insecurity in the region. China recognized this counterproductive international response and adjusted its strategy to emphasize the peaceful intentions underpinning China's rise and the win-win economic benefits stemming from a growing China. This pattern of instrumental learning has also been observed in other avenues of Chinese foreign and security policy.[32] After learning through these experiences that military force was strategically ineffective, China sought to employ economic tools of coercion to pursue its objectives vis-à-vis Taiwan. Using this economic power involved targeting and threatening Taiwanese businesses that were invested in the mainland. China's efforts would be directed at targeting firms and their leaderships to dissuade them from supporting a proindependence agenda.

The next two elections provided multiple instances of China's attempting to use coercive leverage against Taiwanese firms that were invested in the mainland. In the 2000 and again in the 2004 election there were reported instances of coercion, intimidation, or threats against Taiwanese firms. In the run-up to and aftermath of the 2000 election, Chinese attempts to lean on Taiwanese firms were scattered, blunt, and poorly implemented, and, not surprisingly, they seem to have had little effect. During the 2004 election, though, it appears that Beijing refined its implementation tactics and homed in on specific firms and individuals, an approach that generated better results. As noted below, in the aftermath of the 2004 election, China embarked on a reconsideration of how it had been using economic statecraft. This would eventually produce the strategy based not on coercive leverage but on interest transformation. The evolution of China's cross-strait economic statecraft would eventually mature into the long-term interest transformation strategy that we observe today. This strategy is discussed in more detail in chapter 7.

Leaning on Taiwanese Investors

The general practice of economic statecraft at this stage was broad and heavy-handed. China targeted many firms and sought to influence how they and their employees voted. Economic statecraft during these early days of coercive leverage can be roughly characterized as a direct application of the strategic mindset of intimidation and bluster that lay behind China's military coercion simplistically transposed into the economic realm. Still, using economic rather than military power represented something of a de-escalation from China's techniques of 1996. Before delving into the specifics of this case, it is useful to note two characteristics of the 2000 election.

First, as Taiwan democratized throughout the 1990s, its businesses also grew more and more politically active. As is the case in many democracies, political campaign contributions became an important factor of electoral success. In addition, Taiwanese businesses would provide candidates with endorsements, and the support of large employers carried substantial weight for political candidates. Many of Taiwan's most successful multinational firms were viewed as thought leaders and widely admired in Taiwanese society. In addition, Taiwanese firms, like many businesses around the world, often sought to cultivate helpful political connections via active participation in the political process. On the eve of the 2000 election, many of Taiwan's most important firms were playing an advisory role for President Lee Tung-hui (the incumbent president who would retire in 2000). Although Lee was a member of the KMT, his strong sentiments toward Taiwanese independence and efforts to "localize" (*bentuhua*) Taiwan politics made him distrusted by Beijing. Mainland China viewed with suspicion Taiwanese firms that cooperated with Lee.

Second, the 2000 Taiwan presidential election was a tight, three-way race, and mainland China sought to influence the outcome. The establishment KMT had been split by the independent candidacy of James Soong Chu-yu. During the campaign, it was widely suspected that outgoing President Lee's real endorsement was for the Democratic Progressive Party (DPP) candidate, Chen Shui-bian, and not for the official KMT candidate Lien Chan. The mainland Chinese government was clear regarding its own preferences on who should be the next president of Taiwan. A few days before the Taiwanese electorate went to the polls, Zhu Rongji issued stern comments to the effect that Taiwanese voters were not allowed to choose a candidate that would seek independence for Taiwan. This was a thinly veiled attack on Chen Shui-bian, whose DPP had long called for Taiwanese independence. Predictably, these comments angered Taiwanese voters and helped tip the scales in favor of Chen Shui-bian, who had already begun to pull ahead in a tight race. Soong's split from the KMT party (Lien) divided what would have otherwise been the winning majority. In the end, the DPP's Chen inched out Soong and won the election.

The mainland was predictably displeased with this result and issued a public statement criticizing the *taishang*. On April 8, 2000, Li Bingcai, deputy director of China's Taiwan Affairs Office of the State Council, issued a sternly worded statement chastising *taishang* for "scrambling for profit" while "openly clamor[ing] for Taiwan independence and advocate[ing] the 'Lee Tung-hui Line,' which preaches the breakup of the motherland. It has exerted a bad influence."[33] His comments implied further pressure against *taishang* that did not uphold the "one China" principle. His condemnation was echoed by Tang Shubei, executive vice president of the mainland's Association for Relations Across the Taiwan Straits (ARATS).[34]

Even before the election, several prominent *taishang* came under scrutiny. For instance, Stan Shih Chen-jung, chairman of Taiwan's largest personal computer maker, Acer Group, had been a national policy advisor to Lee Tung-hui and seemed to have close ties to Chen Shui-bian. Shih had attracted attention for a DPP campaign advertisement that was using his image.[35] He had to issue a public statement declaring that he would not be present in Taiwan during the elections and that he wished to remain neutral. After Chen's victory, Acer products were removed from mainland shelves and Shih had to make a special trip to the mainland to publicly pledge his support for reunification.[36] Shih, who had normally enjoyed good access to officials and industry leaders, was snubbed during an April 2000 technology conference in Beijing. In responding to this pressure, an Acer executive was quoted as saying, "we definitely consider this is very serious for Acer business group in China. . . . We have to be careful and sensitive in our response."[37] Acer had invested US$150 million in the mainland and planned to expand its facilities there. Shih, like many other *taishang*, eventually tried to distance himself from politics.

Acer was not the only Taiwanese business with political links. Continental Engineering Corporation, China Motor Corporation, I-Mei Foods Company, Ltd., and E. Sun Bank all agreed to join Chen's national policy advisory group. The CEO of Taiwan High-Speed Rail, Nita Ing, and Taiwan Semiconductor Manufacturing chairman Morris Chang also served as policy advisors to Chen Shui-bian.[38] The CEO of Evergreen Shipping, Chang Yung-fa, was another strong Chen supporter and long-time advocate of Taiwanese independence. Chang provided an important endorsement of Chen in the lead-up to the election and agreed to serve on Chen's policy making committee. China's liaison in Hong Kong, He Zhiming, reportedly warned Hong Kong businesses to be wary of choosing Taiwanese partners because proindependence businesses would "face serious consequences."[39] This pressure was significant because a good deal of Evergreen's shipping was routed through Hong Kong (much of Taiwan's mainland shipping moved through Hong Kong because of the lack of direct trade links). After the election, Evergreen retrenched and said it wanted closer economic links with the mainland and that it did not support Taiwanese independence.[40] Evergreen's mainland operations were not materially impacted by Chang's political activities, although he too seemed to lower his political profile in the aftermath of the 2000 election.

One of the most high-profile supporters of Chen Shui-bian was Hsu Wen-lung, the founder and CEO of the petrochemicals and plastics company Chi Mei. Like Shih, Hsu had been an advisor to Lee Tung-hui and was known for his outspoken support of Taiwanese independence. Hsu provided a crucial endorsement to Chen about two weeks before the election. In his endorsement, Hsu noted that Chen was the heir of Lee Tung-hui and was "the candidate best able to follow the departing president's 'line.'"[41] Hsu also agree to serve as a policy advisor to the new Chen administration. Such blatant support infuriated Beijing. After the election, Chi Mei's mainland factories and operations were subjected to surprise inspections, environmental regulations, tax, customs, and labor investigations.[42] "Starting in mid-May, teams of about 40 Chinese investigators descended on three factories run by Chi Mei in China's Jiangsu province and investigated them for a week . . . they [the investigators] intimated strongly that they had been dispatched to the factories because of Hsu's support for Chen . . . The Chinese officials 'were very blunt,' he said. 'They said our president had supported Chen. They had labeled him a Taiwan independence activist.'"[43]

Although Chi Mei did receive harassing investigations, as Scot Tanner noted in his work on the *taishang*, most of these mainland threats against independence-leaning *taishang* did not escalate into substantive actions taken against the offending companies.[44] The primary reason for this was the divergent perspectives between the central government and the local municipalities that hosted the Taiwanese businesses' investments in the mainland. These local officials were much more predisposed toward ensuring that the *taishang* continued to provide important jobs and economic activities in their regions. There were numerous reports of local officials countermanding the centrally issued threats.[45] In the end, the attempt to coerce these firms met with limited (if any) success, although China's coercive tactics did seem to cause most *taishang* to take a lower political profile.

Hsu Wen-lung and the Chi Mei Group was one of the firms that did not buckle and as such continued to receive pressure from the mainland. In 2004, Chi Mei was considering expanding its operations on the mainland to move into liquid-crystal-display (LCD) distribution and assembly. Specifically, Hsu was planning to open another mainland factory in either Shanghai or Ningbo for the Chi Mei TFT/LCD manufacturing subsidiary. The mainland threatened to impose investment restrictions and subject any Chi Mei operations to intense regulatory scrutiny if Hsu persisted in his proindependence advocacy. The chairman of Taiwan's Mainland Affairs Council claims that Beijing had threatened Hsu with "investment restrictions and nonstop regulatory scrutiny of his Mainland operations. 'They applied a lot of pressure.'"[46] In June 2004, Chinese newspapers criticized Hsu Wen-lung by name and noted that all "green" [i.e. proindependence] businesses were no longer welcome on the Mainland. Chi Mei's Taipei Stock Exchange–listed TFT/LCD subsidiary took a 5 percent hit on the news. In the end, Hsu Wen-lung would publish an open letter on March 26, 2005, criticizing Chen for going too far. In his letter, Hsu admitted that Taiwan's push for independence was a "recipe for disaster."[47]

The mainland's decision to focus on one of the most prominent supporters of Chen's independence stance was designed serve as an example to other *taishang*. Hsu made a good candidate to target because he was among the most unrepentant of the pro-DPP *taishang* following the 2000 election. Recognizing that they could not effectively enforce strict measures on all the *taishang*, Beijing sought to single out the most high-profile of them and make an example of him. Hsu's response indicated that this more targeted effort to bring coercive pressure to bear on Chi Mei did have the effect of forcing Hsu to publicly back down from his previous support for Chen. These events provide a good example of how the mainland uses its "king-making" capabilities to encourage or discourage the commercial success of enterprises in the mainland. Those entities that are not seen as being sufficiently supportive are excluded from lucrative contracts, are subject to intrusive regulatory oversight, or may become targets of anticorruption campaigns or any other variety of more subtle discriminatory measures.[48] For those organizations and individuals that toe the line, Beijing can bestow lucrative rewards. Such state favors (or disfavors) are often granted on the basis of political compatibilities with preferred government policy and objectives. The growing asymmetric economic dependence of Taiwan on the mainland make this "king-making" mechanism of coercive leverage seem more likely to be employed in the future. This more sophisticated, targeted strategy presages China's later efforts to employ a strategy that was explicitly designed to not only enforce compliance with Beijing's wishes, but to alter the preferences of the commercial actors so they would *want* what Beijing sought.

By the time the 2004 election had arrived, the mainland had scaled back its heavy-handed interference. This evolution seems to provide some indication that the regime was learning how to more effectively use economic statecraft in its efforts to manage cross-strait dynamics. In 2004, Beijing was much more nuanced in its use of economics to pursue its strategic objectives.[49] The mainland took specific, high-profile measures against the most blatant proindependence *taishang*. This more targeted approach yielded better results as Chi Mei's founder, Hsu Wen-lung, publicly recanted his support for Taiwan's independence. Coercive leverage still failed, however, to prevent Chen's winning re-election in 2004. Coercive leverage—even if used more as a scalpel rather than a sledgehammer—was still not an appropriate economic statecraft strategy to achieve China's objectives. As mentioned above, in the aftermath of Chen's re-election, the mainland reconsidered its coercive approach to economic statecraft. This reorientation marked the origins of the interest transformation strategy that the mainland continues to use today.

Evaluating the Coercive Leverage Strategy

China's primary interest with regard to Taiwan was to prevent further moves toward de jure independence.[50] To do so, China sought to influence Taiwan's elections, specifically to prevent the more independence-oriented candidate from winning. To achieve this objective, China sought to target key business supporters. In 1996, 2000, and 2004 the independence-oriented candidate won. These results suggest that, strictly speaking, China's efforts to lean on the *taishang* did not succeed. That said, China *was* mildly effective at making life difficult for these firms. In the end, there is evidence that the *taishang* will in the future be less likely to actively support contentious political positions. Eventually, after blunt pressure from China, several of the *taishang* seemed to back down or at least take a lower political profile and attempt to "fly below the radar." Overall, though, this coercive approach was strategically not successful because it generated a public backlash among the Taiwanese electorate. China's bullying validated the DPP's independence credentials and triggered nationalist support among the Taiwanese electorate, who did not look favorably on the mainland's efforts to intimidate Taiwan. In the end, China's heavy-handed tactics actually probably helped improve Chen's electoral position. So these attempts at economic statecraft were not successful for the mainland. What went wrong?

The divergent goals of the commercial actors and the state feature prominently in explaining where China's efforts may have faltered. The incentives of the commercial actors (*taishang*) were not aligned with the goals of the state. In the most successful episodes, the state could force *taishang* to hide below the radar to avoid ruffling feathers on the mainland. But the *taishang* that China targeted never *really* wanted to undermine Chen. Moreover, China had no real strategy to alter these commercial actors' preferences. Pressure was simply coercive and designed to ensure compliance (rather than to redefine the *taishang*'s political views). This case shows the limitations of using coercion as economic statecraft. Meaningfully achieving China's goals would require a strategy that was designed to change the political landscape on Taiwan. This was the strategic error that China committed in this case: using the wrong tool for the strategic objective being sought. States must be attuned to what commercial actors want to accomplish and how doing what the state wants to see done might work to the advantage of the firms. In this case, China made it clear that life on the mainland would be better if the *taishang* did what Beijing wanted. But in practice, many *taishang* understood that it was really the local and municipal officials who constituted the "state" who could determine how bad or good the *taishang*'s local mainland operating environment would be.

The state's coercive capabilities were not as powerful as they could have been because the state was not a unitary actor in this instance. The local municipalities and the central government were divided in their respective willingness to actually punish the *taishang*. Many Taiwanese investors had developed deep relationships with local authorities in Xiamen or Fuzhou to help ensure stability and political support for their investments.[51] Indeed, during this period, local authorities' own political advancement increasingly hinged on their local economic performance. In many instances, this economic growth was heavily reliant on continued Taiwanese FDI and management expertise. The local cadre faced strong motivations because their performance evaluation process was heavily weighted toward regional economic performance. This gave them strong incentives to keep the Taiwanese firms, the engine of regional economic growth, happily invested in their region. This narrow interest, however, created tension and divisions between the central government in Beijing and the local municipalities where the *taishang* operated. The result was that the state did not act in a unified manner. As the theory suggests, the Taiwanese commercial actors were able to exploit these divisions to avoid serious punishment. This strategy enabled them to fly below the radar and continue doing business with minimal actual consequences arising from their political actions.

Although there were many *taishang* actively invested in the mainland during this phase, their size and the public nature of their activities helped the state monitor and target firms. When compared to the many small and medium-sized enterprises that constituted the bulk of the early cross-strait commercial actors and the disparate fruit farmers that will be the commercial actors examined in chapter 7, these large *taishang* were relatively easy for the state to monitor and target. This finding tells us something interesting regarding the relative importance of these two variables. Even if there are relatively few firms for the state to monitor, if the state is not unified, it is unlikely that the state will be able to direct the behavior of those firms. Indeed, the evidence from the 1999–2004 period suggests that the problem for China was not so much being able to identify and monitor the *taishang*, but rather the internal divisions within the state that served to undermine Beijing's efforts to coerce the firms.

These internal divisions are also to blame for the ineffectiveness of the state's regulatory capabilities. Although the nature of the relationship between the state and the commercial actors in this case was indirect, this feature alone does not preclude effective government action. China still maintains some indirect, primarily regulatory mechanisms through which it can influence the behavior of firms operating in China. In this case, the regulatory environment had been largely decentralized and was resting mainly on local enforcement efforts. Because the objectives of local officials diverged from those of the central government, the disunity of the state undermined the power of the state to leverage whatever authority it may have been able to wield via the Reporting Relationship IV. This undermined the effectiveness of state enforcement, a necessary tool for a coercive strategy.

From the perspective of the Relative Resources IV, the *taishang* had a good deal of local operating knowledge on the mainland. Although this resource variable did not feature prominently in this case, to the extent that resource endowments did factor in, once again, the center-local divisions within the state does most of the explanatory work. The relative resource disparity between local enforcement capabilities and the central government's more limited resources further undermined the ability of the state to control the commercial actors in this context. The local officials had more of the important bureaucratic resources to facilitate monitoring, compliance, and enforcement than the central government in Beijing was able to bring to bear in this episode.

TABLE 6.1 Coercive Leverage Case Summary Table

	IV CODING	EVIDENCE	DV PREDICTION	DV OUTCOME
Unity of state	Divided	Center-local differences in incentives, enforcement, and preferences regarding leaning on mainland investors from Taiwan	Control unlikely	*Taishang* commercial actors were able to leverage local state relations in mainland China to circumvent central Chinese state efforts to apply economic coercion
Goals	Divergent	The goals of the central state were mutually exclusive to the *taishangs'* preference for independence, but the profit-seeking orientation of *taishang* were quite compatible with the development goals of local mainland political actors	Control unlikely	Very limited ability for the state to control commercial actors; the best the state could do was to force the commercial actors to "fly below the radar"
Market structure	Highly competitive	Many small-, medium-, and large-scale Taiwanese enterprises invested in mainland China, often having established close, personal, business relationships with local host government officials; central government monitoring, coordination, and enforcement were all quite difficult	Control unlikely	Once central state concentrated its efforts at targeting a smaller number of high-profile *taishang* (e.g. Hsu Wen-lung), coercion was a bit more effective, even resulting in some state control over independence advocacy; but the larger strategic intent of shaping the Taiwanese elections away from independence failed
Reporting relationship	Indirect/ nonexistent	Private, Taiwanese firms; regulatory business-government relationship relied primarily on local	Control unlikely	State efforts to control the behavior of commercial actors sympathetic to Taiwanese

	IV CODING	EVIDENCE	DV PREDICTION	DV OUTCOME
		mainland municipal authorities for monitoring and enforcement; local officials were often sympathetic, given the localized economic benefits from these invested enterprises		independence were largely unsuccessful; in fact, the independence issue may have actually benefited electorally from the coercion attempts
Relative resources	Somewhat favors commercial actors	Although not a major driver of the outcome in this case, the evidence suggests the balance of resources favored local governments and the Taiwanese firms operating there rather than the central authorities in Beijing	Not a significant factor	Central state had a difficult time controlling commercial actors and leveraging coercive economic statecraft against Taiwan

During this phase of the cross-strait relationship, China attempted to capitalize on what was becoming an increasingly asymmetrical relationship. China's economic statecraft strategy sought to coerce large Taiwanese firms that had significant operations in the mainland. These firms were targeted because key leaders of these firms supported Chen Shui-bian, the DPP, or proindependence sentiments. China's efforts to prevent independence-oriented candidates from winning presidential elections on Taiwan in these episodes ultimately proved unsuccessful.

China's economic statecraft seems to have suffered from three shortcomings. First, China was trying to change the national preferences of Taiwan via a coercive leverage strategy. This was the wrong strategic tool for such an enormous job. The *taishang* China targeted had strong political views. Rather than recognizing this and designing an interest transformation strategy to address it, China sought to use coercive leverage, a tool suited to enforcing compliance but not to altering preferences. Second, the internally divided nature of the state in mainland China during this phase made enforcement difficult to execute. Even if a coercive leverage approach had been appropriate, the central government authorities were seeking outcomes that were opposed to what the local authorities sought. This friction allowed the commercial actors to find shelter under the protection of local and provincial officials. Third, China's actions against the *taishang* reinforced the belief in Taiwan that China presented a menacing threat to Taiwan. Castigating the *taishang* confirmed suspicions of a China that sought to bully a much smaller Taiwan. Moreover, receiving such pressure seemed to validate the DPP's (and its supporters') antiauthoritarian credentials. In many ways, these firms were seen as standing up to China. China's policies stoked Taiwanese nationalism and on more than one occasion resulted in an electoral lift for the antimainland, proindependence candidate. China's recognition of this counterproductivity would usher in a strategic shift in how China sought to use economic statecraft to pursue its objectives regarding the independence issue on Taiwan. This is the subject of the next chapter.

7

INTEREST TRANSFORMATION ACROSS THE TAIWAN STRAIT

The efforts to shape the electoral outcomes on Taiwan that were discussed in the previous chapter were not merely unsuccessful. In many ways, China's use of coercive economic statecraft actually provoked the opposite of the intended strategic effect. A new approach had to be found. The solution lay in a strategy of economic statecraft called interest transformation.

The heart of this chapter focuses on the mainland's use of economics to alter Taiwan's definition of its own interests. Exactly how does such a strategy work? This chapter examines an episode that helps shed light on this question. At the center of this episode is the spring 2005 visit of Taiwan's opposition party to the mainland and the subsequent elimination of tariffs on Taiwanese fruit.

From April 26 through May 3, 2005, Lien Chan, chairman of the Kuomintang Party (KMT), paid a visit to mainland China. This was a monumentally historic visit as it represented "the first time that Lien personally set foot on the mainland soil since he left in 1945, and also the first-ever visit by a KMT chairman to the mainland in 56 years, ushering in a new stage for the relations between the KMT and the Communist Party of China (CPC)."[1] In the course of this trip, Lien visited Nanjing, Beijing, Shanghai, and his birthplace in Xi'an. While in Beijing on April 29, he met with Hu Jintao, general secretary of the Communist Party. The significance of this handshake for cross-strait relations was considerable: it signaled that the then opposition party KMT was capable of reaching across the strait and making progress in reconciling the two sides of one of the most volatile flashpoints in the Asia-Pacific region. The visit was intended to undermine the credibility of the narrowly re-elected president of Taiwan, Chen Shui-bian, whose policy of seeking independence for Taiwan was an anathema to Beijing. The message was clear: the then-ruling DPP (Chen's party) was not able to meaningfully engage the mainland. Driving home this point was a similar visit by the other significant opposition leader, James Soong Chu-yu, two days later.[2] But perhaps most interesting from the standpoint of the study of economic statecraft was the offer made to Lien at the end of his trip in Shanghai. At the conclusion of that visit, China offered several goodwill "gifts" to Lien (and explicitly to the people of Taiwan). Among these were scholarships for students from Taiwan to study in the mainland, easing of mainland restrictions on mainland tourists that wanted to visit (and spend their money in) Taiwan, lowering of tariffs on fresh fruit exported from Taiwan to mainland China, and two pandas to be given as goodwill ambassadors to Taiwan. These concessions were designed to signal a changed mainland strategy that emphasized "carrots" rather than "sticks." The mainland sought to build bridges directly with the people of Taiwan rather than work with their elected DPP representatives. This strategy was referred to as "public power" (*gong quanli*) and sought to leverage pressure on the DPP by appealing directly to the citizens of Taiwan.[3]

Recall that economic statecraft occurs when the state seeks to generate strategic consequences (in this case, reversing trends toward Taiwanese independence under the DPP leadership) by influencing the behavior of commercial actors (in this case, Taiwanese fruit farmers). The state (in this case, mainland China) has a range of tools at its disposal to incentivize commercial actors to behave in a manner conducive to the state's strategic objectives (in this case, shifting Taiwanese farmers' support away from the traditional, proindependence orientation of the DPP). In this episode of economic statecraft, China eliminated the tariffs on Taiwanese fruit exported to mainland China. This offer was part of a larger set of concessions (like the scholarships for Taiwanese students to study on the mainland) that strategically targeted groups of Taiwanese that traditionally supported Chen Shui-bian and the DPP.[4] China's move was designed to appeal to the fruit producers' economic self-interests and drive a wedge between the DPP and its constituents.[5] The strategy was designed to weaken the DPP's electoral clout on Taiwan.[6]

The effect of this interest transformation strategy has been to create an environment in which DPP candidates now feel the need to moderate their positions so that mainland officials would be willing to work with them. In so doing, the independence movement has been marginalized and is seen as "increasingly irrelevant," a domestic political liability in Taiwan.[7] That said, Taiwanese domestic politics rarely fails to stir passion, and it remains to be seen what role (if any) the independence issue will play in the 2016 presidential contest in Taiwan. Regardless of what the future holds, at least for the period from roughly 2005 to 2014, Taiwan's independence movement largely withered. This chapter examines the fundamentally different approach mainland China took regarding how to most effectively leverage its economic ties with Taiwan. Whereas the previous chapter's economic statecraft sought coercive leverage, this chapter describes how China's economic statecraft sought interest transformation. Understanding precisely how this episode transpired provides a useful window into China's evolving practice of economic statecraft.

Framing the Case

So how did China execute this strategy of interest transformation? We will begin by identifying the key actors in this episode and what their chief objectives looked like. In economic statecraft, the self-interests of the key actors are the linchpin for generating economic behavior that will produce the desired security externalities. In this case, the mainland Communist Party homed in on one of the DPP's key constituencies and sought to demonstrate how shifting its political support would benefit the commercial actors' own narrow economic self-interests. In so doing, the mainland was able to affect the selection of leadership on Taiwan and thus helped derail what had been increasing momentum toward independence. Instead, cross-strait dynamics moved toward deeper and deeper economic integration under the KMT's president Ma Ying-jeou.[8] This section identifies the major groups involved in this episode, their relative priorities, and what the theory leads us to expect in this case.

The overarching goal of mainland China in this episode is, at a minimum, to prevent independence.[9] China's maximal goal is to foster eventual reunification with Taiwan.[10] With the publication of China's 2000 White Paper on Taiwan, the urgency for reunification seemed to take on a greater priority over Beijing's more traditional concerns about Taiwan's moves toward independence. By late 2004, this emphasis on reunification was once again replaced by an expressed desire to simply prevent moves toward independence. Because of Beijing's strategic shift back toward preserving the status quo, China effectively set a much lower bar for what it sought to achieve through economic statecraft in this episode. Dissuading independence and preserving the status quo would be much easier than coercively persuading Taiwan to move toward reunification. This shift also brought China's goals more closely into line with the commercial actors' goals. By reorienting its goals toward preserving the status quo, China made it easier to direct the behavior of the commercial actors. The theory predicts that the state should have an easier time controlling the commercial actors when the goals of the two sides are compatible.

With regard to the Taiwanese business community specifically, China's main objectives were to create "a politically irresistible domestic lobby."[11] The strategy was to create a set of vested domestic interests that would lobby in favor of closer cross-strait ties.[12] To do this, mainland China sought to "further deepen cross-strait economic relations as a source of greater future leverage for Beijing."[13] The opposition party visits, and the subsequent concessions signaled that the KMT (not the DPP) was able to deliver progress on cross-strait issues. These activities were designed to diminish the electoral prospects for the DPP. Scot Tanner concurs that "Beijing's most fundamental and enduring tactical goal ... has been encouraging a subtle form of 'regime change' in Taiwan."[14] Although Tanner notes that Beijing has "sought to exploit the growing cross-strait relationship to undermine the domestic political power of Taiwan officials whom it regards as pro-independence and build support (or at least acceptance) for reunification among Taiwan's citizenry and elite," he does not spend much time exploring exactly how this occurred.[15] This episode sheds more light on the mechanics of this transformative process. Although Tanner touches on interest transformation briefly in his analysis of cross-strait economic statecraft, his work is almost exclusively focused on the coercive leverage elements of the relationship discussed in the previous chapter. He finds (correctly I think) that this tool of economic statecraft was ineffective for Beijing during the late 1990s and early 2000s. What may be more interesting to know is exactly how the mainland sought to transform Taiwan's domestic interests via this longer-term strategy of interest transformation.

Unlike the case of China's coercive leverage strategy discussed in the previous chapter, China's interest transformation strategy was better able to align the interests of the central authorities in Beijing with the proclivities of the localized mainland governmental authorities. In this episode, there were no incentives driving a wedge between the central government and local municipalities, and provinces did not contradict or seek to undermine the center's policies. The state was able to act in a unified way to achieve its objectives largely because the provinces most directly concerned by the strategy (Fujian, Zhejiang, Guangdong) already had good ties to Taiwanese businesses.[16] In addition, these provinces were generally in favor of increased economic interaction given that their consumer markets were getting more and more wealthy and local officials were seeking to enhance consumer access to fruit and other luxury items. There was no evidence of bureaucratic divides within the state either. The Ministry of Commerce followed the cue of China's senior leadership.[17] The Taiwan Affairs Office of the State Council was also on board with the strategy put in place.[18] Finally, in this episode, there was no public evidence of factional divides among senior patrons within the Chinese Communist Party. The policy shift seems to have come after

Hu had completed his consolidation of power.[19] Given the absence of center-local tensions, factional divisions, and bureaucratic frictions in Beijing, the state can be classified as having acted in a unified manner during this episode. The theory suggests that the state should have a much better chance of directing the behavior of the commercial actors when it is acting in a unified manner.

Although the value of the State Unity variable is quite different from the one described in the previous chapter, one area in which these two Taiwan cases are similar is on the Reporting Relationship variable. In both the previous chapter and in this one, the commercial actors described are Taiwan-based, private-sector, commercial firms that are primarily seeking profit. They pay taxes to the government on Taiwan and are not owned, invested in, nor managed by the mainland government. Quite distinct from the Chinese state-owned enterprises that were the commercial actors of chapters 4 and 5, these firms have only indirect reporting relationships with the mainland Chinese state. Indeed, the only real institutional source of state leverage in these cases is through the mainland's ability to influence the regulatory environment in mainland China, the host nation in which these commercial actors operate. The commercial actors in these Taiwan cases are thus fairly distant from the Chinese state. In these cases, the theory predicts that the indirect nature of the reporting relationship should work against state control. As discussed in more detail at the end of this chapter, though, the effect of this variable is overwhelmed by the effect of the mainland state unity, the near-term goal compatibility between the mainland and the commercial actors, and the competitive market structure in this case.[20]

In addition to the mainland Chinese state, the second major political player in this episode is the KMT. At the time of the 2004-2005 visits, the KMT was Taiwan's opposition party, and it sought to undermine public support for the ruling DPP.[21] By targeting one of the DPP's important electoral constituencies that stood to personally benefit from policies that the DPP was ideologically opposed to, the KMT calculated that its electoral prospects would be improved. They wanted to do this by showing that the KMT was able to deliver on issues of political rapprochement with the mainland, which would better position the KMT to build beneficial economic relations across the strait. [22]

Lining up on the other side of this fight was the central government of Taiwan under the leadership of Chen Shui-bian and the DPP. The government wanted to conduct any cross-strait negotiations that might occur as a result of the unofficial, political party visits strictly through official channels. In particular, the Chen government sought to channel talks on the fruit issue through the Taiwan External Trade Development Council (TAITRA) and to a lesser degree through the Mainland Affairs Council (MAC) and the Council of Agriculture (CoA), Taiwan's senior-level, executive branch government body charged with administration and oversight in agriculture. The administration sought to leverage the situation by conducting negotiations in the framework of the WTO, and it worked to frame the discussion as being one of external trade. By internationalizing the talks, the administration apparently sought to use the episode to reinforce the international autonomy of Taiwan. Throughout this episode, the Taiwan government sought to prevent the private-sector actors from getting ahead of the government.

The commercial actors themselves—Taiwan's fruit farmers—sought to secure access to the mainland consumer market, which was attractive both for its future growth potential and as a market capable of absorbing that particular year's bumper crop.[23] To facilitate access to the mainland market, the farmers also sought to build up the supporting trade infrastructure for perishable goods including direct transportation links, quarantine and inspection protocols, expedited customs clearing procedures, etc. The farmers worked through industry associations when interacting with the mainland, in particular the Taiwan Provincial Farmers Association, led by its KMT-affiliated executive secretary, Chang Yung-cheng. Farming on Taiwan is still a fragmented industry (in 2004, there were more than three hundred farmers associations in Taiwan). As a result, the marketplace is fairly competitive, making Taiwan's farmers quick to seize upon any competitive advantage. The farmers are also unlikely to give up or jeopardize an advantage such as access to a new export market once they get it. Thus the Market Structure variable in this case is competitive and diffuse, which the theory suggests should have made it more difficult for the state to monitor and ultimately exercise control over the commercial actors. As this case demonstrates, however, the state can leverage its "king-making" capabilities even under highly competitive market conditions to influence commercial outcomes. In fact, more competitive environments may actually raise the relative value of such state beneficence as firms look for any potential source of competitive advantage. Such state support (or, conversely, disfavor) can spell the difference between business success and failure. An interventionist state is thus able to wade into competitive commercial environments and influence the competitive dynamics by providing preferential market access, uneven regulatory environments, contract awards to favored firms, supportive concessionary financing, tax breaks, or any number of economic policy tools.

Although the theory in this case suggests that the large number of economic actors and their indirect reporting relationship to the state should have made control more difficult, China's "king-making" capabilities helped to mitigate the effect of these variables in this case. In addition, the state unity of this case stands in stark contrast to the divided mainland state actor of the previous chapter. Once again, the balance of relative resources played a minimal role. Before charging into the specifics of the case, let us briefly examine the backdrop against which this episode unfolded.

Context of the Case

There are three important factors that shaped this episode and provide background context for it. The first was the DPP's pattern of electoral successes and Taiwan's growing independence movement of the 1990s and early 2000s. The second factor concerned Taiwan's electoral geography, who votes how and where. The third factor that set the stage for this episode involved mainland China's response to these events and the evolution of China's strategy for leveraging domestic political dynamics on Taiwan.

DPP's Electoral Successes

In this episode, mainland China was seeking to alter the domestic political landscape on Taiwan. A thorough analysis of this episode of economic statecraft ought to place the events of the spring and summer of 2005 in the context of Taiwan's recent electoral history. Of particular importance was the Democratic Progressive Party's (DPP) pattern of increasingly successful electoral victories that can be traced from the origins of Taiwan's democratization in the late 1980s right up to the eve of this episode.[24] Since its founding, the DPP had displayed an ability to consistently demonstrate its growing popularity among the Taiwanese electorate. Mainland China found this to be disquieting and sought to stem the DPP's track record of increasingly significant electoral successes. In particular, mainland China sought to reverse what it perceived as increasingly bold efforts to move toward independence under the leadership of President Chen Shui-bian and the DPP.

The DPP and its proindependence electoral agenda grew more and more politically viable through the 1990s. After first running in the Legislative Yuan (LY) election of 1986 as an illegal party, in the 1989 LY election the DPP won twenty-one seats.[25] This figure was significant because a party needed to hold at least twenty seats in the legislature to be able to propose legislation. In the 1992 LY election, the DPP won fifty seats, and it would continue to build electoral momentum through the 1995 and 1998 LY elections.[26] In the run-up to the 1996 presidential election, the mainland conducted a series of provocative military exercises (including missile launches) in the vicinity of Taiwan.[27] This bullying led to a popular backlash against Beijing that expressed itself as public support for Lee Tung-hui, who was elected with 54 percent of the vote.[28] Although Lee was the KMT candidate, his pro-Taiwan and antiunification sentiments were well-known.[29] During Lee's presidency, "localization" or "indigenization" (*ben-tuhua*) efforts picked up steam. The DPP (and its independence agenda) also gained more and more popularity.

As the century turned, the DPP finally took the reins of power. In the March 18, 2000, presidential election, DPP candidate Chen Shui-bian benefited from a split in the KMT party.[30] The popular James Soong Chu-yu was not given the KMT nomination and chose to run as an independent, while Lien Chan ran as the KMT's candidate. As a result, Chen received 39.3 percent of the votes, beating out Soong (with 36.8 percent) and Lien (with only 23.1 percent) to become the first non-KMT president of Taiwan.[31] The DPP was widely viewed as having moderated its radical independence position to enhance its electability for this election. With the 2001 LY election, the DPP also became the largest political party in the legislature.[32]

The DPP's growing electoral momentum was further solidified with the March 20, 2004, re-election of President Chen Shui-bian and his outspoken independence-oriented vice president, Annette Lu Hsiu-lien. In a tight race, Chen and Lu took 50.11 percent of the vote, narrowly beating the Lien-Soong pan-blue ticket, which garnered 49.89 percent of the vote.[33] Although the final result was likely tipped in the DPP's favor by the assassination attempt on Chen and Lu the day before the election, the result was seen as a watershed for the DPP. The DPP had demonstrated its ability to defeat a unified pan-blue ticket, unlike in the 2000 election, in which the opposition was divided.

Throughout the early 2000s, the KMT sought to stem the DPP's momentum and regain its control over Taiwan's domestic politics. Much of the DPP's popularity emanated from its position as the anti-KMT party. Perhaps most controversially, the DPP had been a longtime supporter of an independent Taiwanese identity, which had manifested as efforts to move Taiwan toward formal de jure independence. Such efforts constituted a red line for mainland China and were the primary reason the DPP's success also frustrated Beijing. The issue of opposing Taiwan's independence provided the initial common cause between Taiwan's opposition parties and the Chinese Communist Party.[34] Chen's re-election in 2004 coincided with Hu Jintao's consolidation of mainland China's top leadership posts and prompted a re-examination of mainland China's strategy toward Taiwan.[35] This strategic shift constitutes the second background factor to which we now turn.

Contemporaneous Political Developments in Mainland China

The offer to drop the tariffs on fruit was not the first attempt by the mainland to use economic tools to undermine the DPP's support base. As discussed in the previous chapter, mainland China had earlier used economic statecraft to threaten Taiwanese investors over their support for Chen Shui-bian and the DPP. Before that Beijing had also engaged in limited and heavy-handed efforts to mobilize "pro-pan-Blue and anti-pan-Green" *taishang* on the mainland. Support included efforts to organize meetings and to facilitate charter flights for pro-Beijing *taishang* to return home to vote in elections. These efforts were largely ineffective, as many fewer actually went home to vote than had been hoped. In addition, China's coercive leverage with the *taishang* seems to have been limited. Anti-DPP harassment of *taishang* on the mainland was publicized in the Taiwanese press and served to underscore the DPP's pro-Taiwan bona fides among the electorate.[36] In 2004, Chen Shui-bian narrowly won re-election. Frustrated, the mainland initially lashed out once again to punish prominent *taishang* that had supported the pan-green efforts. Scot Tanner has noted that despite the tough talk, these efforts had only limited real bite.[37]

The Foundations of Today's Cross-Strait Economic Statecraft

By the fall of 2004, the mainland, after failing to derail the DPP's electoral success using coercive strategies, had begun to shift its economic statecraft strategy to one that emphasized interest transformation on Taiwan.[38] This shift in strategy reflected Hu Jintao's broader emphasis on stability in China's grand strategy.[39] Seen from this perspective, coercion tends to be counterproductive and force falls a bit out of fashion as both represent destabilizing dynamics. Under this line of reasoning, Beijing needed to influence the whole relationship. China's reassessment of the utility of coercive leverage was an important backdrop to the opposition party visits and the fruit tariff discussed below. In particular, there was a renewed emphasis placed on preventing Taiwan's independence as opposed to forcing reunification on Taiwan.[40] On January 28, 2005, Jia Qinglin, chairman of the People's Political Consultative Conference and vice chairman of the Taiwan Affairs Leading Small Group, gave a speech titled "Resolutely Contain 'Taiwan Independence' Separatist Activities; Safeguard Peace and Stability in the Taiwan Strait Region; Continue the Endeavour To Ensure That Cross-Strait Relations Develop Towards Peaceful Reunification," in which he laid the foundation for a strategy that emphasized the prevention of Taiwanese independence.[41] Also, when Hu Jintao took over the CMC, he apparently made it clear that the PRC had no reason to fear Taiwan's procrastination when it came to the issue of reunification.[42] This perspective was also articulated in Hu's March 4, 2005, speech on China's Taiwan policy. In that speech, Hu noted that the current status quo is one in which Taiwan is a part of China.[43] China came to realize that it could afford to play the long game with Taiwan.[44]

The reassessment of China's Taiwan strategy eventually culminated in the legal codification of China's new strategy: the Anti-Secession Law (ASL), which was passed on March 14, 2005. Although this law was initially viewed as aggressive and as providing the legal pretext for China's military resolution of the Taiwan question, it has since been interpreted in a more favorable light.[45] The ASL formally shifted China's strategic perspective on Taiwan. Under the previous paradigm, Beijing felt time was not on China's side and the cross-strait dynamics were moving rapidly toward independence. By the time of the ASL, though, Beijing had changed its strategic view to one in which deepening economic and improving cultural ties worked in China's favor. Over time, Taiwan would become increasingly connected to the mainland. According to this new strategic view, time *was*, in fact, on China's side. The ASL codified a new strategic perspective that held that because Taiwan was actually already a part of China, there was no need to force "unification" but that the imperative ought to be to prevent independence.[46] It is significant that the law was named the "Anti-Secession Law" and not the "Pro-Unification Law." Instead of trying to push for speedy reunification, China had reoriented itself toward maintaining the status quo. This reorientation argued that moves toward formal independence would not be tolerated.[47] The change is an important one. Rather than merely providing justification for impending military action, the ASL was designed to reinforce the existing status quo and to reposition China as a defender of the status quo situation in which Taiwan is a part of China.[48] This shift would also carry important implications for the effectiveness of economic statecraft. By seeking to reinforce the status quo rather than attempting to impose reunification on a short time horizon, Beijing brought its strategic objectives more into line with what economic statecraft could feasibly hope to achieve in the cross-strait context: maintenance of the status quo. In international relations, preserving the status quo is much easier than proactively forcing a target to make a difficult change.[49]

With the ASL, China reoriented away from a short-time-horizon paradigm that sought to pressure Taiwan into reunification. In its place, Hu Jintao installed an emphasis on stability and stressed the need to maintain the status quo across the Taiwan Strait.[50] Both of these favored a longer-term perspective. This shift in strategic perspective in mainland China was the second important contextual factor that would shape the mainland's use of economic statecraft in this episode.

Taiwan's Electoral Geography

The final contextual factor for this episode concerns Taiwan's electoral geography and the historical concentration of the DPP's support base in the southern areas of the island. Popular political support in Taiwan was regionally oriented. Just as there are "blue" and "red" states in the US domestic political landscape, Taiwan has "blue" and "green" counties that have tended to trend toward specific parties

from one election to the next.[51] Although there is some variation from one election to the next, maps 7.1 and 7.2 show that the DPP's bastion of political support
has remained concentrated in southern portions of the island, particularly the
counties of Pingtung, Kaohsiung, Tainan, Chia-I, and Yun-lin.[52] This area was
the crucible of the early democratization movement on Taiwan (while under
the single-party KMT rule) and was the regional basis for the *dangwai* movement and the DPP's consolidation of several disparate opposition groups under
the collective political banner of the nascent opposition Democratic Progressive
Party.[53] This area continues to be the strongest region of DPP support and is
also the area of the country most closely identified with proindependence sentiments.[54] It also happens to be Taiwan's fruit basket, the area that grows many of
the tropical fruits Taiwan produces.[55] This confluence of economics and politics
provides the basic ingredients for this episode of economic statecraft.

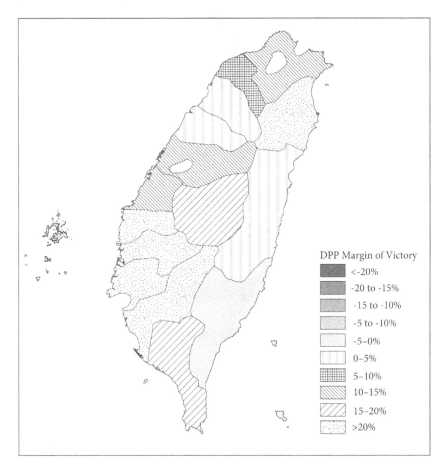

MAP 7.1   Taiwan's 2000 presidential election results

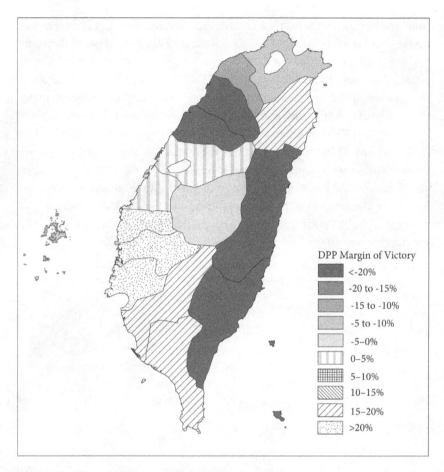

MAP 7.2 Taiwan's 2004 presidential election results

To review, three background conditions are important for contextualizing this episode of economic statecraft. First, in the lead-up to the spring 2005 opposition party visits to the mainland, the DPP had been enjoying increasing electoral momentum. The DPP's electoral success grew from when they first entered the political scene as an illegal party in 1986 to the legislative elections of the 1990s, and they culminated in the 2000 presidential election and then re-election of Chen Shui-bian in 2004. Second, in the aftermath of Chen's 2004 re-election, the mainland revised its strategic approach toward Taiwan and began focusing on using economics as a tool of an interest transformation strategy rather than for coercive leverage. Finally, the DPP support base has been geographically concentrated in the south. The tools of economic statecraft used in this episode sought to leverage this fact.

The next section examines how the Taiwanese farmers were largely responsive to Beijing's efforts to manipulate their narrow self-interests. Beijing sought to use the farmers' self-interests to shift their support away from destabilizing moves toward independence and toward the opposition parties. This had the effect of undermining the more radical, independence-leaning elements within Chen Shui-bian's DPP. The Chen government (like Lee's before it) would prove unable to rein in Taiwan's cross-strait economic engagement with the mainland. The economic activity of these commercial actors generated the security externality of interest transformation on Taiwan. The next section analyzes the business-government dynamics behind the events of 2005 in more detail.

Chinese Manipulation of Fruit Exports

Before 2005, Taiwanese exports of fresh fruit to the mainland were limited. The majority of trade with the mainland was indirect; shipments had to pass through a third-party port, usually Hong Kong. This added costly shipping time to perishable products like tropical fruit, thus restricting the amount of trade.[56] In addition to the logistical constraints on cross-strait trade, the mainland Chinese government had import barriers in place that limited access to China's market. Initially, China only permitted entry for five types of fruits from Taiwan.

Following China's shift to an economic statecraft strategy based on interest transformation, China began to target Taiwan's fruit exports for further expansion. In November 2004, Hsu Hsin-liang (a former DPP chairman who had left the DPP and favored closer ties to China) visited the mainland. Following this visit, China added seven more types of fruit to the list of permissible imports to the mainland, bringing the total to twelve. At the conclusion of Lien's April 2005 visit, China would offer to further reduce barriers by lifting the tariffs on ten types of fruit. In the following months, the list of permitted fruits would be further expanded from twelve to eighteen and tariffs were completely eliminated on another five types of fruit.[57] By the time these measures took effect on August 1, 2005, China had granted tariff-free market access to fifteen of the eighteen types of fruit now permitted to be imported from Taiwan.[58]

The production of this fruit on Taiwan was concentrated in areas that had historically supported the DPP.[59] The earlier discussion of Taiwan's electoral geography showed that Pingtung, Kaohsiung, Tainan, and Chiayi all had a track record of voting heavily for the DPP and favoring Taiwanese independence. As indicated in table 7.1, the permitted fruit with the largest export figures were all concentrated in these traditionally DPP-leaning areas.

TABLE 7.1 Taiwanese Fruit Granted Tariff-Free Market Access[1]

TYPE OF FRUIT	MAJOR PRODUCTION AREA	PEAK HARVEST SEASON	EXPORT GROWTH (TO CHINA 2004 VS. 2005)
Mango[2]	Pingtung County, Kaohsiung County and Tainan County	Summer	11 times ($31,068 vs. $335,921)
Pineapple[3]	Chiayi County	Year-round	89 times greater ($1,740 vs. $154,590)
Custard apple (aka wax apple)[4]	Kaohsiung, Pingtung, Taitung Counties. (Taitung is the largest production area.)	July to February	110 times greater ($1,399 vs. $154,263)
Star fruit (aka Carambola)	Changhua	Year round	Doubled ($69,138 vs. $155,214)
Papaya	Tainan County, Pingtung County and Kaohsiung County	August to October	5 times greater ($10,937 vs. $57,298)
Guava	Throughout Taiwan	November to February	24 times ($6,088 vs. $144,807)

[1] This table shows the top six types of fruit with the largest export volumes. In addition to the six listed in the table, China also granted the following types of fruit tariff-free treatment: pomelo, coconut, plum, jujube/date, betel nut, persimmon, bell fruit, loquat, and peach. Information on specific types of fruit grown in various regions of Taiwan is drawn from information on the Taiwan Council of Agriculture website: http://www.coa.gov.tw/show_index.php or in English at http://eng.coa.gov.tw/list.php?catid=8796. Export data comes from Taiwan's Bureau of Foreign Trade. Although this one-year growth is impressive, it was coming from a low base.
[2] During this period, mangoes were exported mainly to Hong Kong, Singapore, mainland China, and Japan.
[3] The primary export destinations of pineapples were Japan, Hong Kong, Singapore, and Canada.
[4] Taiwan had become the largest custard apple cultivating country in the world.

Mainland China seems to have designed and implemented its strategy of interest transformation in a unified, coordinated manner. The Taiwan Affairs Office, the Ministry of Commerce, the general secretary and the State Council all seemed to be playing from the same sheet of music. Hu Jintao himself provided the strategic guidance for the mainland's strategy vis-à-vis Taiwan. For example, in his March 4, 2005, address, Hu "unequivocally" (*mingque*) proposed that the mainland "earnestly resolve" (*qieshi jiejue*) the problem of Taiwanese produce having a small market share in the mainland.[60] Wen Jiabao also voiced his support.[61] In addition, the provinces like Fujian stood to benefit from enhanced economic ties with Taiwan, So the state was unified in its pursuit of economic statecraft that sought to transform the interests of the Taiwan farmers.[62] China's Ministry of Commerce (MofCOM) led the implementation of the larger national strategic effort to woo the Taiwanese populace directly. Most of the initial contact was between local Taiwanese farmers associations and the Chinese Ministry of Commerce.[63]

The Chen administration was largely cut out of the loop given its strategy of preconditions and attempts to make the issue one of international trade. By trying to treat the issue as a foreign trade issue, even going so far as to seek to conduct negotiations in the WTO forum, the DPP sought to assert the island's sovereignty and international status.[64] Indeed, since March of 2005, senior Chinese MofCom officials had been claiming that the DPP administration was dragging its feet and was opposed to Taiwan farmers selling produce to China.[65] Following the Lien visit, MofCom wanted to negotiate the terms of fast-track customs clearing and quarantine. In response, Chen designated the semiofficial Taiwan External Trade Development Council (TAITRA) to work with the mainland officials on matters of certificates of origin and other bureaucratic matters.[66] Working through TAITRA, however, would make the matter seem like any other of Taiwan's *international* trade negotiations.[67] China refused to talk with TAITRA and instead insisted on talking with the Taiwan Provincial Farmer's Association (TPFA) "in a bid to downgrade Taiwan's status."[68] Beijing was unwilling to treat the matter as an international one, and the result was a diplomatic impasse. From this rhetoric, it is apparent that the issue of Taiwan's fruit exports to mainland China was already highly politicized before the original KMT visit even took place. Being able to wade into this highly charged political environment and deliver favorable results to the farmers in Taiwan further reinforced the KMT's claim that it was more effective at navigating the tricky cross-strait dynamics.

In the wake of the Lien visit, the KMT skillfully used the regionally oriented TPFA as the point of contact to represent the farmers' interests.[69] The Taiwanese fruit farming industry structure is fragmented and consists of mainly small to medium-scale independent farms. These farmers often sell their produce through intermediary brokers who export the fruit. As a result, the industry does not often coordinate its activities closely (as was evidenced by the overplanting and consequent surplus of citrus crops in the late 1990s and early 2000s). To the extent that the industry is organized, it relies on associations like the TPFA to represent its interests. In 2005, the head of the TPFA was Chang Yung-cheng, a KMT-affiliated official. By conducting business through the institutional channel of the TPFA, the KMT was able to achieve three objectives at the same time. First, it could ensure political consistency by routing the liaison through a KMT-controlled body. It could also ensure that credit for any success would rest with the KMT rather than with the DPP administration. Finally, the non-official, substate nature of the TPFA allowed Beijing to make the case that it was not negotiating terms at the national level, but rather with a regional trade association.

Naturally, the DPP wanted to reassert its control of the negotiations. Most of the cross-strait contact had been between Taiwanese farmers associations and the MofCom. Working out matters of inspection and quarantine, however, was clearly a governmental realm. The DPP-appointed chairman of the Mainland Affairs Council, Joseph Wu Chao-hsieh, met with the farmers associations in Kaoshiung in an attempt to persuade them to move more slowly and work more directly through the government in this matter. His efforts would prove fruitless. On the eve of the TPFA's follow-up visit to discuss trade clearing logistics, the DPP threatened that nondesignated groups that negotiated terms of trade with the mainland were potentially conducting illegal operations. "If any civic group takes any actions [sic] that violates the law, the government must take appropriate action."[70] Although this stern warning did result in delaying the delegation's trip by a week, it did not derail the growing momentum. Eventually, China would opt to unilaterally adjust its own tariff policy without any real engagement of officially designated Taiwanese government channels.

In this case study, the Chen administration seems to have been caught flat-footed. They wanted to negotiate the terms of any trade agreement only through their designated semiofficial body, TAITRA. But the administration was never able to wrest control of the momentum. Instead, it struggled to catch up with the local commercial producers who were eager to secure a market for their bumper crop before the peak harvest time of late summer. As is often the case in Taiwanese cross-strait business-government dynamics, the Taiwanese government was unable to effectively control its private, commercial actors. The state actor in this case, the government in Beijing, also did not have any direct authority over the commercial actors, but it was able to exercise some degree of control because it managed the regulatory mechanisms that permitted Taiwan's fruit to gain access to the mainland Chinese market. In this episode, we observe the mainland government using state policy to structure the incentives that the Taiwanese commercial actors faced. By manipulating these incentives, Beijing hoped to undermine Chen Shui-bian's domestic support base by building up the credibility of his main political rival, the opposition party KMT. Mainland efforts to move forward by working with the KMT placed the DPP in a difficult domestic political position. Any attempt by the DPP to reassert its regulatory or governing authority was berated as politicizing the issue or as blocking progress that would otherwise directly benefit Taiwanese farmers, a key DPP constituency.[71]

In the end, the mainland did not wait for a government-sanctioned inter-locutor, but rather unilaterally eliminated its tariffs. On July 28, 2005, China's Ministry of Commerce announced it was unilaterally lifting tariffs on the fifteen fruits listed in table 7.1.[72] The new preferential regulations were to take effect on August 1, 2005, just as Taiwan entered the peak of its major harvesting season. The measures also included fast-track provisions to facilitate rapid customs and quarantine measures. The elimination of the tariff reduced consumer prices paid for Taiwanese fruit in the mainland by 15 to 20 percent.[73] Taiwan's mainland fruit sales were estimated to have gone up 30 to 50 percent in the months following the implementation of the tariff reduction.[74] In addition to eliminating the fruit tariff, the mainland launched an aggressive marketing and promotional campaign touting Taiwan's fruit.[75]

This expedited access to the China market had extra significance because it was a relief to Taiwanese farmers, who had suffered a recent drop in revenues. With the introduction of new farming techniques and improvements in agricultural technology, the supply of high-quality fresh fruit on Taiwan had increased dramatically. In the early 2000s, the domestic market for this produce was saturated, and prices of Taiwanese fruit had fallen by 30 to 40 percent.[76] The reduced prices were passed on directly to the farmers. On the eve of this episode, Taiwan's fruit producers were anxiously searching for new markets in which to off-load their products.[77]

By eliminating the tariffs on these fifteen types of fruit, China effectively provided access to just such a large consumer market for Taiwan's fruit exports. Moreover, the mainland market, a large, relatively untapped source of market demand, held out the promise of considerable future growth. Taiwan had few suitable alternative export markets to turn to for future growth. Japan (the major developed economy located nearby) already accounted for around half of all Taiwanese fresh fruit exports, and that market was well penetrated with little room for growth.[78] The American and Canadian markets were also large, mature markets, but strict quarantine and food safety requirements constrained access for most growers. In addition, the distances involved made transportation logistics a deterrent to further expanding these markets for such perishable goods as tropical fruit. Markets for tropical fruit in Southeast Asia were already highly competitive given the natural climatic advantages producers there enjoyed. Mainland China presented a large, growing population of increasingly wealthy consumers with a common cultural tie in close proximity to Taiwan. Moreover, Taiwanese fruit already enjoyed strong brand recognition as a premium product that could command higher margins than domestically produced Chinese fruit. However, as of 2004, Taiwan's limited access to this market resulted in exporting only US$340,000 of fresh fruit to China.[79] The mainland market was significantly underexploited on the eve of the opposition party visits. The attractive growth potential of China's domestic consumer market is a powerful commercial incentive that China used to good strategic effect in this episode.

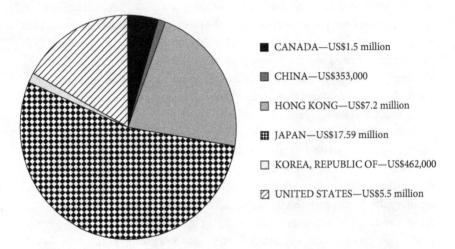

CANADA—US$1.5 million

CHINA—US$353,000

HONG KONG—US$7.2 million

JAPAN—US$17.59 million

KOREA, REPUBLIC OF—US$462,000

UNITED STATES—US$5.5 million

FIGURE 7.1   2004 top fruit export destinations by value. Source: Customs Agency, Ministry of Finance, Executive Yuan, R.O.C. Searchable database: http://www.customs.gov.tw/StatisticsWebEN/IESearch.aspx.

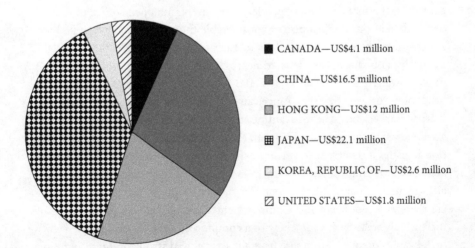

CANADA—US$4.1 million

CHINA—US$16.5 milliont

HONG KONG—US$12 million

JAPAN—US$22.1 million

KOREA, REPUBLIC OF—US$2.6 million

UNITED STATES—US$1.8 million

FIGURE 7.2   2012 top fruit destinations by value. Source: Customs Agency, Ministry of Finance, Executive Yuan, R.O.C. Searchable database: http://www.customs.gov.tw/StatisticsWebEN/IESearch.aspx.

Although fruit production may not be a large part of Taiwan's national exports and at first glance may seem like a relatively insignificant aspect of cross-strait economic interaction, its importance derives from the major role it plays in the regional economies of the counties that make up the DPP's electoral heartland. Because fruit production is concentrated geographically in Taiwan across areas that have traditionally been DPP strongholds, what might otherwise appear to be nationally insignificant amounts of economic interaction take on much greater strategic significance. The move to allow market access to Taiwanese fruit stood to benefit a highly concentrated set of economic interests. These beneficiaries made up a strategic constituency in Taiwanese domestic politics: Chen Shui-bian's support base.[80] The ability of the KMT to break the diplomatic impasse and deliver the export outlet to relieve the farmers' surplus both underscored the inability of the ruling DPP to effectively navigate cross-strait relations and served as a prominent reminder of how the KMT's pragmatic orientation might better suit the farmers' own self-interests in the future.

Results

The data on Taiwan's fresh fruit exports suggest the economic side of the mainland's policy has been successful. As mentioned previously, in 2004 Taiwan exported around US$353,000 worth of fresh fruit to the mainland. In the aftermath of this episode, fresh fruit exports to China showed a fivefold increase in 2005.[81] The mainland market has continued to be a source of export growth for Taiwanese fruit farmers. In 2009, exports of fresh fruit to mainland China hit $5.3 million, almost sixteen times the baseline 2004 figure. By 2011, that figure had more than doubled again to $11.4 million. The first link in the causal chain of the interest transformation strategic logic seems to have been borne out: economic interaction grew considerably as a result of the mainland's policy. But did this interaction engender strategically significant consequences?

The answer lies in the electoral performance of the DPP in the aftermath of this episode. This is not to claim that China's use of economic statecraft is the sole determinant of the KMT's success, but because undermining the DPP's electoral performance was the strategic goal of the mainland, it is only right to examine the subsequent electoral results.[82] The election most immediately following the opposition party visits was the May 14, 2005, National Assembly election. For a variety of reasons, however, this election is an outlier and is not considered in my evaluation of DPP performance.[83]

The May 2005 National Assembly election was followed by two locally oriented elections: the December 2005 "three-in-one" election for county magistrates, councilmen, and township governors and the December 9, 2006, municipal elections for mayor of Taipei and Kaohsiung.[84] These two elections are also problematic as indicators because they are largely local-level contests. To the extent they can be taken as a bellwether of political sentiment on Taiwan, though, the KMT outperformed the DPP in both sets of elections.

In the December 2005 elections, the KMT won control of fourteen of Taiwan's twenty-three counties (with the PFP and the New Party each also winning one county, bringing the total pan-blue counties to sixteen). The DPP won only six counties. Particularly significant was the loss of Chia-yi, a long-time bastion of the DPP and its predecessor democracy movement the *dangwai*. "It was like losing the locomotive of southern Taiwan, where people have been strongly backing the DPP for years."[85] The KMT garnered 50.96 percent of the popular vote while the DPP won only 41.95 percent. "Observers said the outcomes demonstrated voters' disappointment at the DPP, who has failed to break the cross-strait deadlock or revive the economy."[86] Chen's popularity hit an all-time low of 21 percent following the election. Using the previous "three-in-one" election of 2001 as the baseline for comparison, the DPP's share of the popular vote fell from 45.27 percent while the KMT's share increased to 35.06 percent.[87]

In the December 2006 elections, the KMT also handed the DPP significant losses. The KMT won in Taipei (both the position of mayor and a majority of the city councilors), not all that unusual considering that Taipei has historically been a KMT stronghold. A more anomalous result is that the KMT also came close to winning the Kaohsiung mayor election. In this normally DPP stronghold, the KMT received 49.27 percent, almost enough to beat the DPP's 49.41 percent. The difference was a little more than a thousand votes, indicating that the KMT had made significant headway in one of the DPP's key districts. Moreover, the KMT did actually win a majority of the Kaohsiung city councilors seats (seventeen compared to the DPP's fifteen). To the extent that the 2006 municipal elections can be used as an indicator, the results in Kaohsiung suggest that the spring 2005 visits were effective in undermining support in the region for the DPP. The DPP had won the Kaohsiung mayoral election in 2002 with a comfortable 50.04 percent of the vote vs. the KMT's 46.82 percent, and in 1998 when it first wrested control of the city from the KMT with 48.71 percent of the vote vs. the KMT's 48.13 percent.

Although the elections in December of 2005 and 2006 may indicate an eroding DPP grip on power, confirmation of the DPP's electoral downfall came in the next cycle of national level elections in Taiwan in 2008. The results of these two elections (the January 12, 2008, Legislative Yuan election and the March 22, 2008, presidential election) show a clear defeat for the DPP and a validation of the KMT's cross-strait policies. The electoral maps 7.3 and 7.4 depict the erosion of support for the DPP.[88]

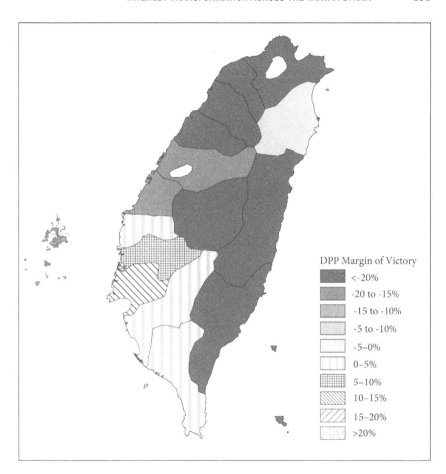

DPP Margin of Victory

■ <-20%

■ -20 to -15%

■ -15 to -10%

■ -5 to -10%

□ -5–0%

□ 0–5%

□ 5–10%

□ 10–15%

□ 15–20%

□ >20%

MAP 7.3   Taiwan's 2008 presidential election results

Of particular significance is the loss of regional areas of traditional pan-green support in the counties targeted in this episode of economic statecraft. The twenty-three counties are shaded to indicate the popular vote: darker shades represent a larger margin of support for pan-blue in that county. As expected, the pan-blue won by the largest majorities in their traditional strongholds of the north. But what is most striking was the weakness of pan-green support among their traditional base in the south.

In the Legislative Yuan election, the pan-greens fared poorly. Even among the counties in which the pan-green won a plurality, in only two counties did they manage to win more than 50 percent of the vote. This stands in striking contrast to the pan-blue margin of victory, which garnered greater than 60 percent of the popular vote across six counties and swept up a total of eighteen of

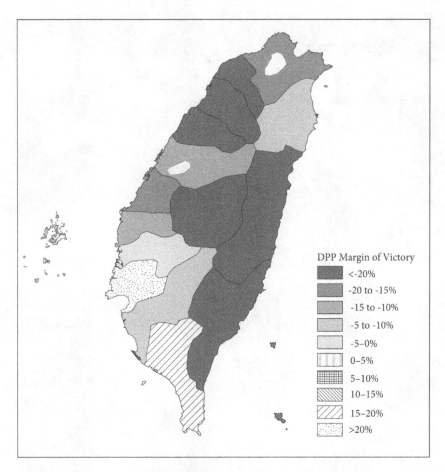

MAP 7.4 Taiwan's 2008 Legislative Yuan election results

the twenty-three counties. This resulted in a supermajority—86 of the total 113 legislative seats—for the pan-blue alliance. The remaining 27 seats went to the DPP.[89] The DPP's major pan-green partner, the independence-issue-driven TSU, won no seats in this election.

A similar story is told by the presidential contest between the pan-blue candidate Ma Ying-jeou and the pan-green candidate Frank Hsieh Chang-ting. In this election, the pan-blue candidate took 58.45 percent of the popular vote, winning in a landslide over Frank Hsieh.[90] Taiwan's presidential elections have historically been closely fought elections, which made this margin of victory unusual. As was the case in the Legislative Yuan election, the pan-blue carried more regions with a greater margin of victory than did the pan-green. Even in the areas that make up the pan-green base of support, the pan-green won by more than 55 percent in only one county.[91] The shift away from the pan-green agenda is striking when the 2008 elections are juxtaposed with the comparable 2004 LY and presidential elections.

But perhaps the most effective display of the success of the mainland's interest transformation strategy lies in the 2012 presidential contest, in which the incumbent Ma Ying-jeou defeated Tsai Ing-wen, the DPP candidate. Although Ma succeeded in winning re-election, the most helpful evidence for the causal theory lies in the DPP's electoral strategy of consciously toning down its earlier stance on Taiwanese independence.[92] Recognizing the reality that a strong position in favor of independence was no longer a feasible electoral option, Tsai Ing-wen went to great lengths to stress this aspect of her candidacy.[93] Taiwan's growing economic ties with the mainland provided the general electoral public on Taiwan with economic equities in maintaining and solidifying a stable, cross-strait relationship. These economic ties now effectively precluded drastic shifts toward independence. Mainland China had achieved its goal.

Baselining the Results

These strategic results ought to be considered in reference to some baseline for economic statecraft in this context. In particular, rigorous analysis would seek to establish a baseline along three aspects of the episode. First, were the results meaningful? Second, how do we know that economic statecraft generated these strategic results? Finally, how do we know that this episode constituted economic statecraft as opposed to simple commercial calculations? In other words, to examine economic statecraft, one must be able to distinguish what constitutes economic statecraft from simple, straightforward, "normal" commercial activity.

On the first issue of whether the economic statecraft in question generated strategic results, the evidence shows that a significant electoral shift from the DPP in favor of the KMT took place in Taiwan. This change suggests that China's economic statecraft undermined one of the DPP's key support bases. Second, how much of that change can be attributed to the economic statecraft? Although the results of this episode are clearly shown in the subsequent electoral behavior, it is difficult to establish how large an impact the issue of fruit tariffs per se had in determining voter behavior. Voters were likely already getting unhappy with Chen (especially regarding corruption issues and his administration's economic mismanagement), and that certainly lowered the DPP's popularity going into the 2008 elections. It is interesting to note, however, that slowing economic prospects might have actually increased the saliency of the fruit tariff because the affected parties would have been that much more sensitive to *any* source of economic relief. Fruit exports constitute only a small portion of Taiwan's overall exports (with fruit exports to China being smaller still). The concentrated nature of the beneficiaries in Taiwan and the growth potential of the Chinese market, however, do seem to suggest strategic importance in this episode.[94]

One helpful indicator is the amount of attention paid to the issue by the highest-ranking leaders in both China and Taiwan. Hu Jintao specifically outlined the strategic significance of relieving Taiwanese farmers, and Wen Jiabao also echoed these points.[95] Of course, leading KMT officials sought to score political points throughout this episode. But perhaps most tellingly, Taiwan president Chen Shui-bian himself indicated that this matter of granting Taiwan fruit tariff-free status was an important one: "China's recent announcement of duty free treatment for exports of certain fruits by Taiwan's farmers to the Chinese market is just a decision unilaterally taken by Beijing based on political needs."[96] To the extent national leaders must prioritize their limited time and attention, we can interpret the attention they afforded to this episode as indicative of its significance.

So if the effect was strategically important and the economic statecraft was a major contributor to generating that result, how should the reader know if the observed economic interaction is actually the result of strategically manipulated economic statecraft as opposed to normal economic interaction performed for purely commercial reasons? At the heart of this challenge lies distinguishing between the normal economic behavior of commercial actors and the state's strategically motivated manipulation designed to achieve foreign policy objectives by using commercial actors.

In this episode, the evidence suggests that the decision to lower tariffs on the fifteen types of fruit was a strategically motivated one designed to influence the political outcome in Taiwan rather than a purely commercially driven desire to improve the terms of trade. Perhaps most importantly from the point of view of distinguishing between the two is that tariffs were not lowered on bananas. This fact is important because bananas are by far Taiwan's single largest fruit export.[97] Any *commercially* driven effort to expand Taiwan's fruit exports should have included its largest type of exported fruit. Lychees, Taiwan's third-largest fruit export, were also excluded while mangoes, the second-largest, were included.[98] The reason for this can be found in the confluence of Taiwan's electoral geography and where certain types of (mainly tropical) fruit are produced in Taiwan. For example, the production of mangoes is concentrated in Pingtung, Tainan, and Kaohsiung Counties, all DPP strongholds. Consequently, mangoes were slated for tariff elimination while bananas and lychee, both of which lacked this sort of strategic geographic concentration, were not.

If mangoes played this strategic role, one should have observed a disproportionate electoral impact in areas that were highly reliant on mango production. To explore this hypothesis, let us look at the three largest mango-producing townships in Tainan, Chiayi, and Kaohsiung counties, all DPP strongholds. These townships were Nanxi, Yujing, and Nanhua.[99] Not only did these townships demonstrate the strongest shift away from DPP support (among mango-reliant townships in these three DPP-leaning counties) during the 2008 presidential election, but they also most strongly rejected the DPP candidate in the 2008 Legislative Yuan election.[100] This shift is made even more dramatic when one considers that Tainan consistently ranked first among Taiwan counties in percent of voter support for the DPP in presidential elections, as well as first or second in overall support for the DPP in Legislative Yuan elections, between 2000 and 2008.[101]

Another indicator of the strategic rather than commercial orientation of this economic statecraft policy was that mainland China did not seek to gain access to Taiwanese markets for its own fruit producers. If the tariff reduction were part of a larger commercially oriented effort to remove barriers to trade, one might have expected to see tariff reduction on China's side as part of a more comprehensive bargain to increase cross-strait trade. Instead the tariff reduction targeted specific types of fruit and there was no effort to seek reciprocity for China's own producers.

Finally, oranges—one of the types of fruit most prone to overproduction in Taiwan—were not even permitted entry into China.[102] If the purpose of lowering the tariffs on certain types of fruit were actually commercial (i.e. to help relieve overproduction), one would have expected to see oranges, the type of fruit that was arguably most prone to overproduction, included in the relief effort as well. The evidence suggests that the intent in this episode was not simply to help relieve all Taiwanese farmers, but rather to relieve *strategically significant* farmers. By demonstrating the benefits that the targeted farmers stood to gain from a KMT-led cross-strait relationship, the mainland sought to undermine the DPP's support.

Each of these elements indicates that mainland China's move to grant access to some types of fruit had noncommercial, strategic motives. The evidence suggests that the lowering of tariffs was a deliberate policy of economic statecraft specifically calculated to alter the domestic electoral interests of a key support base for Chen Shui-bian. By undermining Chen's support, the mainland hoped to curb Taiwan's proclivity toward independence. This strategic objective was one of Beijing's paramount goals vis-à-vis Taiwan. In this episode, mainland China pursued that goal by instrumentally using commercial actors to help achieve its strategic objectives.

Evaluating the Case

This section evaluates this episode of China's economic statecraft in light of the theoretical framework presented earlier. The evaluation begins by reviewing the coding of this episode in terms of the independent variables that account for the mainland's ability to motivate the commercial actors to behave in a manner that generated the strategic effects it sought. These values are summarized in table 7.2. In terms of the overall effectiveness, China's use of economic statecraft in this episode seems to have been effective at destabilizing the Chen administration and undermining public support for the DPP in some of its key support bases.[103] The most important factor accounting for China's success seems to have been the mainland's ability to pursue a unified approach to implementing a strategy that made the most of political divisions within Taiwan. Mainland China identified a vulnerability in Taiwan's ruling party and instituted trade policies that sought to drive a wedge between the Taiwanese government and some of its key supporters. By providing economic benefits to an influential domestic constituency and by working through the opposition party to deliver these benefits, the mainland was able to pursue a strategy that sought to alter Taiwan's definition of its interests.

Although a strategy based on exploiting this type of security externality is generally a long-term one (national interests do not tend to turn on a dime), this episode offers a concrete illustration of exactly how this sort of transformation takes place over a condensed time scale. Given Taiwan's historically close electoral environment, shifts of support among key constituencies can have important effects on shaping political outcomes. By focusing on one particular series of events, we can better understand exactly how economic statecraft actually works in practice.

Examining the goals of China and the goals of the commercial actors in this episode is interesting because they seem to be compatible in the short term (both sides sought to enhance the farmers' access to the China market) but their longer-term goals (farmers' desire for Taiwanese independence and China's desire for reunification) are mutually exclusive. By shifting its emphasis toward preventing independence and de-emphasizing the reunification aspect, China was able to find common ground with the commercial actors. Although the long-term consequences of cross-strait economic relations remain unknown, the observable near-term effects seem to suggest that Taiwan no longer pursued de jure independence. Altering the target states' definition of its interests lies at the heart of this type of security externality. The hope is that the economic activity, which establishes strong stakes in stability, provokes these commercial actors to revisit their political priorities. In this way, the mainland's strategy diminished the attractiveness of the independence issue as a salient political position on Taiwan.

In this episode, there are many small fruit farmers. The market would be characterized as highly fragmented, which, as expected, poses some challenges for the state when it comes to coordinating the commercial actors. Although it was not the primary principal in this case study, the Taiwanese government found it particularly difficult to monitor and enforce its preferences on the fruit farmers. For example, efforts on the part of the ruling DPP to reassert its leadership over the cross-strait negotiations were unsuccessful. This is a theme that one observes over and over when examining Taiwan's efforts to rein in its commercial actors. Because the commercial actors are numerous and agile and because the commercial attraction of the mainland is such a strong draw, the actors often find ways to circumvent the Taiwanese state's efforts to control their behavior. The mainland, however, is able to exert some control over these actors by manipulating the commercial actors' business operating environment. This provides the state with what I call "king-making" capabilities, the ability to determine commercial winners and losers. By targeting the commercial incentives and influencing the conditions under which the private Taiwanese firms operate, the mainland is able to channel the firms' behavior.

The state's acting in unison was one of the main factors that accounted for the ability of the mainland to manipulate the commercial actors in this episode. The strategic orientation for China was articulated at the highest levels of national leadership, and their vision was echoed throughout the implementation of the strategy. Finally, unlike in previous attempts to use coercion to manage cross-strait commercial actors, there were no incentives for local municipalities to undermine the central government's objectives.

Because the commercial actors in this episode of economic statecraft were farmers on Taiwan, and because mainland China does not really have any jurisdiction over them beyond regulating the mainland's customs and tariff regulatory regime, the reporting relationship between the commercial actors and the state in this episode is indirect. The relationship can be characterized as a light regulatory relationship that takes place mainly at the point of import entry into mainland China. The state in this case study has the ability to regulate customs requirements and not much else. Unsurprisingly, this is exactly where we see the state using its policy tools. Taiwanese farmers are not Chinese state-owned enterprises like those examined in the previous chapter, nor are they extensions of the Chinese government as is the case for the sovereign wealth funds examined next. The Taiwanese farmers are privately managed, privately capitalized, and privately owned enterprises. For the Chinese state to control their behavior would require that the state manipulate the commercial conditions under which they conduct their normal pursuit of profit. The reporting relationship between the mainland Chinese state and Taiwanese farmers is about as indirect as possible. From the perspective of the reporting relationship independent variable, this episode should be a hard case for economic statecraft to have worked. Because these business-government dynamics are so fundamentally different from those examined in other chapters, this case is an instructive one to explore from a theory-building perspective.

Finally, although they were not a significant factor, the relative resources in this episode seem to have been slightly skewed toward the mainland. In terms of expertise, it determined the conditions under which the fruit would or would not be granted access to the Chinese market. The state had a larger budget, better organizational capacity, and more personnel than the Taiwanese farmers did. In addition, the large number of farmers complicated effective coordination beyond their common interests represented by the various professional associations. That said, the evidence does not suggest that this IV was particularly salient in this episode.

These observations are summarized in table 7.2. This case identified a discrete instance of economic statecraft that used a strategy based on interest transformation, thus demonstrating how this type of economic statecraft actually works in practice. Through process-tracing focused on microlevel empirics, this case demonstrated exactly how states conduct such a strategy and the mechanisms by which particular instances of economic interaction may be converted into strategic consequences. Operationally, China has pursued this strategy beginning with the historic hosting of Taiwan's opposition party visits to the mainland in the spring of 2005. Subsequently, China eliminated tariffs on specific fruits exported from Taiwan to the mainland. By altering the commercial self-interest calculus of Taiwan's fruit farmers, Beijing sought to undermine the key support base for independence-minded president Chen Shui-bian and the DPP. This strategy was more effective than the previous one emphasizing coercive leverage for several reasons. First, mainland China was simply seeking to reinforce the status quo, a much more attainable goal, rather than proactively pursue reunification as suggested by the 2000 White Paper. Second, the competitive dynamic of the domestic market on Taiwan gave mainland China the ability to leverage its market access to craft an attractive opportunity for Taiwanese fruit. Third, the actual short-term political cost to farmers for going along with the mainland offers was relatively low. Staunchly proindependence farmers could still maintain their positions because the mainland had no real direct enforcement mechanisms for monitoring farmers' personally held beliefs. In this subtlety lies the brilliance of the mainland strategy. By virtue of the very public role the KMT played in facilitating access for Taiwan's fruit farmers, the commercial actors simply felt that they had economic interests that were more effectively served by the KMT. To remain electorally competitive, the DPP was compelled to moderate its positions

TABLE 7.2   Interest Transformation Case Summary Table

	IV CODING	EVIDENCE	DV PREDICTION	DV OUTCOME
Unity of state	Unified	Effort was coordinated and led from top with no competing bureaucratic arguments from ministries; Hu Jintao's consolidation of power limited potential for competing personal factions to undermine; municipal/ provincial centers of authority also wanted to see improved Taiwan economic ties	Control likely	Control was achieved via a coordinated state policy
Goals	Compatible for near term; mutually exclusive re: Taiwan independence in the long-term	China wants to minimally prevent Taiwan independence, maximally promote reunification; Taiwan farmers want an export market, and also prefer Taiwan independence. Both farmers and China's goals can be achieved on the economic front in short-term;	Control likely (at least in the near-term)	Commercial actors did what state wanted them to do; observed near-term erosion of support for independence-oriented DPP stemming from disillusionment with DPP governance especially cross-strait policies that do not deliver the benefits that the KMT demonstrate

(Continued)

TABLE 7.2 (Continued)

	IV CODING	EVIDENCE	DV PREDICTION	DV OUTCOME
		e.g. China can open market and farmers can gain access, but mutually exclusive re: larger issue of Taiwan independence in the long term.		capacity to deliver to farmers. Long-term behavior remains to be seen
Market structure	Competitive	Many small-scale Taiwanese fruit farmers; over 300 professional associations	Control difficult	Control was still achieved by leveraging the competitive dynamics among fruit producers (e.g. no one can afford to be shut out of Chinese market). However, monitoring farmer behavior (e.g. whether they vote for KMT instead in next election) was not feasible
Reporting relationship	Indirect; only able to exercise regulatory control at point of entry	Government ownership: none; private-sector actors Management: None; private-sector actors with no funding or investment from mainland. Only required reporting is regulatory compliance with customs/ quarantine/ inspection regime	Control difficult	The tools of control were fairly blunt (e.g. allow market access or not) since the structure of this relationship permitted minimal points for calibration. That said, despite these conditions making this a "hard case" the state was successful

	IV CODING	EVIDENCE	DV PREDICTION	DV OUTCOME
				in getting the commercial actors to do what it wanted
Relative resources	Somewhat favored state	Mainland had most relevant expertise since market access granted by mainland government/ customs; mainland government had larger budget and personnel resources given scale of MofCom and difficulties coordinating among the many disparate Taiwan farmers	Control likely (but not a significant factor)	Relative resources between the Chinese state and the Taiwanese farmers almost completely favored the Chinese state (organizational scale, fiscal, etc.); it was the only one in a position to eliminate the tariffs. That said, relative resources did not seem to be a very important factor in this episode

so that the mainland would also be willing to work with them.[104] The immediate results were a dramatic restoration of the KMT to positions of power in Taiwan's domestic politics.

While the short-term effect may have been decreased electoral support for the DPP in this region of Taiwan, the more impressive consequences may have been longer-term. First, targeting constituents' narrow economic self-interests seems to have lessened the political viability of policies that stand to jeopardize economic benefits like mainland market access for Taiwanese commercial interests. As a result, the issue of Taiwanese independence seems to have lost some of its luster within the DPP.[105] Second, even if the economic benefits to fruit farmers is a relatively small portion of Taiwan's overall economic activity, the "demonstration effect" of this episode sent a clear signal to Taiwan's existing and potential economic interests related to mainland China. Arguably, the mainland's interest transformation strategy not only paved the way for a KMT resumption of power on Taiwan, but it also enabled Ma Ying-jeou to move forward with deeper cross-strait economic engagement across the board. These efforts eventually led to the Economic Cooperation Framework Agreement (ECFA), which promised even deeper cross-strait economic integration in the years to come.

Economics plays an important role in mainland China's contemporary relationship with Taiwan. This chapter and the previous one explored the evolution of that relationship. This examination of the development of cross-strait relations suggests that China has undergone a process of tactical learning and has employed a gradually more sophisticated approach to economic statecraft. Chapters 6 and 7 focused on several specific episodes in which the mainland sought to use economic statecraft to pursue its strategic objectives vis-à-vis Taiwan.

As economic ties grew and Taiwan became increasingly dependent on the mainland, mainland China attempted to use its economic position as a coercive tool. Chapter 6 examined specific attempts to use coercive leverage in which Taiwanese investors came under pressure from the mainland authorities. In this chapter, we observe a mainland China that has become more nuanced in its employment of economic statecraft. Today, mainland China is mainly focused on transforming the interests of Taiwan and using economic ties to deter independence. The foundations of this policy can be seen in the case examined in this chapter.

China continued to strengthen economic ties in an attempt to alter the interests of Taiwan. The ECFA promised to tie Taiwan even more closely to the mainland economy. Over the long term, this strategy of engagement seeks to encourage Taiwan to redefine its own national interests in such a way that makes de jure independence counterproductive and encourages eventual reunification with the mainland. By creating increasingly numerous and powerful vested interests in Taiwan that seek at a minimum continued stability (i.e., no moves toward de jure independence) and perhaps eventual reunification, China is engaged in a strategy of economic statecraft that is designed to achieve its long-term strategic goals with respect to Taiwan.

Whereas this chapter was primarily focused on understanding how China employed economic statecraft via trade concessions to key constituencies on Taiwan, the final part of this book addresses another growing and important potential channel for China's economic statecraft: its sovereign wealth funds.

Part IV

CHINA'S SOVEREIGN WEALTH FUNDS

Part 4 of the book focuses on China's deployment of state capital. In the next three chapters, I examine one of the major sources of China's state capital: China's sovereign wealth funds, the government financial entities charged with investing funds directly on behalf of the state. These cases involve economic entities that are actually extensions of the state itself, and many are disproportionately predisposed toward state control. Under such circumstances, it may be reasonable to ask whether it is even possible for these kinds of commercial actors to engage in economic activity that is *not* economic statecraft. Although many of the following cases do result in instances of state control, there are some circumstances in which control is more difficult, indicating that there is more to Chinese economic statecraft than simple reporting relationships. By examining instances when Chinese sovereign wealth funds have and have not been used to pursue strategic objectives, we can develop some insight into what a state can do to limit the propensity for sovereign wealth funds to be used as instruments of economic statecraft. If there are measures that can succeed even under these conditions in which the state-firm relations are so predisposed toward state control, similar strategies to lower the likelihood of state control may help mitigate strategic concerns in other arenas that might otherwise be conducive to economic statecraft.

As China seeks to liberalize its economy and ostensibly bring greater market forces to bear on state-owned enterprises and other economic actors, the venue of state finance promises to provide a mechanism for the state to retain some control over commercial actors. As the Chinalco–Rio Tinto episode suggested, one of the most effective mechanisms for retaining state influence over the behavior of these semiprivatized economic actors is through the financing channel. Despite some liberalization efforts, it is not surprising to observe that the banking and financial sector has been one of the key sectors in which the state has retained an active (and influential) role. By retaining its ability to control the flows of capital, the state is able to ensure that economic actors dependent upon state capital remain largely beholden to state preferences. In this study of Chinese economic statecraft, it seems logical, then, to take a closer look at the important and growing phenomenon of Chinese state capital.

An accurate assessment of this potential tool of economic statecraft ought to consider the full range of entities that are charged with allocating capital internationally on behalf of the state. To this end, the cases in this part of the book examine not only China's official sovereign wealth fund, the China Investment Corporation (Zhongguo touzi youxian zeren gongsi), but also the National Social Security Fund Council (Quanguo shehui baozhang jijin lishi hui), and the State Administration of Foreign Exchange (Guojia waihui guanli ju).[1] I examine their institutional origins, missions, and investment activity from the perspective of economic statecraft. Are these entities well-suited as instruments of Chinese economic statecraft, and have they been used this way?

Although each of these entities is responsible for investing government funds, they differ from each other in important ways. The goals and missions of these actors vary, as does the degree to which their activities support China's foreign policy objectives. All share the unifying quality of being nonprivate, state-owned, state-managed or state-funded commercial actors responsible for investing state funds. This allows for analyzing the differences among them to determine how those differences may account for observed outcomes. To varying degrees, their activities are influenced both by commercial and strategic foreign policy objectives. Understanding these differences provides us with a better understanding of how the state is able (or not able) to effectively control the deployment of investment capital to achieve its foreign policy objectives.

The first two cases are useful from a theory-building perspective for their ability to illustrate extreme values.[2] The time period covered by these cases runs from China's World Trade Organization (WTO) entry to the onset of the 2008 financial crisis. The origins of China's contemporary economic statecraft can be traced to this period. The institutional architecture of China's state investment apparatus that was laid during this time provides the foundation for China's ability (or inability) to effectively leverage the sovereign wealth aspect of its monetary power. This power ultimately stems from China's considerable foreign exchange reserves. Although China's decision to maintain its dollar peg in the face of the East Asian financial crisis dates to 1997, China's massive buildup of foreign exchange reserves really begins its dramatic growth only after China entered the WTO in 2001. The buildup is a result of China's trade surplus and its nonconvertible currency policy. During this period, China has built up its "economic gunpowder" to the point that it can now afford the luxury of using economics to pursue its foreign policy objectives, as opposed to using its foreign policy to ensure that its economic objectives are met.[3] Understanding the limits of that economic power and how it gets mobilized involves a closer examination of the particular interaction between the Chinese government and its commercial actors. These three chapters focus on how this interaction takes place in the realm of the investment of state capital. In the case of NSSF, we observe an unambiguously commercial agent with little potential for economic statecraft, while SAFE presents evidence of a commercial actor being used to achieve China's foreign policy objectives. My analysis of the CIC suggests that its potential usefulness as an instrument of Chinese economic statecraft lies somewhere between the two extreme cases of SAFE and NSSF.

In the final empirical chapter I draw on the theory to address a specific contemporary concern about Chinese economic statecraft: namely whether China's official sovereign wealth fund will be used in a noncommercial way to advanced Chinese strategic interests. China's current structural macroeconomic situation suggests that it may continue to build up its foreign exchange reserves, which raises a host of concerns. Although China will certainly maintain some of these holdings as traditional central bank foreign exchange reserves, some portion of this capital will be reallocated into China's sovereign wealth funds. The size and activities of these sovereign wealth funds spark a number of strategic concerns. In fact, much of the US domestic political debate surrounding China's foreign-exchange-supported sovereign wealth fund involves concerns about the security externalities its activities may generate.[4] As demonstrated by the case study of SAFE that follows, such concerns are not without merit. At the same time, it would be a mistake for host nations to implement irrationally protectionist policies that unduly restrict the international flow of capital out of paranoia about the strategic effects of sovereign wealth. What is missing from the contemporary discussion is an analytical framework for dispassionately evaluating when such concerns are warranted. The theory of economic statecraft presented in part 1 provides this sort of framework. In the final chapter, I apply the theory to determine whether the CIC presents cause for strategic concern.

8

STATE ADMINISTRATION OF FOREIGN EXCHANGE

A SAFE Tool of Economic Statecraft

Given the unusually high levels of retained earnings on Chinese corporate balance sheets, its exchange rate regime, and the large amount of national savings more generally, it seems likely that Chinese outward-bound investment is likely to grow.[1] According to China's Ministry of Commerce, by 2020 China will be the largest overseas investor in the world.[2] This growth in outward investment activity has been a source of concern to others, given the potential or actual security externalities that result from the activities of commercial actors. Specifically, it is the strategic implications of large flows of government-directed investment capital that raise the fear of this particular form of economic interaction being used to further politically motivated, strategic goals.[3] Of particular concern, given the prominent role played by the state, are the financial activities of the sovereign wealth funds and the state-owned banks. To the extent that these state investment decisions are used to pursue foreign policy goals, such behavior is an example of economic statecraft being conducted through financial channels. The empirics that follow illustrate how these types of economic statecraft do or do not play out in practice.

This chapter examines China's State Administration of Foreign Exchange (SAFE). SAFE primarily serves to manage China's foreign exchange reserves. In addition, SAFE has demonstrated its utility as an instrument of Chinese economic statecraft. This chapter examines one episode in detail to show exactly how the state was able to use SAFE to pursue its strategic foreign policy objectives. That episode involves Costa Rica's 2007 derecognition of Taiwan.

In this case, many of the values across the independent variables indicated that state control would be likely. The state was acting in a unified manner with regard to its Taiwan priorities, and although the goals between the state and the economic actor were not entirely compatible, the market structure had recently shifted to introduce a competing entity. This resulted in an oligopolistic market dynamic that would lend itself to state control. As the theory suggests, when the state is unified but the goals are divergent, the outcome of whether the state can control the commercial actor(s) is determined largely by the market structure. The direct reporting structure and the relative balance of resources also favored state control in this instance.

The remainder of the chapter first examines SAFE as a state financial entity and then explores the Costa Rica case, in which SAFE used its financial resources to pursue China's foreign policy objectives. The chapter concludes with a discussion of how this case maps back to the theory. The next chapter will examine China's National Social Security Fund (NSSF). In striking contrast with SAFE, the NSSF's institutional design seems consciously designed to maximize its commercial rather than strategic value. Understanding how this was done offers a helpful counterpoint to the case of SAFE.

Overview of the State Administration of Foreign Exchange (SAFE)

Although specific information regarding SAFE's internal reporting structure is not widely available, it seems that SAFE is "a bureau with vice-ministerial rank under the PBoC [People's Bank of China]."[4] The history of SAFE's institutional development is really the story of China's evolution on foreign exchange policy—a gradual and experimental liberalization of its capital account. SAFE has had investment operations dating at least to 1997, when its Hong Kong office was established to conduct open market operations to defend China's currency peg in the face of the East Asian financial crisis. Today, SAFE still maintains the renminbi's (RMB) peg range. Its primary duties also include allocating foreign exchange for clearing China's foreign trade and managing China's capital account liquidity. It functioned as an independent entity until 1998, when it was rolled up under PBoC as part of the larger reorganization of China's financial sector. Even after it reported to PBoC, there was a division of labor between SAFE and PBoC that saw SAFE enjoy a substantial degree of autonomy in its management of China's foreign exchange reserves, while the PBoC focused on domestic macroeconomic management, building up its central bank functions, and steering China's domestic monetary policy. This functional division of labor and SAFE's history as a previously autonomous entity partly account for why SAFE may have been accustomed to operating relatively autonomously under the PBoC.[5]

SAFE has traditionally been secretive about its investment activity. This disposition has valid commercial reason: because of SAFE's size, knowledge of its capital allocations could move markets. Unfortunately, such a shroud of secrecy also makes it easier for the state to direct such institutions to conduct noncommercial (often political) activities out of the public's eye. Despite SAFE's secrecy, there is evidence that SAFE had begun diversifying away from US treasuries, its default investment asset. By 2007, these treasuries had been producing negative real returns given the anticipated RMB appreciation and China's domestic inflation. As a result, SAFE began diversifying away from US-dollar-denominated assets. These efforts directed SAFE's investments both into other currencies and into alternative asset classes with greater risk-reward profiles (such as equities as opposed to fixed income government bonds). As discussed in more detail in the CIC chapter, the CIC was created in part because the Ministry of Finance (MOF) was critical of PBoC's (and thus SAFE's) foreign exchange management and investment of what by 2007 had amounted to a good deal of China's store of its national wealth.

According to available estimates, SAFE apparently managed an investment portfolio of at least $311.6 billion—mainly in US treasuries and bonds around the time of the Costa Rica episode.[6] Details of SAFE's portfolio are not available, but we know it is big. China ended 2009 with approximately $2 trillion in foreign exchange reserves and by mid-2010 these had grown to $2.5 trillion.[7] As of the end of 2013, China had approximately $3.66 trillion of foreign exchange reserves. Because Chinese banks must clear their foreign exchange and convert all foreign currency to RMB exclusively through SAFE, SAFE is left holding a large stockpile of foreign currency. Generally speaking, most trading countries tend to hold enough foreign exchange reserves to cover three to four month's worth of trade.[8] Beginning in 2004 or early 2005, China found itself with "excess reserves," an economic condition in which reserves exceed the amount of foreign currency needed to underwrite and clear about one quarter's worth of trade (plus some cushion for investments, direct conversion, and capital flows). This quickly led to a domestic consensus in China that SAFE now had more reserves on hand than was needed to underwrite China's international trade and defend its currency peg, even under conservative assumptions. This naturally prompted discussions over what China ought to do with its excess reserves.[9] Eventually China decided that a portion of the reserves would be used to recapitalize China's banking sector, which since the late 1990s had become weighed down by bad debts.[10] SAFE also faced increasing pressure to generate a higher return on its asset base.[11] As a result, China decided to create the China Investment Corporation (CIC).

The creation of the CIC was a direct bureaucratic encroachment into SAFE's traditional turf that prompted SAFE to alter its behavior. Part of SAFE's response was to demonstrate that it, too, could provide higher returns by moving a portion of its holdings out of low-yielding treasuries.[12] One of the consequences of this more aggressive investment stance appears to have been a series of ill-timed, clandestine stock purchases made on the London exchange in late 2007 and the first half of 2008.[13] Shortly after SAFE made these purchases, the market experienced a precipitous decline. Analysts have estimated that SAFE lost approximately $80 billion by buying in at the top of the market.[14] Although SAFE does not disclose its investments, some of its holdings publicly reported having SAFE as a major stockholder. Among these are the French petroleum company Total, some European private equity funds, and several large-cap UK companies including British Petroleum. SAFE has also been identified as a shareholder in the US private equity group TPG.[15] Apparently, SAFE often uses intermediaries to conduct its purchases to help conceal SAFE's involvement in the transactions. For instance, SAFE allegedly used its Hong Kong office, which in turn directed a third-party manager to conduct many of these transactions on the open market in London.[16] Such a predilection for secrecy, a lack of public accountability, and an absence of transparency make SAFE well-suited to be used to pursue non-commercial activities. At the same time, the competitive dynamic introduced by the creation of the CIC seems to have prompted SAFE to become a more pliable agent for the state, willing to pursue national goals that may not be strictly commercial in nature.[17] To get a better sense of exactly how such economic statecraft works in practice, the next few sections examine one such episode regarding China's use of SAFE to pursue its strategic foreign policy objectives.

SAFE's Purchase of Costa Rica's Bonds

On June 1, 2007, Costa Rica formally ceased to recognize the Republic of China and announced that it would instead recognize the People's Republic of China.[18] This represented the culmination of considerable diplomatic efforts on the part of the PRC. The State Administration of Foreign Exchange (SAFE) played a key role in financing the eventual deal in the form of a two-stage purchase of $300 million dollars worth of US-dollar-denominated Costa Rican government bonds.[19] The first purchase occurred in January 2008 for $150 million worth.[20] The second purchase seems to have occurred in January 2009 for another $150 million. The bonds were twelve-year notes with a "way below market" interest rate of 2 percent.[21] The terms of these bonds are significant. Such noncommercial terms provide evidence that this episode was a "hard test" for government control, a case in which SAFE had to act contrary to its own business interests to achieve the state's foreign policy objectives. Such cases are often the best examples of economic statecraft. In addition to this bond purchase, China promised $130 million in aid to Costa Rica.

The terms of the switch in recognition were apparently made an explicit part of the agreement that Yang Jiechi, China's then foreign minister, and Bruno Stagno Ugarte, foreign minister of Costa Rica, signed on June 1, 2007.[22] Although the deal was intended to remain secret (apparently against the wishes of the Costa Rican diplomats),[23] documents detailing the agreement were subsequently made public as a result of a Freedom of Information Act–style inquiry by a Costa Rican journalist.[24] Although the documents have since been removed, for a time the Costa Rican Foreign Ministry had posted copies of the June 1, 2007, agreement between the PRC and Costa Rica on its website.[25] In addition to the agreement, the Foreign Ministry posted "several subsequent letters" that laid out the terms of the deal (e.g., an additional $130 million of direct foreign aid). The Chinese Ministry of Foreign Affairs did not contest the validity of these documents.[26]

These revelations are significant in two ways. First, as Stephen Van Evera likes to emphasize, secret government documents that later become public can often provide good academic source material and make for particularly compelling case evidence. Because the contents were not originally intended to be made public, policy makers are generally more free to reveal true intentions without regard to public or political costs. Second, the attempt to keep such activities out of the public eye suggests that similar episodes may be occurring secretly (although secrecy also implies that "smoking gun" evidence of other such activity will generally be thin).

Changing recognition in exchange for economic benefits should not be viewed as a particularly notable event.[27] Costa Rica's switch was simply the most recent chapter of what has been called "checkbook diplomacy," a strategy through which Beijing and Taipei vie for international support by providing economic concessions to other nations in exchange for recipient nations' formal diplomatic recognition.[28] This phenomenon is not new. Since the origins of the Chinese Civil War, both sides have sought international legitimization from third parties. The significance of the Costa Rican episode lies in the fact that there is clear evidence that the PRC successfully used SAFE to pursue its foreign policy objectives.[29] In this case the state mobilized its monetary assets—not fiscal assets—to achieve its foreign policy goals.[30]

In this case, SAFE's goals were to ensure that it maintained a monopoly over China's foreign exchange management. In order to do this, it needed to isolate, marginalize, and if possible, eliminate the CIC. One of the best ways to accomplish this was to demonstrate how useful SAFE could be to China's political leadership. In this instance, SAFE demonstrated its usefulness by providing an important element of economic inducement to Costa Rica. Unlike more transparent, commercially oriented sovereign wealth funds, SAFE does not seem to be concerned with appearing to be politically motivated in its allocation of state investment capital. On the contrary, it seemed particularly eager to demonstrate its usefulness in the face of the creation of an alternative rival institution (CIC) that was encroaching on its bureaucratic turf.

So what were the goals of the state in this instance? China sought to limit the number of countries that provide diplomatic recognition to Taiwan. Limiting Taiwan's diplomatic space has been a long-standing objective of the PRC. One of the ways the PRC pursues this objective is to use economic inducements to woo Taiwan's allies away, often using multiple avenues of economic engagement (trade, investments, aid, etc.). In the lead-up to the SAFE purchase, Chinese economic ties with Costa Rica had been growing rapidly. In fact, Costa Rica had been one of the few countries to run a trade surplus with China. Trade with China in 2007 was up more than 25 percent while exports were up more than 30 percent over a year earlier, making China Costa Rica's second-largest trading partner. Costa Rica was also China's second-biggest trading partner in Central America.[31] China often takes advantage of such deepening economic ties to improve diplomatic relations. It is important to view the SAFE deal in the larger context of China's growing economic relationship with Costa Rica. Although economic interaction is important in its own right, China also leverages its economic relations for strategic ends. In this case, China sought to convince Costa Rica to switch its official diplomatic recognition from Taiwan to the PRC.[32] SAFE, China's official custodian of its foreign exchange reserves, secretly used a portion of those reserves to pursue one of China's core strategic interests. The result was economic statecraft.

Beyond SAFE: Other Aspects of the Costa Rica Deal

The SAFE bond purchase was part of a larger pattern of economic inducements collectively designed to strengthen Costa Rica's ties to the PRC while severing its connection to Taiwan.[33] As is common in such episodes of Chinese use of economics, China also financed the construction of a new, forty-thousand-seat national sports stadium for San Jose. Estimates of the cost for the stadium range from $25 to $83 million.[34] China also promised a new science and technology park.[35]

The Costa Rica deal also involved natural resource development and exploration. Hu Jintao signed a contract to modernize and expand the capacity of Costa Rica's Moin refinery from twenty-five thousand barrels per day to sixty thousand.[36] The financing of this $1 billion project is illustrative of the interconnectedness of many of the commercial actors discussed in this book. CNPC and Costa Rica's state-owned refinery, Recope, were to each contribute $150 million to capitalize a $300 million mixed capital, joint-venture entity. The remaining $700 million would be provided to China National Petroleum Corporation (CNPC) in the form of credits "from a bank in China."[37] Large Chinese policy banks have often been required to extend such credits to finance government-designated projects. In this way, the Chinese government is able to effectively direct economic activity (like project finance) to facilitate foreign policy objectives. Additionally, CNPC and Recope planned to establish a $6 billion refinery that would have a daily processing capacity of two hundred thousand barrels.[38] It also appears that a subsidiary of CNPC was engaged in negotiations to conduct oil exploration in Costa Rica's territorial waters.[39]

Such government-backed economic activity is not limited to extractive industries. Huawei Technologies Co., Ltd. (Huawei) was chosen over Ericsson to deploy Costa Rica's first 3G network.[40] The $235 million contract was awarded by Costa Rica's Electricity Institute (ICE), a Costa Rican state-run electrical company. Generally, China's economic engagement also entails a cultural component as well. Such activities are intended to foster deeper understanding and closer cultural ties between China and its foreign partners. In the case of Costa Rica, such activities have included the founding of the Confucius Institute for Chinese-language studies at the University of Costa Rica as well as an invitation to participate in the Shanghai Expo in 2010.[41] Large-ticket capital projects and high-profile public works are also often combined with personal benefits for key decision makers.[42] Such activities skate dangerously close to bribery and corruption, often exacerbating already problematic governance conditions in smaller, developing economies.

The case of Costa Rica is just one example of how China seeks to use its economic engagement to improve ties with countries. China gradually seeks to build on these economic links to foster greater diplomatic cooperation. Over time, as economic ties grow and deepen, they generate interest transformation security externalities that China often seeks to capitalize on to further its longer-term strategic goals. To specify the relevant conditions that enabled the state to control SAFE and direct its behavior in this episode, we return to the five factors presented in chapter 2.

Evaluating the SAFE Case

The state in this episode was not divided on the strategy nor on the particular instruments used to engage Costa Rica. The timing and announcement of various aspects of the strategy indicate a good deal of senior-level coordination. For instance, trade and investment deals were often coordinated with a senior official's state visit. The foreign ministry took the lead in ensuring smooth coordination across various functional lines. There is no evidence of cross-cutting local or provincial vested interests that stood in opposition to closer ties with Costa Rica. Likewise, there were no obvious factional politics or apparent bureaucratic turf battles over Costa Rica's recognition policy. As a result, the state principal exhibited a good deal of unity in this episode.

This case exhibited a fair amount of divergence along the dimension of the Goal Compatibility IV. As mentioned earlier, this condition of state unity and divergent goals implies that this case should have been a "hard case" for state control. As such, it represents a useful test for the theory. The goals of SAFE (to profitably invest a portion of China's foreign exchange reserves and marginalize an upstart competitor) did not necessarily correspond to the state's goals in this case. Although the state acted in a unified manner, furthering the goals of the state (diplomatically isolating Taiwan) would have required that the economic actor (SAFE) offer below-market rates to Costa Rica. This type of irrational behavior is an example of unprofitable commercial activities that tend to serve as observable indicators of economic statecraft. For economic actors to engage in this sort of behavior often requires that the state be able to direct the economic actor to conduct activities that run counter to the economic agent's own natural, commercial interests. Under such conditions, the theory suggests that the outcome of whether the state is able to control the commercial actor will often turn first on the competitive dynamics among the economic actors and second on the balance of relative resources and the nature of the reporting relationship.

The reporting structure for this case—and, incidentally, for all of China's sovereign wealth funds that are the focus of this portion of the book—is direct. SAFE is a wholly government-owned, managed, financed, and operated state investment entity. This extreme value on the Reporting Relationship IV reinforces the government's ability to direct SAFE's activities. SAFE is run by managers who serve at the pleasure of the CCP, and the senior management team is approved by the central Communist Party Organization Department.[43] SAFE nominally reports to the PBoC, and while it is able to enjoy some degree of discretion in its investment decision making,[44] it has only limited independent agency and, as discussed above, no real incentive in this case to resist State Council directives given the bureaucratic incentive to recapture its exclusive position as sole asset manager of China's national reserves.

The relative resources were evenly distributed between the central government and SAFE in this episode. Because the engagement with Costa Rica was at its core a foreign policy issue, the State Council in conjunction with the Ministry of Foreign Affairs were the natural government entities leading the coordination efforts. In terms of the purchasing, pricing, and structuring of the actual deal to buy Costa Rica's bonds, however, the government would likely have relied on SAFE's expertise. There was not any obvious resource asymmetry in this episode.

That said, SAFE has traditionally enjoyed a good deal of unique financial expertise, given its history of managing China's foreign exchange reserves. Prior to the existence of CIC, SAFE enjoyed an unchallenged monopoly over the administration and investment of China's foreign exchange reserves. This was coupled with SAFE's institutionally concentrated financial expertise that provided SAFE with power vis-à-vis the less knowledgeable state. For a considerable portion of its existence, this relative resource asymmetry coupled with an absence of institutions competing for SAFE's mission provided SAFE with some degree of autonomy vis-à-vis the state. With the introduction of the CIC, SAFE lost a good deal of this agency. The emergence of the CIC significantly undermined SAFE's monopoly and predictably increased the state's control over SAFE. SAFE's poorly timed equity investments (e.g., the UK stock purchases mentioned earlier) are an example of the competitive dynamics brought about by the creation of the CIC. With the Costa Rica episode, SAFE wanted to show its superiors that it could act as a useful policy arm for the senior decision makers. These points suggest that since the creation of the CIC, SAFE has been playing institutional defense against the encroachment on its traditional sphere of influence: investing the state's hard currency assets.[45] The existence of the CIC created direct competition for SAFE, and as a result SAFE may have been more willing to act as a dutiful agent of the state.

These dynamics suggest that after SAFE learned there was an alternative institutional competitor for investing state foreign exchange reserves, it became more likely to listen to the wishes of the principal. The most conducive situation for state control is one in which there are a small number of commercial agents who can be pitted against one another, effectively jockeying for the good graces of the state.[46] In this case, a change in the value of the Market Fragmentation IV (shifting from a monopoly to an oligopoly) contributed to SAFE's willingness to act as an agent for the state to achieve China's strategic objectives vis-à-vis Costa Rica.

This episode provides a clear case of the state using economic tools to achieve a foreign policy goal. SAFE became an instrument of Chinese foreign policy when it used monetary assets to purchase Costa Rican bonds on commercially unattractive terms. Hard tests for economic statecraft include instances when the state is able to exert enough control over commercial actors to direct them to pursue

TABLE 8.1 SAFE Case Summary Table

	IV CODING	EVIDENCE	DV PREDICTION	DV OUTCOME
Unity of state	Unified	There was little bureaucratic or factional disagreement within the state regarding Taiwan; no evidence of center-local tensions	Control likely	Control was achieved via a coordinated state policy
Goals	Somewhat divergent	SAFE sought to profitably invest a portion of China's foreign exchange reserves and marginalize an upstart competitor; the state was trying to diplomatically isolate Taiwan	Control possible	Control was achieved and SAFE offered below-market interest rates to Costa Rica
Market structure	Oligopolistic	SAFE's relative monopoly on administering China's foreign exchange reserves was recently eroded by the criticism of its returns and recent creation of the competing entity CIC; in addition, CDB's ambitious footing may have helped to foster a competitive spirit in China's state finance sector	Control likely	Control was enabled by the introduction of CIC; prompted SAFE to forgo its traditional autonomy in favor of demonstrating its utility as a tool of economic statecraft
Reporting relationship	Direct	SAFE is a wholly government-owned, - managed, - financed, and - operated state investment entity	Control likely	This extreme value on the Reporting Relationship IV reinforced the government's ability to direct SAFE's activities

IV CODING	EVIDENCE	DV PREDICTION	DV OUTCOME
Relative resources Fairly even	SAFE had some foreign asset-related experience advantages; but the State Council and the Ministry of Foreign Affairs were also well-resourced within government	Not a significant factor	State control of SAFE's behavior, but probably not due to the balance of relative resources

strategic objectives that run against the commercial actor's economic interests.[47] How did the state do this? The state was able to generate the desired behavior using an incentive structure that can be conceptualized using the factors presented in chapter 2. The state acted in a unified manner; shifting diplomatic recognition faced little internal resistance or dissent within China. At the same time, the goals of the principal and the agent diverged. The goals of SAFE (maximizing return on its investments) were at odds with goals of the state (diplomatically isolating Taiwan). According to the theory, the outcome of whether or not the state would be able to control the economic actor under such conditions should hinge on the market structure. In this case, SAFE's use as an instrument of Chinese economic statecraft corresponds to a shift in the market structure from one in which SAFE was "the only game in town" to one in which the CIC was created as an alternative economic actor competing to perform a similar mission. The limited competition with the emergent CIC created a market in which these two entities could be played off one another, and this competitive dynamic facilitated state control over SAFE. The move toward a more competitive market structure provides a useful illustration of the theory, and, as the theory suggests, we observe state control. In addition to these dynamics predicted by the theory, this episode also involved a lack of transparency, which seems to be another condition conducive to having noncommercial factors play a larger role in influencing the behavior of the agent. There are also efforts in this case to keep the state manipulation of commercial activity secret, which implies that other cases of Chinese economic statecraft may not exhibit such obvious "smoking guns."

Taken together, the independent variables indicate a high likelihood that the commercial actor in this case would do what the state wanted. It should not come as a surprise then that the outcome in this episode is that the state was able to control SAFE. In this episode, we can clearly observe that SAFE was directed to purchase $300 million of Costa Rican bonds at below-market rates as part of China's effort to entice Costa Rica to switch diplomatic recognition away from Taiwan.[48] As indicated above, the empirics of this episode provide evidence of state control. In this instance, China was able to use a state investment entity as a strategic tool to effectively achieve a foreign policy objective.

9

WHAT RIGHT LOOKS LIKE

The National Social Security Fund

If the SAFE-Costa Rica episode illustrates how China's sovereign wealth funds can be used to pursue Chinese strategic interests, the National Social Security Fund (NSSF) case demonstrates the opposite extreme. The NSSF is a relatively commercially driven state investment entity that is not easily used as a tool of China's economic statecraft. In contrast to the SAFE case, this case explores the factors that make the NSSF unlikely to be a source of strategic concern. Because this case is an instance of a "dog that did not bite," there is no particular historical episode to analyze. Instead, the analysis of this case focuses on the NSSF's institutional and structural characteristics as well as on its investment activities, the observable manifestation of its behavior.

In the case of the NSSF, the five factors introduced in chapter 2 all seem to suggest that the NSSF will not be easily used as a tool for Chinese economic statecraft. The broad bureaucratic representation in the NSSF's governance structure suggests that many state voices have a say in the orientation and direction of the NSSF. This institutional representation makes effective state coordination more complicated and state unity that much more elusive. There does seem to be consensus, however, around the primary mandate for the NSSF. The NSSF is primarily designed to support China's social security system with reliable, conservative investment returns. Although there seems to be much complementarity between the goals of the NSSF and of the state, the fundamentally commercial nature of these goals also suggests little cause for economic statecraft concerns. The NSSF enjoys a monopoly presence as China's sole national sovereign wealth fund focusing on social security. Being the only entity charged with ensuring future national social security funding provides the NSSF with some leverage to resist potential state efforts to direct its investing activities away from anything but the most commercially profitable opportunities. Likewise, the NSSF's extensive use of third-party asset managers adds an additional layer of principal-agent coordination challenges that the state would have to overcome if it sought to control the NSSF's international allocation of state capital to pursue strategic rather than commercial goals. Finally, as China's most professional sovereign wealth fund, the NSSF enjoys a human capital resource advantage over many other parts of the state. Few of the Communist Party's top officials have the detailed financial experience and expertise the NSSF enjoys. This talent asymmetry also helps ensure that the NSSF is unlikely to be used as a tool of Chinese economic statecraft.

The rest of this chapter begins with a historical overview of the NSSF, followed by an examination of the NSSF's financing sources and uses. I then look at the NSSF's mandate and activities before evaluating how the theory maps on to the case of the NSSF. My analysis suggests that the NSSF does not have much potential as an effective tool of Chinese economic statecraft. The conclusion revisits the NSSF/SAFE case juxtaposition and sets the stage for the next chapter's focus on the China Investment Corporation.

The National Social Security Fund (NSSF)

The National Council for the Social Security Fund was established in November 2000 to oversee a special supplementary fund (the National Social Security Fund, NSSF) used by the central government to help ensure adequate funds to cover its social security needs. It was originally intended to backstop liabilities and potential investment losses of municipal and province-level social security funds that had been investing the pension assets that workers paid into state-owned enterprises (SOEs). In many ways, the NSSF was a pioneer for China. It was China's first explicit sovereign wealth fund, and the NSSF was the first to use third-party asset managers. It was originally set up to both act as a national resource to bail out potentially failed local and provincial pension funds and to provide a nationally sanctioned model of pension investment upon which other local funds around China could pattern their operations. The management of the National Social Security Fund is based on the State Council's "Provisional Rules of Management for the National Social Security Fund." The annual report the NSSF publishes as part of its statutory duties clearly specifies the convergence between the goals of the state, to provide adequate funds to cover future social security liabilities, and the goals of the fund, to maximize investment returns while protecting the initial capital investment. As a result, the fund is professionally operated and conducts commercially motivated investment activity. Of the entities that invest capital on behalf of the state, the NSSF is the least motivated by noncommercial goals. For this reason, the NSSF case makes an interesting juxtaposition with the SAFE case just examined; the two cases lie at opposite ends of the spectrum and thus provide useful illustrations of the theory.

The government set up the NSSF to provide funding for the projected social security obligations that the government would face in the near future.[1] As a result, there was a strong incentive to focus the NSSF on generating respectable returns while protecting the initial capital entrusted to it.[2] The goals of the state (to ensure adequate funding for future social security obligations) depended on the goals of the commercial actor (to pursue investment returns while preserving the capital base entrusted to NSSF). Complementary goals result in the state being able to effectively control the activities of the NSSF. The NSSF's activities, however, are oriented around largely commercial goals, thus substantially mitigating the likelihood that the NSSF's activities will be used to generate explicitly political security externalities.

The NSSF is run by a board of directors that reports to the State Council. The State Council can appoint and dismiss the NSSF's chairman, vice chairmen, and any of the sixteen directors on the board. As a "governmental agency at the ministerial level," the NSSF institutionally reports directly to the State Council. At the same time, the Ministry of Finance and the Ministry of Labor and Social Security are mandated to "supervise the investment operations and custody" of the NSSF. In practice, Ministry of Finance personnel occupy the key operational positions while the Ministry of Labor and Social Security is able to voice its preferences or concerns regarding particular investments, portfolio allocation, or practices. Although these reporting relationships evidence a significant role for the state in monitoring and enforcing compliance with national goals, the multiple institutional interests that have a voice in the administration of NSSF suggest the potential for a lack of state unity.

The National Social Security Fund (NSSF): Financing Sources

The NSSF has grown to about RMB 1.11 trillion (or about US$182 billion) in assets under management at the end of 2012.[3] The source of these funds has largely been "fiscal surpluses" that have been allocated to NSSF from the central government. Its other important sources of funds are shares of publicly listed SOEs, individual worker contributions, and investment returns. The annual funding comes from the central budget (hence an important source of the Ministry of Finance's influence). The NSSF has also often received proceeds or stock in SOEs just before their initial public offering (IPOs).[4] This has generally been seen as a government vote of confidence and support as well as acting as a stabilizing influence for the IPOs because the NSSF traditionally does not sell its shares (normally around 10 percent of the total number) right away. The third source of funds for the NSSF comes directly from individual worker contributions. Finally, the NSSF retains and reinvests its returns it has earned on previous NSSF investments.

Over time, the relative importance of these sources has shifted. Initially, almost 100 percent of the NSSF's funding came from state budget allocations. But as more and more SOEs went public in the early to mid-2000s, a greater and greater share of the NSSF's annual funding was coming from proceeds from these IPOs.[5] Today, investment income usually accounts for most of the annual increase in the NSSF's assets. In addition, the NSSF has gotten increasingly more and more independent and self-sustaining over time. Its purview of permitted investments has also expanded to include private equity and alternative investment classes and to investing a portion of its capital internationally. The NSSF operates with a long-term investment horizon, fifteen to twenty years.[6] This enables it to take advantage of short-term price fluctuations and act as a market stabilizing force.

The National Social Security Fund (NSSF): Financing Uses

The gradual evolution of the NSSF's asset allocation provides evidence for a sustained pattern of commercially driven diversification and investment activities. The NSSF was launched in 2000 with RMB 20 billion (US$2.9 billion). In its early days, the NSSF's returns were primarily driven by the interest paid on its bank deposits. But that was soon to change. It first ventured away from short-term, fixed-income investments with a RMB1.27 billion pre-IPO equity investment in Sinopec and Yangtze Power when those companies listed domestically in 2001.[7] Since these early investments, the NSSF has shown a desire to move out of fixed income and into more equities. In 2002 a statute was passed stipulating that SOEs would contribute 10 percent of their IPO proceeds to the NSSF (generally in the form of direct equity stakes). The government's objective in having the NSSF take these stakes was mainly to provide a stable government owner that would not sell the newly listed shares right away. It also allowed the NSSF to scale up its assets under management and partake in the monetization of the state's crown jewels. In June 2004, the NSSF used RMB10 billion to buy pre-IPO shares of Bank of Communications just before it went public on the Hong Kong exchange.[8] During 2005, the NSSF also bought US$2.6 billion of the Industrial and Commerce Bank of China's (ICBC's) pre-IPO stock and US$1.4 billion of Bank of China's (BOC's) stock before each of their Hong Kong listings. Buying in at this time (usually at or close to book market value, i.e., undervalued) just before the public listing allows the NSSF to ensure relatively safe, high returns on its investments. In addition, the NSSF was receiving 10 percent of the shares of SOEs that were listing in Hong Kong. As a result of the 10 percent pre-IPO "tax," during this time, the NSSF acquired a portfolio of small stakes in twenty-one recently IPO'd SOEs. Eventually, this "IPO tax" was limited to SOEs that were listing on foreign exchanges because it was thought that the "IPO tax" was contributing to the cooling of China's domestic stock market in the mid-2000s.

The NSSF was also an early innovator of using third-party asset managers, another important factor favoring commercial, arms-length investment strategies in which the government has a limited voice (further restricting its ability to use the investment activities to realize strategic foreign policy objectives). The NSSF continued to expand this practice. After its first two years of operation, the NSSF displayed a preference for incrementally expanding its use of third-party asset managers. In 2003, the NSSF first sought out local fund managers to manage assets on its behalf. It hired six Chinese third-party asset managers to manage funds split 1:2 (stocks:bonds).[9] These mandates managed about RMB32 billion or approximately 24 percent of the NSSF's total assets at the end of the year. During 2004, the NSSF also increased its number of third-party asset managers to ten and increased their share of assets under management to 36 percent.[10] By the end of 2005, the third-party asset managers were in charge of RMB73 billion (about US$9 billion, or 34 percent of the NSSF's total assets). Between 2005 and 2007, the NSSF also added one securities company and three fund managers to its original ten third-party asset managers. With the State Council's passage of the Interim Measures on Overseas Investment by Social Security Fund in the late spring of 2006, the NSSF was authorized to begin investing abroad. Although this move into international investing greatly enhanced the NSSF's potential to generate strategic security externalities, the NSSF mitigated concerns by appointing ten foreign third-party professional fund managers in late 2006. By 2007, the NSSF was investing internationally under commercial conditions. As of the end of 2012, the NSSF had entrusted 41 percent of the investments to third-party asset managers.[11]

As the NSSF has ramped up its assets under management, it seems to be looking to continue this commercially driven strategy. At the end of 2012, the NSSF had a little over RMB1.106 trillion or about US$182 billion in total assets. This consisted of about RMB651 billion of assets that were directly invested by the NSSF while the other RMB455 billion was sourced to third-party asset managers.[12] In 2012, the fund had a return of 7.01 percent, although since inception the NSSF has averaged an 8.29 percent annual return. Chasing returns rather than scoring diplomatic points provides a strong incentive for the agent to pursue purely commercial objectives.

The NSSF is primarily invested in domestic Chinese assets. This domestic distribution of the NSSF's investments further mitigates the likelihood that the NSSF will be used to pursue strategic foreign policy goals.[13] At the end of 2012, the NSSF held about RMB28 billion in bank deposits. Another RMB312 billion was held as tradable securities. The largest category of assets was "investments held to maturity," which stood at RMB432 billion at year's end. There is little evidence of significantly sized direct foreign investments, acquisitions, or controlling interest stakes that were purchased or managed directly by the NSSF.[14] Avoiding such concentrated investments also reduces the potential for security externalities. During the 2008 financial crisis, the value of the NSSF's largely third-party-managed equity investments fell from RMB125 billion at the beginning of the year to RMB69 billion by year's end, reflecting the general decline in the value of equities in 2008.[15] This result was very much in line with the losses suffered by other commercial investors.

The NSSF's pioneering use of investment mandates issued to third-party domestic asset managers was an important source of professionalism for the NSSF. This practice significantly lowered the possibility that the NSSF would be used as a strategic tool for realizing China's foreign policy objectives. The use of third-party asset managers introduced another layer of state-commercial actor relations into the situation. Now the state would have to not only manage the NSSF if it wished to use it to support non-commercial goals, but the NSSF would then also need to direct or control these third-party asset managers to get them to support noncommercial goals. Such layers of agency provide a considerable firebreak against any sort of noncommercial behavior. Importantly, the NSSF's practice has also become the template for the CIC's use of third-party asset managers. To the extent China is looking to reassure recipient nations who may be concerned about the noncommercial orientation of China's outwardly bound investment flows, it may wish to consider using professional, transparent, third-party asset managers that provide a convincing element of commercial rather than political or strategic motivation.

The National Social Security Fund (NSSF): Mandate and Activities

The NSSF seeks to achieve "capital appreciation of assets on the basis of protecting capital [principal]."[16] The inherently commercial nature of this primary mission provides the NSSF with a solid commercial footing. Despite the absence of independent directors on the board, the NSSF has been able to remain relatively free from the politicization of its investments. This is due largely to the intrinsic goal compatibility between the government and NSSF around its explicit function: to focus on earning safe, reliable returns while protecting its capital base as part of the state's effort to meet its outstanding social security, retirement, and pension obligations.

The net effect of the NSSF's commercial orientation is to significantly reduce the possibility of the NSSF's investment activity being used to further China's foreign policy objectives. There are several rationales for this. First, the NSSF seems suffused with a strong conservative bias to protect its investment capital, which serves to reassure investment targets of NSSF's position as a conservative long-term investor. This helps to allay fears of the NSSF posing a destabilizing investment influence. By minimizing the NSSF's proclivity for destabilizing recipients of its funds, this investment strategy also reduces the possibility that the NSSF will be used as an instrument of coercive leverage, thus helping to limit potential security externalities. Second, the NSSF is deliberately seeking to outsource almost half of its total assets and already outsources the majority of its tactical investment decision making (acting like a "fund of funds"). This is especially true in the area of its international investments. Relying on private-sector, third-party international asset managers introduces another layer of principal-agent coordination challenges that the state would need to overcome if it were to wield the NSSF as an instrument of economic statecraft.

Finally, the NSSF has been able to avoid efforts to exert noncommercial pressure by claiming that the NSSF must operate on a strictly commercial basis to achieve its mission to fund the pension system against China's demographic projections.[17] This primary tasking for the NSSF enjoys considerable political buy-in among China's elite leadership. The compatibility of goals between the state and the NSSF enables the NSSF to pursue commercial objectives and conduct its business on commercial grounds. Although this goal compatibility makes state control more likely, the commercial nature of these mutual goals limits the security concerns stemming from the NSSF's activity.

Evaluating the NSSF Case

With respect to the Goals IV, the state and the NSSF are in agreement regarding the NSSF's commercially oriented objectives because both the state and the commercial actor seek to maximize risk-adjusted return on the NSSF's investments. The NSSF pursues commercially oriented goals. It is not a source of significant security externalities, as a large portion of its assets are invested domestically in China. What foreign investment it does conduct is done through professional, third-party asset managers (like JP Morgan Chase, Invesco, LaSalle, PIMCO,

Fidelity, T. Rowe Price, etc.). Such reliance on arms-length asset managers decreases the likelihood that they will be used to support specific foreign or strategic policy objectives.[18]

Of course, if the NSSF's investment mandates were to constitute a significant portion of these third-party manager's portfolio of assets, it would not be unreasonable to ask whether these third-party managers might become beholden to the NSSF. Indeed, to the extent that a firm is largely reliant on NSSF (or any other entity's) funding, we might expect it to defer to the preferences of the large investor. To date, there does not seem to be any specific instances of this. I suspect that is because most investment mandates that have been placed with third-party managers are relatively small amounts in comparison to the total assets under management at these large multinational investment houses. But as placements grow in size and as sources of capital tighten (perhaps as a result of a credit crunch) we can expect the influence of China's outward-bound capital to grow.[19]

The NSSF is governed by a Board of Directors whose chairman and vice chairman are appointed by the State Council. The state in this case is fairly divided under the State Council, with the Ministry of Finance and the Ministry of Labor and Social Security providing input and guidance in their respective contexts. Although the Ministry of Civil Affairs and the Ministry of Human Resources and Social Security play an advisory role, the Ministry of Finance seems to be the key supervisory entity. For day-to-day operations, the Ministry of Finance and the Ministry of Labor and Social Security also have a voice at the table. As the oldest of China's sovereign wealth funds (dating back to 2000), the NSSF has had a relatively long period to resolve matters of bureaucratic influence and establish clear lines of authority. That said, the presence of so many interests in NSSF governance suggests that state unity may be very fragile. These wide-ranging bureaucratic interests represented at the NSSF would make it hard for any one interest to hijack the NSSF and direct its investments for narrow political goals. Thus, commercially motivated goals provide consensus objectives that further reinforce the NSSF's commercial proclivity. In addition, the NSSF has taken on a greater role in the assumption and management of provincial-level social security funds in recent years. This dynamic has introduced yet another dimension of state division: center-local cleavages. Given that the primary driver behind this expansion of the NSSF's purview was to professionalize the management of these state investment assets, this move likely reinforces two elements of the NSSF that make it unlikely to be a useful tool of Chinese economic statecraft: strictly commercial goals and a divided state.

The NSSF is the only national social security fund. In this sense it operates in a concentrated market. Of course there are other Chinese sovereign wealth funds, but only one NSSF with a clear commercial and fiduciary mandate.[20] Therefore, the NSSF lacks the competitive dynamic observed in the SAFE case that compelled the commercial actor to engage in noncommercially motivated activities. Moreover, the state has clearly signaled that it does not seek anything but commercial returns from the NSSF. Even if the state did seek to use the NSSF as an instrument of financial economic statecraft, that effort would be complicated by the NSSF's use of third-party professional asset managers. The state would need to control not only NSSF but also the NSSF's third-party asset managers. This is the equivalent of adding another layer of principal-agent challenges into the equation. Thus the Reporting Relationship IV indicates that it would be hard for the state to direct the NSSF to achieve strategic objectives.

Being the oldest of China's sovereign wealth funds, the NSSF has considerable institutional knowledge, which also tilts the Relative Resources IV in its favor. At the CIC and NSSF, the familiarity with international investment banking operations and world-class asset-management skills endow these agents with a significant resource advantage over the state.[21] Moreover, these entities have attracted a significant share of the Chinese Communist Party's limited financial management talent. Both of these factors suggest that these commercial actors will enjoy a degree of expertise asymmetry that would be likely to cause the state to defer to the agent. Interestingly, it seems that both of these entities have worked hard to place their organizations on as commercially oriented a footing as possible. Such a disposition would play to their technical expertise and provide the commercial actor with even greater autonomy, free from political interference.

To summarize, the NSSF's efforts to provide public transparency, regular reporting, and disclosure as well as its clear, commercially driven goals all suggest that the security consequences of the NSSF's activities will likely be minimal. The diverse interests of the state represented in the NSSF's governance structure make it difficult to direct the NSSF to pursue any one constituency's narrow political agenda. As a result, maintaining the NSSF's commercial orientation provides a consensus mission on which all parts of the state can agree. In addition, the NSSF enjoys an information and expertise asymmetry vis-à-vis the state in matters of financial expertise. This and the lack of any alternative bureaucratic rivals strengthen the NSSF against any state attempts to control its activities. Lastly, the extensive use of third-party asset managers makes it much more difficult for the state to direct or even influence the NSSF's investment activities. This facet of the reporting relationship makes the use of NSSF funds to pursue strategic state security objectives unlikely. Although the NSSF case displays some state control (largely due to convergent goals), in this case the goals of the state are largely commercial, with little effective pressure for anything other than commercial objectives. NSSF's commercial orientation therefore provides a good baseline for comparison. The NSSF stands out as an extreme case of how state investment could be institutionally structured to limit its propensity to be used as a tool of economic statecraft. Just as SAFE represented a set of extreme values that resulted in its effective use as an instrument of Chinese economic statecraft, so too does the NSSF case study represent a commercially oriented Chinese sovereign wealth investment fund.

TABLE 9.1 NSSF Case Summary Table

	IV CODING	EVIDENCE	DV PREDICTION	DV OUTCOME
Unity of state	Divided	Broad bureaucratic representation in the NSSF's governance structure suggests that many state voices have a say in the orientation and direction	Control unlikely	No evidence of effective state control of NSSF's behavior beyond normal commercial operations
Goals	Convergent	Commercially driven goals; although there seems to be a high degree of complementarity between the goals of the NSSF and the state, the fundamentally commercial nature of these goals also suggests little cause for economic statecraft concerns	Control likely	Since goals were in agreement around commercial objectives, possibility for NSSF to be used for economic statecraft was limited
Market structure	Monopolistic	"Only game in town" for the state to provide a national financial support to China's social security scheme; although this simplifies the	Control unlikely	Being the only entity charged with ensuring future national social security funding provided NSSF with leverage to resist potential

	IV CODING	EVIDENCE	DV PREDICTION	DV OUTCOME
		state's monitoring and compliance tasks, such concentration provides the commercial actor with leverage against the state		state efforts to direct its investing activities away from anything but the most commercially profitable opportunities
Reporting relationship	Indirect	Public transparency; regular reporting and disclosure; NSSF's extensive use of third-party asset managers adds an additional layer of principal-agent coordination challenges that would have to be overcome if the state sought to control the NSSF's international allocation of state capital to pursue strategic rather than commercial goals	Control unlikely	Extensive reliance on third-party asset managers insulated NSSF from most forms of politicized investing (the major exception being NSSF support for high-profile IPOs of SOEs—but even these potentially noncommercial effects were largely confined to the domestic realm); the third-party institutional arrangement seems to have outweighed the fact that NSSF was nevertheless an official arm of the state
Relative resources	Favors NSSF	Widely viewed as China's most professional sovereign wealth fund during this	Control unlikely	NSSF's resource asymmetry meant that (if necessary) it would be able to resist

(Continued)

TABLE 9.1 (Continued)

IV CODING	EVIDENCE	DV PREDICTION	DV OUTCOME
	period, the NSSF enjoyed a human capital resource advantage over many other parts of the state; NSSF budgets were well-resourced and most of the small number of top party officials with relevant financial skills supported or were directly involved with NSSF		any attempt to control or steer its behavior away from its strictly commercial mandate; no evidence found of economic statecraft attempts

These two case studies are useful from a theory-building perspective in that they resulted in extreme opposite outcomes: economic statecraft is illustrated in the case of SAFE (a result that is explained largely by values on the Market Fragmentation IV, Reporting Relationship IV, and Unity of State IV), and limited state control with little potential for economic statecraft in the case of the NSSF. Its strong commercial orientation suggests it is significantly less likely to be used as an effective tool of economic statecraft.

In terms of the book's theory, SAFE and the NSSF provide useful case studies with extreme values across the IVs. Such extreme cases facilitate checks of internal validity; in other words, does the theory work as we would expect given the extreme value on the IVs? As we observe, the extreme values in the case of SAFE suggest that the state would be able to direct the behavior of the agent.[22] Although perfect experiments are rarely possible in international relations, the theory's causality does play out as expected in the case of SAFE. In the comparable case of the NSSF, the values are also extreme, but in the opposite direction. As the theory predicts, the NSSF case suggests that the state would have a difficult time trying to control the investment activity of the NSSF and direct it toward pursuing China's foreign policy objectives. The institutional structure of the NSSF makes it difficult to be used as a tool of effective statecraft. These specific cases of China's state investment offer an in-depth examination of how the state can (or cannot) achieve state control. In both the cases of the NSSF and SAFE, the theory operates as we would expect it would.

But what about China's only officially designated sovereign wealth fund, the China Investment Corporation? Will the CIC act more like SAFE and become a pliable tool of Chinese economic statecraft, or will it seek to mimic the NSSF's commercial orientation? The next chapter focuses an analytical lens on the origins, evolution, and trajectory of the CIC in an effort to answer these questions.

10

THE CHINA INVESTMENT CORPORATION

The previous two chapters examined SAFE and the NSSF, two sovereign wealth funds whose extreme values on the IVs served to illustrate the theory in the empirical context of China's state finance. SAFE was directed to use foreign exchange reserves as part of an integrated economic foreign policy designed to achieve China's strategic interests, whereas the NSSF was seen as an exclusively commercially oriented sovereign wealth fund. This chapter examines the China Investment Corporation (CIC), another Chinese sovereign wealth fund whose empirics suggest it lies somewhere between the two extremes of SAFE and the NSSF.

The evaluation of the CIC can be parsed into two separate minicases. In the early days of the CIC, the state was quite divided about the CIC's mission and goals. Not surprisingly, there was little state control over CIC (and its predecessors). As the 2008 financial crisis unfolded, the State Council (and the Ministry of Finance in particular) consolidated its control of the CIC. This consolidation marked the second phase of the CIC case. The chapter begins by briefly examining the origins, structure, and leadership of the CIC. This is followed by a detailed review of the sources and uses of the CIC's financing. The final portion of the chapter applies the theory to better understand the CIC case as an instrument of Chinese economic statecraft.

Origins of the CIC

The CIC came about as an institutional response to mounting criticism that the People's Bank of China (PBoC) (via SAFE) was not maximizing the returns on China's growing foreign exchange reserves. The macroeconomic structural imbalances suggested that China would continue to build up foreign exchange reserves for the foreseeable future. This problem of managing China's foreign exchange reserves was not going away, and critics of the PBoC argued that China needed to proactively address how best to use its excessive reserves. Of course, one can imagine how many institutional interests came out of the woodwork to lay claim to excess national resources! Eventually, China's leadership determined that it would set up a sovereign wealth fund primarily modeled on Singapore.[1] Thus the idea of the CIC was born.

The China Investment Corporation formally commenced operations on September 29, 2007. The intention to create a sovereign wealth fund, however, was first publicly announced as early as March 2007.[2] Apparently, there were some delays in getting the organization stood up initially.[3] In fact, the first official sovereign wealth investment occurred in May 2007, when China Jianyin Investment Limited (a government holding company charged with managing any asset purchases until the sovereign wealth fund was stood up) purchased a 9.9 percent non-voting stake in the Blackstone Group for US$3 billion. China Jianyin (along with its Blackstone stake and other assets) would eventually be rolled into the CIC.

The evidence suggests that at the time of the Blackstone purchase the commercial actor enjoyed considerable independence from the central government. This stemmed from a lack of a clear reporting structure to the senior leadership of the CCP. At that time, Jianyin was part of the Ministry of Finance (MOF). As a bureaucratic entity, MOF was actively engaged in critiquing the PBoC for its paltry returns on China's increasing foreign exchange reserves.[4] This was part of an effort to wrest greater control over the management of China's foreign exchange reserves from the PBoC that dated back four or five years prior to the launch of the CIC. By mid-2007, the state was clearly divided along bureaucratic lines, and the division provided the commercial actor with considerable room to maneuver. This condition was exacerbated by the relative absence of financial expertise among senior party leadership.[5] The state therefore had little choice but to rely on the professional judgment of the few senior leaders in the CCP that had established financial credentials. The result was that Jianyin bought a 9.9 percent stake in Blackstone Group for $3 billion as part of Blackstone's IPO. This action would later come under fire for its lack of due diligence and proper vetting.

So what was China Jianyin? How did it come to enjoy so much autonomy in the months leading up to the creation of the CIC? China Jianyin Investment Limited was created out of China Construction Bank (CCB) on September 17, 2004. Its creation was part of the CCB's reorganization in preparation for its public listing as a joint-stock company. Because of legal limitations on what the CCB could own once it was reorganized, it was required to spin off its ownership of China International Capital Corporation (CICC).[6] China Jianyin Investment Limited was created to own 43.35 percent of CICC.[7] Because the CCB was wholly owned by Central Huijin at this time, China Jianyin also became a subsidiary of Central Huijin. China Jianyin later would become the primary vehicle for the government to recapitalize and restructure China's domestic stock brokerages following the 2004–2005 collapse in that sector.[8] As a result, China Jianyin would eventually come to serve as a holding company for several Chinese financial companies (mainly brokerages). These assets eventually came under the CIC when the CIC initially acquired Central Huijin. Indeed, the CIC can trace its roots to the early recapitalization efforts of Central Huijin and China Jianyin.

To complete the picture of the CIC's roots, we must go back to 2003, when the PBoC—China's central bank—acting through its subsidiary, SAFE, dedicated US$45 billion of China's foreign exchange reserves to create the Central Huijin Investment, a vehicle designed to recapitalize China's largest domestic banks.[9] The move was a controversial one at the time because valuable foreign currency was being used to prop up bad assets on the books of China's domestic banks. Moreover, the move signaled a bureaucratic power shift away from the Ministry of Finance (which had previously been the dominant government bureaucracy with respect to China's banking entities) to the People's Bank of China (the central bank, which managed China's foreign currency reserves). On January 6, 2004, the PBoC announced that earlier in December 2003 it had used $45 billion of US government bonds and other foreign-currency-denominated assets in its coffers (taken from what would have otherwise been an even higher $403.3 billion foreign exchange reserve reported at year's end 2003) to take an equity stake in Central Huijin Investment. The newly created Central Huijin then turned around and made subordinated loans to the Bank of China (BOC) and China Construction Bank (CCB) so that these banks could count the value of these loans as their own assets (equity capital) on their 2003 year-end books. The purpose of this shell game was to help clean up the balance sheets of these banks (i.e., lower their nonperforming loans ratio) to enable them to have successful IPOs. This operation was done in December 2003 with a view to eventually retiring the Central Huijin loans via an exchange for stock when the banks went public in two or three years' time. A similar maneuver was used to recapitalize ICBC.[10]

The move enabled the relatively weak commercial banks to use China's official dollar-denominated assets to support their balance sheets, thus permitting the PBoC to help them without requiring the PBoC to issue any additional RMB-denominated bonds (i.e., "real money" domestically in China). Issuing the banks more RMB would likely have added to the domestic inflationary pressure, while reallocating foreign reserves would help relieve pressure for letting the RMB appreciate, thus making the maneuver a win-win proposition. Of course, the only catch was that these assets could not really be spent in China (because the banks would have first needed to convert them to RMB, which the PBoC was not going to let them do). But these assets *could* be used on dollar-denominated investments. Over next few years, Central Huijin would come to develop some limited expertise in assisting the banks with placing some of their capital in overseas, dollar-denominated investments, because these sorts of investments did not require conversion to RMB.

The December 2003 operation ought to be understood in the context of the broader effort to reform China's domestic banking sector. Previously, in 1998, the PBoC had injected RMB270 billion (about US$32.6 billion) into the "Big Four" banks to help stave off collapse. Again in 2000 and 2001, it allowed them to essentially write off RMB1.4 trillion of bad loans by transferring these nonperforming loans to asset-management companies that were designed to recover as much of the bad debt as possible. By using the foreign exchange reserves to set up Central Huijin, the PBoC was able to use these assets to achieve an important domestic reform priority at a time when low interest rates in the United States meant that the opportunity cost of using these foreign exchange reserves was not very high.

I begin the CIC case with this brief discussion of the CIC's roots in China's domestic bank recapitalization to provide context for the domestic bureaucratic competition between the MOF and the PBoC, which would color the CIC's early experience. Under the planned economy, the MOF directed China's banks to provide credits as dictated by the plan, which meant that China's banks were national instruments of economic planning. With the advent of the bailouts of nonperforming loans, the PBoC took on a larger role in the ownership and management of the banking sector. As the PBoC played a larger role, MOF ceded bureaucratic territory. Frictions between MOF and PBoC have characterized much of China's recent macroeconomic reforms.[11] The CIC grew out of a series of moves to mobilize foreign exchange reserves to achieve the domestic political goals of recapitalizing China's banks. Although the CIC today seems to be trying to move toward a purely commercial footing, this has certainly not always been the case. To understand whether the CIC can be used as an effective instrument for furthering China's foreign policy objectives, it is important to identify the factors that enable the state to control the activities of the CIC. To answer this, let us take a closer look at the leadership, structure, and activities of today's CIC.

The China Investment Corporation (CIC): Structure and Leadership

To understand the dynamics driving the values on the Unity of State IV and the Reporting Relationship IV for this case requires examining the organizational

architecture and changes in the leadership of the CIC.[12] At the top of the organization is the CIC's Board of Directors, which essentially serves as the senior
leadership organization for the CIC.[13] As needed, the board may notify the State
Council of "major issues." These are usually decisions on investment of more
than US$1 billion.[14] The CIC's Articles of Association stipulate the composi-
tion of this eleven-person Board of Directors. The chairman (Ding Xuedong)
and vice chairman (Li Keping) are both appointed directly by the State Council
of the PRC.[15] The third and final executive director for years had been Zhang
Hongli, who was also the executive vice president and COO of the CIC until
his retirement in July 2011. The third executive director then became the chief
investment officer, Li Keping. When Li Keping was promoted to vice chairman,
the third executive director position was given to Zhang Xiaoqiang, a veteran of
the National Development and Reform Commission (NDRC), who previously
served as secretary general of the NDRC's predecessor, the State Development
and Planning Commission. The five nonexecutive directors (directors who do
not also concurrently hold a senior operational management position in the
company) must consist of one individual nominated by each of the following
stakeholders: the National Development and Reform Commission, the Ministry of Finance, the Ministry of Commerce, the People's Bank of China, and the
State Administration of Foreign Exchange. The State Council must approve their
nominations. There are also two independent directors who cannot have any
ties to the CIC "that may influence his or her independent objective judgment."
The final member is the "employee director" that is supposed to "represent the
employees" on the board.

The board composition reflects the diverse range of institutional interests
that have a stake in the CIC, but the overall impression of the CIC's leadership
is that (1) this is clearly a government entity with direct lines of authority to
senior state leadership, (2) former Ministry of Finance officials occupy most of
the top executive posts, and (3) there has been a trend toward professionalization and commercialization in the operations and executive management of the
CIC. The five nondirector positions are allocated to the entities that are directly
concerned with the CIC to ensure that each stakeholder gets a voice at the table.
Both the chairman and the vice chairman, however, are appointed by the State
Council (headed by Premier Li Keqiang). Ding Xuedong (current chairman),
Lou Jiwei (previous chairman), and Zhang Hongli all came out of the Minis-
try of Finance. Jin Liqun (who until May 2013 was chairman of the Board of
Supervisors, the auditing and oversight portion of the management) also came
out of the Ministry of Finance.[16] The company management and the Executive
Committee—responsible for the day-to-day operations of the CIC—have both
been dominated by the Ministry of Finance although more recent hires feature

individuals with previous asset-management experience, particularly at the NSSF (e.g., Li Keping).

While the Ministry of Finance may have strong representation at the CIC, it is certainly not the only voice at the table. Almost every other major government institutional stakeholder in the world of Chinese finance is represented at the CIC. Moreover, many of these personnel are increasingly reflecting a trend toward international technocratic education and experience. For example, Gao Xiqing (the former vice chairman and president) is a graduate of Duke Law School and came to the CIC from the National Council for the Social Security Fund.[17] When Li Keping (another NSSF veteran) was brought to the CIC, he was given the chief investment officer role from Gao Xiqing's portfolio.[18] The former president of Central Huijin and the current deputy chief investment officer, Xie Ping, a reformer from the PBoC, is also a member of the executive committee. Until June 27, 2013, Wang Jianxi—previously chairman of China Jianyin—was the chief risk officer at the CIC.[19] By 2013, the Executive Committee included individuals who during their careers had been with ICBC, the NSSF, China Construction Bank, PBoC, Export-Import Bank, and National Development and Reform Council (NDRC). This diversity of institutional allegiances throughout the governance structure of the CIC is an important factor in light of the Unity of State IV.

Particularly in the early days of the CIC, there seemed to be a considerable bureaucratic struggle between the MOF, PBoC, and NDRC over the CIC's mandate and how it should deploy its capital.[20] At the core of this debate was a difference over the degree to which the CIC ought to use its resources to support national policy versus using them to maximize its risk-adjusted return on investment. While this struggle was taking place, the CIC's precursor entities (China Jianyin and Central Huijin) were actively seeking out investment opportunities abroad (Blackstone and Morgan Stanley). These investments were characterized by their chummy characteristics and later came under fire for their lack of due diligence and subsequent losses. The details of the investments suggest that the commercial actor was taking the initiative and acting relatively independently of the state. Later efforts to consolidate state power over the CIC were partly based on arguments claiming that this loosely supervised CIC of the early period needed to be reined in with proper investment review processes and risk-management procedures. Without such mechanisms of more centralized control, it was argued, the CIC would continue to engage in poorly timed investments that lose half their value in a few years. Indeed, Lou Jiwei was successful in putting these more formalized institutional procedures in place.[21]

Although the data seems to suggest that diverse institutional interests continue to be represented at the CIC (indicating a divided state, especially in the

formative days of the CIC), there is also strong evidence that the MOF consolidated its dominance of the organization, potentially paving the way for tighter
state control in the future.[22] Subsequent personnel changes in some of the top
positions at the CIC seem to suggest that the MOF continues to try to consolidate its grasp.[23] In addition, there seems to be a trend toward professionalization and international technocratic financial expertise among the more recently
appointed management. Ten of the eleven members of the management team
have graduate degrees. More than half have doctorates in economics and five
of the eleven obtained degrees in the United States.[24] This, in conjunction with
previous professional experience (banking, finance, the NSSF, etc.), augurs for a
strongly commercial orientation for the CIC's future.

The evolution in the structure and leadership of the CIC thus suggests two
phases. In the first, we observe less state control (relatively unsupervised deals
like Blackstone and Morgan Stanley) during the CIC's initial formative period
when the State Council was more divided about what the CIC's mission ought to
be and who would lead the organization in what direction. To the extent that the
state actor has become more unified in the second phase (consolidated leadership by MOF and a consensus in the State Council on the CIC's primarily commercial international mission), the theory leads us to expect additional control.[25]
Although the organization chart and the backgrounds of senior leadership might
provide important information on the values for the Reporting Relationship IV
and the Unity of State IV, these are only some of the factors that must be considered when determining what drives the outcomes observed in the CIC case.
Understanding the CIC case more fully requires examining its funding sources
because these play an important role in shaping the CIC's own interests.

The China Investment Corporation: Financing Sources

The CIC was initially capitalized with $200 billion using three tranches of fixed-
coupon special treasury bonds denominated in RMB. The first tranche (ten-year,
paying a 4.3 percent coupon) was worth 600 billion yuan (about US$77 billion)
and was sold to the PBoC on August 28, 2007.[26] The second tranche was actually
a series of six "public" offerings of ten- and fifteen-year bonds with coupon rates
in the range of 4.41 to 4.68 percent. Most of these were (semiforced) purchases
by commercial banks for a total of about 199 billion yuan (about US$26 bil-
lion) between mid-September and mid-December 2007.[27] The third tranche
(fifteen-year, paying a 4.45 percent coupon) was worth 750 billion yuan (about
US$97 billion) and was sold to the PBoC (again via the Agricultural Bank of

China [ABC] intermediary) on December 10, 2007.[28] In addition to this initial $200 billion capitalization, it appears that the CIC has received an additional $30 billion "injection" from SAFE that was recorded as an "Other Liabilities" line item on the 2011 balance sheet.[29] The 2012 Corporate Overview states that the CIC has received a total of $49 billion in additional capital since it began.[30] This implies that the CIC received another $19 billion in 2012; presumably this was also reflected on the balance sheet since the "Other Liabilities" line item went up by roughly $20 billion between 2011 and 2012.

This financing structure has three implications. First, the investment returns that the CIC had to generate to make its scheduled interest payments were considerable. Not only did it face fixed debt payments on the original $200 billion regardless of the performance of its investment portfolio, but it was expected to invest in international assets while its debt payments were to be made in the appreciating RMB currency.[31] Even though the interest on this debt was only around 4.5 percent (considerably less than a 6 percent domestic inflation rate), by its own estimate the CIC needed to generate aggregate returns of about $14.6 billion per year, or about 7.3 percent on its $200 billion asset base, just to break even.[32] This financing structure suggests that the CIC was provided with a strong commercial incentive to focus on generating investment returns to meet its financial obligations. Second, by seeding the CIC in this way, the PBoC was able to soak up perceived excess liquidity from the system.[33] This suggests that to the extent the CIC will be used as an instrument for the state to pursue policy preferences, those priorities will be largely domestically oriented macroeconomic priorities as opposed to expansive foreign policy goals. Third, the PBoC was forced to bear the brunt of the currency risk, because the MOF could hold the RMB proceeds from the bonds for a period of time and collect the risk-free returns resulting from the RMB appreciation. As the counterparty to the transaction, this financing arrangement forced the PBoC to hold the relatively devalued foreign exchange.[34] This provides further indication that MOF was in the bureaucratic driver's seat.

This examination of the financing and management structure both suggested that MOF gained control of the CIC after an initial period when the state was divided across bureaucratic lines. Another implication of this data is that the CIC was constituted in such a way that it faced a number of incentives to perform as a commercially viable investment entity going forward. This commercial orientation was reinforced by a major institutional restructuring that took place in 2011. By 2015, the CIC was clearly segmented into three operational elements: Central Huijin, focusing on stewardship of the domestic banking assets; CIC Capital, focusing on the CIC's direct investments; and CIC International, covering the nondirect investment international activities.

On September 28, 2011, CIC International was created to take on all of the CIC's international investing mission, assets, personnel, and responsibilities. Effectively, this sectioned off Central Huijin and its domestically focused banking work from CIC's internationally oriented investing.[35] As its operational capabilities grew, CIC established offices in Hong Kong and Toronto.[36] CIC annual reports went to great lengths to stress the commercial nature of the CIC's (and later CIC International's) investing activities. There was a genuine effort to build up industry best practices regarding risk management, vetting of third-party asset managers, and the CIC's investment process. Each of these institutional changes reinforced the propensity for the CIC to act in a professional, commercial manner. Unfortunately, in January 2015, CIC Capital was established with what appears to be a decidedly less commercial mandate focusing more on "long-term financial returns" and promoting "international investment cooperation."[37] The holdings of the CIC provide another important source of information about its behavior and intentions. Let us now turn to a more detailed look at the CIC's investment activities.

The China Investment Corporation: Financing Uses and Activities

By far, the majority of the CIC's investments have been in the finance sector. Specifically, the capital raised by the initial bond issuances discussed above was put to use in three ways. These allocations serve as costly signals that reveal the CIC's goals and priorities and make for excellent empirical material for analyzing whether the CIC will be used as an instrument of China's economic statecraft. The largest allocation was used to acquire Central Huijin from the PBoC. Another large allocation was used to continue the recapitalization of the domestic banks (in this case, Agricultural Bank of China and China Development Bank). The final portion of the capital was designated to be used for investing abroad. Although the CIC would likely have preferred to have had a purely internationally oriented, exclusively commercial investment mandate, the central government directed the CIC to take on the mission of recapitalizing the banking sector.

In November 2007 the newly created CIC purchased Central Huijin from the PBoC for US$67 billion.[38] This valuation of Central Huijin was approximately at book value, which indicated a relative bargain for the Ministry of Finance and another bureaucratic setback for the PBoC. With the acquisition of Central Huijin, the CIC had used about one-third of its $200 billion of investment capital and picked up a considerable portfolio of China's domestic banking assets. Central

Huijin's holdings at the time included a 35.33 percent stake of the Industrial and Commercial Bank of China (ICBC) and a 70.69 percent stake (this included the 9.21 percent owned by China Jianyin) of the China Construction Bank (CCB).[39]

How did Central Huijin come to hold such a large stake in China's largest banks? Throughout the 1980s and early 1990s, China's state-owned banks underwrote many of China's inefficient and failing state-owned enterprises. By providing favorable loans and extending credit to these otherwise unsustainable enterprises, the banks eventually accumulated considerable portfolios of non-performing loans (NPLs) on their balance sheets. As these NPLs built up on the banks' balance sheets, fears of systemic banking collapse grew. With the 1998 creation of the CCP's Central Financial Work Commission after the East Asian financial crisis, the PBoC embarked on a plan to reduce the NPLs and gradually commercialize the banks. Doing this involved a complicated (and often non-transparent) reallocation of central bank assets and off-balance-sheet recapitalization vehicles. The CIC (and as of 2011, the Central Huijin portion of the CIC) inherited at least a majority (if not the entirety) of this function. This domestic banking sector recapitalization mission is reflected in the CIC's second large transactional allocation of its capital, to which we now turn.

In addition to the acquisition of Central Huijin's and China Jianyin's assets, the CIC was tasked to provide future capital injections to banks preparing to list their stock publicly as part of the ongoing recapitalization of China's banking system.[40] Also, in November 2007 the CIC announced it would provide US$67 billion to two of China's state-owned banks: the Agricultural Bank of China (ABC) and the China Development Bank (CDB).[41] In December of 2008, the CIC (via Central Huijin) injected US$19 billion into the ABC in preparation for its anticipated 2010 public listing. This resulted in ownership of ABC being split fifty-fifty between the Ministry of Finance and the CIC.[42]

Unlike ABC, which is the last of China's "Big Four" commercial banks to be readied for partial public listing, China Development Bank is a "policy bank," meaning that it functions as a legally mandated, explicit policy arm of the central government, rather than on a commercial basis.[43] At the end of 2007, Central Huijin provided US$20 billion capital to shore up the CDB's balance sheet.[44] Central Huijin provided an additional $21 billion at the end of 2008 as part of the CDB's reorganization into a joint stock company (i.e., no longer a policy bank). By 2009, Central Huijin owned 48.7 percent of the CDB, with the other 51.3 percent residing at the Ministry of Finance. By the end of 2012, the CIC's share had dropped slightly to 47.63 percent as a token portion of the CDB's equity was allocated to the NSSF.

The acquisition of Central Huijin and the recapitalization of ABC and the CDB account for approximately $135 billion of CIC's initial $200 billion capitalization, which would mean that only about $65 to $70 billion remained for the CIC to use as foreign investment capital.[45] The likelihood that this much smaller figure could have a significant, sustained foreign policy effect decreases considerably. Although the CIC's $200 billion top-line figure and billing as "China's Sovereign Wealth Fund" conjure up frightening possibilities of large waves of government-directed foreign investment, the $65–$70 billion figure represents considerably less international economic gunpowder that may be used to gain influence.

So what exactly does the CIC own and how are these assets structured? Although China Jianyin's purchase of US$3 billion of Blackstone during Blackstone's IPO and the CIC's acquisition of $5 billion of Morgan Stanley both attracted considerable public attention, these holdings represented a comparatively small fraction of the CIC's investments. The majority of the CIC's holdings have been concentrated in China's state-owned banks.[46] These fall into two groups: "commercial banks" and "policy banks." The commercial banks are the "Big Four." As of the December 31, 2008, the CIC (via Central Huijin) owned 67.5 percent of the Bank of China, 35.4 percent of ICBC (the other 35.4 percent is with MOF), 48.2 percent of China Construction Bank, and 50 percent of ABC (pending public listing).[47] As of December 2012, CIC's share of the Bank of China had increased slightly to 67.72 percent—perhaps the result of reinvested earnings—35.46 percent of ICBC, 57.21 percent of China Construction Bank, and 40.21 percent of ABC. These, in addition to its 47.63 percent ownership of China Development Bank, make up the majority of the CIC's assets.[48] Exactly how much of the CIC's asset base they make up is more difficult to determine. These assets are difficult to value since much of the equity is locked up in nontradable shares, but based on the $67 billion Central Huijin acquisition plus the roughly $60 billion of publicly announced capital that was invested into the ABC and CDB recapitalizations, these assets accounted for between one-half and two-thirds of the CIC's assets and clearly indicate a domestic banking-reform focus.[49] This portion of the CIC's work seems unlikely to generate serious security concerns since this capital is not directly involved in international activities.

The remaining third of the CIC's assets are those assets that have been earmarked for foreign investment. The investment of these assets seems to be the root cause of much of the trepidation surrounding the activities of the CIC. Based on my calculations, the total amount of capital CIC was originally looking to deploy internationally would have been between $45 and $70 billion. CIC president Gao Xiqing has since announced, though, that "CIC will invest between $80 billion and $90 billion outside China, up from its original target of deploying $66 billion overseas." Apparently, the additional funds stem from capital that had been earmarked for recapitalizing state-owned banks but was no longer necessary.[50] In addition, the higher figure most likely includes some portion of the CIC's early investment profits. Analysts opined that this amount would likely grow as the CIC demonstrated its ability to generate returns and would be given further allocations of state capital to manage.[51] This happened in December 2011 with an additional $30 billion "injection" into the CIC.[52] Based on the CIC's 2012 Annual Report, the CIC also received an additional $19 bil- lion by December 2012, bringing the CIC's total funding (excluding any retained earnings) to $249 billion. As mentioned above, the majority of this funding was directed domestically to recapitalize China's domestic banking system. But from the point of view of economic statecraft, the CIC's international investments are the activities most likely to generate security externalities. My estimates put that figure around $95 to $120 billion by December 2012, with the most likely esti- mate of internationally deployable capital at around $110 billion for the CIC.[53] As of year-end 2012, little of this capital base remained in cash.

CIC's Direct Investments

I suggest that this capital has been deployed by the CIC in two phases that cor- respond to the course of its institutional maturation. In the first phase, the CIC (and its institutional predecessors) enjoyed little state control and the CIC invested without much State Council oversight. Many of these investments were in the financial sector and often reflected the inexperience of government offi- cials unaccustomed to asset management.

The largest investment stake of this early period of the CIC was the $5 billion purchase of 9.9 percent of Morgan Stanley on December 19, 2007.[54] This CIC came under considerable criticism for its haphazard approach to this investment. "Before CIC committed about $5US billion for a 9.9 per cent stake in the US bank in 2007, it did not even bother to adhere to the international practice of hiring an independent financial adviser. Neither did Morgan Stanley."[55] Despite the significant stake, the CIC also waived any rights to a board seat or an active role in the management of the company. The CIC has continued to maintain its substantial ownership stake in Morgan Stanley, and when Morgan Stanley was reorganized as part of the bailout from the 2008 financial crisis, the CIC main- tained its stake.[56]

The next largest allocation of this early investment activity was the April 2008 announcement of the CIC's $3.2 billion placement with J. C. Flowers for 80 percent of a new private equity fund. The third-largest commitment was the May 2007 China Jianyin purchase of a $3 billion IPO stake of Blackstone. Recall that this stake (along with the other China Jianyin holdings, including the

43.35 percent ownership of CICC) came over to the CIC as part of the Central Huijin acquisition. The Blackstone and Morgan Stanley purchases were made partly with an eye toward learning more about international investing and internal due diligence and risk-management practices. In addition, these investments were seen as building strategic partnerships for the CIC as it entered into relatively uncharted waters for Chinese central bankers: large-scale asset management of foreign exchange reserves.[57] Because of the good deal of public and private criticism that CIC received about these investments, "CIC has been discouraged from taking more direct stakes, at least for the time being."[58] The only other major early purchases were the relatively small $200 million IPO purchases of VISA and the $100 million IPO stake in China Railroad Group, announced on November 21, 2007.[59] The Hong Kong Railroad buy was a largely symbolic gesture of support in line with what has become common practice for state-owned companies that are listing on major exchanges.[60]

Following these initial direct investments, which together amount to a little more than $16 billion, the CIC was still left with around $70 billion waiting to be invested overseas at the end of 2008 and the beginning of 2009.[61] Most of this would be quietly deployed via third-party asset managers, but a fraction of it was used to make an impressive number of "direct investments."

In the second phase of the CIC's investment activities, state control of the CIC was consolidated, with the Ministry of Finance playing the lead role. During this phase, the CIC engaged in a substantial deployment of its capital, often investing directly in assets that had been hit by the 2008 financial crisis. Although the CIC performed as a more closely state-controlled entity during this period, the CIC deliberately attempted to restrict its investment activity to a commercial orientation as part of its ongoing attempts to maximize its bureaucratic autonomy. Through increasing reliance on third-party asset managers, portfolio diversification management, and a strong commitment to risk management, the CIC has sought to consciously pre-empt state attempts to direct the CIC's investments toward political or strategic goals.

According to publicly available reports, the bulk of the CIC's international investment activity has been to place asset-management mandates with third-party commercial asset managers.[62] The majority of the CIC's pool of internationally deployable investment capital thus seems to have been competitively awarded to third-party investment managers across a range of asset types and investment strategies.[63] For example, there were reports that the CIC awarded Blackstone a $500 million mandate for its fund of funds asset-management business.

This kind of capital-management strategy adds a significant degree of commercialization to the CIC's activities and thereby reduces the potential for politicization. By putting its capital with third-party fund managers, as the NSSF had done, and essentially becoming a "fund of funds," the CIC effectively ties its hands by adding another layer of relationships between the state and the commercial actor in which the international third-party fund manager has the CIC as its principal. Introducing this additional layer of commercially oriented autonomy significantly increases the distance between the State Council and the commercial actors ultimately responsible for deploying the state's capital. This reduces the ease with which the CIC can be used as an instrument of economic statecraft. Put differently, it would become considerably more complicated to enforce effective state control over the CIC *and* for the CIC, in turn, to effectively ensure control over the third-party asset manager. If China decides to use third-party fund managers to manage the vast majority of its foreign-invested capital, this would be an important measure in insulating such activities from many security consequences that might otherwise result from state-sponsored investment flows on such a large scale.

From the perspective of economic statecraft, the CIC's "direct investments" pose a greater risk because these forms of investing do not enjoy the additional arms-length insulation of a third-party asset manager. Although the CIC's direct investments may only make up a third of its international capital base, given the significant size of the investment dollars in play, a closer look at the CIC's direct investments is warranted. The table below reflects the publicly disclosed transactions the CIC has made. For a more detailed description of these activities, see appendix 2.

Direct investments like these constitute the largest source of concern from a security externalities standpoint because they represent concentrated positions from which the CIC could influence the behavior of the invested enterprises.[64] Although it is too early to tell, these recent moves may be a bellwether of the CIC's more active deployment of capital overseas, particularly with concentrated positions in the sectors the CIC has designated as "strategic." These include energy, mining, infrastructure, and agriculture.[65]

There is some risk of strategic transfer given dual-use technologies and valuable knowledge that might be transferred as a result of acquisitions in sensitive security areas.[66] For instance, the information technology sector is the second most heavily weighted sector (after financials) in the CIC's equities portfolio, at 11.6 percent. In addition, there is evidence that China's state-sponsored investment activities are at least partly guided by a desire to secure what the Chinese government views as strategic access to resources and technologies.[67] Tapping Morgan Stanley's and Blackstone's institutional knowledge seemed to be at least part of the motivation behind the CIC's initial investments. In addition, the CIC's investments in Teck, PT Bumi, Noble Group, Nobel Oil Group, SouthGobi,

TABLE 10.1   China Investment Corporation's Disclosed Direct Investments

YEAR	TARGET	DATE	TRANSACTION AMOUNT (USD, UNLESS SPECIFIED)	ASSET	SECTOR
2007	Blackstone	May	$3 billion	9% equity	Financial
	Morgan Stanley	December	$5 billion	9.9% stock purchase	Financial
	VISA	November	$200 million	IPO	Financial
	China Railroad Group	November	$100 million	IPO	Rail industry
2008	J. C. Flowers	April	$3.2 billion	80% equity of fund	Financial
2009	Morgan Stanley	June	$1.2 billion	Common stock	Financial
	Teck Resources	July	$1.5 billion	Stock	Mining
	KazMunaiGas	July	$940 million	10.6% equity	Natural gas
	PT Bumi Resources	September	$1.9 billion	Debt	Coal
	Noble Group	September	$858 million	14.9% equity	Financial
	Nobel Oil Group	September	$270 million	45% equity	Oil and gas
	SouthGobi Energy Resources	November	$500 million	30-yr secured convertible debt	Coal
2010	AES	March	$1.58 billion	15% equity	Power and utility
	Chesapeake Energy	June	$200 million	Convertible shares	Oil and gas
	Peace River Oil Partnership	June	$329 million	45% joint venture	Oil and gas
	Penn West	June	$416 million	5% stock	Oil and gas
	BTG Pactual	December	$300 million	Equity	Finance
	BUMA	December	$73 million	8% stock	Mining
2011	Diamond S Shipping	July	$100 million	10.5% equity	Shipping
	AES-VCM Mong Duong Power	September	$93 million	19% equity	Power and utility
	Horizon Roads	October	$300 million AUS	13.84% equity	Infrastructure
	China Construction Bank	November	$1.75 billion	H-shares	Financial
	Shanduka	December	2 billion Rand	25.8% equity	Mining
	GCL-Poly Energy	December	$717 million	20.1% equity	Renewable energy
	Goodman Group	December	$200 million AUS	Stock	Real estate
	GDF Suez Exploration and Production	December	$3.15 billion	30% stake in gas exploration assets	Natural gas

YEAR	TARGET	DATE	TRANSACTION AMOUNT (USD, UNLESS SPECIFIED)	ASSET	SECTOR
	Atlantic LNG	December	$850 million	10% equity	Natural gas
2012	Thames Water Utilities	January	£276 million	8.68% equity	Utilities
	EP Energy	May	$300 million	9.9% equity	Oil and gas
	Polyus Gold	May	$424.5 million	5% equity	Gold
	Eutelsat Communications	June	€386 million	7% equity	Telecommu- nications
	Heathrow Airport Holdings	November	£450 million	10% equity	Infrastruc- ture
	Moscow Exchange	December	$187 million	4.58% share	Finance

This list may not be exhaustive as CIC is always careful to note that these public disclosures are "selected" direct investments, not necessarily all—nor even the largest—of the CIC's direct investment activities.

BUMA, Shanduka Group, Penn West, Peace River Oil Partnership, Chesapeake Energy, EP Energy, GDF Suez, and Atlantic LNG all share a resource-oriented dimension. The CIC could also potentially use its privileged access to gain technical expertise and build industry knowledge by participating as a shareholder in these businesses. Through shareholder meetings, industry conferences, proxy filings, and in some instances board seats, the CIC is able to build human capital, skills, industry expertise, and insider knowledge.[68] In fact, it would be hard for the CIC to be a smart investor *without* learning about the businesses and industries in which these portfolio companies operate.[69] If the CIC were really concerned with limiting its potential security externalities, we would see a strong preference for international third-party asset managers and virtually no direct investments managed in-house. But given the massive expansion of the CIC's in-house investment staff and the CIC's intent to conduct direct investments in "strategic" sectors, one suspects this will not be the case.[70] As a result, the potential for concerns over security externalities will remain hanging over the head of the CIC.

Such concerns about strategic transfers will be even more justified if the CIC shifts to a more active investment style or if it leverages its unique status to "create value" in its holdings (that is, facilitate deals for its portfolio companies, fund promising investment technologies, direct lucrative market opportunities in China's developing market toward portfolio partners, etc.). This sort of "value creation" is precisely what many strategic private equity investment funds do, and there seems to be little outside constraint on the CIC's ability to eventually do the same. Even if the CIC initially starts down this path out of a purely commercial orientation, it is a short leap from there to outright economic statecraft, particularly given the institutional context of China's sovereign wealth funds.

The CIC's Mandate and Coding the DV for the CIC Case Study

The above examination of the CIC's assets indicates that the majority of its capital has been dedicated to recapitalizing China's domestic banking sector. The portion of assets that is available for international investment is the source of most of the international trepidation regarding possible security externalities. Of this capital base, the CIC's "direct investments" raise more concern than does its use of international third-party asset managers. Specifying the conditions under which the state is or is not able to direct the behavior of the CIC along foreign policy—as opposed to commercial—interests lies at the heart of whether China's state-directed investment is likely to be a matter of strategic concern.

To code the DV, we first need to identify the goals of the state and compare them to what the commercial actor does in practice. In this case study, factional frictions and bureaucratic battles prevented a clear, consistent set of the state's goals from being specified during the CIC's early days. Particular factions and bureaucratic interests would vie with each other for defining the goals of the "state" with respect to the CIC as a commercial agent of the state.[71] One vision of China's interests with respect to the CIC stressed the macroeconomic utility of the CIC. This group tended to stress the importance of a commercial orientation for the institution. The other perspective emphasized the larger national strategic interests of China and wanted to see the CIC actively supporting China's stated political goals and priorities. While this struggle was especially pitched early on in the process of creating the CIC, it now seems that many of these power struggles were resolved in favor of the MOF, particularly when it was backed by Wen Jiabao at the level of the State Council. As a result, I code this case as exhibiting a lack of state control in the initial period. Since about mid-2008, however, MOF had increasingly been consolidating its power. The result was that by the end of 2008, the state was largely unified and control was present. Thus, for the post-2008 CIC case, I code the DV as exhibiting state control.

The CIC's initial mandate reflected the internecine power struggle that characterized the CIC's formation.[72] This mandate had three different components. First, as is evidenced by its asset allocation up to that point, the CIC has been primarily tasked with completing the recapitalization, limited privatization, and ongoing management of China's state-owned banks.[73] The government had already decided that a portion of its excess reserves would be used to recapitalize the domestic banking sector, which was on unstable grounds because of the bad lending policies the banks had. Interestingly, these loans were provided to otherwise insolvent and inefficient state-owned enterprises. Since the government did not want these firms to collapse (for fear of rising unemployment and a lack of an alternative social welfare safety net to the *danwei*), it leaned on the banks to extend credit. The result was a portfolio of nonperforming loans that later required bank recapitalizations. As per the central government's wishes, the CIC continued to play an important role in recapitalizing the domestic banks.

The second main goal of the CIC was to provide a vehicle for China to diversify its highly concentrated holdings of US-dollar-denominated government debt. The CIC was tasked with managing an important part of the diversification strategy for China's excess foreign reserves. Due the relatively low yield on US treasuries, China sought to improve the returns on a portion of its foreign exchange reserves. Indeed, as noted earlier, the origins of the CIC can be traced in part to the Ministry of Finance critiquing the PBoC's management of the foreign exchange reserves.[74] Although a portion of these reserves were used to recapitalize China's domestic banks, the rest of the capital was to be invested abroad. How these investments were to be made (whether on a commercial or political basis) became an important bone of contention.

The final (initially contested and since repudiated) mandate of the CIC was to support the outward expansion of Chinese firms.[75] Traditionally, China's state-owned banks served as dispersing conduits for state-directed capital allocation (for example, CCB specialized in project financing while the ABC provided credit to the agricultural sector). There have been suggestions that the National Development and Reform Council (NDRC) and several large state-owned enterprises have pressured the CIC to continue to play such a role underwriting the international investments, acquisitions, and projects of China's SOEs as they go abroad.

To the extent the CIC can facilitate the economic activities that generate security externalities in line with China's objectives, it may be a useful agent for furthering China's strategic interests. Activities like underwriting acquisitions of strategic assets abroad, subsidizing militarily significant firms and industries, or using CIC's investment clout to lean on holdings or potential partners to cooperate with China's national interests are just some of the ways one could imagine the CIC could play a constructive role in furthering China's strategic interests. To the extent the CIC operates as an independent, commercially driven entity with a significant distance between itself and the central government (or even better, between the CIC's overseas third-party asset managers and the central government), it will be difficult to use the CIC as a tool of China's foreign policy. Such a commercially oriented firm would mainly consider an investment's potential for return rather than its strategic significance.

In an effort to directly address international concerns stemming from Chinese government involvement in international investment, CIC leaders have gone to great pains to publicly commit themselves to a purely commercial set of goals. For instance, Wang Jianxi (then chairman of China Jianyin and later the CIC's chief risk officer) stated on September 10, 2007, "The mission for this company is purely investment-return driven."[76] On the day the CIC was created, Yang Qingwei (formerly NDRC's director general of the Department of Investment, then CIC's deputy chief investment officer) claimed, "The company's principal purpose is to make profits."[77] CIC chairman and CEO Lou Jiwei has also consistently emphasized the commercial nature of CIC's activities: "We will adopt a long-term and prudent investment principle and a safe, professional portfolio strategy that adapts to market changes, which will put emphasis on a rational match of returns and risks."[78] Such public statements seemed designed to both reassure nervous host nations about the CIC's investment presence in their markets as well as reinforce Lou Jiwei's vision of the CIC's commercially driven mission, free from the interference of noncommercial interests. Many of the CIC officials' statements have sought to explicitly address sensitive areas of international concern. For example, Lou originally indicated that the CIC would not invest in infrastructure, while the vice minister of finance, Li Yong, committed not to make acquisitions in foreign airlines, telecommunications, or oil companies.[79] Although subsequent direct investments have shown how fragile such reassurances can be, these statements signified the CIC's intent to be a largely commercially driven institution. Perhaps more importantly, their public nature signified the consolidation of the CIC under a leadership that sought to publicly commit itself to a commercial as opposed to a political agenda.

In sum, the state goals were not unified initially in this case study because of the factions and bureaucratic divisions among competing domestic financial governmental institutions. Without a coherent, unified set of goals from the state, it was difficult to exercise effective state control over the CIC. Once MOF had consolidated its power over the CIC, it was able to shape and manage the CIC's agenda, processes, and activities. The commercial actor in this analysis had four key goals: recapitalize the banks, diversify China's foreign exchange holdings, and support outward expansion of Chinese SOEs (though this seemed to have been later dropped as part of CIC's mission). In addition to these three, the CIC must continuously struggle to prove its ongoing viability as a new bureaucratic institution. Such new entities are subject to rivals' efforts to "kill the baby in the cradle."[80] The commercially oriented vision for the CIC was useful for consolidating MOF control and marginalizing those factions that advocated a stronger role for the CIC as a strategic tool for pursuing noncommercial state objectives. This fourth goal of institutional survival is perhaps the most important goal for the CIC.

As evidenced by the allocation of the CIC's capital, its management, and its investment activities, it seems that the CIC was set on a largely commercially oriented path that emphasized its task of managing a portion of China's excess foreign exchange reserves. An examination of the evidence on the CIC's goals suggests that while state control may have been lacking in the early stages of the CIC's existence, processes and institutions have since been put into place that facilitate ongoing, limited principal-agent control in the future. The CIC will also likely take the political preferences of the senior leadership into consideration as it executes its capital allocation duties. This is reflected in the CIC's reporting structure, which ultimately is directly accountable to the State Council under Li Keqiang. Finally, its investment decision process suggests that large investments will need direct State Council level approval before they can proceed. The CIC today seems to be largely fulfilling the interests of the State Council, which is to conduct commercially oriented diversification of China's foreign exchange reserves.

That said, the CIC has taken a number of steps to maximize its own agency and provide it with some room to pursue its own bureaucratic interests and to maintain its freedom of action as much as possible. Although this is unlikely to result in an outright loss of state control, the CIC's pursuit of a more commercial orientation would make it increasingly difficult for the government to effectively wield the CIC as a political instrument of China's foreign policy. The next section moves beyond the question of whether the state has been successful at controlling the CIC to a closer examination of the factors that facilitate or hinder state control of the CIC.

Evaluating the CIC

As discussed above, evidence from the CIC case suggests that in the early days of the CIC, there was relatively little state control. As the CIC has matured, there has been more evidence of state control. What explains this variation? In this section, we examine the IVs presented in chapter 2 in light of the CIC case.

In the CIC case, the state was initially divided across bureaucratic and factional lines, which provided the commercial actor with an opportunity to play one portion of the state against the other to maximize the commercial actor's own preferences. It is mainly because of the divided state that we observe the lack of state control in the early days of the CIC. The Ministry of Finance's commercially oriented vision for the CIC, however, won out at the State Council, and as a result the state principal became more unified. The CIC's early investments provide evidence of free-wheeling deal makers exercising considerable freedom of action. In the Morgan Stanley investment, the commercial actors took initiative and acted on their own interests. Likewise, the Blackstone purchase is also often cited as a case where state control was absent.[81] In both instances, the government was divided among competing visions for the CIC (or its predecessor institutions).

There were numerous reports of a bureaucratic struggle between the Ministry of Finance, the PBOC, and the NDRC for control over the CIC. These battles were particularly pitched during discussions regarding the CIC's design and creation.[82] While the PBoC under Zhou Xiaochuan had generally pushed for greater central bank independence and a liberal economic orientation (both of which would enhance its bureaucratic stature), the NDRC sought to preserve its own power within the government bureaucracy by resisting moves to limit the state-directed allocation capital and the NDRC's ability to "guide" the economy. Part of the critique over generating a higher return on China's foreign exchange reserves, which led to the creation of the CIC, was an effort by the Ministry of Finance to wrest the management of the banking sector away from the PBoC.[83] Before the banking recapitalizations of the early 2000s, the MOF enjoyed unchallenged control of China's banking sector. As the PBoC began to tap foreign exchange funds to recapitalize the banks and prepare them for eventual public listings, the PBoC increasingly gained control over more and more of China's financial sector. The MOF resented this erosion of its influence and sought to regain control over China's banks. By late 2008, this strategy had largely worked and the MOF once again controlled, either directly or indirectly (largely via the CIC), almost all the state's banking assets. The MOF was in the driver's seat at the CIC, with a clear chain of control led by the State Council.[84] The unification of the state thus enabled the political leadership to exercise more effective control over the CIC.[85] With the promotion of Lou Jiwei to minister of finance in 2013, the leadership of the CIC began turning over. Given the prevalence of Jiang Zemin–affiliated leaders in senior party posts alongside Xi Jinping, it will be interesting to see if the CIC tacks back toward the NDRC's original preference for the organization: playing a strategic role in supporting Chinese state priorities.[86]

The goals of the CIC largely reflected the goals of the factional forces within the state leadership. In this sense, there was relative compatibility on the Goals IV. Because the state itself was initially divided over its vision for the CIC, however, we observe that the commercial actor had some space to emphasize and define its own interpretation of what its goals ought to be. Initially, the divisions at the top made state control more difficult. As the CIC became institutionally consoli-

THE CHINA INVESTMENT CORPORATION

dated, the more commercially oriented mission took on a more dominant role. This consolidation anchored the CIC to more explicit, commercially oriented goals. Although this consolidation would seem to facilitate greater state control in the future, the commercial nature of these goals limits the instrumental usefulness of the CIC as an agent to support the strategic foreign policy preferences of the state. The CIC was established to help diversify China's foreign exchange reserves. That goal does not conflict with the CIC's desire to earn a respectable rate of return on its portfolio. Although the CIC's goals of establishing itself as a viable bureaucratic player entail less than national-level priorities, these more narrow bureaucratic interests do not necessarily undermine the state's macroeconomic goals for the CIC. The most divisive source of goal friction revolved around the CIC's using its resources to provide additional support for national Chinese strategic interests. Although this goal was discussed early in the CIC's bureaucratic life, it was resisted by the CIC leadership and is no longer officially a part of CIC's mandate. As discussed above, such "national" goals were largely the product of a divided leadership that was later consolidated around commercial goals that were in line with the CIC's own institutional interests.

From a Relative Resources IV perspective, the CIC's financial expertise provided it with a considerable advantage. The state was dependent on the CIC to source investment opportunities, conduct due diligence, negotiate investment terms, and execute capital placements. In all these matters, the CIC was working with a relative information asymmetry that undermined state control and maximized the CIC's discretion. In addition, because there was a lack of financial expertise at the highest levels of government (most of that expertise was in the commercial actor), the state was forced to rely on and trust the commercial actor.[87]

The case of the CIC was probably best categorized as an "oligopolistic" market structure because the only real alternative to the CIC for investing China's foreign exchange reserves was SAFE.[88] As mentioned in the SAFE case study, the CIC was created partly with a view toward generating an alternative commercial actor for managing some of China's foreign exchange reserves.[89] In this sense, SAFE and the CIC are two semicompetitive investment arms of the state and thus the Market Fragmentation IV has a slightly competitive value. The bureaucratic rivalry that simmered between the PBoC and the MOF seems to have spilled over and was being continued between SAFE and the CIC.[90] Such bureaucratic competition facilitates effective state control because it provides the state with an alternative commercial actor to execute its wishes. The existence of an alternative commercial actor waiting in the wings that may be more willing to do the wishes of the state lends a certain amount of discipline to the state-CIC relationship (just as it did to the state-SAFE relationship).

In terms of the Reporting Relationship IV, the CIC, like all the commercial actors examined in these two chapters, is a wholly owned, managed and operated government entity.[91] The CIC's organizational structure was loosely modeled on the NSSF. It, too, was governed by a board of directors that was responsible to the State Council. In turn, the State Council can nominate the chairman of the CIC. All of these factors favor state control over the CIC. The institutional architecture seems to suggest that the CIC will be likely be subject to continued state control. This is especially true for large, high-profile investments. At the same time, the entity also seems to want to fight for its autonomy by stressing the commercial orientation of its activities and thus the need for the state to rely on the CIC's professional judgment regarding its activities. Moreover, the relatively scarce technical subject matter expertise within the senior ranks of the party provides the CIC considerable weight.

The coding of the theory's independent variables for the early and later CIC cases is summarized in tables 10.2 and 10.3.

TABLE 10.2   Early CIC Case Summary Table

	IV CODING	EVIDENCE	DV PREDICTION	DV OUTCOME
Unity of state	Initially divided bureaucratically and factionally	Competing bureaucratic interests: MOF vs. PBoC vs. NDRC; competing personal factions: Wen Jiabao's protégés vs. Zhu Rongji's vs. Jiang Zemin's	Control unlikely	State control was limited during periods of divided state as seen by early CIC behavior and investments
Goals	Divergent	Goals are defined by state; divergence over CIC independence and commercial incentive vs. supporting foreign policy goals and/ or the outward expansion of Chinese firms	Control unlikely	Given divided state, the CIC's goals did correspond to some elements of the state's vision, but there was enough contestation to enable the CIC to carve out its own institutional identity

	IV CODING	EVIDENCE	DV PREDICTION	DV OUTCOME
Market structure	Oligopolistic	Mainly bureaucratically competitive with SAFE and to a lesser degree SS Fund, but as state entity, the CIC faces limited real commercial competition	Control likely	State control was not strong during this period suggesting that the divided state was more important in explaining the outcome than the competitive dynamic with SAFE
Reporting relationship	Fragmented and poorly defined	Precursor entities were loosely supervised with few investment processes in place	Control unlikely	State control was weak as expected given the divided state
Relative resources	Asymmetric in favor of CIC	Financial/investing expertise: state almost completely reliant on talent at the CIC. Budget Endowment and Personnel count: initially small but "entrepreneurial" vs. State Council's overstretched and nontechnical staff	Control unlikely	State control weak as evidenced by early investments in Morgan Stanley and Blackstone when resources were almost entirely concentrated at the CIC (and its pre-cursors, Central Huijin and Jianyin)

TABLE 10.3 Late CIC Case Summary Table (2008–2012)

	IV CODING	EVIDENCE	DV PREDICTION	DV OUTCOME
Unity of state	Unified (weak?)	State principal was consolidated under Wen's State Council institutionalization of CIC with clear reporting & commercial goals for CIC; MOF now seemed to be dominant (still have some factional and bureaucratic undercurrents but no longer seem to be defining feature); no evidence of municipal/provincial centers of authority as the CIC is a central government organization	Control likely But potentially weak going forward	State control was institutionalized as evidenced by risk-management and review procedures; institutionalization and reporting structure might shift toward weak control if post-Wen MoF consolidation of the CIC breaks down; also divided State Council might lead to a divided principal again
Goals	Compatible	Goals are defined by state; CIC mission was largely resolved in favor of commercialization; both agent and principal goals were able to be achieved	Control likely	CIC publicly committed to commercial orientation; supportive State Council affirmed the CIC's goals with Articles of Association; generated institutional procedures for ensuring commercial investment behavior
Market structure	Oligopolistic	Mainly bureaucratically competitive with SAFE and to a lesser degree SS Fund, but as state entity, the	Control likely	State control seemed to have been implemented, but around relatively benign commercial

	IV CODING	EVIDENCE	DV PREDICTION	DV OUTCOME
		CIC faced limited real competition		goals; future leadership and factional balance likely to determine whether this commercial orientation continues
Reporting relationship	Direct for large activities; indirect for day-to-day	Government ownership: direct and complete. State management: indirect via CIC senior management with only limited (also governmental) "independent" oversight; as CIC commercializes, expect reporting relationship to become more indirect as use of international third-party managers expands	Weak control	State control likely as a result of effective and clear reporting structure that enabled oversight/ political interference in high-profile cases but largely meant that the CIC operated autonomously in the NSSF model; commercial orientation and third-party mandates
Relative resources	Asymmetric in favor of CIC	Financial/investing expertise: state almost completely reliant on talent at the CIC. Budget endowment and personnel count: empirics are unclear, although the CIC's permanent staff and HQ suggest advantage over State Council's overly taxed management resources	Control unlikely	State sought to overcome asymmetry through institutionalization of reporting, processes, and senior leadership appointments; a growing cadre of technical expertise in the upper echelons of the CCP over time

The CIC as an Instrument of Chinese Economic Statecraft

Are there legitimate economic statecraft fears surrounding the CIC's activities? The answer turns on whether the CIC operates on a commercial basis. To the extent the CIC can increase the distance between itself and the state, it will be less easily controlled or used to support the political, foreign policy, or noncommercial objectives of Beijing. Currently, the CIC goes to great pains to ensure that it is driven purely by commercial interests, as that orientation maximizes the CIC's own narrow preferences. The reality, however, is that the CIC controls a large pile of money that has been earmarked to be invested, that is, allocated by the state. The natural result is that there will be competing claims about how that allocation happens. One might expect that competition to intensify as the quantities of capital to be invested increase and factional equilibria are destabilized by personnel changes resulting from the 18th Party Congress and Wang Qishan's anticorruption drive.

Several structural elements make politicization not an unlikely outcome in the future. First is the mixed institutional structure of the management team. While the CIC seemed to be MOF-dominated from 2008 to 2012, there are other voices inside and outside the room (and even upstairs). Second, the CIC must still vet its largest investments with the State Council, which then has the ability to exercise control over the CIC's behavior. There is also some danger that the CIC will be pressured into supporting China's larger national interests. Although increasing professionalization reinforces greater commercialization and moves the CIC away from acting as a policy arm of the central government, China's institutional memory of similar state financing policy mechanisms and the statutory design of the CIC both leave open the possibility of the state's leveraging its greater control over the CIC to pursue noncommercial goals.

This question may very well be resolved by two key dynamics. The first is the degree to which the CIC is able to institutionally lock in a purely commercial orientation. To accomplish this, it is critical that the recent efforts to improve transparency be continued. A lack of transparency hurts efforts to place the CIC on a purely commercial footing because secrecy allows for more effective politicization and organizational hijacking. The CIC's adoption of (and leadership role in) the Santiago Protocols on sovereign wealth funds and the CIC's continued publication of a transparent annual report are two important steps in improving the CIC's organizational autonomy and limiting the likelihood that CIC will be used as an instrument of economic statecraft. Nontransparent operations strengthen the hand of hard-line NDRC officials who would prefer to hold onto to the reins of the economy in order to direct plan-based, strategic allocations of capital. In order for the CIC to solidify its own bureaucratic autonomy, it ought to move toward locking in transparency and commercially oriented independence from noncommercially motivated political interests. If the State Council seeks to provide international reassurance to the host nation recipients of China's outward direct investment, it ought to provide the CIC with an arms-length, insulated, commercial space in which to pursue profitable returns for the state.

The second key dynamic to watch is the factional struggle for power, in particular the competition between domestic political factions that favor a plan-oriented, government-directed strategic approach to China's economic development and the more liberalizing, reform-oriented elements of China's leadership. If reform-oriented, commercially driven interests remain at the helm, it is likely that the CIC will continue to liberalize and effectively increase the distance between the state and the commercial actor. If statist interests are ascendant in the senior ranks of the party, the institutional structure and China's history of state-directed central planning and capital allocation are conducive to permitting the CIC to be used to serve the foreign policy interests of the state. With an increasing base of capital to be invested abroad, the potential dollar figures at stake are large (though not as large thus far as some may have feared) and have the potential to generate significant impact. Having this capital directed in a noncommercial manner could raise significant strategic concerns for other countries. There are some indications that reform-minded, liberalizing elements within China's central leadership have been forced to retrench in light of the 2008 economic crisis and the subsequent discrediting of a more liberalized economic development model. If the CIC veers from its current commercializing path, the likelihood of the CIC being used to pursue strategic national interests will increase substantially.

This chapter set out to determine whether the CIC posed a strategic security threat as an instrument of Chinese economic statecraft. While this chapter's analysis suggests that the CIC is capable of producing security externalities, the CIC's current development path indicates a relatively commercially motivated orientation that should limit the strategic consequences of its activities. A close inspection of the CIC's resource allocation shows that only a portion of its total capitalization has been dedicated to foreign investment, with the rest being used primarily to reorganize the domestic Chinese banking system. This fundamentally limited the size of the CIC's internationally deployed capital, thus also limiting its strategic impact. Perhaps more importantly, evidence suggests that the CIC's current development path puts it on a commercial footing that helps to limit the degree to which the state can control its investment as part of an economic statecraft strategy. Improvements in transparency, an incentive structure that supports a commitment to commercial operations, and increasing reliance on third-party mandates for foreign capital allocation all suggest that the CIC will not be an effective tool for achieving China's foreign policy interests.

Several characteristics of the CIC case study suggest it may be difficult to use the CIC as an instrument of economic statecraft. First, the CIC was at the epicenter of a bureaucratic struggle for control and influence over China's finances. As a result of this divided state during the CIC's early operations, state control was weakened and the CIC enjoyed a good deal of relatively independent agency in conducting its affairs. Once more centralized control was consolidated, the ability of the state to direct the behavior of the CIC was strengthened. By this time, however, a consensus was reached at the State Council regarding the CIC's commercial mandate, limiting the likelihood that the CIC would be asked to act as an instrument of China's economic statecraft. Second, the CIC leadership has a strong incentive to carve out a bureaucratic living space for its existence as a new financial institution charged with investing China's assets (particularly in light of SAFE, which already had the mission of managing China's foreign exchange reserves). This led to a preference for professionalism, autonomy, and a strong commercial orientation, all of which undermined tight state control. Third, the CIC was led by a considerable coterie of senior CCP financial talent. The senior administration of the CIC included some of the brightest financial stars of the Communist Party leadership. This talent pool has helped skew the Relative Resources IV in favor of the CIC, affording it additional room to avoid tight state control.

Of course, the CIC remains an arm of the state responsible for investing billions of dollars around the world, so the door remains open to direct political state control over the CIC. If ideas favoring increased roles for the state in the management of China's economic activity gain popularity among China's leadership, the CIC will likely come under increasing pressure to act in support of national objectives, even if they have little commercial merit. Under these conditions, the formal reporting structure and processes of the CIC's institutional architecture would make it difficult for the CIC to avoid political interference. Although the 2012 CIC leadership seemed to be effectively consolidated under the influence of a reformist-oriented segment of the Ministry of Finance, there are few permanent fixtures of the CIC that guarantee that its future investment behavior will not stray from a strictly commercial orientation. In addition, SAFE's direct investment of a small portion of its considerably larger foreign exchange reserves provided the government with an alternative commercial actor that is capable of performing CIC's work should CIC prove unwilling to abide by the government's preferences. This competitive dynamic also suggests that CIC might be more easily brought to heel to do the state's bidding.

Despite a good deal of initial trepidation over the Chinese government's ability to use the China Investment Corporation (CIC) for strategic purposes, the evidence suggests that using the CIC as an effective instrument of economic statecraft may be more difficult than some fear. This chapter's exploration of the empirics provides reason for optimism regarding the CIC's future direction. Although it is still much too early to draw definitive conclusions, the CIC may be on a path of professionalization and commercialization. The increasing distance between the state and the commercial actor makes it increasingly unlikely that the CIC can be used as an effective tool to realize Chinese foreign policy objectives. The CIC is unlikely to constitute an economic statecraft threat assuming that it continues to evolve in the direction of its current commercial orientation. At the same time, there are a number of aspects of the CIC case that suggest caution may yet be warranted. The framework presented in chapter 2 provides a useful analytical approach to monitor and assess developments in the evolutionary path of the CIC and other commercial actors that might be used as tools of economic statecraft.

CONCLUDING IMPLICATIONS

What Was Learned from the Cases?

Stepping back from the specifics of each case, we can distill a few observations about Chinese economic statecraft as well as economic statecraft more generally. First, state control is an essential and often overlooked prerequisite of economic statecraft. Most of the work on economic statecraft in international relations has either neglected this issue through an overly narrow focus on state actors as the units of analysis or has simply assumed away the state's ability to control the behavior of commercial actors. Both approaches are problematic, and this book serves to fill this gap in our understanding of economic statecraft. By problematizing this part of the mechanism (control), we get a more accurate accounting of Chinese economic statecraft, both successes and failures. Without state control, commercial actors may certainly still engage in behavior that carries with it strategic ramifications. For example, China National Petroleum Corporation's early forays into Sudan generated unwelcome diplomatic and strategic liabilities for China. But the state must be able to control or direct the activities of commercial actors to harness economic power into an effective tool to realize foreign policy objectives. Such was the case when SAFE was used as an instrument of economic statecraft to help persuade Costa Rica to shift its diplomatic recognition from the ROC to the PRC or when Chinalco prevented foreign iron ore supply consolidation. In order for economics to be used as an active instrument of statecraft, nations must be able to control or direct the behavior of the economic actors that carry out the international economic activity.

Second, state unity is the most important determinant accounting for when state control is likely. The theory presents five factors that determine when state control is more or less likely. Of these factors, state unity is the most critical for state control because without it, the state cannot control actors. Of all the cases in this book, not one exhibited state control of commercial actors in the absence of a unified Chinese state. A state that is divided often cannot even agree on what is in "China's" best national interests, let alone pursue those interests via economic channels of national power.[1] These cases suggest that state unity is fundamental for state control, which in turn is a prerequisite for economic statecraft.

If state unity was the most important independent variable, the balance of relative resources seemed to be the least significant of the five. In both Taiwan cases and the Rio Tinto case, this factor appeared not to have played a decisive role in explaining the outcome. That said, the research design never intended to rigorously identify the relative importance across the five IVs. Rather, the case-work was designed to test whether the causal mechanisms operated the way that the theory suggested they should. The observation that the balance of resources seemed to less frequently be a significant driver is simply an assessment that seemed to emerge from the empirics of these cases. It may very well prove to be anomalous to these particular cases. On the other hand, it might suggest that this variable could productively be dropped from future explanations of state control.

Another observation that might be made across these cases involves what I have termed the "king-making" capabilities of the state. In countries like China, where government support and positive relationships with officials are critical for commercial ventures to succeed, there appears to be another arrow in the quiver for state control. By backing only those commercial actors that curry favor or prove amenable to advancing government agendas, the state is able to at least partially compensate for the problematic principal-agent challenges stemming from a fragmented market structure. Initially, the theory suggested that a state would have a difficult time monitoring and enforcing compliance with state goals in a highly fragmented and competitive sector. But China's "king-making" capabilities allow it to bestow favor on those commercial actors that prove eager to pursue state goals. The state simply needs to let its preferences be known and those same competitive dynamics will drive some firms to actively court state favor as a key competitive edge. This dynamic seemed to play out in the Taiwan interest transformation and SAFE cases. In addition to bestowing positive favors, the state's "king-making" capabilities can also actively discriminate against commercial actors. By publicly identifying and punishing high-profile offenders as it did in the latter episodes of coercive leverage against the *taishang*, China sends powerful signals to commercial actors. When the state plays such an important, direct role in the domestic political economy, "king-making" capabilities provide an important element of economic statecraft.

These types of dynamics extend well beyond the cases covered in this book. Google's high-profile departure from mainland China was driven largely by its frustration at what it found to be an unfair playing field in which the state tilted the competitive environment in favor of domestic rivals like Baidu. More recently, China's enforcement of its Anti-Monopoly Law has received attention for allegations that it has been used to unfairly target foreign multinationals.[2] This behavior helped to contribute to the pessimistic views of a 2014 American Chamber of Commerce in China survey of its members in which 60 percent of the respondents felt that foreign business was less welcome in China.[3] A similar survey from the US-China Business Council found that "86 percent of firms surveyed expressed some level of concern about competition enforcement activities in China."[4] Whether or not foreign firms were being unfairly targeted, the perception by foreign multinationals was that they were no longer welcome in China. "Although foreign companies including Microsoft, Qualcomm and Daimler have in recent months been subjected to surprise raids, lengthy investigations and increasing fines by China's government antitrust enforcers, they have had little recourse against such actions."[5] Episodes like these illustrate the ongoing importance of Chinese economic statecraft. In the coming decades, there will likely be no shortage of material for scholars of economic statecraft to study and dissect as we seek to enhance our understanding of this important phenomenon in international relations. While this book may be the first, it will certainly not be the last word on the subject of Chinese economic statecraft.

Policy Implications

This project grew out of real-world questions about how China actually exercises its international economic power under contemporary conditions of globalization. Not surprisingly, the work carries important policy implications. First, there is a set of policy implications for China and the world beyond its borders concerning China's reform and liberalization, its rise, and its use of economic power. Second, there are more narrow, case-specific policy implications that are idiosyncratic to the particular empirical contexts examined in this book.

Big-Picture Implications

There are two main policy implications for China stemming from this research. First, *China must reform to reassure*. States are worried about the strategic consequences of China's growing power.[6] Such fears are particularly acute in the economic and security realms. To what extent will China be able to leverage its growing economic clout to pursue strategic objectives abroad? This research suggests that the answer lies in the ability of the state to control the behavior of economic actors. To the extent that the Chinese state continues to hold (or expands) its active management of China's economy and is able to direct the behavior of economic actors, it will be more able to engage in economic state-craft. Conversely, observers of China should be reassured by efforts to extract the state from its active roles in directing China's economic activity. Explicit efforts to limit the role of the state in controlling or directing the activities of economic actors should go a long way toward limiting the potential for China to leverage its economic power for noncommercial goals.

This finding carries important implications linking China's domestic political economic reform effort to China's rise on the international stage. If China wishes to allay concerns over its use of economic tools of statecraft in the international realm, China must continue to increase the distance between the state and the economic actors at home. For the past thirty-five years, China has been engaged in a massive reform and liberalization effort that has fundamentally reoriented its economy (and society). This effort has generated considerable economic growth and unlocked Chinese potential that had lain dormant for more than 150 years. The Opening Up and Reform period has fundamentally been about extracting the state from the active direction of China's economy, instituting market-based reforms, and freeing up the productive capacity in China. An important impli-cation of this book is that China ought to continue liberalization and ongoing economic reform efforts. I argue that for China to best realize its own national interests, it must continue on the path of economic liberalization and integration into the global economic order as the most efficient and productive (and by exten-sion the most stabilizing) path toward great power status. A natural outgrowth of this transformation should be a reduction in the capabilities of (and the tempta-tion for) the state to direct the behavior of commercial actors toward strategic objectives. The market mechanism should indeed play a larger role in China's economy. As China continues to liberalize and reform its economy, traditional avenues of direct state control seem likely to weaken. Massive, state-controlled finance entities like SAFE, the CDB, and the CIC, however, provide a tempting lever for exerting continued state influence over the conduct of strategic com-mercial activities. The last cluster of cases helps to illuminate how institutional design can facilitate state control or—perhaps more importantly—can credibly tie the hands of the state in a manner that can reassure wary partner nations of an *absence* of strategic state control. This holds out the possibility for a rising China to assuage a nervous world concerned about Chinese economic statecraft.

Such institutional designs can effectively "spike the guns" of economic statecraft by deliberately exacerbating the principal-agent challenges that would be facing a state that potentially sought to control economic actors.

In the wake of the 2008 financial crisis, classical liberal ideas of economics in which the state plays a minimal role in the economy fell out of favor. This sentiment was particularly pervasive in China, where a relatively mild dip was followed by a rapid recovery. This prompted some to view the financial crisis as hastening and affirming China's rise to great power status. By extension, China's resilience seemed to have reaffirmed the advantages of its blended economic model. Debunking the attractiveness of liberalization strengthened the case against further economic reform. A stall of the current reform effort and the government leadership deciding to maintain a heavy hand in guiding the economy would carry significant implications for China's economic power. An active role for government would imply that the state would more easily be able to direct China's economic power. As mentioned at the outset of this study, however, extensive state direction of the economy leads to long-run inefficiencies that would eventually limit China's "economic gunpowder." This is a key trend to watch in the future. Will China move forward and continue to reform and liberalize, or will it fall victim to the "middle income trap" under a hybrid model of state capitalism?

China's leadership ought to be aware that its rapid economic growth has also enabled a significant expansion of China's potential to use economic power to pursue its strategic goals. Slipping into mercantilist habits or defensive economic planning that seeks to extend and reassert state control over what are viewed as strategically vital sectors of China's economic landscape will lead other nations to (rightly) fear noncommercial motives behind China's growing economic presence in the world. Even if China does not intend to use its growing economic clout for strategic purposes, the outside world suspects the worst given existing perceptions of China's domestic political economy, particularly in the most strategically sensitive areas. The best way for China to reassure a nervous world and to lock in its own continued economic success is to institutionalize a more limited role for the state in directing and controlling commercial behavior. Continuing economic liberalization should result in China's commercial actors being motivated more by profit rather than by governmental directive. If these liberalization efforts stall and China becomes locked in some partial model of state capitalism, it may possess enough "economic gunpowder" to be dangerous while also enabling the state to retain the capabilities to direct that economic power.[7]

"Reforming to reassure" is likely the only real way for China to ingrain meaningful assurances that it will not seek to use its growing economic power to realize strategic objectives. To the extent China genuinely seeks to reassure the international community about its growing economic might, it must also proceed with the liberalization of its domestic political economy. Only by increasing the scope of unfettered commercial activities for China's economic actors and limiting the role of the state can China credibly commit to pursuing international economic interaction on purely commercial grounds. Such a path forward would have the added benefit of enhancing the long-term competiveness of China's emerging world-class firms by freeing them from distorting and distracting political objectives.[8]

This project makes explicit the links between China's domestic political economy and international economic power. Although a liberally oriented political economy may be less easily manipulated to achieve narrow political goals, it has proven to be the most powerful model for maximizing national economic productivity over the long run.[9] To the extent China's grand strategy relies on continued economic growth, the reform effort that has been responsible for unleashing its incredible economic potential ought to be deepened. In the process of removing the heavy hand of the state, China will also be able to reassure anxious partners that its growing economic power will be used to seek commercial rather than political gains.

A second policy implication flowing from this work is that *domestic battles over the future direction of China's political economy carry clear strategic implications in the international realm*. Actions that may be undertaken for purely domestic political reasons or narrow factional or ideological contests have real international repercussions for China. Even if policies within China are pursued for purely domestic or even localized political rationales, to the extent these stall liberalization efforts or otherwise enhance the role of the state in directing China's economy, they will feed into international fears of a rising China intent on using economic power to pursue its strategic objectives. It would not be a stretch of the imagination to see how interbureaucratic rivalries like those observed in the case of the CIC or interfactional competitions for influence could derail Chinese reform efforts or even enhance the ability of the state to control economic actors in certain strategic industries. Domestic political economic outcomes in China have strategic repercussions in the international realm. This international dimension will only increase as China takes on a more prominent role in international affairs.

Domestic Chinese elites may well be preoccupied with China's domestic challenges. There is certainly no shortage of them, and appropriate solutions are likely going to be hotly contested issues in Chinese domestic politics over the coming decade. Most of these political-philosophical battles will be played out on a domestic stage for a domestic audience. There will be fighting over the distribution of domestic costs and benefits. The outcomes of these battles will be driven primarily by domestic logics, but the international community will be watching. These ostensibly domestic political economic dynamics will have international consequences as the outcomes will determine the institutional shape and tenor of China's domestic preferences for years to come. These preferences, in turn, will be translated into national interests, which will eventually be pursued by China in the international system.

This book connects China's domestic political economy and domestic-level factors to China's international strategic security environment and the ability of China to use economics to influence outcomes on the international stage. By extension, I suggest that China's strategic international considerations also carry implications for China's domestic political economic reforms. Similarly, China's domestic political economic reforms have a bearing on China's international credibility. Seen in this light, China's domestic political economic reforms perform an important signaling function, communicating information about China's future economic statecraft capabilities and the general thrust of its broader intentions in the international system. Will China seek to become a revisionist great power intent on using economic tools of national power, or will China signal its intention to support a largely status quo international system predicated on commercial interests?

Case-Specific Implications

In addition to these large-scale policy implications concerning China and its position in the international system, there are particular policy implications that are grounded in the specific empirical contexts of the cases examined in this book. The analysis of China's "going out" strategy implies that the Chinese state *can* effectively coordinate its commercial actors' search for raw materials, but such coordination often requires high-level attention from senior leadership to overcome internal divisions within the Chinese state and information asymmetries between the state and the commercial actors conducting the economic activity. State control is thus unlikely to be consistent enough to adequately micromanage China's supply of raw materials. Rather, state influence is likely to be concentrated on the largest, most visible deals. China has embarked on a path of liberalization and commercialization. This transition is an ongoing process and ought to continue. As the state cedes greater and greater decision making to the commercial actors, the state will need to grow more comfortable with a market-based provision of goods and services to meet China's needs. This transition will likely be most difficult for those goods and services China considers to be "strategic." Failure to move toward more efficient market-based solutions, however, will likely result in long-term inefficiencies in exactly those areas that are most strategically sensitive for China. The most secure and reliable sources of strategic raw materials for China may be found in deep and liquid international commodity exchanges. These may also ultimately be the most affordable, stable, efficient, and sustainable mechanism for supplying China's needs. Paradoxically, developing such a secure position for China will likely require that the state become comfortable with letting go of its direct involvement in these "strategic" sectors and allowing the market to play a greater role.

China will likely broaden and deepen its engagement with Taiwan to create vested interests in Taiwan favoring amicable cross-strait relations.[10] Strategies based on interest transformation have proven to be much more effective for China than those based on coercive leverage. Interest transformation efforts offer the most efficient path toward eventual reunification. Given Taiwan's geographic realities, Taiwan's best policy may very well be to cooperate with Beijing at developing closer economic ties. Taiwan must be keenly aware, however, of the gradual interest transformation security externalities that such cooperation will likely produce. Proactive measures to institutionalize Taiwan's core values might help defend against eventual erosions of the de facto sovereignty Taiwan enjoys today.

Finally, my work on sovereign wealth funds implies that if China wishes to assuage foreign partners regarding its growing outward-bound investment flows, these flows ought to be as commercially oriented and transparent as possible. Specific institutional measures that increase the distance between the Chinese government and the investment decision making are the most effective way to credibly achieve this type of reassurance. This study suggests that if China is intent on using its sovereign wealth funds to pursue strategic national objectives, a lack of transparency and public accountability as well as close political control over the use of state capital are important characteristics that would enable economic statecraft. As illustrated by the CIC, China must first decide what it would like to achieve with the CIC before the state can hope to control the investment behavior of this sort of financial entity. If China only seeks to improve the returns on its excess foreign exchange reserves, then China's interests should not suffer any harm from a policy of full disclosure and exclusive use of third-party asset managers. In-house asset management and direct, concentrated investment positions open the door to noncommercial behavior that leverages China's massive reserves of state capital and the use of these funds to pursue China's strategic interests.

In conclusion, three major implications stand out from this research. First, commercialization of the actors responsible for conducting economic activity is the key to avoiding state use of economic power. Such nonpoliticized orientation of commercial actors is the strategic equivalent of "spiking the guns" of economic statecraft. This is not to say that commercial activities may not generate security externalities, but merely that the state's ability to direct such security externalities is difficult if the state does not control the commercial actors. Second, economic statecraft is not an easy lever of national power for states to wield. To be effective, many factors need to align. This book suggests that the most important factor is state unity. In situations where China is starkly divided it is unlikely that the state will be able to exercise effective control. That said, mixed, hierarchical, state capitalist systems like China's are predisposed to have the necessary institutional characteristics for the pursuit of national objectives through economic means. For these reasons, China will need to work hard to tie its own hands if it is to convince others that they need not fear China's use of economic power. The analysis of China's sovereign wealth funds provides an example (NSSF) of how institutions and mechanisms can be designed to limit the ability of the state to use these funds as tools of economic statecraft. Finally, in the absence of meaningful economic reforms that further remove the state from its ability to direct China's economic actors, China is likely to continue to seek to use economic power to pursue its strategic objectives.

Economic Statecraft beyond China

The intersection of economics and security is a critical, continuously changing landscape. This study has sought to organize and theorize one aspect of that field, China's economic statecraft. Although focused only on China's economic statecraft, many of the ideas presented in chapters 1 and 2 might also apply beyond the empirical context of China.

This study was originally motivated by a puzzle about Chinese economic statecraft. Sometimes the Chinese state could exercise control over economic actors and was able to achieve state strategic goals, and at other times the state was unable to control the economic actors. Why? In answering this puzzle, this book links microeconomic, firm-level behavior with the grand strategy of states. Such a framework also suggests a more general theory of economic statecraft that might apply beyond the context of China.

Seen in this light, this project might also help to understand precisely how states use economics to pursue their strategic objectives. An innovative part of this theory is that it links domestic political economy conditions and behaviors to larger questions of international relations and grand strategy, thus bridging the microlevel behavior of firms with macrolevel outcomes of national grand strategy. China is a good case for understanding this phenomenon and for exploring the causal mechanisms of this new theory, but the study of economic statecraft in international relations need not be limited to China. China's domestic political economy lends itself to state control. Because of this, cases taken from the Chinese context should be predisposed toward economic statecraft. This makes China a useful empirical context to look at if one wants to learn how economic statecraft works. The project is a theory-building effort, and these case studies have been selected to tease out the causal mechanisms driving the outcomes on the dependent variable. But that does not imply that this theory could not be productively employed beyond China, which naturally prompts one to wonder whether a more general theory of economic statecraft can be distilled from this work.

The first step in deriving a more general theory of economic statecraft from this study would likely be to see how well the theory holds across the universe of cases (or suspected cases) of Chinese economic statecraft. The cases in this study were selected for their ability to tell us something useful about the causal mechanisms of the proposed theory. They were helpful in establishing the internal validity of the theory (step one in building a theory). The next step would be to test the theory's external validity across all cases of Chinese economic statecraft. This could be done by building up a dataset of cases of Chinese economic statecraft and testing how well the hypothesized relationships hold up across this universe of cases.

Once the theory's external validity is established in the context of Chinese economic statecraft, we might think about how well it travels to other "mixed regimes," states with an institutional history of active government control of its domestic political economy. States like Russia and India may share similar scale and domestic political economic characteristics to China that make it likely for the theory to travel well to those empirical contexts. Although the results might certainly fit well (perhaps even best) to these kinds of "mixed regimes," there is no theoretical reason to limit the theory's domain exclusively to "mixed regimes." If a nation has a more liberalized domestic political economy, the theory might still apply because such cases will simply have different values across many of the independent variables. In this manner, applying the theory to more liberal regimes (such as the United States or Britain) simply relaxes some of the fundamental business-government assumptions and the domestic political economic context conditions that are present in the China cases.

The framework presented here could be used to generalize a middle-range theory of economic statecraft that bridges the theoretical lacuna between behavior of commercial actors and the grand strategies of nation-states. Developing a better understanding of how states employ economics in their grand strategy would be important not only as a theoretical exercise designed to fill gaps in the field, but also as a useful tool for understanding the important role economics plays in the practical applications of a nation's grand strategy. Practitioners as well as scholars seek a deeper understanding of the possibilities of exercising economic tools of national power. Economic power is often a difficult lever of international power to wield, but when it is used it can be very important. Economic elements of American power featured prominently in the post–World War II containment strategy (Marshall Plan, Bretton Woods, GATT, the rebuilding of Japan and Germany, etc.). For a variety of reasons, states often prefer to use economic rather than military tools of statecraft. Indeed, at different times throughout history, various countries ranging from Britain (efforts to support its continental allies in the late 1700s) to Japan (in the 1980s) have displayed a preference for using economic power to pursue their strategic objectives. Reasons for pursuing national strategic objectives via economic rather than (or in conjunction with) military power vary widely. For example, exercising military power may be an unattractive option because of alliance obligations (Suez Crisis of 1956), a lack of force projection capabilities (numerous cases of UN sanctions), fear of escalation, etc. In other cases, economic power may be a particularly attractive option because of asymmetric dependence (pre–World War II Japanese reliance on US oil), the lulling effects of perceived benefits of economic ties (nineteenth-century railroad investment in the Far East), or relative ease of implementation (2006 freezing of DPRK assets at Banco Delta in Macao). Over time and across geographic spaces, economics has been employed as a tool of national power; understanding exactly how states employ economics in practice to achieve their grand strategic objectives is a useful contribution to policy makers' understanding of how states behave in the international system. A general theory of economic statecraft could offer insight into real-world challenges policy makers face when attempting to strategically use economic interaction.

Considering the importance of economic tools of grand strategy, the economic statecraft topic is not well developed in the field of security studies. Compared to our understanding of the nature, limitations, and mechanics of how military power operates and is used by states, we know relatively little about the economic dimensions of national power. Given the strategic importance of the economic dimension of security, much more work needs to be done on this topic. At the same time, China's growing economic clout and unique domestic political economy enable it to continue to exercise economic statecraft in its conduct of international affairs. China will remain a fascinating source for years to come for studying how economic power is applied in the international system. As a field that cares about real-world outcomes and phenomena that can change the course of history, we ought to be focusing more efforts to understand economic statecraft as it is practiced in the twenty-first century.

Rising states and the dynamics of great power transitions lay at the root of some of the world's greatest wars and have historically been a source of systemic danger. The aggregate national power of rising states fundamentally rests on economic foundations. In addition to fueling military capabilities, that economic power can itself be instrumentally directed to pursue national strategic objectives. Understanding how this happens has been the basic driver of this study. Economic statecraft is likely to continue to occupy a prominent role in China's grand strategy in the future. The rising importance of China in world affairs is unlikely to fade anytime soon, and the strategic significance of international economic relations continues to be an influential feature of international relations. These topics provide ample opportunities for continuing exploration.

CODING OF THE INDEPENDENT VARIABLES

This appendix provides a greater specificity of classification for the independent variables used in this study. For each variable, I provide the range of values that the variable can take on as well as three observable indicators that help determine that variable's value in any particular case. These independent variables are each continuous and vary across a spectrum of values between the two extremes depicted in the table found at the end of this appendix. Given the inherently qualitative nature of many of these phenomena, it is difficult to provide a rigid quantification for the valuations of these variables. That does not mean, however, that we cannot strive for rigor and clarity in how values in this study are assigned. Throughout the empirical chapters, I provide specific evidence that speaks to the variable coding for that particular case. It might be useful for readers to think about the independent variables in a qualitative, historical study like this as specifying *where to look* in a given case if one seeks to understand the relevant drivers, rather than looking to the variables to signal *how much* of a given factor was driving the outcomes.

Market Structure

One of the key features of the principal-agent challenge is whether the principal is able to effectively monitor the agents. It is intuitive that the greater the number of agents the principal has to keep track of, the harder it becomes to track all of the agents' behavior. For purposes of coding, the Market Structure

Independent Variable (Market IV) can range from a concentrated market structure to a fragmented, competitive one. There are three attributes that we can observe about a market that tell us whether it is concentrated or not: the number of firms, the share of the market that is concentrated at the very top, and the pricing power enjoyed by the largest firms in that space. In the cases in this book, I try to distinguish between highly concentrated markets dominated by one to three noncompetitive, monopolistic firms and oligopolistic market structures that are dominated by more than just one or two rival players. The concentration of market share among the top firms provides a second indicator that can be examined to provide a sense for whether a particular market space is concentrated or not. If at least half of the total market belongs to the top five or six firms, the space is likely to be fairly concentrated. Finally, one could study the pricing power in a given market. If the top firms are price makers or if they engage in cartel pricing behaviors, that would be another indicator that the market is concentrated. If the market enjoys competitive pricing, that would be a sign that the market is more fragmented.

Unity of State

Just as the agent side of this relationship can be divided among multiple economic agents, so too can the principal side involve multiple actors. The state principal may not be acting in a coordinated, unified fashion. Such division typically occurs along three lines: along bureaucratic lines, between competing personal or ideological factions, and among central and municipal or provincial centers of authority. Variation across these dimensions is captured by the State Unity Independent Variable. Bureaucratic and institutional friction is frequently observed in the case of China. These can be manifested in bureaucratic reorganizations, contests over jurisdiction in a particular issue area or topic, and classic organizational competitions for budget and personnel. Factional conflicts often overlay bureaucratic struggles in China. Factional contests can be indicated by promotion patterns, purges, elite networks and known rivalries, corruption cases, and a host of other publicly observable manifestations of ideological inclinations and personal ties at the top of the Chinese state hierarchy. Finally, the state can be divided along geographic lines. Kenneth Lieberthal famously expounded on the consequences of the center-local tensions in the Chinese system of governance.[1] This type of state division can be understood as the local state interests diverging from the national state interests. There could also be interregional divisions between the wealthier eastern and southern provinces and the poorer central and western provinces.

Like the other independent variables, in the real world the values of this variable span a continuous spectrum. The State Unity variable can range from being deeply divided to highly unified. From time to time in the casework, I have tried to identify relative degrees of division and to specify the type of ways the state may be divided when referential comparisons may be useful. But the fundamental variation that explains the theory is whether or not the state is acting in a unified way. Thus, for purposes of this study, the State Unity variable has been operationalized as a simple dichotomous value of either a unified state or a divided state.

Nature of the Reporting Relationship

The nature of the reporting relationship between the state and the commercial actors is another important factor influencing the likelihood of state control. Values on the Reporting Relationship IV range from a direct reporting relationship between the economic actor and the state to complete independence from the state. In situations with no direct state relationship, the only types of reporting ties are indirect (for example, regulatory or tax enforcement relationships between the firms and the state). If there is a direct reporting relationship, the principal-agent literature suggests it should be easier for the state to exercise control over the economic actors. There are several observable indicators for this variable that assist the particular coding in a given case. First, one can look at the ownership structure. Does the state have a controlling interest in the ownership of the economic actor? Is the economic actor entirely or majority held by the state? Is there no state ownership at all? Second, one can study the management structure and reporting relationships of the economic actor's leadership. Are the individuals state employees? Are senior posts in the entity appointed by the Organization Department of China's Communist Party or another government body? Does the firm have to report to SASAC, the State Council, or some other portion of the Chinese party-state? Is there an explicit consultative role for the state in firm decision making? Does the firm operate in a heavily regulated sector? Finally, one can examine the role of state financing to get some purchase on the nature of the reporting relationship between the economic actor and the state principal. Is the firm fully funded by the state? Does the economic actor derive the majority of its financing from state sources? Does the firm receive any state resources at all? The role of the state across all three of these dimensions (ownership, management, and financing) provides observable indicators that aid in coding whether the Reporting Relationship IV is direct or not.

Relative Balance of Resources

The balance of resources between the state and the economic actors is another independent variable that in practice varies along a continuous spectrum from being lopsidedly in favor of the state to being lopsidedly in favor of the economic agents. To help maintain theoretical simplicity, I also operationalize this variable as a dichotomous one when coding various episodes in this book. There are three types of observable indicators the assessment of which can provide some guidance regarding whether the overall balance of resources favors the state or the economic actors. The first is the distribution of human capital and knowledge. For example, does the technical know-how in a particular industry reside exclusively at firms in that sector? Do government regulators have enough experience to understand the field they are trying to manage? Is an industry changing so rapidly that any understanding outside the organizations driving the innovation is quickly made obsolete? There are other similar questions that can be used to assess whether the distribution of expertise and technical knowledge favors firms or the state. What does the state's organizational capacity look like? How does that compare with the organizational capacity of the economic actors? The more advanced the principal's organizational capacity to monitor, enforce, and regulate its agents, the more likely that principal-agent challenges will be overcome. The other two indicators of the relative balance of resources can be more easily measured (that is, of course, assuming that the data is publicly disclosed). If the balance of expertise can be thought of as the quality metric of human capital, the balance of personnel refers to the quantitative distribution of human capital resources. What does the raw total of warm bodies look like when the principal and agent are compared? Are there physically enough people at the state to effectively monitor and enforce desired behavior on the part of the economic agents? Finally, the last resource indicator has to do with comparing budgets and endowments between the principal and the economic actors. Are they roughly equivalent or does one dwarf the other? Do their respective allocations provide any other relevant information that can speak to the ability of the state to control the commercial actors?

Intrinsic Compatibility of Goals

The final independent variable has to do with the compatibility of the state's goals with those of the economic actors. How closely are the goals of the agents aligned with those of the principal? If the basic objectives of the commercial actors are closely compatible with the basic goals of the state, one would expect to observe less principal-agent friction. The values for this variable in practice are of course continuous along a spectrum ranging from highly complementary to highly divergent, but like the other independent variables in this study, it too can be usefully dichotomized for the sake of simplicity. Thus, episodes in the cases are coded as being either compatible or not. When the state and the economic actors have incompatible goals, the likelihood of state control will go down, ceteris paribus. To determine goal compatibility, there are several indicators that can be examined. For example, does the commercial agent face strong, short-term-oriented profit incentives that force it to optimize its activities for maximum returns? In such instances, does the state seek goals that are largely driven by political or strategic rather than commercial considerations? These are the sort of first-order inquiries that an analyst ought to perform when assessing whether goals are compatible. But there are other indicators as well. For instance, if the state has a significant role in defining the goals of the economic actor or even if the state is in a regulatory position to substantially alter the firm's commercial success through discretionary authority, one might expect that the goals between the state and the firm align more closely. Another way one could approach the coding of intrinsic goal compatibility would be to ask whether the state's and the economic actor's goals could both be attained or if their goals are mutually exclusive. To the extent that state and economic actor goals may actually be complementary, there would be greater intrinsic goal compatibility.

TABLE A.1 Summary Table of Independent Variable Coding

INDEPENDENT VARIABLE	OBSERVABLE INDICATORS	RANGE: LOW VALUE	HIGH VALUE
Market structure	Number of firms, market share, pricing power	Highly competitive	Concentrated
Unity of state	Bureaucratic divides, personal factions, center-local tension	Fragmented	Unified
Reporting relationship	Government owner, state management, state funding	Nonexistent	Direct
Relative resources	Expertise/knowledge, budget endowments, personnel counts	Favors commercial actor	Favors state
Goal compatibility	Profit motive, state defines goals, mutual exclusivity of state and actor goals	Divergent goals	Convergent goals

CHINA INVESTMENT CORPORATION'S DIRECT INVESTMENTS IN THE AFTERMATH OF THE FINANCIAL CRISIS

In the summer of 2009, with asset prices reflecting a substantial discount as a result of the global economic crisis, the CIC went on a buying spree, investing more than $58 billion in 2009 alone.[1] In July, the CIC purchased $1.5 billion of Teck Resources, Canada's largest diversified mining firm specializing in copper, metallurgical coal, and zinc.[2] Also in July, the CIC invested $940 million to acquire 10.6 percent of ISC KazMunaiGas Exploration and Production based in Kazakhstan. In September 2009, the CIC bought $1.9 billion of PT Bumi Resources' debt.[3] PT Bumi is Indonesia's largest thermal coal mining company. Earlier that month, the CIC bought a 14.9 percent stake in Noble Group, a Singapore-based commodities trader, for $858 million. The CIC also bought 45 percent of Nobel Oil Group LTD, a Russian oil and gas production player in West Siberia, for $270 million.[4] In November 2009, the CIC acquired $500 million of thirty-year secured convertible debt of SouthGobi Energy Resources Limited, a Canadian listed firm whose major assets include large coal mines in Mongolia near the Chinese border. In December 2010, the CIC announced that it had invested $300 million in BTG Pactual, a Brazilian investment bank actively expanding into commodities finance, and $73 million for an 8 percent stake in BUMA, an Indonesian mining services company. In December 2011, the CIC acquired 25.8 percent of Shanduka Group—a South African mining group—for two billion rand. GCL-Poly Energy is a Hong Kong–listed renewable energy company in which the CIC invested $717 million for a 20.1 percent equity stake. CIC was also active in real estate, taking part in a GBP800 million consortium that helped bail out London's Canary Wharf and investing AUS$200 million in Goodman Group, an Australian real estate investment trust. Apparently, the CIC also awarded $800 million to Morgan Stanley to coinvest in a projected $5 billion global property fund. These purchases all seem timed to capitalize on the relatively low asset valuations brought on by the financial crisis.

The buying spree continued (although in smaller increments) in 2010.[5] The CIC purchased 15 percent of AES, a US power generation and utility company with significant international operations, in March 2010 for $1.58 billion. In September 2011, the CIC would go on to coinvest another $93 million for a 19 percent stake in AES-VCM Mong Duong Power in Vietnam. In June 2010, the CIC completed three more investments in the oil and gas sector. The CIC acquired 5 percent of Alberta-based Penn West for $416 million. CIC also inked a tar sands joint venture (in which it owned a 45 percent stake) in the Peace River Oil Partnership for $329 million.[6] Finally, the CIC bought $200 million worth of Chesapeake Energy's convertible shares. Chesapeake is a leading player in the US shale oil and natural gas industry. In May 2012, the CIC would continue to feed its US shale oil appetite by buying a 9.9 percent stake in EP Energy—a Houston-based shale oil exploration and production company—for $300 million. In December 2011, the CIC invested $3.15 billion in GDF Suez Exploration & Production International, SA for a 30 percent stake in its gas exploration assets. That same month, the CIC invested $850 million for a 10 percent share of the Atlantic LNG Company, a liquefied natural gas producer and distributor operating on the southwest coast of Trinidad. A few months prior to that in July 2011, the CIC provided $100 million as part of a syndicate to finance Diamond S Shipping's build out of energy shipping tankers. The move garnered the CIC a 10.5 percent share in Diamond S. In October 2011, CIC made a AUS$300 million purchase of 13.84 percent of Horizon Roads, an Australian toll road operator.

In 2012, a greater effort was placed on diversifying the CIC's portfolio into international infrastructure and other "defensive" stocks.[7] For example, in June 2012, the CIC bought 7 percent of Eutelsat Communications, SA—a European communications satellite provider—for 386 million euros. It also bought an 8.68 percent share of Thames Water Utilities in January 2012 for £276 million. In November of that year, the CIC purchased 10 percent of London's Heathrow Airport holdings for £450 million.[8] Although impressive, this listing of the CIC's direct investments is likely not complete (the CIC makes a point of noting that it does not publicly declare all of its direct investments). This listing does, however indicate the breadth and extent of the CIC's direct investment activity.

Despite the element of prestige attached to the CIC's direct investment portfolio, the commercial wisdom of this sort of direct investment activity is questionable from a strict asset-management perspective. There are several challenges that are likely to make the CIC's direct investment activity difficult to sustain. First, the CIC's direct investments attract disproportionate public and intergovernmental scrutiny both at home and abroad. Direct investment activity is rife with pitfalls ranging from concentrated, illiquid positions and disappointing returns to suspicions of nefarious intent. Direct investments act like a lightning rod in a politically charged atmosphere. Second, there is a fundamentally structural problem of ensuring consistent, respectable returns at scale. Very large direct investors like Berkshire Hathaway or sovereign wealth funds frequently find themselves limited to considering only large-scale investments that are capable of absorbing the volume of capital they seek to deploy. Typically, the highest growth and greatest potential for capital gains, however, are found in the small cap and start-up space. The returns on the CIC's direct investment activity might look underwhelming by comparison. Similarly, timing sectoral downturns is notoriously difficult. Purchasing shale plays when oil is trading at one hundred dollars per barrel looks regrettable when the price of oil falls by half. Third, the CIC's direct investments have the playing field stacked against them. Unlike large private equity firms, the CIC must consider the political costs of taking board seats and actively managing its portfolio companies.[9] This precludes an important avenue of "value creation" that would be otherwise available to most other direct investors at this scale. While it might be compared against other private direct investors pursuing a similar investment style, it might not have access to the same advantages those investors can use. Fourth, because of the scale of the CIC's direct investments, it often must take a fairly large position in the target companies and this creates another set of challenges. Such large positions are often difficult to exit successfully. Large positions can be quite illiquid and selling them off runs the risk of devaluing the asset in the process. Finally there is a problem of talent. Not only is it difficult for CIC to profitably deploy such large-scale capital in a nimble manner, but it is competing against the rest of the world's top asset managers to source and execute the best deals. There is no reason to assume that even the most talented fiscal and monetary experts in China's government and party apparatus will be gifted and experienced portfolio managers. In addition, the CIC faces the problem of how to attract and retain top talent. The best asset managers can command high salaries, but having the government employ individuals at those rates would seem to run against the spirit of Xi Jinping's anticorruption efforts. While none of these challenges is insurmountable, they do amount to a considerable headwind that might dampen enthusiasm for the CIC's direct investment activity.

Notes

INTRODUCTION: OIL, IRON, MANGOES, AND CASH

1. See for instance Daniel W. Drezner, "Bad Debts: Assessing China's Financial Influence in Great Power Politics," *International Security* 34, no. 2 (Fall 2009): 7–45, in which Drezner argues that China's foreign exchange reserves will be of limited strategic use. For other good treatments of China's economic power see David M. Lampton, *The Three Faces of Chinese Power: Might, Money, and Minds* (Berkeley: University of California Press, 2008); and David Shambaugh, *China Goes Global: The Partial Power* (New York: Oxford University Press, 2013).

2. Specifically, as defined in greater detail in chapter 1, economic statecraft refers to state manipulation of economic interaction to capitalize on (or reduce) the associated security effects.

3. "They [Chinese SOEs] are designed to facilitate the goals of China's Communist Party and to help achieve the goals of the country's 12th Five Year Plan. They are guided by the government rather than by market principles," according to Michael R. Wessel, "Opening Statement of the Hearing Co-Chair," from US-China Economic and Security Review Commission, *Chinese State-Owned and State-Controlled Enterprises: Hearing before the U.S.-China Economic and Security Review Commission*, 112th Congress, 2nd session, February 15, 2012, 5. In that same hearing, an international lawyer, Timothy Brightbill, added, "Because SOEs 'often behave as instruments of Chinese foreign policy,' SOE investments and operations in the U.S. market also raise national security and other strategic concerns. The primary motive of SOEs often is not merely economic, but rather to further the objectives of the government, whether it be to obtain advanced technologies, secure access to raw materials, maximize production output or achieve geopolitical influence." From "Written Statement of Timothy C. Brightbill before the U.S.-China Economic and Security Review Commission Hearing on Chinese State-Owned and State-Controlled Enterprises," ibid., 84.

4. See for example Ian Bremmer, "State Capitalism Comes of Age: The End of the Free Market?" *Foreign Affairs*, May/June 2009, 40–55; and Souvik Saha, "CFIUS Now Made in China: Dueling National Security Review Frameworks as a Countermeasure to Economic Espionage in the Age of Globalization," *Northwestern Journal of International Law & Business* 33, no. 1 (Fall 2012): 199–235. Another work that portrays a rising China as threatening and destabilizing is John Mearsheimer, "China's Unpeaceful Rise," *Current History* 105, no. 690 (April 2006): 160–62.

5. For variants of this line of reasoning see Susan Shirk, *China: Fragile Superpower* (New York: Oxford University Press, 2008); and Shambaugh, *China Goes Global*.

6. A more complete theory of economic statecraft would connect the microlevel behavior of global commercial actors with the larger, macrolevel strategic consequences of that economic interaction for nation-states. Norrin M. Ripsman and T. V. Paul, *Globalization and the National Security State* (New York: Oxford University Press, 2010), systematically test various claims in the globalization literature regarding national security, but they mainly test particular hypotheses derived from the globalization literature rather than generating an integrated theory of economic statecraft.

7. While military aspects play a key role in a country's grand strategy, grand strategy also includes an economic element. See especially discussions of the full spectrum of tools available to states in the introduction of Paul M. Kennedy, *The Rise and Fall of the Great Powers: Economic Change and Military Conflict from 1500 to 2000*, 1st ed. (New York: Random House, 1987); and Barry R. Posen and Andrew L. Ross, "Competing Visions for U.S. Grand Strategy," *International Security* 21, no. 3 (1996): 8 n. 2.

8. Following an internal debate, China's senior leadership decided to change the name of its grand strategy from "Peaceful Rise" (which was seen as too destabilizing) to "Peaceful Development" (which carried less threatening connotations). Although still in its early stages, initial policy indications of Xi Jinping's "China Dream" motif, his "New Silk Road Economic Belt," and his "21st Century Maritime Silk Road" all suggest a prominent, continuing role for economics in China's grand strategy. See, for instance, Xi's September 7, 2013, speech at Nazarbayev University in Astana, Kazakhstan, in which he first proposed his "New Silk Road Economic Belt" vision, or his October 3, 2013, speech to the Indonesian parliament in which he laid out his ideas for a "21st Century Maritime Silk Road." Incidentally, President Obama was forced to cancel his plans to attend this APEC summit because of a US government shutdown, poignantly underscoring regional concerns about the permanence of the US presence in Asia.

9. See Russell Ong, *China's Security Interests in the Post-Cold War Era* (Richmond, Surrey: Curzon, 2002); and Russell Ong, *China's Security Interests in the 21st Century* (New York: Routledge, 2007).

10. Lampton, *The Three Faces of Chinese Power*.

11. Phillip C. Saunders, "China's Global Activism: Strategy, Drivers, and Tools," Institute for National Strategic Studies Occasional Paper No. 4 (Washington, DC: National Defense University Press, 2006).

12. See for instance Da Wei, "Has China Become Tough?" *China Security* 6, no. 3 (2010): 97–104; and Linda Jakobson and Dean Knox, "New Foreign Policy Actors in China," *SIPRI Policy Paper*, no. 26 (September 2010).

13. See Adam Segal, "Chinese Economic Statecraft and the Political Economy of Asian Security," in William W. Keller and Thomas G. Rawski, *China's Rise and the Balance of Influence in Asia* (Pittsburgh: University of Pittsburgh Press, 2007). Segal also grapples with the question of whether China's use of economics is effective. See his "China's Economic Statecraft: Markets, Trade, Power, and Influence," a paper he presented at the Assessing China's Rise: Power and Influence in the 21st Century Conference at MIT (February 9, 2009).

14. For Kastner's quantitative complement to Segal's paper see "Buying Influence? Assessing the Political Effects of China's International Economic Ties," a paper he presented at the Assessing China's Rise: Power and Influence in the 21st Century Conference at MIT (February 9, 2009). For additional work on China's influence see Anders S. Johansson, "China's Growing Influence in Southeast Asia—Monetary Policy and Equity Markets," *The World Economy* (2012): pp. 816–37, and papers presented at the 2013 International Studies Association annual meeting by Evelyn Goh, "The Forms of Chinese Influence"; Michael Glosny, "Chinese Perspectives on the PRC's Influence"; Scott Kastner, "Measuring the Effects of China's Influence"; Rosemary Foot and Rana Inboden, "China's Influence on Asian States in the UN Human Rights Council"; and John Ciorciari, "China's Influence on Monetary Policy in Developing Asia." For an optimistic assessment of China's growing regional role see Arvind Subramanian and Martin Kessler, "The Renminbi Bloc Is Here: Asia Down, Rest of the World to Go?" Peterson Institute for International Economics Working Paper 12–19 (October 2012).

15. For a good example of such scholarship see Deborah Brautigam and Xiaoyang Tang, "Economic Statecraft in China's New Overseas Special Economic Zones: Soft Power, Business, or Resource Security?" *International Affairs* 88, no. 4 (2012): 799–816.

1. WHAT IS ECONOMIC STATECRAFT?

1. In some instances, states themselves may directly engage in economic transactions (foreign aid, procurement, etc.) but for the most part, states write the rules of the game and define the conditions under which firms operate.

2. Joanne Gowa and Edward D. Mansfield, "Power Politics and International Trade," *American Political Science Review* 87, iss. 2 (1993): 408–20.

3. Intentionality is merely likely to impact the degree to which *manipulation* of the externality occurs; such manipulation is defined as economic statecraft and is conceptually distinct from the notion of security externalities (see my definition of "economic statecraft" below). What really matters from the point of view of the strategic outcomes are the security externalities themselves; whether they were deliberately generated or simply the unintended by-product of normal commercial behavior does not really affect the security consequences. Whether intended or not, the causal logic of security externalities holds; that is, commercial actors can and do generate security consequences as a result of economic interaction. When states seek to deliberately manipulate that economic interaction, they are engaging in economic statecraft.

4. Conversely, when states are unable to control the behavior of commercial actors, commercial actors may engage in activities that produce security externalities that are counterproductive for a state's strategic interests.

5. David A. Baldwin, *Economic Statecraft* (Princeton, NJ: Princeton University Press, 1985).

6. Previous work has tended to conceive of economic statecraft in terms that frequently limited treatment of economic tools of national power to those phenomena like sanctions, which could be easily observed and for which convenient datasets already exist. Today, there is a tendency to equate *economic coercion* with *economic statecraft* as being one and the same. They are not. This book argues that coercion is just the tip of the iceberg when it comes to the phenomenon of contemporary economic statecraft.

7. Baldwin, *Economic Statecraft*, p. 30. Baldwin actually introduces this definition on page 13–14 of chapter 2, but develops it more fully in chapter 3, "What Is Economic Statecraft?"

8. See ibid., 8–9, in which he borrows from Harold and Margaret Sprout and K. J. Holsti.

9. Ibid., 31–32.

10. David Baldwin, conversations with the author, at the September 2011 annual meeting of the American Political Science Association, Seattle, Washington.

11. Eugene Staley, *War and the Private Investor; a Study in the Relations of International Politics and International Private Investment* (Garden City, NY: Doubleday, Doran & Co., Inc., 1935). This work was an early attempt to systematically examine cases in which commercial actors behaved in ways conducive to states' strategic objectives. Staley was also keen to note that his research often found governments doing the bidding of their commercial actors as well.

12. Albert O. Hirschman, *National Power and the Structure of Foreign Trade* (Berkeley: University of California Press, 1945).

13. See Herbert Feis, *Europe the World's Banker, 1870–1914* (New Haven, CT: Yale University Press; London: Oxford University Press, 1931). Feis would later document the American and British efforts to support China's currency against Japanese attempts to undermine the currency as part of Japan's strategy to fracture China into more easily conquered autonomous regions. Herbert Feis, *The Road to Pearl Harbor: The Coming of the War between the United States and Japan* (Princeton, NJ: Princeton University Press, 1950).

14 See especially Staley, *War and the Private Investor*, and Hirschman, *National Power and the Structure of Foreign Trade*, 170.

15. See Klaus Eugen Knorr, *Power and Wealth: The Political Economy of International Power* (New York: Basic Books, 1973); Klaus Eugen Knorr, *The Power of Nations: The Political Economy of International Relations* (New York: Basic Books, 1975); Klaus Eugen Knorr and Frank N. Trager, *Economic Issues and National Security*, vol. 7 (Lawrence: Published for the National Security Education Program by the Regents Press of Kansas, 1977). Also see Robert Gilpin, *U.S. Power and the Multinational Corporation: The Political Economy of Foreign Direct Investment* (New York: Basic Books, 1975); Robert O. Keohane, *After Hegemony: Cooperation and Discord in the World Political Economy* (Princeton, NJ: Princeton University Press, 1984); and Robert O. Keohane and Joseph S. Nye, *Power and Interdependence: World Politics in Transition* (Boston: Little, Brown, 1977).

16. See especially chapter 4, "International Economic Leverage and Its Uses," in Knorr and Trager, *Economic Issues and National Security*, and chapter I, "International Power and Influence" in Knorr, *The Power of Nations*.

17. Knorr, *The Power of Nations*, 28.

18. In *The Power of Nations*, Knorr discusses multinational corporations chiefly in the context of a brief refutation of neo-Marxism. See chapter IX, "Imperialism and Neocolonialism," in ibid., 239–309.

19. Ibid., 28.

20. Susan Strange, *States and Markets* (London: Pinter Publishers, 1988). Although the systemic architectural designs of the international regime do clearly confer a significant source of power to the hegemon, like other works in the hegemonic theory literature, Strange's focus on the third level of analysis prevents her from directly engaging the role of commercial actors. Cheryl Christensen also discusses the importance of structural power in the context of economics and security in "Structural Power and National Security," in Knorr and Trager, *Economic Issues and National Security*, 127–59.

21. See Richard N. Cooper and Council on Foreign Relations, *The Economics of Interdependence; Economic Policy in the Atlantic Community*, 1st ed. (New York: Published for the Council on Foreign Relations by McGraw-Hill, 1968), especially chapter 6, "National Economic Policy in an Interdependent World."

22. Keohane and Nye, *Power and Interdependence*.

23. "[T]his book argues that the international political order created by dominant powers primarily in their security interests has provided the favorable environment for economic interdependence and corporate expansionism." Gilpin, *U.S. Power and the Multinational Corporation*, 19.

24. Examples of works making the case for a significantly diminished national state in the era of globalization abound. See for instance Kenichi Ohmae, *The End of the Nation State* (New York: Free Press 1995); Susan Strange, *The Retreat of the State: The Diffusion of Power in the World Economy* (Cambridge: Cambridge University Press, 1996); Keith Suter, *Global Order and Global Disorder: Globalization and the Nation-State* (Westport, CT: Praeger 2003); Jan Aart Scholte, *Globalization: A Critical Introduction* (London: Palgrave, 2000); Martin Wolf, "Will the Nation State Survive Globalization?" *Foreign Affairs*, January–February 2001; Walter B. Wriston, *Twilight of Sovereignty: How the Information Revolution Is Transforming Our World* (New York: Scribner Book Company, 1992); William Greider, *One World, Ready or Not: The Manic Logic of Global Capitalism* (New York: Simon & Schuster, 1997); Thomas L. Friedman, *The World Is Flat: A Brief History of the Twenty-First Century* (New York: Farrar, Straus and Giroux, 2005); Richard O'Brien, *Global Financial Integration: The End of Geography* (London: Pinter, 1992). In response to a frequent assumption in this literature on globalization that the state has become irrelevant in the face of multinational corporations, my work argues that the mechanisms of state influence may have changed over time, but states remain powerful international actors. For a similar theoretical perspective see Sean Kay, "Globalization, Power, and

Security," *Security Dialogue* 35, no. 1 (2004): 9–25. Contemporary conditions of complex, interdependent global economic interaction require that we understand the ways in which states continue to exert their influence.

25. Richard N. Rosecrance, *The Rise of the Trading State: Commerce and Conquest in the Modern World* (New York: Basic Books, 1986).

26. See for example Daniel W. Drezner, *All Politics Is Global* (Princeton, NJ: Princeton University Press, 2007); Suzanne Berger and Ronald Philip Dore, *National Diversity and Global Capitalism* (Ithaca, NY: Cornell University Press, 1996); Maria Gritsch, "The Nation-State and Economic Globalization: Soft Geo-Politics and Increased State Autonomy?" *Review of International Political Economy* 12, no. 1 (2005): 1–25; and Peter Evans, "The Eclipse of the State? Reflections on Stateness in an Era of Globalization," *World Politics* 50, no. 1, fiftieth anniversary special issue (1997): 62–87. Ripsman and Paul, in *Globalization and the National Security State*, also address some of these claims that the nation-state and national security have been fundamentally altered as a result of globalization.

27. Indeed in recent years, there has been an effort to consciously articulate a distinctly "Chinese" school of international relations that is explicitly non-Western. See for instance Wang Jisi, "International Relations Theory and the Study of Chinese Diplomacy," in *An Assignment for the New Century: International Relations Studies in China (Revised Edition)*, ed. Yuan Ming (Beijing: Peking University Press, 2007), 322–40 (in Chinese). These attempts have largely failed to produce a uniquely Chinese theoretical paradigm. See Gustaaf Geeraerts and Men Jing, "International Relations Theory in China," *Global Society* 15, no. 3 (July 2001): 251–76.

28. For more on this internal/external dichotomy in China's economic security and grand strategy, see Wang Zhengyi, "Understanding China's Transformation: International Strategic Objectives, System Adjustment and International Power," in *World Politics—Views from China, Volume 6: Non-traditional Security*, ed. Zha Daojiong (Beijing: New World Press, 2007), 41–56 (in Chinese).

29. See, for example, Chen Jiagui and Huang Qunhui, "Industrial Development, the Changing National Situation and the Strategy of Economic Modernization: An Analysis of the National Situation for China's Growth into a Large Industrial State," *Social Sciences in China*, iss. 4 (2005): 4–16 (in Chinese).

30. See, for example, Liu Xinhua and Qin Yi, "China's Oil Security and Strategic Choices," *Contemporary International Relations*, iss. 12 (2002): 35–46 (in Chinese); and Liu Yujiu, "Present State and Main Task of Development of Rare Earth Industry in China," *Journal of the Chinese Rare Earth Society* 25, iss. 3 (June 2007): 257–62 (in Chinese).

31. Securing access to natural resources like oil is a frequent theme in Chinese writings on economics and strategy. For a sampling of this work, see Zha Daojiong, "Interdependence and China's Oil Supply Security," *World Economics and Politics*, iss. 6 (2005): 15–21 (in Chinese); Liu Jun and Jin Shuyun "The Actuality and Countermeasure of the Iron Ore Resource in China," *China Mining Magazine* 18, iss. 12 (Dec. 2009): 1–2, 19 (in Chinese).

32. I discuss China's broad national interests in more detail in chapter 3. Also see Wang Yizhou, ed., *World Politics—Views from China, Volume 2: National Interests* (Beijing: New World Press, 2007) (in Chinese), especially part 3, "China's National Interests Examined," on 197–328.

33. "China's recently more active and positive approach in Asian regional economic, security, and political organizations seems to reflect the strong recent priority of the Chinese administration to ensure that China's rising power and influence not be seen by China's neighbors and the region's dominant outside power, the United States, as a danger." Robert G. Sutter, *Chinese Foreign Relations: Power and Policy since the Cold War* (Lanham, MD: Rowman & Littlefield Publishers, 2008), 113. An example of this strategy was China's pre-financial-crisis strategy toward Southeast Asia. See Deng Yingwen, "On the

Recent ASEAN Trade Relations with Japan," *Journal of Jinan University* (Philosophy and Social Sciences), iss. 3 (2008): 28–33 (in Chinese), for a revealingly competitive account of Japan's economic-based influence in the region.

34. For an example of this sort of strategic logic, see Men Honghua, "The Construction of China's National Strategy System," *Teaching and Research*, iss. 5 (2008): 13–20 (in Chinese), in which he argues for an integration between China's domestic, regional, and global strategy focusing on continued "opening up" efforts that have underpinned China's modern strategic success.

35. One of the most comprehensive treatments of this idea can be found in Zhou Yongsheng, *Economic Diplomacy* (Beijing: China Youth Press, 2004) (in Chinese); another good source on the topic is He Zhongshun, *Research on China's Economic Diplomacy: Theory and Practice* (Beijing: Current Affairs Press, 2007) (in Chinese).

36. Although both usages can be found in the literature, any given author will normally use it to mean *either* the use of diplomacy to further economic goals *or* the use of economics to further diplomatic goals.

37. For an example of a type of work that uses the term in this way see Tsinghua University Institute of International Studies & Research Center of Economy and Diplomacy, *China's Economic Diplomacy 2006* (Beijing: Renmin University Press, 2007) (in Chinese).

38. Put another way, this use of the term can be thought of as using economic means to achieve diplomatic results. See Zhou Yongsheng, "The Opportunities and Challenges Confronting Economic Diplomacy: A Conceptual Study of Economic Diplomacy," *World Economics and International Politics*, iss. 7 (2007): 39–44 (in Chinese); Ruan Zongze, "Let China's Economic Strength Cement Its Diplomatic Power," *Global Times*, October 22, 2012 (in Chinese). Another good example of this type of work is Wu Baiyi, "China's Economic Diplomacy: Continually Transforming External Integration," *Foreign Affairs Review*, no. 103 (2008): 11–19 (in Chinese), in which he argues that China has shifted the emphasis of its foreign policy toward economics and is seeking to maximize China's power through global economic integration. Interestingly, this piece explicitly makes note of state-firm cooperation to pursue China's strategic objectives.

39. It should be noted that the Chinese term *jingji fanglue* may be the closest direct translation of the English term "economic statecraft," but most of the Chinese literature employing that term focuses on internally oriented, domestic Chinese state economic planning and guidance. *Jingji fanglue* does not have the connotation of external orientation that the term carries in the English-language international relations literature. *Jingji waijiao* may therefore be a better way to discuss this economic component of national power.

40. See Zhao Kejin, "The Rise of Economic Diplomacy: Connotation, Mechanism and Trends," *Teaching and Research*, iss. 1 (2011): 56–62 (in Chinese).

41. This partly because much of the work is highly empirical in nature. See for example Wang Shuchun, *Economic Diplomacy and the Sino-Russian Relationship* (Beijing: World Affairs Publishing House 2007) (in Chinese). Scholars of economic diplomacy are also frequently regional experts (e.g., Zhou Yongsheng is primarily a Japan specialist). Another example is China's use of economics in its relations with Southeast Asian states; see for example Zhang Shengjun, "East Asian Economic Convergence and Chinese National Interests," in *World Politics—Views from China, Volume 2: National Interests*, ed. Wang Yizhou (Beijing: New World Press, 2007), 295–306 (in Chinese); also see National Defense University, *International Strategic Analysis 2006–2007* (Beijing: Current Affairs Press, 2007), esp. chap. 2 (in Chinese). China is also concerned with Japan's deep economic ties with the region. See Deng, "On the Recent ASEAN Trade Relations with Japan." This focus on what other nations are doing in the realm of economic statecraft is not limited to Japan.

For more on how economics features in Russian strategy see Wang Lijiu, "Russia's Eurasian Union Strategy and Its Impact on Sino-Russian Relations and SCO," *Contemporary International Relations* 22, iss. 2 (2012): 86–96.

42. As will be explained in greater detail in the next chapter, these units are the locations where we can observe the variation that explains changes in whether the state is or is not able to control the economic actor(s).

43. See for example Edward Hallett Carr's discussion of economic power. ("In the pursuit of power, military and economic instruments will both be used.") Carr, *The Twenty Years' Crisis 1919–1939*, 2nd ed. (Edinburgh: R. & R. Clarke, Ltd., 1946), 113–32. For more on the blending of national strategic interests and commercial actors, see the discussion of Feis, Knorr, Staley, and Hirschman earlier in this chapter.

44. Karen M. Sutter, "Business Dynamism Across the Taiwan Strait," *Asian Survey* 42, no. 3 (May/June 2002): 522.

45. A refreshing exception is Bryan Early's work. See Bryan R. Early, *Busted Sanctions: Explaining Why Economic Sanctions Fail* (Stanford, CA: Stanford University Press, 2015); and Bryan R. Early, "Unmasking the Black Knights: Sanctions Busters and Their Effects on the Success of Economic Sanctions," *Foreign Policy Analysis* 7, iss. 4: 381–402.

2. THE CHALLENGE OF STATE CONTROL

1. The specific instruments of state control may be laws, regulations, and policies, but it may also include a range of less formal institutional state policy mechanisms as well.

2. Bates Gill and James Reilly, "The Tenuous Hold of China Inc. in Africa," *Washington Quarterly* 30, iss. 3: 37–52. More recently, Reilly has also applied a principal-agent approach to understand the decentralized nature of Chinese economic relations with North Korea. See James Reilly, "China's Economic Engagement in North Korea," *China Quarterly* 220 (December 2014): 915–35.

3. For more on dependent and independent variables see John Gerring, *Case Study Research: Principles and Practices* (New York: Cambridge University Press, 2007), 21; Stephen Van Evera, *Guide to Methods for Students of Political Science* (Ithaca, NY: Cornell University Press, 1997); and Alexander L. George and Andrew Bennett, *Case Studies and Theory Development in the Social Sciences* (Cambridge, MA: MIT Press, 2005), esp. chap. 1.

4. Indeed, these two conditions reflect the basic premise of principal-agent theory: a unified, rational principal whose goals are divergent from the agent(s) responsible for conducting the activity.

5. This is likely to be true even though the limited number of commercial agents makes the government's monitoring and enforcement challenges relatively easier.

6. The lines between these three types of market structures are blurry in practice, but for coding purposes, I used three aspects of the market structure to determine whether a given empirical context was competitive, oligopolistic, or concentrated. Concentrated markets were typically dominated by one or two colluding firms that control at least half of the market. In economics terms, such firms are typically price makers (rather than price takers). I defined competitive market structures as those in which more than seven major firms actively compete and at least half of the market lies beyond the top six firms. Firms in competitive markets are often "price takers" with no single firm able to unilaterally set prices. Oligopolistic markets are dominated by two to six competitive firms that tend to control at least half the market. Such market structures often exhibit cartel pricing. For more on the coding of independent variables, see appendix 1.

7. Business-government relations need not only vary by state. They may also vary over time, or by region, industry, or even by firm, as mentioned earlier.

3. ECONOMICS AND CHINA'S GRAND STRATEGY

1. For example, China's engagement strategy with Taiwan continues to yield improvements in cross-strait ties. China's sovereign wealth funds continue to build up their coffers while there is some indication that their investments have had some success in advancing China's goals of energy diversification and technology transfer.

2. Michael D. Swaine, "Does China have a Grand Strategy?" *Current History* 99, no. 638 (2000): 274; Michael Pillsbury, *China Debates the Future Security Environment* (Washington, DC: National Defense University Press, 2000); Raffaello Pantucci and Alexandros Petersen, "China's Inadvertent Empire," *National Interest*, iss. 122 (Nov/Dec. 2012): 30–39.

3. This does not mean that China lacks a basic consensus about the grand strategic goals and vision of the state. For a good synopsis of China's grand strategy and supporting rationale under Hu Jintao, see Avery Goldstein, *Rising to the Challenge: China's Grand Strategy and International Security* (Stanford, CA: Stanford University Press, 2005).

4. The canon of classical realist works include theorists like Carr, Kennan, and Morgenthau, who, while holding true to realism's enduring insights, tend to accord considerable weight to domestic drivers of a state's foreign policy. There are also strains of neoclassical realism that stress domestic sources of foreign policy. For a synopsis of neoclassical realism in contemporary international relations scholarship, see Steven E. Lobell, Norrin M. Ripsman, and Jeffrey W. Taliaferro, *Neoclassical Realism, the State, and Foreign Policy* (New York: Cambridge University Press, 2008).

5. Barry R. Posen, *The Sources of Military Doctrine* (Ithaca, NY: Cornell University Press, 1986), 13.

6. Goldstein, *Rising to the Challenge*, 17 (italics added). For an excellent brief discussion on the nature of grand strategy, see Goldstein, *Rising to the Challenge*, 17–20.

7. States will try to pursue their preferences in the international environment. See Goldstein's footnote 6 on page 17: "[L]eading states have usually sought to shape, and not just survive in, their international environment, typically in ways that will further enhance their wealth, power, and status." Goldstein, *Rising to the Challenge*.

8. For a tidy comparative perspective of China as a "Leninist party-state," see Sujian Guo, *Chinese Politics and Government: Power, Ideology, and Organization* (New York: Routledge, 2013).

9. Goldstein offers a terrific synopsis of these characteristics in *Rising to the Challenge*. Preservation of the Communist Party's continued grip on power is a primary concern. One of the key legitimating factors that enables this is continued economic growth, which helps ensure domestic stability. In addition, China's international economic interaction helps pave the way for its rise to great power status. Economics features prominently in China's grand strategy. See, for instance, Wang Jisi, "Studying China's International Strategy: Model Reconsideration and Construction," *International Politics Quarterly*, iss. 4, no. 106: 1–8 (in Chinese). For a good introduction to a variety of perspectives on China's grand strategy, see that entire dedicated issue of *International Politics Quarterly*.

10. This assumption of how national interests are defined in communist regimes is shared by Knorr. See chapter 2 in "Foreign Policy and National Interest, Klaus Eugen Knorr, *The Power of Nations: The Political Economy of International Relations* (New York: Basic Books, 1975), esp. 36–37.

11. Although an oversimplification, one way to think about the division of labor is that the state provides the institutional mechanisms by which the party can implement its policies.

12. See Cheng Li, "China's Communist Party-State: The Structure and Dynamics of Power," in *Politics in China: An Introduction*, ed. William A. Joseph (Oxford: Oxford University Press, 2010), 165–92; Tony Saich, *Governance and Politics of China* (New York:

Palgrave, 2011). For a seminal text on China's political system, see Kenneth Lieberthal, *Governing China: From Revolution Through Reform*, 2nd ed. (New York: Norton, 2004), esp. chaps. 6 and 7.

13. This quote was originally attributed to Rufus Miles, an American federal administrator whose career spanned Roosevelt's New Deal to Johnson's Great Society. It is often called "Miles's Law." Richard Stillman, "'Where You Stand Depends on Where You Sit': (Or, Yes, Miles's Law also Applies to Public Administration Basic Texts)," *The American Review of Public Administration* 29, no. 1 (1999): 92–97. For a nice introduction to such concepts, see James Q. Wilson, *Bureaucracy: What Government Agencies Do and Why They Do It* (New York: Basic Books, 1989).

14. Examples of such organizations include other members of the Central Committee of the Politburo (particularly the other members of the Standing Committee), each of whom generally represents an important power base within Chinese domestic politics; the State Council (and its constituent members' institutional interests); and the Central Military Commission (and by extension the various regional, service, and organizational bureaucratic equities represented there). In addition to these "pinnacle players," various other organizational and institutional centers of power may weigh in on specific aspects of Chinese grand strategy. For example, the Ministry of Finance, the People's Bank of China, the various policy banks (e.g., China Development Bank, China Import-Export Bank, etc.), the Ministry of Commerce, National Development and Reform Commission (NDRC), the Big Four Chinese banks, the State Assets Supervision and Administration Commission (SASAC), and China's sovereign wealth funds all influence economic aspects of China's grand strategy.

15. This dynamic was highlighted and stressed by several interlocutors during the course of my fieldwork.

16. Despite evidence of occasional lack of coordination, Hu Jintao and the premier, Wen Jiaobao, maintained a strong enough control over China's international behavior to consider China as a rational and unitary strategic actor. Thus far, the evidence suggests that Xi Jinping and Li Keqiang will be able to exercise at least as much control. Xi's early administration seems to offer support for considering China as a rational and unitary strategic actor for the foreseeable future. Of course, no state is ever *perfectly* "rational" nor "unitary" given the realities of domestic politics and the myriad other factors that shape international behavior. But I assume (like many other mainstream analyses of international relations) that, for the most part, China normally behaves like other state actors acting to rationally pursue its interests. In this sense, examples like China's 2007 ASAT test are the exceptions that prove the rule. To the extent this assumption does not hold true, my Unity of State IV is designed to capture such meaningful variation in the casework.

17. An example of this is the delayed release of the 2010 White Paper. One of the alleged reasons behind the delay was the lack of consensus over the "Strategic Outlook" preamble section.

18. This type of tension is reminiscent of the frictions present in a federal system of government, although it should be noted that China has a central (not federal) domestic governmental structure. The regional latitude stems from informal and bureaucratic monitoring, enforcement and compliance challenges rather than from a formal center-local federalism.

19. For example, in 2013–2014, Xi Jinping first announced and subsequently elaborated on the implementation mechanisms for his "New Silk Road Economic Belt" to link Central Asia more closely to China.

20. Bates Gill, *Rising Star: China's New Security Diplomacy* (Washington, DC: Brookings Institution Press, 2007); Goldstein, *Rising to the Challenge*; Wang Yizhou, ed., *Volume on National Interests* (Beijing: New World Press, 2007) (in Chinese); C. Fred Bergsten,

Charles Freeman, Nicholas R. Lardy, and Derek J. Mitchell, *China's Rise: Challenges and Opportunities* (Washington, DC: Peterson Institute for International Economics, 2008), esp. chap. 2, "China Debates Its Future."

21. Technically, this preference is the CCP's preference but by virtue of being able to determine the national interests, it has also become the overriding national objective as well. See my first assumption in the section above.

22. "One profound consequence of China's reform and opening up is that the Communist ideology has lost its appeal and economic growth has become the primary legitimizer and stabilizer of the Chinese political system." Bo Kong, *China's International Petroleum Policy* (Santa Barbara, Calif.: Praeger Security International, 2010), 141. Wang Zhengyi traced how economic growth became fused with national security and ongoing regime stability in his 2004 piece "Conceptualizing Economic Security and Governance: China Confronts Globalization," *The Pacific Review* 17, no. 4: 523–45.

23. Since the accession of Hu Jintao, there has been an emphasis on stability as being the other important foundation for preserving the CCP's grasp on leadership. Partly to differentiate himself from his predecessor, Xi Jinping has not emphasized stability. It will be interesting to observe whether Xi Jinping relies more heavily on nationalistic sentiment given China's more assertive defense of its maritime territorial claims that have coincided with Xi's early time in leadership.

24. In addition to maintaining stability in China's international and domestic environments, Bates Gill notes that "China's new security diplomacy obviously aims to augment China's wealth and influence, but in a way that reassures its neighbors of its peaceful and mutually beneficial intent." Gill, *Rising Star*, 10.

25. Gill, *Rising Star*, 10.

26. Needless to say, Chinese strategists were none too pleased with Obama's "Asian pivot," which was largely seen as a form of anti-China containment. See Kai Liao, "The Pentagon and the Pivot," *Survival: Global Politics and Strategy* 55, iss. 3 (2013): 95–114.

27. Evan S. Medeiros, "China's International Behavior: Activism, Opportunism, and Diversification," *Joint Forces Quarterly*, no. 47 (2007): 34–41.

28. See Goldstein, *Rising to the Challenge*, 22–29.

29. Ibid., 12.

30. Ibid.; also see his chap. 7, "China and the Major Powers."

31. For more on this element of China's strategy see ibid., chap. 6, "China Adjusts."

32. Medeiros, "China's International Behavior" (italics in the original), 36.

33. Chinese strategic thinkers frequently use the term *jingji anquan* (economic security) in discussions of China's economic vulnerabilities. For a comprehensive treatment of this concept, see the China Institutes of Contemporary International Relations (CICIR) book by that name, *National Economic Security* (Beijing: Current Affairs Publishing House 2005) (in Chinese). Also see Zha Daojiong, ed., *World Politics—Views from China, Volume 6: Non-traditional Security* (Beijing: New World Press, 2007) (in Chinese) esp. 39–84.

34. Discussions of *jingji anquan* (economic security) usually emphasize China's raw material dependence vulnerabilities. See Lin Xionghui, *Research on Economic Globalization and Army Political Thought Education* (Beijing: Military Science Publishing House, 2004) (in Chinese). For an example of a scholar arguing that China's security is threatened by its reliance on an American-dominated globalization regime, see Zhang Wenmu, "China's National Security Problem from the Perspective of Globalization," *World Economics and Politics* 2002, iss. 3: 4–9 (in Chinese).

35. The Chinese literature seems to be especially sensitive to natural resource vulnerability, particularly China's dependence on imported sea-borne petroleum. See Men Honghua, "The Strategic Significance of Ensuring China's Energy Security," *Asia Pacific Journal* 2005, iss. 1: 33–44 (in Chinese), in which he argues that China should project sea

power capabilities to secure its energy security. For more on sea power and its relationship to China's national and economic interests, see Wang Lidong, *A Theory of National Maritime Interests* (Beijing: National Defense University Press, 2007), esp. chap. 6 (in Chinese).

36. A strong conqueror would unite the lands of China into an empire. This conqueror would then become emperor and a dynasty would be established that would last for a period of time. The high-water marks of Chinese civilization (Tang poetry, Ming trade, Song arts) flourish when the empire is strong and well governed. But eventually, fissures emerge that spell the beginning of the end of a dynasty. Dynastic collapse would introduce a chaotic period of localized warlord states often plagued by banditry. Eventually, outside conquest or an internally generated warlord would reconsolidate the empire and a new dynasty would begin. For an accessible history of modern China (with helpful attention to the historical relationship between the mainland and Taiwan), see Jonathan D. Spence, *The Search for Modern China*, 2nd ed. (New York: W. W. Norton, 1999).

37. Of course this is not the only reason Taiwan occupies an important place in China's strategic thinking, but the issue is a complicated one. Exploring this topic properly requires volumes.

38. "As ever, China's current grand strategy first attends to potential threats to vital interests (territorial and political integrity)." Goldstein, *Rising to the Challenge*, 23.

39. This internal-external linkage of regime threats reflects Chinese strategic thinking that was manifested in the creation of a National Security Council in China. See Jane Perlez, "New Chinese Panel Said to Oversee Domestic Security and Foreign Policy," *New York Times*, November 13, 2013.

40. For more on China's broad national interests see Wang Yizhou, *Volume on National Interests*, esp. 197–328 (in Chinese).

41. Between 1978 and 2005, China's GDP grew at an average annual rate of 9.6 percent. See Carsten A. Holz, "China's Economic Growth 1978–2025: What We Know Today About China's Economic Growth Tomorrow," *World Development* 36, no. 10 (2008): 1665–1691. Although more recent data may yet be subject to restatement, it seems that China's GDP has grown by an average of approximately 10.6 percent per year since 2005, although most recent estimates predict that this rate will decline to 6 or 7 percent (and perhaps lower) as China attempts to reach a "sustainable rate of economic growth" in the near future. For official data see China's National Bureau of Statistics, *China Statistical Yearbook 2014* (Beijing: China Statistics Press, 2015).

42. Even if growth slows, China is already the world's second largest economy and a massive regional actor in Asia.

43. Such works frequently highlight the intrinsic connections between economic growth and increasing military capabilities. See for instance Ye Zicheng and Mu Xinhai, "A Few Thoughts on the Chinese Sea Power Development Strategy," *International Politics Quarterly*, iss. 3 (2005): 5–17 (in Chinese); Lin Xionghui, *Research on Economic Globalization and Army Political Thought Education*.

44. See for example Ye Zicheng, "The International Environment's Relationship to China's Peaceful Development: Some Thoughts," *International Politics Quarterly*, iss. 1 (2006): 20–30 (in Chinese).

45. For example in Men Honghua and Hu Angang, "Five Years after Entering the WTO: China Ought to Further Open to the Outside," *Opening Herald*, iss. 1, no. 130 (February 2007): 68–73 (in Chinese), the authors argue that China's entry into the WTO has been a successful extension of China's thirty-year Reform and Opening Up effort. This strategy has produced considerable results for China, prompting the authors to call for further opening up.

46. For instance, see Yuan Chengzhang, "A Discussion of Deng Xiaoping's International Strategic Ideological Disposition: Ten Essential Elements," in *World Politics—Views*

from China, Volume 3: Strategies of the Great Powers, ed. Jin Canrong, 71–84 (Beijing: New World Press, 2007) (in Chinese).

47. John Whalley and Xian Xin. "China's FDI and Non-FDI Economies and the Sustainability of Future High Chinese Growth," *China Economic Review* 21, no. 1 (March 2010): 123–35.

48. Xu Zhanchen and Chen Wenling, "On the Strategies of China's Economic Diplomacy to Major Countries in the New Period," *Globalization*, no. 7 (2014): 26–37 (in Chinese); Jiang Ruiping, "The Current Opportunities and Challenges Facing China's Economic Diplomacy," *Foreign Affairs Review*, no. 5 (2009): 40–55 (in Chinese).

49. Economic goals are still a central component of China's foreign policy, and a good deal of China's foreign policy will continue to be directed toward enabling China's ongoing economic integration for the reasons highlighted above. Given China's history, ambitions, and domestic institutions, however, it is reasonable to expect that some portion of China's growing economic power will be used to pursue foreign policy goals, and this new, important phenomenon has not received appropriate analytical attention.

50. In particular, Chinese authors have begun to call attention to the need for inter-agency coordination when implementing Chinese economic statecraft. See, for example, Song Guoyou, "China's Near-Abroad Economic Diplomacy: Coordination Mechanisms and Strategies," *International Studies*, no. 2 (2014): 41–52 (in Chinese).

51. Of course, China can seek ways to insulate itself from unipolarity (multilateral organizations, norms such as sovereignty, balancing, prestige, etc.), and China makes little secret about its efforts to actively encourage the "multipolarization" and "democratization" of the international system, but ultimately, China's post–Cold War foreign policy has had to be implemented under the shadow of American unipolarity for the last quarter-century.

52. These are often referred to as "spikes of excellence" and generally are platform-specific capabilities focused on exploiting perceived weaknesses in the American military's order of battle rather than representing a holistic, integrated combat force.

53. Economics is a critical component of Beijing's "New Security Concept," and economics seems likely to continue to play an important role in China's pursuit of its strategic objectives. See C. Fred Bergsten et al., *China: The Balance Sheet* (New York: Public Affairs, 2006).

54. In 2003 and again in 2006, China apparently had "technical problems" on a Chinese oil pipeline that supplies North Korea. In both instances, the "problems" were conveniently timed to send a strong signal of Beijing's displeasure. In addition, there may have been another instance of China at least threatening to cut off oil to North Korea in 2009. At various times, China has sought to lean on North Korea over its missile tests, nuclear program, and North Korean reticence to rejoin the six-party talks.

55. For an example of such strategies, see China's "indigenous innovation policy" (*zizhu chuangxin zhengce*) that was launched in 2006 but gained steam in the second half of 2009 and reached a peak in 2010.

56. Although the data seem to suggest that the antimonopoly law has been used to target domestic Chinese companies as well as foreign enterprises, the international perception of the law's enforcement is that it provides a mechanism for the state to target less-favored commercial entities. See US-China Business Council, "Competition Policy and Enforcement in China" September 2014, available online at https://www.uschina.org/sites/default/files/AML%202014%20Report%20FINAL_0.pdf.

57. Deborah Brautigam and Xiaoyang Tang, "Economic Statecraft in China's New Overseas Special Economic Zones: Soft Power, Business, or Resource Security?" *International Affairs* 88, no. 4 (2012): 799–816.

58. Of course, much of this positive tone can be quickly squandered when Beijing is seen as engaging in provocative actions in the region. Even if China feels that it is merely

responding to others' aggression, the mere fact that the region views China's actions as belligerent is what generates the strategic effect.

PART II. SECURING STRATEGIC RAW MATERIALS

1. The State Council has defined seven industries as "strategic." They are defense, power generation and distribution, oil and petrochemicals, telecommunications, coal, aviation, and shipping. See "Guiding Opinion on Advancement of State-Owned Capital Restructuring and Reorganization of State Owned Enterprises," issued by SASAC on December 18, 2006, available (in Chinese) at: www.sasac.gov.cn/gzjg/xcgz/200612180138.htm.

2. Mikael Mattlin, *The Chinese Government's New Approach to Ownership and Financial Control of Strategic State-Owned Enterprises* (Helsinki: Suomen Pankki [Bank of Finland], 2007), 25–26.

4. "GOING OUT" AND CHINA'S SEARCH FOR ENERGY SECURITY

1. Robert G. Sutter, *Chinese Foreign Relations: Power and Policy since the Cold War* (Lanham, MD: Rowman & Littlefield, 2008).

2. China's surging growth has also created significant increases in its demand for raw materials. "Though China's demand for these imports certainly will go up and down with economic cycles, from 1995 to 2003, China accounted for 68 percent of global demand growth for oil, 82 percent of steel, 100 percent of copper, 100 percent of aluminum, and 73 percent of nickel." David M. Lampton, *The Three Faces of Chinese Power: Might, Money, and Minds* (Berkeley: University of California Press, 2008), 91.

3. From Ian Taylor, *China's New Role in Africa* (Boulder, CO: Lynne Rienner Publishers, 2009), 18, citing Ian Taylor, "China's Oil Diplomacy in Africa," *International Affairs* 82, iss. 5 (2006): 937–59.

4. Jianhai Bi and David Zweig, "China's Global Hunt for Energy," *Foreign Affairs* 84, no. 5 (2005): 25.

5. Securing raw materials (including oil) has been a dominant theme among China's leadership. See, for instance, Premier Zhu Rongji's March 5, 2001, comments on the draft outline of the Tenth Five-Year Plan: "Report on Economic and Social Development of the Tenth Five-Year Plan." Available (in Chinese) at www.sdpc.gov.cn/fzgh/ghwb/gjjh/W020050614801666916182.pdf. In that plan, China also developed its first "Energy Development Key Special Plan" as a complement to the Tenth Five-Year Plan. Available (in Chinese) at http://www.sdpc.gov.cn/fzgh/ghwb/zdgh/t20050714_36295.htm.

6. The specific name and scope of the line ministry that was charged with administering China's petroleum (and often chemical) assets changed a number of times since October 1, 1949, as a result of various reorganizations. The original ministry was called the Ministry of Fuel Industry. What matters for the purposes of this chapter, however, is that the assets were always managed, owned, and operated directly by the state ministry.

7. Such pathologies include the lack of meaningful price signal, under- or overplanning estimates, absence of commercial incentives, shirking, and a host of other deadweight losses. The issues that frequently bedevil planned economic systems are well depicted in János Kornai, *The Socialist System: The Political Economy of Communism* (Princeton, NJ: Princeton University Press, 1992). For a helpful discussion of similar pathologies in the Chinese context, see Nicholas R. Lardy, "Recasting of the Economic System: Structural Reform of Agriculture and Industry," in *China in the Era of Deng Xiaoping*, ed. Michael Ying-Mao Kau and Susan Marsh (Armonk, NY: M. E. Sharpe, 1993), 103–20.

8. Virtually all of China's petroleum assets resided in the ministry. The major exception was the China National Chemicals Import and Export Corp (SinoChem), which was a state-owned enterprise created in the 1950s to conduct international oil trading. Since China's economy was a closed economy, only certain entities were authorized to conduct international economic activities.

9. Jin Zhang, *Catch-Up and Competitiveness in China: The Case of Large Firms in the Oil Industry* (London: Routledge Curzon, 2004).

10. MPI was abolished when the CNPC was created in 1988.

11. The liberalization of China's oil sector provides a useful illustration of the "paradox of economic statecraft." States seeking to exercise economic power need to be able to direct that economic behavior. But the more states try to direct the economic activities of commercial actors, the greater the risk of distortion and eventual erosion of "economic gunpowder" the state has at its disposal. If states seek to increase their productivity by giving commercial actors free rein, it becomes that much more difficult for a state to direct its economic might.

12. Taylor, *China's New Role in Africa*, p. 167, citing his interview with a Chinese trader, in Praia, Cape Verde, November 5, 2007.

13. From the point of view of the reporting relationship these bureaus were bureaucratically outranked by the ministerial level authority held by the heads of CNPC and SinoChem. As discussed in more detail below, this disparity added to the difficulty faced by the state regulators.

14. "Increasingly, China is relying on its oil companies to provide the means of securing energy security, linking itself to a market-based form of energy security." Pauline Kerr, Stuart Harris, and Yaqing Qin, *China's "New" Diplomacy: Tactical Or Fundamental Change?*, 1st ed. (New York: Palgrave Macmillan, 2008), 220.

15. Such frictions and state-commercial coordination challenges are typical across all avenues of Chinese economic statecraft. The hybrid model of government involvement with commercial actors is what makes China such an interesting case to explore to understand exactly how states actually practice economic statecraft.

16. "As a result, the SPCIB [State Petroleum and Chemical Industry Bureau] often deferred to the three NOCs over policy problems. Further, SPCIB suffered from an asymmetry between the amount of personnel it had and the amount of tasks it was assigned. Staffed with only 90 people, the SPCIB was responsible for planning and devising overall development strategies for the oil and petrochemical industry as well as promoting continued restructuring of the 7,500 SOEs under CNPC and Sinopec." Bo Kong, *China's International Petroleum Policy* (Santa Barbara, CA: Praeger Security International, 2010), 16.

17. Zhou would succeed Wang as CNPC's general manager and was later promoted to the Standing Committee of the Politburo. He later directed the Public Security Commission. Leadership of Chinese NOCs is considered a prestigious post for up-and-coming darlings of the CCP.

18. This phrase is often translated as "going out," "stepping out," or "going global." This policy encourages firms to move into international markets and compete in the global marketplace. It is part of the Chinese leadership's effort to improve the quality of Chinese enterprises by the stimulation of competitive pressure, adoption of international quality standards, diffusion of technology, and management practices through multinational competition. The goal is to create world-class, Chinese multinational corporations.

19. The government did eventually give its official imprimatur to these efforts. See Xu Xiaojie, "Chinese NOCs' Overseas Strategies: Background, Comparison and Remarks," March, 2007 paper prepared in conjunction with the James A. Baker III Institute for Public Policy, Rice University, and Japan Petroleum Energy Center. Available at http://www.rice.edu/energy/publications/docs/NOCs/Papers/NOC_ChineseNOCs_Xu.pdf. Xu Xiaojie was the director of the Institute of Overseas Investment at CNPC Research Academy of Economics and Technology in Beijing.

20. For more on Jiang's remarks see Chen Huai, "China's Oil Security Strategy Ought to be Based on 'Going Out,'" *Economic Research Review*, no. 25 (2001) (in Chinese).

21. The four objectives of the policy are to provide markets for Chinese products, improve resource security, enable technology transfer, and promote research and development. China's oil projects overseas often meet more than one of these objectives and frequently receive state support.

22. Even relatively small investments would need to secure approvals from SAFE, Mof-Com, and often the State Council, among other bodies.

23. Bi and Zweig, "China's Global Hunt for Energy." This dynamic also seems to lay behind China's substantial investments in Iran, limiting its ability to cooperate with the United States on other priorities.

24. "'China confronts foreign competition' said Chen Fengying, an expert at the China Contemporary International Relations Institute, which is based in Beijing and affiliated with the state security system. 'Chinese companies must go places for oil where American [and] European companies are not present. Sudan represents this strategy put into practice.'" Peter S. Goodman, "China Invests Heavily in Sudan's Oil Industry; Beijing Supplies Arms used on Villagers," *Washington Post*, December 23, 2004.

25. The GNPOC "consortium's Heglig and Unity oil fields now produce 350,000 barrels per day, according to the U.S. Energy Department. Separately, CNPC owns most of a field in southern Darfur, which began trial production [in 2004], and 41 percent of a field in the Melut Basin, which is expected to produce as much as 300,000 barrels per day by the end of 2006. Another Chinese firm, Sinopec Corp., is erecting a pipeline from that complex to Port Sudan on the Red Sea, where China's Petroleum Engineering Construction Group is building a tanker terminal." Goodman, "China Invests Heavily in Sudan's Oil Industry."

26. Taylor, *China's New Role in Africa*, p. 50. The precise size of China's involvement is difficult to determine. A World Bank study "recorded six confirmed oil-related projects" between 2001 and 2007 "amounting to some $645 million" of confirmed (although not by Chinese sources) commitments. The same study "also has information on another six unconfirmed oil projects, amounting to an additional $789 million of possible finance commitments." Vivien Foster, *Building Bridges: China's Growing Role as Infrastructure Financier for Sub-Saharan Africa* (Washington, DC: World Bank: Public-Private Infrastructure Advisory Facility, 2009), 50.

27. Goodman, "China Invests Heavily in Sudan's Oil Industry."

28. In particular, AVIC I transferred flight simulators for their K-8s to Sudan. Six of these training jets were delivered to the Sudanese Air Force in 2006 and another six were to follow soon thereafter. The K-8 is a trainer for fighter jets. After undergoing basic training on these jets, pilots would progress to the Chinese NAMC Q-5 (A-5 is the export version) Fantan. At least three A-5 Fantan ground attack fighters have been photographed on runways in Darfur. See May 8, 2007, Amnesty International report titled "Sudan: Arms continuing to fuel serious human rights violations in Darfur," Available at http://www.amnesty.org/en/library/info/AFR54/019/2007, esp. 7–8 and 12–17. Also see February, 2006 Amnesty International report titled "China: Sustaining conflict and human rights abuses—the flow of arms accelerates," Available at http://www.amnesty.org/en/library/asset/ASA17/030/2006/en/be25c03a-d42b-11dd-8743-d305bea2b2c7/asa170302006en.pdf. The Sudanese Air Force has also been supplied with "US$100 million worth of Shenyang fighter planes, including a dozen supersonic F-7 jets." Taylor, *China's New Role in Africa*, 120. "Many of the helicopter gunships in Khartoum's arsenal were obtained from China, often using projected receipts from oil extractions in the regions where fighting took place." Ibid., 123.

29. "The Chinese National Petroleum Corporation (CNPC) . . . is one of the main oil concession-holders in Sudan with the largest share (40%) in GNPOC, which exploited

Blocks 1 and 2 (the Heglig and Unity oilfields); and a concession over the most productive field, Block 4. In July 2006 China started output from Blocks 3 and 7 (in the Melut basin, northern Upper Nile State in South Sudan), which will produce an estimated 200,820 barrels a day. The early exploitation of oil fields Block 1 and 2 in Unity State, in South Sudan, at the time that China was a member of this consortium, was accompanied by mass forced displacement and killings of the civilian population living there. Sudanese planes bombed villages and Southern militias, supported by Sudanese armed forces, attacked villages, killing people and destroying homes until the area was depopulated, in an apparent aim to clear the area of people for oil exploration and extraction. . . . CNPC also directly benefited from the 'security' provided by the Sudanese army against rebel groups in the oilfields—the same forces responsible for the massive force displacements of civilians in the oilfields." (From "Sudan/China: Appeal by Amnesty International to the Chinese Government on the Occasion of the China-Africa Summit for Development and Cooperation," published November 1, 2006. Available at http://www.amnesty.org/en/library/info/AFR54/072/2006/en.)

30. For example, "China is said to have sold the government of Sudan SCUD missiles at the end of 1996 in a deal underwritten by a $200 million Malaysian government loan against future oil extraction, according to a high-level Sudanese defector, who claimed the deal, which he said he witnessed, was arranged by Sudan's state minister for external relations, Dr. Mustafa Osman Ismail." See *Sudan: Global Trade, Local Impact; Arms Transfers to all Sides in the Civil War in Sudan* (Human Rights Watch, 1998), esp. section IV. Concerning the SCUD transfer, the report references footnote 83: "Human Rights Watch interview with Abdelaziz Ahmed Khattab, The Hague, November 15, 1997. Khattab also claimed, in a written statement, that the Malaysian national oil company was used as a cover to ship arms to Sudan: 'Arms deals agreed upon have been shipped by sea in the name of the Malaysian National Petroleum Company and that of the Chinese National Petroleum Company, under the guise of petroleum exploration equipment according to an agreement concluded between the government in Khartoum and these companies in Kuala Lumpur under which they provide weaponry and military equipment in exchange for being given concessions for oil explorations.' *Statement by the Administrative Attaché, Embassy of Sudan, Kuala Lumpur, Malaysia: To the People of the Sudan and World Public Opinion*, signed by Abdelaziz Ahmed Abdelaziz Khattab, the Netherlands, September 29, 1997. Human Rights Watch has been unable to independently confirm this allegation. The Canadian oil company Arakis Energy Corporation is known to have been involved with a number of partners in an oil-exploration and development scheme in Sudan, the Sudan Petroleum Project, since November 1996. According to news reports, two of Arakis's partners in the project, China National Petroleum Corp. and Petronas, the Malaysian state oil company, have covered start-up costs, giving credit to Arakis for its spending from 1993 until the formation of the consortium in November 1996." (Available at http://www.hrw.org/legacy/reports98/sudan/Sudarm988–05.htm#P566_98312.)

31. "Even when the Chinese leadership may want certain outcomes from China's engagement in Africa, it may not have all the leverage or control over a fast-expanding network of state and private actors who have entered these markets following the logic of globalization and profit maximization." Wenran Jiang, "Fueling the Dragon: China's Rise and its Energy and Resources Extraction in Africa," *China Quarterly* 199 (2009): 585–609. Quote is from page 608.

32. See May 8, 2007, Amnesty International report titled "Sudan: Arms continuing to fuel serious human rights violations in Darfur," Available at http://www.amnesty.org/en/library/info/AFR54/019/2007.

33. Taylor, *China's New Role in Africa*, 175.

34. China would eventually send 435 engineers as peacekeepers into Darfur.

35. See Mark Turner and Guy Dinmore, "US Defends China Over Darfur Diplomacy," *Financial Times*, Apr. 12, 2007, 7; and Richard McGregor, "Beijing's Africa Envoy to Focus on Darfur," *Financial Times*, May 11, 2007, 11.

36. "China's Africa Policy Changing for the Better," *Japan Times*, September 11, 2008.

37. Kevin Carey, Ulrich Jacoby, and Sanjeev Gupta, *Sub-Saharan Africa: Forging New Trade Links with Asia* (Washington, DC: International Monetary Fund, 2007).

38. See: Harry G. Broadman and Gozde Isik, *Africa's Silk Road: China and India's New Economic Frontier* (Washington, DC: World Bank, 2007), 120, esp. table 2A.4, "Africa's Top 20 Exports to China: Products and Leading Exporters."

39. Matthew Green, Richard McGregor, and William Wallis, "Nine Chinese Oil Workers Killed in Attack at Ethiopia Exploration Site," *Financial Times*, April 25, 2007, 1.

40. Taylor, *China's New Role in Africa*, 49.

41. Sinopec reportedly received a 75 percent share and Sonangol held a 25 percent share of three offshore fields from the 2006 deal.

42. The terms of this loan were very favorable to Angola: $2 billion at an annual interest rate of 1.5 percent payable over seventeen years. Allegedly, this package convinced Angola to reject Royal Dutch Shell's intention to sell its stake in an Angolan oil field to the Oil and Natural Gas Corporation Videsh Ltd. (an Indian firm) in favor of Sinopec. Apparently, this same aid package was responsible for a separate decision to award a different stake in Angola to Sinopec. See Peter C. Evans and Erica S. Downs, "Untangling China's Quest for Oil through State-Backed Financial Deals," *Brookings Policy Brief*, no. 154 (May 2006): 3.

43. "Blast Kills 46 at a Copper Mine in Zambia," *New York Times*, April 21, 2005, sec. A; foreign desk, 5; Michael Wines, "World Briefing Africa: Zambia: Anger After 50 Die in Chinese Plant," *New York Times*, April 22, 2005, sec. A; foreign desk, 8.

44. Joseph J. Schatz, "Zambian Hopeful Takes a Swing at China; Presidential Challenger Stirs Resentment at Asian Power's Growing Influence in Africa," *Washington Post*, September 25, 2006.

45. See Bonnie Glaser, "Ensuring the 'Go Abroad' Policy Serves China's Domestic Priorities," *China Brief* 7, no. 5 (2007): 2–5; "While most of the previous reform efforts resulted in enhanced managerial and/or local government control over enterprise management and financial decisions, several recent initiatives by SASAC specifically and central government more generally appear aimed at reestablishing central government authority over the *crème de la crème* of SOEs." Mattlin, "The Chinese Government's New Approach to Ownership and Financial Control of Strategic State-Owned Enterprises," Bank of Finland Institute for Economies in Transition Discussion Paper Number 10 (2007), 44.

46. People's Republic of China, Ministry of Commerce, "Explanation regarding 'Mechanisms for Strengthening Chinese Overseas-Invested Enterprises' and 'Guidelines for Worker Safety and Protection,'" August 31, 2006. Available (in Chinese) online at http://hzs.mofcom.gov.cn/aarticle/bk/200608/20060803022750.html.

47. This was also designed to prevent counterproductive competition among Chinese bidders for international assets.

48. It should be noted that China is not unique in this regard. Other states often support their firms' large international commercial deals as well.

49. Chris Alden, "China in Africa," *Survival: Global Politics and Strategy* 47, no. 3 (2005): 147.

50. For an in-depth treatment of Chinese investment in Africa (including a detailed focus on China's aid ties) see Deborah Brautigam, *The Dragon's Gift: The Real Story of China in Africa* (Oxford, UK: Oxford University Press, 2009).

51. This type of structure strikes me as odd, but it seems consistent with China's general obsession over supply risk in its petroleum strategy. A similarly unusual logic seems

to drive China's desire to secure equity oil and ensure that Chinese oil is transported via Chinese-flagged tankers.

52. In particular, "loans-for-oil" along the lines of the Angola Model have proliferated. For example, the China Development Bank (CDB, discussed in more detail in the next chapter) provided $25 billion in exchange for Russian petroleum in February 2009. That same month, CDB loaned $10 billion to Brazil and $8 billion to Venezuela in two other massive oil-backed deals. In April, CDB invested another $1 billion in Angolan oil and the Export-Import Bank provided $5 billion to Kazakhstan. In July, CDB once again invested $1 billion in Ecuador and another $4 billion in Venezuela.

53. Eight of the nine members of the Politburo Standing Committee (the apex of China's leadership) traveled to Africa between 2005 and 2010. Hu Jintao visited nineteen African countries between 2004 and 2010. For excellent data on senior state leadership visits see Chinavitae.org.

54. "As the Chinese leadership has pursued its (admittedly uneven) post-Mao economic liberalization policies, they have encountered increasing difficulties in controlling—or even keeping abreast of—the diverse activities in which various Chinese corporations and individual merchants are engaged overseas." Taylor, *China's New Role in Africa*, 178–79. In addition to undermining China's reputation, CNPC and Sinopec frequently competed over the same international assets, initial Chinese acquisitions seemed prone to overpaying for assets, and the government often seemed to be running to catch up with its fast-moving NOCs.

55. This has the effect of creating a default screening process for issues that warrant the attention of China's top leadership.

56. Although this generally only seems to happen when events have already escalated to the point that they warrant the attention of China's senior leadership.

5. RIO TINTO AND THE (IN)VISIBLE HAND OF THE STATE

1. Lucy Hornby, "China iron ore imports grow 10% in 2013," *Financial Times*, January 10, 2014, available at http://www.ft.com/intl/cms/s/0/9914dac0-79b7-11e3-8211-00144feabdc0.html#axzz2v0pYO7n9; Glenys Sim and Rebecca Keenan, "China Iron Ore Imports to Near Record This Year, Shougang Says," *Bloomberg Businessweek*, March 24, 2010, available at http://www.businessweek.com/news/2010-03-24/china-iron-ore-imports-to-near-record-this-year-shougang-says.html.

2. See October 25, 2007, company press release, available at http://www.riotintoalcan.com/ENG/media/media_releases_1033.asp.

3. The BHP-Rio merger would have combined the world's second- and third-largest producers of iron ore. "If Australia's BHP Billiton succeeds in ensnaring Rio Tinto, steelmakers—led by the Chinese—will find themselves trying to bargain down a miner which produces more than one-third of the world's iron ore. Add in CVRD of Brazil and the trio would account for almost three-quarters. Faced with such a prospect, it is not difficult to understand why government-owned China State Development Bank has reportedly started building a stake in Rio Tinto" "Orefull Realities," *Financial Times*, November 12, 2007, 14.

4. Shai Oster and Rick Carew, "China Inc.'s Top Deal Maker Provokes a Backlash Abroad," *Wall Street Journal* (Eastern edition), April 16, 2009, A1.

5. Paul Glasson, "Regional Focus to Global Push: The China Syndrome," *The Australian*, March 4, 2009, available online at http://www.theaustralian.com.au/business/latest/regional-focus-to-global-push/story-e6frg90f-1111119022238; also see Oster and Carew, "China Inc.'s Top Deal Maker Provokes a Backlash Abroad."

6. Aluminum Corporation of China (Chinalco, also known as Chalco) was founded in 2001 as a rollup of the state-owned aluminum sector. At the time, it had about 200,000

employees and twenty-five subsidiaries. "As a national champion with more than 40 per cent of Chinese alumina and aluminium production in 2007, Chinalco was an obvious candidate for the mission, even if lossmaking companies with a $9bn equity base don't ordinarily get $20bn loans—in this case from China Development Bank." "Chinalcrio," *Financial Times*, February 13, 2009, 12. Chinalco had in fact recently led a number of international acquisitions (though none this large). In addition, Chinalco's goals of multi-metal diversification fit nicely with the needs of the state.

7. Chinalco had a well-respected track record of postacquisition success domestically in China, having been created as part of a plan to roll up the fragmented domestic aluminum producers in the early 2000s. In 2004 Chinalco outbid ten rivals to make what was at the time China's largest investment in Australia (a bauxite mine). In May 2007, Chinalco invested in a Saudi joint venture smelter. Chinalco also acquired 49 percent of Yunnan Copper Industry Group, China's third-largest copper producer, and in June of that year Chinalco completed the purchase of Canada's Peru Copper, which enabled Chinalco to diversify into other metals. Baosteel, by contrast, had a reputation for acrimonious and poorly managed consolidation.

8. Alcoa lent $1.2 billion, and perhaps more importantly its name, to the "Shining Prospect" acquisition vehicle, providing some political cover against an anti-Chinese political backlash to the deal. At the end of February 2009, Alcoa formally pulled out of the JV vehicle and received $1.021 billion in cash from Chinalco plus its pro rata share of dividends paid by Rio while "Shining Prospect" owned the shares. Despite the considerable loss in value of the Rio shares after BHP withdrew its bid, Alcoa only had to claim a $120 million noncash after-tax loss on the venture, given Chinalco's obligation to underwrite Alcoa's stake. That Chinalco afforded Alcoa such a degree of downside protection indicates the political rather than financial value that Alcoa brought to the venture.

9. Xiao described the move as one of "unimaginable complexity" in an interview he had with Caijing three weeks later. Zhao Jianfei, "Chinalco's General Manager on the Rio Tinto Buy," *Caijing*, March 3, 2008. Available in English at http://english.caijing.com.cn/2008–03–03/100050605.html

10. See Wang Hengli's Xinhua news report titled, "Zhongmei lianshou 140 yi meiyuan rugu li ta zhongguo zuida haiwai touzi" (cleverly, this can be translated either as: "'Chinalco & Alcoa' jointly invest US$14 billion in Rio Tinto China's largest overseas investment" or as "'China-US' jointly invest . . ." since Chinalco's and Alcoa's Chinese names both include the characters for China and the United States as their first character. Newspaper headlines often employ such abbreviations to save space. In this instance, use of the convention also seems to belie the intent of Alcoa's involvement in the first place.) Available (in Chinese) at http://news.xinhuanet.com/fortune/2008–02/02/content_7548886.htm.

11. See Jiang Yuxia, "Chinalco, Alcoa buy 12% of Rio Tinto's UK-listed firm," available at http://news.xinhuanet.com/english/2008–02/01/content_7545423.htm.

12. Author's interviews #2008620 and #2008625a, Beijing. Daniel Drezner suggests that such reticence is to be expected in the area of economic statecraft and is not necessarily unique to the Chinese case. See Daniel W. Drezner, "The Hidden Hand of Economic Coercion," *International Organization* 57 (2003): 643–59.

13. Oster and Carew, "China Inc.'s Top Deal Maker Provokes a Backlash Abroad."

14. Ibid.

15. "As a triple-B borrower, Rio has secured debt financing at a size and rate for which it would have otherwise struggled. The valuation of assets that Chinalco is buying into, meanwhile, is ahead of most analysts' estimates." Ibid. "Rio says it could have raised $10bn from a rights issue. But that would have left it needing more, forcing it to sell prized assets

at firesale prices. Chinalco's bid, it argues, is generously priced and offers access to Chinese cash and minerals," David Pilling, "Do Not Reject Chinalco's Bid for Bogus Reasons," *Financial Times*, February 26, 2009, 9.

16. Xiao was subsequently promoted to deputy secretary general of the State Council and made an alternative member of the 17th CPC Central Committee. In 2012, he was once again promoted, this time to full member status of the 18th CPC Central Committee and given a spot on the powerful Central Commission for Discipline Inspection.

17. Shareholders grew more and more displeased with company management and the Chinalco deal that threatened to dilute existing shareholders by not adequately providing them with an opportunity to maintain their current equity stake.

18. Oster and Carew, "China Inc.'s Top Deal Maker Provokes a Backlash Abroad."

19. This episode is discussed in more detail below.

20. Antonio Regalado, "Corporate News: Beijing Considers Financing Petrobras," *Wall Street Journal*, February 20, 2009, B3.

21. "China reached a long-term deal to lend $25 billion to two Russian energy companies in exchange for an expanded supply of Russian oil, highlighting how the world's No. 3 economy is using its financial muscle to lock up access to natural resources." David Winning, Shai Oster, and Alex Wilson, "World News: China, Russia Strike $25 Billion Oil Pact—in Third Deal in a Week, Beijing Moves to Lock Up Natural Resources at Bargain Prices to Fuel its Growth," *Wall Street Journal*, February 18, 2009, A8.

22. At the time, China imported about half of the oil it was using.

23. Winning, Oster, and Wilson, "World News: China, Russia Strike $25 Billion Oil Pact," A8.

24. Erica Downs, "In China-Russia Gas Deal, Why China Wins More," *Forbes*, June 20, 2014, available online at http://fortune.com/2014/06/20/in-china-russia-gas-deal-why-china-wins-more/.

25. "Brazil's government has pressed the oil giant, the country's largest company, to increase spending ahead of elections in 2010 and as a tonic against the economic crisis ... it will spend $28 billion through 2013 exploring and drilling in the deep-water fields." Regalado, "Corporate News: Beijing Considers Financing Petrobras."

26. Ibid.

27. "*Guojia kaifa yinhang*" is more accurately translated as "Nation Development Bank," but I have adopted the common naming convention of "China Development Bank" or "CDB" that more often appears in English-language sources.

28. The Big Four are ICBC (which was primarily engaged in providing industrial and commercial credit), Agricultural Bank of China (which provided credit primarily to rural areas), Bank of China (which handled foreign currencies), and China Construction Bank (which specialized in medium- to long-term domestic infrastructure project finance). With the 1994 reforms, these fiscal policy activities began to be transitioned to the policy banks, and the Big Four were made ready for public stock listings as commercial-oriented banks.

29. Regarding the role of China's policy banks in supporting national priorities, see He Fan, Xu Qiyuan, and Xuxiu Jun, "Strategic Options for Development Finance in Promoting Financial Cooperation in China's Near Abroad," *China Market*, iss. 16 (2011): 4–6 (in Chinese).

30. In 2008, CDB had assets of $540 billion. The World Bank had approximately $58.8 billion in 2009 (38.2 in 2008) while the Asian Development Bank had only about $52 billion. See http://web.worldbank.org/WBSITE/EXTERNAL/NEWS/0,,contentMDK:22233771~pagePK:34370~piPK:34424~theSitePK:4607,00.html, and http://www.adb.org/Documents/Others/Financial_Profile/default.asp?p=orgfrs respectively. By 2012, CDB's assets had topped the $1 trillion threshold.

31. Jamil Anderlini, "Illegal Lending Scandal Hits China Development Bank," *Financial Times*, August 30, 2008, 9.

32. See chapter 10 for more on the CIC's origins.

33. CDB was recapitalized at $20 billion. See Brad Setser, "The Implications of Sovereign Wealth Fund Investments for National Security," Testimony before the US-China Economic and Security Review Commission, February 7, 2007, 9; Xin Zhiming, "Huijin to Inject $20b into China Development Bank," *China Daily*, December 31, 2007. On December 11, 2008, CDB officially changed its organizational structure to a corporate stockholding structure similar to the sort the Big Four commercial banks have used to go public. As part of this reorganization, Central Huijin provided RMB 146.1 billion and the Ministry of Finance provided a RMB 153.9 billion registered capital injection, again similar to the efforts to shore up commercial banks' balance sheets before public listing. As a result, CDB's 2008 Annual Report lists Central Huijin as owning 48.7 percent of CDB while the Ministry of Finance (MoF) holds the remaining 51.3 percent. That figure remained relatively unchanged (except for a small stake given to China's Social Security Fund) according to CDB's 2012 Annual Report, which lists Central Huijin as owning 47.63 percent of CDB while the National Council for Social Security Fund now owns 2.19 percent and the MoF holds the remaining 50.18 percent.

34. CDB's 2008 Annual Report available in English at http://www.cdb.com.cn/English/Column.asp?ColumnId=91.

35. CDB's 2012 Annual Report available in English at http://www.cdb.com.cn/english/Column.asp?ColumnId=91.

36. "The State Council has become more active in communicating its wishes to key departments and companies of late. . . . In some instances, the State Council has itself been the driver of investments abroad." Paul Glasson, "Regional Focus to Global Push: The China Syndrome," *The Australian*, March 4, 2009, 22.

37. These will be discussed in more detail in part 4 of the book.

38. "China's State Council, the country's cabinet, also announced measures yesterday to stimulate lending and mitigate the impact of the global slowdown on China's slowing economy. The council said it would work to ensure there was sufficient liquidity in the banking system and would allow the country's three 'policy' banks—China Development Bank, China Export and Import Bank and China Agricultural Development Bank—to make a further Rmb100bn ($14.5bn, EUR11.5bn, pound(s)9.9bn) of loans." Jamil Anderlini, Geoff Dyer, and Raphael Minder, "Western Banks Face Snub from China Fund," *Financial Times*, December 4, 2008, 3. "China Development Bank (CDB), a joint-stock commercial lender reformed from policy one, relied on its project reserve advantage to further expand credit in 2008, in line with the domestic demand expansion policy. 83.3% of its loan was provided for the nation's coal, electricity, and oil supply, agriculture, forestry, animal husbandry and fishery, telecommunications, and public infrastructure fields, as well as central, west, and northeast China enjoyed 64.5% of the total money loaned by CDB. In addition, the Beijing-located bank aggregately lent CNY 83.3 billion to the domestic environment protection, energy saving, and emission reduction projects, and around CNY 17 billion was loaned to disaster areas attacked by the 8.0-magnitude earthquake on May 12, 2008." "China Development Bank Expanded Credit in 08," *SinoCast China Business Daily News*, January 12, 2009.

39. "Barclays strengthened its bidding power for ABN Amro by raising Euros 3.6bn from China Development Bank and Singapore's Temasek, in return for stakes of 3.1 and 2.1 per cent respectively." John Willman, "Yesterday's Bad Guys Ride to the Rescue," *Financial Times*, January 23, 2008, 4. CDB invested approximately $2.9 billion.

40. "Barclays will train CDB commodities traders and bankers and will become the Chinese bank's preferred provider of commodity market risk hedging. . . . The bank also

264   NOTES TO PAGES 102–112

said it will help CDB develop commodity products, focusing initially on corporate clients rather than investors, trading capabilities and commodities risk management infrastructure. . . . Gao Jian, deputy governor of CDB, said Barclays was the right long-term partner for the bank. The agreement, which runs to 2012 and could be extended for another five-year period, is part of the banks' alliance started in July when CDB became one of Barclays' largest shareholders." Javier Blas, "Barclays to Form Alliance with CDB," *Financial Times*, October 10, 2007, 17.

41. Apparently, one of the factors that enabled CDB to be tapped to finance the Chinalco-Rio deal was CDB's relationship with international bankers.

42. CDB's structure as a policy bank entails a statutory obligation to implement state policy rather than operate on purely commercial terms.

43. Large transactions often signal important data points for the study of economic statecraft in these sectors. They also generally involve relatively high levels of public visibility, which provides instructive transparency in what can otherwise be murky terrain.

PART III. CROSS-STRAIT ECONOMIC STATECRAFT

1. Other such regional approaches have focused on China's relations with ASEAN/ Southeast Asia, Africa, Central Asia, Latin America, etc.

2. Scott L. Kastner, *Political Conflict and Economic Interdependence Across the Taiwan Strait and Beyond* (Stanford, CA: Stanford University Press, 2009). See also Scott L. Kastner, "When Do Conflicting Political Relations Affect International Trade?" *Journal of Conflict Resolution* 51, no. 4 (August 2007): 664–88.

3. Murray Scot Tanner, *Chinese Economic Coercion Against Taiwan: A Tricky Weapon to Use* (Santa Monica, CA: RAND Corporation, 2007).

4. See Chen-Yuan Tung, "Cross-Strait Economic Relations: China's Leverage and Taiwan's Vulnerability," *Issues & Studies* 39, no. 3 (September 2003): 137–75.

5. For a more detailed treatment of the full range of ways economic interaction can affect security, see William Norris, "Security Externalities: A Theoretical Framework for Understanding the Relationship Between Economics and National Security" (unpublished manuscript).

6. COERCIVE LEVERAGE ACROSS THE TAIWAN STRAIT

1. These periods are not really as neat as this conceptual abstraction makes them out to be. In the real world, various tools of economic statecraft may be in operation throughout these historical periods. For purposes of empirical analysis, though, the periods can be usefully distinguished from each other by the broad underlying strategic logic and the dominant theory of victory that underpinned China's approach to economic statecraft during that particular phase. Indeed, strands of both a "carrot" and "stick" approach have long been present in the mainland's Taiwan strategy. By drawing the distinction between China's coercive leverage strategy and its interest transformation strategy, this periodization seeks to highlight the different causal logics underpinning the respective strategies' use of tools of economic statecraft.

2. "During the relatively early years of cross-strait engagement, when China relied more heavily on Taiwan for investment, Chinese officials—especially local officials—went out of their way to reassure Taishang investors that their businesses would be insulated from downturns in Beijing-Taipei relations." Murray Scot Tanner, *Chinese Economic Coercion against Taiwan: A Tricky Weapon to Use* (Santa Monica, CA: RAND Corporation, 2007), 113.

3. Although it should be noted that mainland China does seem to exhibit some degree of learning across these three election cycles. In the run-up to the 1996 election, China

fired missiles alarmingly close to Taiwan as part of a series of exercises. This did have a crude, destabilizing economic impact (particularly on Taiwan's stock market), although most analysts would argue that the attempt to intimidate Taiwan resulted in greater public support of Lee Tung-hui. In the 2000 election, there were broad efforts to punish "green" businesses (those that supported the DPP/Taiwanese independence) as well as strongly worded statements by Zhu Rongji. But by 2004, China had focused its coercive strategies on specific individuals and targeted businesses. Taken together, these three cycles provide support for the notion that China's use of coercive leverage became more sophisticated as lessons from previous efforts were analyzed and incorporated.

4. Recall the discussion of security externalities in chapter 1. For more on interest transformation types of security externalities, see William Norris, "Security Externalities: A Theoretical Framework for Understanding the Relationship Between Economics and National Security" (unpublished manuscript).

5. Tanner, *Chinese Economic Coercion against Taiwan*, 111.

6. Abdelal and Kirshner also call attention to what Albert Hirschman called influence effects. Both works note the need for additional scholarship designed to understand exactly how this sort of economic statecraft works in practice. For more see Rawi Abdelal and Jonathan Kirshner, "Strategy, Economic Relations, and the Definition of National Interests," *Security Studies* 9, no. 1 (1999): 119; and Albert O. Hirschman, *National Power and the Structure of Foreign Trade* (Berkeley: University of California Press, 1945).

7. Karen M. Sutter, "Business Dynamism Across the Taiwan Strait," *Asian Survey* 42, no. 3 (May/June 2002): 522, 527; Richard C. Bush, *Untying the Knot: Making Peace in the Taiwan Strait* (Washington, DC: Brookings Institution Press, 2005), 28, also highlights the appreciation of the new Taiwan dollar in addition to the rising costs of land and labor in Taiwan, as well as growing domestic demand for stricter environmental regulations.

8. For a good case study of such dynamics see Laurids S. Lauridsen, "Policies and Institutions of Industrial Deepening and Upgrading in Taiwan I—the Basic Industry Strategy in Petrochemicals," vol. 4 (Working paper no. 10, produced for the GlobAsia Research Group, International Development Studies, Roskilde University, Denmark, 1999).

9. Tse-Kang Leng, "The State and Taiwan's Mainland Economic Policy," *Asian Affairs: An American Review* 23, no. 1 (Spring 1996): 31.

10. "Increased political competition enabled civil society, especially business interests, to gain greater voice relative to the state than it had during the earlier period of state-guided export-led industrialization." Steve Chan, "The Politics of Economic Exchange: Carrots and Sticks in Taiwan-China-U.S. Relations," *Issues & Studies* 42, no. 2 (2006): 6.

11. This domestic political economy development on Taiwan is an important precursor of the inability of the Taiwanese government to control its commercial actors, a dynamic observed later in the 1990s and 2000s. This makes it easier for commercial actors to avoid tight control as opposed to the earlier period of tight state control of the economy. As Taiwan liberalized and the economy became more and more privatized, the state had less ability to maintain control over its commercial actors, whose cross-strait engagement generated strategic externalities with which Taiwan's administrations would later have to contend. China continues to seek to take advantage of these economic ties to further its strategic objectives.

12. Seanon S. Wong, "Economic Statecraft Across the Strait: Business Influence in Taiwan's Mainland Policy," *Asian Perspective* 29, no. 2 (2005): 41–72, highlighted the need for the DPP to moderate its position and tack to the center, but what may be more interesting is how winning elections in Taiwan became so dependent on campaign contributions and the important role of Taiwan's large corporations as a source of these contributions.

13. By the late 1970s, the Chinese Communist Party faced public alienation after four decades of failed economic policies. Under the leadership of Deng Xiaoping, the party

turned to economic growth based on liberalization that required massive amounts of foreign investment. Taiwan business owners were an obvious source because they had capital and because they were culturally Chinese. Bush, *Untying the Knot*, 28.

14. Ibid., 28

15. As early as Marshall Ye Jianying's Nine Points speech in 1981, the PRC has been taking specific steps to facilitate private-sector Taiwanese investment in mainland China. Nancy Bernkopf Tucker, *Dangerous Strait: The U.S.–Taiwan–China Crisis* (New York: Columbia University Press, 2005), 102; also see Bush, *Untying the Knot*, 36–38.

16. These articles contained all the special inducements offered to foreign investors, but went several steps further by allowing Taiwanese investors to sell stock in projects, rent government-owned factories, and take over and operate state enterprises by guaranteeing a certain amount of earnings to the state. See Leng, "The State and Taiwan's Mainland Economic Policy," 29, and Tucker, *Dangerous Strait*, 102.

17. Yu-shan Wu notes that during this post-Tiananmen period, the PRC's cross-strait economic strategic behavior was driven more out of economic necessity stemming from suspended investment flows rather than by any serious motivation to use economic interaction to unify Taiwan. See Wu, "Mainland China's Economic Policy Toward Taiwan: Economic Needs Or Unification Scheme?" *Issues and Studies* 30, no. 9 (September 1994): 29–49.

18. Weng notes that Taiwan offered only "half-hearted condemnation" of the Tiananmen crackdown. B.S.J. Weng, "The Evolution of a Divided China," in *The Chinese and Their Future: Beijing, Taipei and Hong Kong*, ed. Z. Lin Thomas W. Robinson (Washington, DC: American Enterprise Institute Press, 1991), 373. Instead of an expected cooling of cross-straits economic activity, investment activity actually picked up steam during this period as Western capital flows dried up. The degree of China's isolation should not be overstated, however. In addition to Taiwanese FDI, Japan was also fairly quick to reinstate much of its economic aid and loans.

19. Ibid.

20. Ibid.

21. Cheng notes that Deng's South China Tour is also likely to have been responsible for attracting Taiwanese FDI during this period. See Tucker, *Dangerous Strait*, 97.

22. It should also be noted that during this time, the Taiwanese government relaxed its position on prohibited investments in mainland China. In this more relaxed atmosphere, a higher level of investment was officially reported to the government. Thus the unusually high levels of FDI reported in 1993 are in part due to the belated registration with the Taiwanese Investment Commission (part of the Ministry of Economic Affairs) by firms that invested surreptitiously in China previously. For more on this see Cheng in Tucker, *Dangerous Strait*, 97.

23. Frequently, supporting legal infrastructure was locally based and relied on maintaining good relations with local municipal authorities. Until the Koo-Wang talks and the Regulations for Encouraging Investment, there was little nationally based law to govern the security of private property rights and other issues of ownership and transfer.

24. Tax concessions included two years of corporate tax exemption and three years of 50 percent reduction. Land concessions filled out the offering with government-led development of industrial estates to facilitate the benefits of larger technology parks.

25. Defining and ensuring enforcement of private property rights was a key source of uncertainty and insecurity that Beijing tried to address in its development of a supporting legal and economic infrastructure in mainland China. For more on the centrality of property rights in economic development see Douglass Cecil North and Robert Paul Thomas, *The Rise of the Western World; a New Economic History* (Cambridge, UK: Cambridge University Press, 1973); Douglass Cecil North, *Structure and Change in Economic History*, 1st ed. (New

York: Norton, 1981); Oliver E. Williamson, Sidney G. Winter, and R.H. Coase, *The Nature of the Firm: Origins, Evolution, and Development* (New York: Oxford University Press, 1991).

26. "Similarly, Beijing gained the support of Hong Kong's business community in opposing democratic reforms by the last British governor, Chris Patten, with threats to ruin their businesses after 1997." Bruce Gilley and Julian Baum, "Crude Tactics," *Far Eastern Economic Review* 163, no. 26 (2000): 25.

27. "The implicit threat is to close Taiwan out while the rest of the world is rushing in." Bob Ross as quoted in ibid.

28. "During the 1995–1996 and 1999–2000 Taiwan Strait incidents, the localities—particularly in the coastal areas—reiterated their pledge to protect the interests of TIE [Taiwan Invested Enterprises]." Chen-Yuan Tung, "Cross-Strait Economic Relations: China's Leverage and Taiwan's Vulnerability," *Issues & Studies* 39, no. 3 (Sept. 2003): 137–75, 169. Although to be fair, Tung is correct to note that it is uncertain to what degree these local preferences determined (or at least constrained) Beijing's behavior.

29. "'The cross-straits economic and trade co-operation and other exchanges are in the fundamental interests of the people on both sides of the Taiwan Straits and *have an important bearing on the development and prosperity of the Chinese nation*. Therefore they are not to be affected by political disparities across the Taiwan Straits,' said Chen Yunlin, Deputy Director of the Taiwan Affairs Office of the State Council, at a meeting with Taiwan investors in Fujian, a province facing Taiwan. 'No matter what happens, the rights and interests of Taiwan business people investing in the mainland will always be protected and will not be harmed.' . . . China's mainland 'is committed to provide better investment environment for Taiwan business people *for the prosperity of the Chinese nation in the 21st Century*,' Chen said." Xinhua News Agency, "Political Disparities Won't Affect Taiwan Investors: Official," August 7, 1995 (italics added). For evidence of additional reassurances, also see speeches of other senior mainland officials and government media coverage at the time Xinhua News Agency, "Wang Daohan Pledges to Protect Legitimate Rights of Taiwan Investors," October 29 1995; Xinhua News Agency, "Taiwan Investors' Interests on Mainland Reassured," September 7, 1995; Xinhua News Agency, "Wang Daohan: Situation Across Straits Will Not Affect Investment," October 16, 1995; Xinhua News Agency, "Taiwan Investors' Interests Well Protected," September 26, 1995; Xinhua News Agency, "China's Pledge to Taiwan Investors," March 25, 1996.

30. China's coastal economic engines of growth, particularly Fujian, were still highly reliant on Taiwanese capital and management expertise.

31. The last paragraph of the document begins, "As the Chinese government has successively resumed the exercise of sovereignty over Hong Kong and Macao, the people of the whole of China are eager to resolve the Taiwan issue as early as possible and realize the total reunification of the country. They cannot allow the resolution of the Taiwan issue to be postponed indefinitely." For the full text of the 2000 White Paper see http://english.gov.cn/official/2005–07/27/content_17613.htm.

32. See for instance E. S. Medeiros and M. T. Fravel, "China's New Diplomacy," *Foreign Affairs* 82, no. 6 (2003): 22–35.

33. Xinhua General News Service, "China Will Not Yield on Matter of Principle—Official," April 8, 2000.

34. Tang stated that *taishang* did little to promote reunification while reaping profits. Chung-yan Chow, "Business Leaders Warned on Independence," *South China Morning Post*, April 10, 2000.

35. Dermot Doherty, "Taiwan's Business Leaders Take Sides before Vote," *Dow Jones Newswire*, March 16, 2000.

36. Mure Dickie and James Kynge, "Business in Taiwan Heeds Warning on Independence," *Financial Times*, April 11, 2000, 12.

37. Ibid.

38. Doherty, "Taiwan's Business Leaders Take Sides before Vote."

39. "'Individual leading business figures have, on the one hand, openly supported Taiwan independence on the island, and on the other, obtained advantages from their economic activities in the mainland,' the official, He Zhiming, told a group of pro-Beijing businessmen. 'This is absolutely not permitted. I believe all of you, on listening to these remarks, will know how to choose when seeking Taiwan trading partners.'" John Pomfret, "China Warns Taiwan Firms Not to Back Sovereignty; Beijing Says Businesses Risk Losing its Trade," *Washington Post*, June 3, 2000, sec. A, 9. The Hong Kong government denied this position, "but the damage was already done." See the June 5, 2000, editorial in the *Asian Wall Street Journal* titled "China's Threats—Withholding Economic Opportunities to Influence Taiwan Will Backfire," 8. Also see J. R. Wu, "Taiwan Businesses Can Still Seek the Good Earth but Wary," *Dow Jones International News*, June 25, 2000.

40. Dickie and Kynge, "Business in Taiwan Heeds Warning on Independence."

41. Mure Dickie and James Kynge, "China in Warning to Taiwan Businesses," *Financial Times*, April 10, 2000, 10.

42. Gilley and Baum, "Crude Tactics."

43. Pomfret, "China Warns Taiwan Firms Not to Back Sovereignty."

44. Tanner, *Chinese Economic Coercion against Taiwan.*

45. See for instance "Business Trumps Politics," *The Economist* (U.S. Edition), July 28, 2001.

46. Brian Bremmer and Matt Kovac, "China's New Taiwan Tack," *BusinessWeek*, May 16, 2005.

47. Ibid.

48. I use the term "entities" to denote that targets of this type of economic power are not limited to the Taiwan case. Local governments, businesses, specific individuals, newspapers, or NGOs are some examples of entities that may be targets of such practices. The Hong Kong case provides several illustrations of how Beijing uses this sort of economic power.

49. "Throughout most of the campaign, moreover, Beijing appeared to demonstrate much greater sophistication about influencing democratic politics than it had shown in the past. . . . Beijing largely refrained—though not entirely—from the type of finger-wagging public threats against the Taiwan electorate that had proven disastrously counterproductive in the 1996 and 2000 elections." Tanner, *Chinese Economic Coercion against Taiwan*, 118.

50. It deserves to be noted that China's 2000 White Paper on Taiwan suggested that the mainland's patience with the status quo was wearing thin and that delays of the eventual reunification would not be tolerated "indefinitely." This suggests that China may have been revising its objectives for the portion of this case spanning the period roughly from 2000 to 2004.

51. Such local support is critical in successful investments. According to Taiwanese businessmen, "policies, negotiations, or agreements signed by Taipei and Beijing help very little; what really controls the daily life is the local city or county government." Leng cites his interview with Liu An-kuo, a Taiwanese lampmaker, in August of 1994. Leng, "The State and Taiwan's Mainland Economic Policy," 26.

7. INTEREST TRANSFORMATION ACROSS THE TAIWAN STRAIT

1. Xinhua General News Service, "Taiwan Fruit Arrives in Wake of Lian-Soong Visits to Chinese Mainland," May 15, 2005.

2. Soong was chairman of the People First Party (PFP) in Taiwan, a party that split from the KMT just before the 2000 presidential election. It and the KMT were the two

main opposition parties making up the "pan-blue" alliance that opposed Chen's DPP-led "pan-green" alliance. Soong's delegation visited the Chinese mainland from May 5 through May 13. Like Lien, it was the first time Soong had returned to the mainland since leaving in 1949. Soong also met Hu and visited the cities of Xi'an, Nanjing, Shanghai, and Changsha. "Taiwan's Soong Due in Beijing Amid Ray of Hope," *Agence France Presse—English*, May 10, 2005.

3. For how the lowering of fruit tariffs fit into the broader strategy of "public power" see PRC Ministry of Commerce, "Ministry of Commerce Spokesman Announces Implementation of Zero Tariff Handling Measures for 15 Types of Taiwanese Fruit," July 28, 2005, press release (in Chinese). Available at www.mofcom.gov.cn. Also, Jia Qinglin (chairman of the People's Political Consultative Conference and vice chairman of the Taiwan Affairs Leading Small Group) set out China's emerging Taiwan strategy in his January 28, 2005, speech. Available in Chinese at http://news.sina.com.cn/c/2005-01-28/20344978641s.shtml.

4. China offered to allow more Taiwan students to study in China and stated it would recognize Taiwan-issued degrees for purposes of mainland employment. Beijing also pledged to grant scholarships to Taiwanese students as well as extend to Taiwanese students the privilege of paying similar (i.e., reduced) tuition fees, equivalent to those that mainland Chinese students were charged. See Chua Chin Hon, "Taiwan Gets More Sweeteners from China," *Straits Times* (Singapore), May 14, 2005. In addition to the educational concessions, China also permitted a greater number of mainland tourists to visit Taiwan (although the Taiwanese government still had its own restrictions on the number of mainland visitors it would permit to enter). It also offered to establish direct air cargo links to help facilitate the transportation of perishable fruit. Finally, China offered a gift of two pandas to the Taipei Zoo. This offer was eventually declined by Taiwan on the grounds that international trafficking of endangered species is not permitted. "By rejecting these offers, the ruling Democratic Progressive Party is putting itself in a difficult position. Almost all these policies benefit segments of the Taiwanese population. When this adds up, the ruling party is going to face the consequence of losing the support of these people." Professor Emile Sheng of Taiwan's Soochow University, as quoted in Chua Chin Hon, "Taiwan Gets More Sweeteners from China," 4.

5. Wang Feng, "'Lien-Soong' Land, Seek New Cross-Strait Economic/Trade Breakthrough," *Caijing*, May 16, 2005 (in Chinese).

6. "Since its red-carpet welcome of Taiwanese opposition leaders Lien Chan and James Soong in late April and early May, the Mainland's strategy has been to try and win the hearts of the Taiwanese people while isolating the island's pro-independence forces. The farm benefits target south Taiwan—a key support base for the island's pro-independence government and a major fruit-growing area." Clarissa Oon, "China Scraps Import Tariffs on Taiwan Fruits; Beijing Acts on Pledges Made during Taipei Opposition Visits," *Straits Times* (Singapore), June 2, 2005.

7. For a convincing treatment of this perspective see Robert S. Ross, "Taiwan's Fading Independence Movement," *Foreign Affairs* 85, no. 2 (2006): 141.

8. A prominent example of Ma's efforts is the Economic Cooperation Framework Agreement (ECFA), which lowered the tariffs and permitted access to the mainland market for about five hundred Taiwanese goods.

9. Formal independence has been a red line for China for quite some time. See for example Chong-Pin Lin, "More Carrot than Stick: Beijing's Emerging Taiwan Policy," *China Security* 4, no. 1 (2008): 1–27; Emerson M. S. Niou, "Understanding Taiwan Independence and its Policy Implications," *Asian Survey* 44, no. 4 (2004): 555–67.

10. As Tanner puts it, "But Beijing's predominant tactical concern remains trying to reshape the political mainstream in Taiwan's emerging democracy, so that Beijing's

anti-independence demands and pro-reunification overtures to Taipei will be greeted with increasing political acceptance." Murray Scot Tanner, *Chinese Economic Coercion against Taiwan: A Tricky Weapon to Use* (Santa Monica, CA: RAND Corporation, 2007), 105.

11. Ibid., 111.

12. For an illustrative description of such dynamics see Rawi Abdelal and Jonathan Kirshner, "Strategy, Economic Relations, and the Definition of National Interests," *Security Studies* 9, no. 1 (1999). Their discussion of the Hawaii case is particularly useful.

13. Tanner, *Chinese Economic Coercion against Taiwan*, 111.

14. Ibid., 105.

15. Ibid., 105.

16. For example, Fujian had already attracted some $1.9 billion of Taiwanese investment in the agricultural sector. In the wake of this episode, there were plans to create "cross-strait agricultural co-operation experiment zones" between the cities of Fuzhou and Zhangzhou.

17. MofCom frequently referred to China's larger strategic approach to Taiwan in its policy statements. See for example PRC Ministry of Commerce, "Ministry of Commerce Spokesman Announces Implementation of Zero Tariff Handling Measures for 15 Types of Taiwanese Fruit," July 28, 2005, press release (in Chinese).

18. Chen Yunlin, minister of the Taiwan Affairs Office, reportedly referred to the "tariff-free entry of Taiwanese fruit" as "a concrete effort by the Mainland to promote the fundamental interests of Taiwan compatriots." "Mainland Drops Taiwan Fruit Tax," *China Daily*, July 29, 2005. This language is similar to that used in Hu's March 3, 2005, speech.

19. Jiang had already handed over chairmanship of the Central Military Commission in mid-September 2004 to Hu Jintao.

20. The last variable, reflecting the balance of relative resources, also does not seem to factor strongly in this case. Although it may have slightly favored the state by virtue of having China's well-resourced Ministry of Commerce acting as the gatekeeper, these resources ought to be assessed relative to the fragmented and relatively underresourced fruit farmers.

21. Goh Sui Noi, "KMT Win a Victory for Ties with Beijing," *Straits Times* (Singapore), December 5, 2005; Xinhua General News Service, "KMT Spokesman: Development of Cross-Straits Relations Trend of Times," May 2, 2005.

22. "The tactical considerations behind the visit are simple. Mr. Lien wants to send the message to [the] Taiwanese that he and his party can manage cross-strait relations better than President Chen and his DPP, a message Beijing is happy to reinforce." "A Historic Visit to China," *Japan Times*, May 5, 2005..

23. "In the case of commerce across the Taiwan Strait, China has deliberately reached out to select groups or sectors in Taiwan, such as fruit farmers, airline companies, petrochemical firms, and the tourist industry, that have a particular interest in gaining or maintaining access to the mainland market." Steve Chan, "The Politics of Economic Exchange: Carrots and Sticks in Taiwan-China-U.S. Relations," *Issues & Studies* 42, no. 2 (2006): 4.

24. The DPP's origins are intertwined with the story of Taiwan's democratization. Charles Chi-hsiang Chang and Hung-mao Tien, *Taiwan's Electoral Politics and Democratic Transition: Riding the Third Wave* (Armonk, NY: M. E. Sharpe, 1996).

25. John Fuh-sheng Hsieh and Emerson M.S. Niou, "Issue Voting in the Republic of China on Taiwan's 1992 Legislative Yuan Election," *International Political Science Review / Revue Internationale De Science Politique* 17, no. 1 (1996): 13–27, esp. 21.

26. Andrew J. Nathan, "The Legislative Yuan Elections in Taiwan: Consequences of the Electoral System," *Asian Survey* 33, no. 4 (1993): 424–38, figures taken from page 425.

27. For more on these events see Nancy Bernkopf Tucker, *Dangerous Strait: The U.S.–Taiwan–China Crisis* (New York: Columbia University Press, 2005); Suisheng Zhao, *Across*

the Taiwan Strait: Mainland China, Taiwan, and 1995–1996 Crisis (New York: Routledge, 1999); Chen Qimao, "The Taiwan Strait Crisis: Its Crux and Solutions," *Asian Survey* 36, no. 11 (1996): 1055.

28. Tun-jen Cheng, "Taiwan in 1996: From Euphoria to Melodrama," *Asian Survey* 37, no. 1, A Survey of Asia in 1996: Part I (1997): 43–51, figures taken from page 44.

29. Eventually Lee would form his own proindependence Taiwan Solidarity Union (TSU) party and leave the KMT. The TSU would later join with the DPP to anchor what would become known as the "pan-green alliance."

30. Yu-shan Wu, "Taiwan in 2000: Managing the Aftershocks from Power Transfer," *Asian Survey* 41, no. 1, A Survey of Asia in 2000 (2001): 40–48, esp. 41.

31. E. Niou and P. Paolino, "The Rise of the Opposition Party in Taiwan: Explaining Chen Shui-bian's Victory in the 2000 Presidential Election," *Electoral Studies* 22, no. 4 (2003): 721–740, figures taken from note 14, p. 733.

32. In response, the KMT forged a "pan-blue" alliance with Soong's People First Party (PFP) and the pro-China New Party (NP) in a desperate move to maintain control of the Legislative Yuan. This coalition stood in opposition to the "pan-green" alliance between the DPP and the TSU. The best the KMT could do was to create a blocking coalition to deadlock the legislature and block President Chen's DPP agenda.

33. Ching-hsin Yu, "The Evolving Party System in Taiwan, 1995–2004," *Journal of Asian and African Studies* 40, no. 1–2 (2005): 105–23, table 1, 110.

34. During his visit, James Soong signed an agreement with Hu Jintao opposing Taiwanese independence. See Xinhua General News Service, "No Taiwan Independence, No Military Conflicts: Communique," May 12, 2005.

35. "In Beijing, Chen Shui-bian's reelection touched off a bitter internal debate over how much political leverage Beijing is getting from its economic ties with Taiwan." Tanner, *Chinese Economic Coercion against Taiwan*, 126.

36. Tanner, *Chinese Economic Coercion against Taiwan*, 119–20. This result provides a good illustration of how policies designed to achieve coercive leverage (harassment of the DPP-leaning *taishang*) can often undermine interest transformation strategies.

37. Ibid., esp. 113–26.

38. Chen Shui-bian's re-election as president in 2004 seems to have been the catalyst prompting this strategic re-evaluation of China's approach to Taiwan. Chow Chung-yan and Josephine Ma, "Beijing 'to Rethink its Cross-Strait Strategy,'" *South China Morning Post*, March 22, 2004, 4; Chong-Pin Lin, "More Carrot than Stick: Beijing's Emerging Taiwan Policy," *China Security* 4, no. 1 (2008): 1–27. Lin was formerly Taiwan's deputy minister of national defense and previously served as the first vice chairman of Taiwan's Mainland Affairs Council.

39. With the assumption of chairmanship of the Central Military Commission, Hu completed his consolidation of leadership around this time. This provided Hu with greater latitude to establish guiding principles for China's strategic direction. "On Sept. 24, 2004, five days after Hu took over the chairmanship of the Chinese Communist Party's Central Military Commission, he reportedly approved at an internal meeting a new guideline on Taiwan Policy which reflected his patience: 'strive for negotiation, prepare for war, and fear not Taiwan's procrastination' (*zhengqu tan, zhunbei da, bu pa duo*)." Ibid., 25, note 9.

40. For an example of China's previous efforts to push for reunification sooner rather than later see "One Country Principle and the Taiwan Question," White Paper in the *People's Daily*, Feb. 22, 2000, 1, available (in Chinese) online at http://www.people.com.cn/GB/channel1/14/20000522/72540.html. Before that, Jiang Zemin articulated his Eight Points in a January 30, 1995, speech.

41. He gave the speech in the context of "updating" the mainland's commitment toward Taiwan. See Speech at the Meeting Marking the 10th Anniversary of the Issue of Comrade

Jiang Zemin's Important Speech, "Continue the Struggle to Promote the Accomplishment of the Great Cause of Reunification of Our Motherland." Available in Chinese at http://news.sina.com.cn/c/2005–01–28/20344978641s.shtml. For an indication of its significance, see Xinhua General News Service, "Chen Calls Jia's Speech Important Guide on Taiwan Issue," January 29, 2005.

42. Suisheng Zhao noted this on page 92 of Suisheng Zhao, "Conflict Prevention Across the Taiwan Strait and the Making of China's Anti-Secession Law," *Asian Perspective* 30, no. 1 (2006): 79–94. It comes from a personal interview that he conducted in Beijing in October of 2005. Lin Chong-Pin corroborates this perspective: "[T]he timetable for cross-Strait unification, constantly discussed under Jiang's tenure, has been shelved under Hu." Lin goes on to note, "A number of dates for unification, to be achieved with force if necessary, were considered at different stages including 2002, 2005, 2007, 2010, and 2020, although Jiang never publicly ruled a final decision on it." Lin, "More Carrot than Stick: Beijing's Emerging Taiwan Policy," 3. Lin notes that these dates were not reported officially via Xinhua or Renmin Ribao but rather through Hong Kong media outlets.

43. See Xinhua General News Service, "Four-Point Guideline on Cross-Straits Relations Set Forth by President Hu," March 4, 2005; Xinhua General News Service, "Do Best to Seek Peaceful Reunification, but Never Tolerate Taiwan Independence: President," March 4, 2005.

44. This contrasts with the previous policy that stressed the need for reunification. For a useful overview of Hu Jintao's "new thinking" in China's Taiwan policy see Guo Weifeng, ed., *Hu Jintao and New Thinking on Cross-Strait Relations* (Hong Kong: China Review Academic Press, 2005) (in Chinese).

45. See, for instance, J. Adams et al., "Taiwan: The Cold Shoulder; Beijing Is Setting Up Legal Cover for an Attack on the Island, and Unnerving Leaders in Taipei," *Newsweek*, Feb. 20, 2005, 32. On the more favorable interpretation see John Q. Tian, *Government, Business, and the Politics of Interdependence and Conflict Across the Taiwan Strait* (New York: Palgrave Macmillan, 2006), 52. "[R]ather than intimidate the Taiwanese, the ASL was meant more to unshackle the hands of Beijing's Taiwan Affairs officials to promote cross-Strait engagement from internal hawkish opposition." Lin, "More Carrot than Stick: Beijing's Emerging Taiwan Policy," 5.

46. See Guo, *Hu Jintao and New Thinking on Cross-Strait Relations*.

47. In the event that Taiwan attempted to declare independence, then the ASL would provide a legal pretext for military options.

48. Zhao, "Conflict Prevention Across the Taiwan Strait and the Making of China's Anti-Secession Law," esp. 92–93 in which Zhao discusses Hu Jintao's new Taiwan policy.

49. Recall Schelling's deterrence versus compellence logic in Thomas C. Schelling, *Arms and Influence* (New Haven, CT: Yale University Press, 1966).

50. Edward Friedman, "China's Changing Taiwan Policy," *American Journal of Chinese Studies* 14, no. 2 (October 2007): 119–34; and Lin, "More Carrot than Stick: Beijing's Emerging Taiwan Policy."

51. Election Study Center, National Chengchi University. "The Elections for Public Offices in the Republic of China." Comparative yearly results demonstrate strongest DPP support in southern counties. http://vote.nccu.edu.tw/engcec/vote4a.asp.

52. Memories of KMT abuse run deep in this part of Taiwan. See for example Ray Cheung, "Where the Kuomintang Is Despised; in Pingtung, Elderly Voters Remember the Party's Brutal Rule," *South China Morning Post*, December 8, 2004, 6.

53. Shelley Rigger, *Politics in Taiwan: Voting for Democracy* (London: Routledge, 1999).

54. J. Lay, K. Yap, and Y. Chen, "The Transition of Taiwan's Political Geography," *Asian Survey* 48, no. 5 (2008): 773.

55. Council of Agriculture, Executive Yuan, Republic of China. *2004 Statistics on Fruit Production by County*. http://eng.coa.gov.tw/content_view.php?catid=9565&hot_new=9529.

56. Although a limited direct trade link had been established between Fujian Province and Taiwan in July 2003, this route was only authorized for shipments weighing less than one hundred tons and with a value of less than US$100,000. These were fairly small amounts by international shipping standards.

57. PRC Ministry of Commerce, "Association for Cross-Strait Economic Exchange: We By No Means Unilaterally Appointed Taiwan's Consultative Representative to the Talks on Implementation of the Zero-Tariff Measures for Taiwanese Fruit," July 28, 2005, press release. Available (in Chinese) at www.mofcom.gov.cn.

58. PRC Ministry of Commerce, "Effective August First: Mainland to Formally Implement Zero Import Tariff for 15 Types of Taiwanese Fruit," July 28, 2005, press release. Available (in Chinese) at www.mofcom.gov.cn.

59. Council of Agriculture, Republic of China. *Agricultural Statistics Yearbook, 2004*, 74, table 5.

60. See Xinhua General News Service, "Do Best to Seek Peaceful Reunification, but Never Tolerate Taiwan Independence: President," March 4, 2005, for excerpts of his speech. Hu's quote was frequently cited both in official mainland press releases covering the fruit tariff developments and in policy statements from the Ministry of Commerce. See for instance PRC Ministry of Commerce, "Ministry of Commerce Spokesman Announces Implementation of Zero Tariff Handling Measures for 15 Types of Taiwanese Fruit," July 28, 2005, press release (in Chinese).

61. "He [Wen Jiabao] declared that Beijing 'will take measures to boost sales on the Mainland of farm produce from Taiwan, *particularly from southern Taiwan*. We will do whatever benefits the Taiwan people,' he emphasized." Ting-I Tsai, "Taipei: Yes, We Have No Bananas," *Asia Times*, October 28, 2006 (italics added).

62. Xinhua General News Service, "Agricultural Exchange Conforms to Aspiration of People Across Taiwan Straits," September 9, 2005.

63. Although MofCom was important (especially with regard to implementation and execution), the mainland's strategy was clearly coordinated from the top, specifically via the Taiwan Affairs Office of the State Council. Xinhua General News Service, "Mainland Association Invites Taiwan Counterparts to Talk about Fruit Sale," June 1, 2005; Xinhua General News Service, "Chinese Mainland Hopes Taiwan Authorities to Push Fruit Exports to Mainland," July 8, 2005.

64. Lilian Wu, "Taiwan Not Restricting Fruit Exports, Wants Cross-Strait Talks," Central News Agency–Taiwan, July 22, 2005.

65. "DPP's Ideology Hinders Fruit Trade," *Business Daily Update*, July 28, 2005, 27; "DPP Plays Politics with People's Interests," *China Daily*, June 28, 2005.

66. See Mainland Affairs Council's daily briefings for June 17, 2005, and July 8, 2005, available at http://www.mac.gov.tw/ct.asp?xItem=47565&ctNode=6462&mp=3 and http://www.mac.gov.tw/ct.asp?xItem=47561&ctNode=6462&mp=3 respectively.

67. "The most important reason for this is that TAITRA has rich experience in the international arena and is specialized in assisting negotiations with foreign countries," MAC vice chairman, as quoted in "Mac, Coa Decline Opposition's Invitation," *China Post*, July 7, 2005.

68. Joseph Wu, DPP-appointed chairman of Taiwan's Mainland Affairs Council, as quoted in "PRC Scraps Tariffs on 15 Taiwan Fruits," *Taiwan News*, July 29, 2005; also see "China Using Fruit Trade to Downgrade Taiwan: Official," *Asia Pulse*, July 27, 2005.

69. "Taiwan Farmers Group to Send Team to China for Talks on Fruit Exports—Report," *AFX—Asia*, June 19, 2005; "Farmers' Group to Visit China, Discuss Exporting Fruits," *China Post*, June 19, 2005.

70. Straits Exchange Foundation vice chairman You Ying-lung, as quoted in "MAC, CoA Decline Opposition's Invitation," *China Post*, July 7, 2005. According to the government's official position, "civic groups were free to visit the mainland provided they did not make any unauthorized deals. He [You] said violators would be punished by law."

71. In meetings on the issue with farmers at the time, there was "a call from opposition Kuomintang (KMT) Chairman Lien Chan and some legislators who said that the government should put aside its anti-China ideology for the benefit of Taiwan's farmers. Lien said the government should respond quickly to China's offer to allow 18 categories of Taiwan fruits into the mainland duty free without politicizing or complicating the issue so that Taiwan's farmers can reap the benefits." "Farmers Interested in Exports to China," *China Post*, May 13, 2005. Although China did offer access for eighteen categories of fruit, only fifteen of these were given tariff-free treatment. On the issue of politicization, also see "KMT Defends Farmers Delegation," *China Post*, June 24, 2005; Jacky Hsu, "Taipei Tries to Soothe Angry Farmers," *South China Morning Post*, July 28, 2005, sec. NEWS, 6.; "DPP's Ideology Hinders Fruit Trade," *Business Daily Update*, July 28, 2005, 27.

72. PRC Ministry of Commerce, "Ministry of Commerce Spokesman Announces Implementation of Zero Tariff Handling Measures for 15 Types of Taiwanese Fruit," July 28, 2005, press release (in Chinese).

73. PRC Ministry of Commerce, "Cross-Strait Agricultural Produce Trade to Gradually Enter a State of Ecstasy," August 1, 2005, press release (in Chinese) (Heilongjiang Province Edition).

74. "Fruit Exports to Mainland China," Customs Administration, Ministry of Finance. Searchable database: http://www.customs.gov.tw/StatisticsWebEN/IESearch.aspx.

75. See for instance Xinhua General News Service, "Measures to Help Sell Taiwan Fruits on Mainland Market Effective," September 28, 2005; "China Spokesman Says Measures Taken to Aid Taiwan Fruit Market," *BBC*, September 28, 2005; and "Taiwan Tariff-Free Fruit Sales Brisk; Pose No Pressure on Hainan Fruit," *People's Daily*, August 12, 2005 (overseas ed.). Available (in Chinese) at http://news.xinhuanet.com/taiwan/2005–08/12/content_3342317.htm. Also see Xinhua General News Service, "Fruit Show Adds Market Value to Chinese Farm Produce," November 12, 2005; and Xinhua General News Service, "China's Mainland to Set Up Business Zones for Taiwan Farmers," June 1, 2005.

76. Xinhua General News Service, "Fruits from Taiwan Embark Mainland with Wider, Easier Access," May 19, 2005.

77. "Farmers Interested in Exports to China," *China Post*, May 13, 2005.

78. Taiwan's largest destination market was Japan ($18.2 million) followed by Hong Kong ($8.1 million), the United States ($5.7 million), Singapore ($2.5 million), Canada ($1.7 million) and mainland China ($340,000). Taiwan Bureau of Foreign Trade, Statistical Database on Foreign Trade.

79. In 2004, Taiwan exported some $38 million worth of fresh fruit in total but only $340,000 to the mainland. Taiwan Bureau of Foreign Trade, Statistical Database on Foreign Trade.

80. "In reaching out to Taiwan's business community, Beijing has not only sought to attract the relocation of large companies such as those in the petrochemical industry or to establish business links with others such as airlines, but it has also promoted ties with the island's fruit farmers and medium sized firms engaged in labor-intensive production. The latter groups constitute key supporters for the DPP." Chan, "The Politics of Economic Exchange," 17. Also see Joel Wuthnow, "The Integration of Cooptation and Coercion: China's Taiwan Strategy since 2001," *East Asia* 23, no. 3 (2006): 26.

81. As is often the case when working with Chinese statistics, I have encountered a number of discrepancies in the course of my research. The most reliable, consistent, and complete figures are those provided by the Customs Agency of Taiwan. Customs Agency, Ministry of Finance, Executive Yuan, R.O.C. http://www.customs.gov.tw/StatisticsWeb EN/IESearch.aspx.

82. Voter behavior is obviously driven by a wide range of factors and considerations.

83. This election is not a reliable indicator for four reasons. First, the vote was a de facto referendum on the proposed constitutional amendments that were designed to move Taiwan's political system toward favoring large, nationwide parties as opposed to the plethora of smaller, largely single-issue or locally driven political parties. The vote was largely treated as a technical matter related to consolidation of Taiwan's democratization. Unlike most elections in Taiwan, this vote was not really about cross-strait ties or even about explicit public policies, rather it was a largely procedural referendum. Second, the election was not campaigned along traditional coalition lines (i.e., pan-blue versus pan-green). Rather, the election fissures were between large parties (the KMT and the DPP) on one side and the smaller parties (TSU, PFP, and a host of other, smaller parties) on the other. The proposed reorganization of the government would consolidate power in the hands of the larger national parties and make it more difficult for smaller parties to play an influential role in national politics. As a result, the smaller parties unsurprisingly aligned against the two (normally opposing) largest parties. Third, most politicians, parties, and the general public treated the vote as a relatively unimportant matter of institutional housekeeping. In comparison to most Taiwanese elections, the political parties and candidates did not spend much money on the election. Finally, record low turnout makes this election an inappropriate indicator. Only about 23 percent of an otherwise historically participatory Taiwanese electorate voted in this election. Taiwanese voter participation is regularly well over 50 percent, and it is not unheard of to see voter turnout of greater than 80 percent. Bad weather in the north also likely kept voters at home, further skewing any meaningful results beyond the constitutional amendments. For these reasons, this election will not be considered when assessing the results of this episode of economic statecraft.

84. These two largest of Taiwan's municipalities are administered directly under the central government and hold elections on their own independent schedule.

85. Lin Hung-chan, spokesman for defeated DPP candidate Chen Li-chen, at Chen's election headquarters, admitting that losing Chia-yi was a significant defeat for the DPP. Hsiu-chuan Shih, "KMT Makes History in Chiayi City," *Taipei Times*, December 4, 2005, 2.

86. "KMT Wins in a Landslide," *China Post*, December 4, 2005.

87. It should be noted that the KMT's 2001 figure is not a good baseline for comparison because the PFP-KMT split was near its height in 2001 and a significant portion of the "pan-blue" vote was likely siphoned off from the KMT's share of the popular vote in 2001.

88. Taiwan's Political Geography Information System, National Cheng Chi University. http://tpgis.nccu.edu.tw/NccuEng/.

89. T. Gold, "Taiwan in 2008: My Kingdom for a Horse," *Asian Survey* 49, no. 1 (2009): 89.

90. Alexander C. Tan, "The 2008 Taiwan Elections: Forward to the Past?" *Electoral Studies* 28, no. 3 (2009): 505.

91. Ibid., esp. 505–6. Perhaps not surprisingly, that county—Yunlin—was not a major producer of any of the tropical fruits that had been targeted. Yunlin was a major producer of *only* oranges (*liucheng*) in 2004, producing 79,000 of the national total of 211,000 metric tons. Yunlin produces less than 5 percent of the national output of all other targeted fruits. Council of Agriculture Yearbook, 2004.

92. Author interview with local DPP official in southern Taiwan, May 2011; "Contents of Tsai Ing-wen's post-election press conference," DPP webpage (in Chinese), January 15, 2012, http://www.dpp.org.tw/news_content.php?&sn=6013; "Frank Hsieh: DPP Should Lean towards KMT's Cross-Strait policy," KMT News Network [from Taipei papers], February 8, 2012, http://www.kmt.org.tw/english/page.aspx?type=article&mnum=112&anum=10855.

93. See for instance Voice of America, "Taiwan Opposition Candidate, in US, Promises Moderate China Policy," VOA, September 14, 2011; Alan Romberg, "All Economics Is Political: ECFA Front and Center," *China Leadership Monitor*, no. 32 (May 2010): 8. On May 4, 2010, Tsai Ing-wen asserted that the DPP's plan to gradually develop relations with the mainland, keeping issues related to sovereignty and political freedom in mind, was more responsible than the aggressive rapprochement pursued by the KMT. While not exactly embracing the mainland, this stance is a far cry from the confrontational Chen.

94. It is also important not to underestimate the significance of signaling in this episode. Improved cross-strait economic ties were important to sectors of Taiwan's economy well beyond fruit or even agriculture more broadly.

95. "When talking about the marketing of Taiwan's farm produce in the mainland, Hu said the issue 'involves the fundamental interests of the broad masses of the Taiwan farmers,'" as quoted in Xinhua General News Service, "Do Best to Seek Peaceful Reunification, But Never Tolerate Taiwan Independence: President," March 4, 2005; "He [Wen Jiabao] declared that Beijing 'will take measures to boost sales on the mainland of farm produce from Taiwan, particularly from southern Taiwan. We will do whatever benefits the Taiwan people,' he emphasized." Tsai, "Taipei: Yes, We Have no Bananas."

96. President Chen made these comments during a meeting with board members of the Outstanding Farmers Association of the ROC. His speech was perceived as defensive in response to what he clearly viewed as strategically threatening overtures from the mainland. See Luis Huang, "China's Duty Free Entry of Taiwan Fruits a Political Need: President," Central News Agency–Taiwan, May 11, 2005.

97. Ting-I Tsai, "The Beijing-Taipei Fruit Fracas," *Asia Times*, August 26, 2005. Taiwan exports more bananas than any other type of fruit. According to Taiwan's Bureau of Foreign Trade, banana exports in 2004 were more than double the next largest type of exported fruit.

98. According to Taiwan's Bureau of Foreign Trade, in 2004, Taiwan exported about US$4.5 million worth of lychee.

99. The townships of Nanxi, Yujing, and Nanhua (ranked first, second, and third, respectively) produced more metric tons of mangoes than any other townships in Tainan, Chiayi, and Kaohsiung counties. Each of these townships produced more than twice the amount of the fourth-ranked township. Mango production figures are drawn from the respective county Accounting, Budget and Statistics Bureau data.

100. Election Study Center at National Chengchi University, "The Elections for Public Offices in the Republic of China," http://vote.nccu.edu.tw/engcec/vote4a.asp. These three townships reside in the Second Constituency of Tainan County. While the KMT fielded no candidate in the Second Constituency, a third-party candidate, Li He-shun, won a large majority of the popular vote (Nanxi: 65.4 percent, Yujing: 58.03 percent, Nanhua: 59.25 percent) *only* in Nanxi, Yujing, and Nanhua, while losing in the rest of the townships. His party, Non-partisan Solidarity Union, makes a point of rejecting Taiwan's political status as an electoral issue. This party espouses the principle that Taiwan's political status vis-à-vis China should not be given primacy at the expense of economic and welfare issues. "Sincerely Defuse Hostility to Resolve Cross-Strait Disputes," NPSU party website (in Chinese), http://www.taconet.com.tw/npsu. The NPSU believes the issue of Taiwan's future political status should be decided at an unspecific future date. "NPSU: Let New President Handle UN Bid," *China Post*, February 2, 2008, http://www.chinapost.com.tw/print/141610.htm.

101. Election Study Center at National Chengchi University: "The Elections for Public Offices in the Republic of China," http://vote.nccu.edu.tw/engcec/vote4a.asp.

102. Because of improvements in fertilizers and pesticides as well as the long lead time for growing oranges and the high sunk costs of uprooting planted trees, this type of fruit has been particularly prone to overproduction in Taiwan.

103. "If this strategy is intended to divide and confuse, it seems to be working. Taiwan's independence-leaning president, Chen Shui-bian, has appeared far less assured in dealing with the goodwill gestures than he did shrugging off the earlier verbal and legal attacks. His ratings have fallen and his ruling Democratic Progressive Party has never looked more divided." Jonathan Watts, "Beijing's Panda Hug Divides and Confuses Taiwan," *Manchester Guardian Weekly*, May 13, 2005–May 19, 2005, sec. 172, 10.

104. Eventually, the DPP representative, Frank Hsieh, did have contact with the mainland in an effort to signal the DPP's ability to also work with the mainland if elected.

105. "Contents of Tsai Ing-wen's post-election press conference," DPP webpage (in Chinese). http://www.dpp.org.tw/news_content.php?&sn=6013; "Frank Hsieh: DPP Should Lean Towards KMT's Cross-Strait policy," KMT News Network [from Taipei papers], February 8, 2012, http://www.kmt.org.tw/english/page.aspx?type=article&mnum=112&anum=10855; DPP Foreign Affairs Department, "National Security Strategy 2011," http://www.scribd.com/doc/62902537/National-Security-Strategy-2011. The document states, "The Democratic Progressive Party believes that Taiwan and China must reach an understanding that is based on reality and the fact that the two sides are different, yet at the same time express a shared desire for seeking commonality and strategic mutual interests, all with the goal of developing a stable mechanism that would benefit the pursuit of peaceful development on both sides." It goes on to highlight mutual trade exchanges as key to this goal. The word "independence" is used once in the three-page outline of national security objectives, not in reference to Taiwan, but referring to "the independence of our sovereignty."

PART IV. CHINA'S SOVEREIGN WEALTH FUNDS

1. The other international commercial actors that are similarly tasked with investing China's state capital are two of China's three "policy banks" (the China Export-Import Bank—Zhongguo jinchukou yinhang—and the China Development Bank—Guojia fazhan yinhang). Although the China Investment Corporation (CIC) is widely considered to be China's *official* sovereign wealth fund, each of these government entities is charged with investing a portion of the state's wealth abroad. Although the US Treasury officially only recognizes the CIC as China's sovereign wealth fund, from an analytical point of view there is a strong case to be made for expanding the analysis to cover the full range of entities that function as sovereign wealth funds. The US Treasury's classification carries certain obligations and legal stipulations that, for political reasons, it may wish to avoid. Ted Truman, a widely recognized authority on global sovereign wealth funds, suggests a more inclusive definition along the lines of the one I am using. See Edwin M. Truman, "Rise of Sovereign Wealth Funds: Impacts on US Foreign Policy and Economic Interests," testimony before the Committee on Foreign Affairs, US House of Representatives, May 21, 2008. Available at http://peterson-institute.org/publications/papers/truman0508.pdf.

2. Selecting cases that exhibit extreme values on the IVs offers an opportunity to observe how such values cause outcomes in the DV. Such process tracing enables tests of internal validity, an important initial step in theory building.

3. I am indebted to Barry Naughton, Charles Freeman, and Tony Lake for pointing out this distinction in our conversations. During much of the 1990s and early 2000s, China's foreign policy mainly served its economic interests. There is still some of that going on today, but the growth and progress China has made economically has sparked concern that China will now be able to leverage its economic power to pursue an expanding set of foreign policy preferences. For more on how expanding capabilities tend to lead to expanding national aims, see Arnold Wolfers, *Discord and Collaboration; Essays on International Politics* (Baltimore: Johns Hopkins University Press, 1962), 89–91.

4. Such worries run the gamut from strategic resources transfer as a result of equity stakes in mineral deposits and sensitive technology transfer as a result of joint ownership

in dual-use technologies to fears of coercive leverage stemming from dependence on Chinese sources of capital and the longer-term transformation of interests that results from international investment flows. For instance, in its January 22, 2008, report to Congress on China's sovereign wealth fund (the CIC), the Congressional Research Service provided at least seven areas of concern: "There is concern that China may use the CIC to secure energy resources or purchase strategic assets for geopolitical purposes. There are also market apprehensions that the CIC could seek to increase its market share in important industries via targeted acquisitions or takeovers. Others are concerned that CIC might make investments in particular companies in order to obtain access to sensitive technology or information. . . . There are also apprehensions about the potential for abuse or corruption created by the greater proximity SWFs create between governments and the private sector. As the existing investments of the CIC reveal, there is a growing network of interlinked investments between banks and other financial firms within China and overseas. . . . These potential economic risks are seen as including financial market instability, undesirable foreign control or influence over key industries or companies, access to sensitive technology, and other forms of unfair competitive advantages." (Michael F. Martin, "China's Sovereign Wealth Fund," CRS Report for Congress, January 22, 2008, 17–19 inter alia.) All these concerns can be usefully conceptualized as security externalities that stem from the behavior of these commercial entities.

8. STATE ADMINISTRATION OF FOREIGN EXCHANGE

1. "In the year 2007, China entered into 108 bilateral investment agreements with foreign countries all over the world and China's foreign investment amounted to USD 20 billion. Most of the money went into the developing countries in Asia and Latin America." "China Foreign Investment Spree to Continue," *SinoCast China Business Daily News*, April 9, 2008. Compare this with the growth in 2008 and 2009, when CDB announced (in a single instance) a $30 billion loan to CNPC for financing acquisitions abroad. By 2012 China's outward direct investment had risen to more than $74 billion.

2. Paul Glasson, "Regional Focus to Global Push: The China Syndrome," *The Australian*, March 4, 2009, 22.

3. Angel Gurria, secretary general of the Organization for Economic Cooperation and Development, in his March 27, 2008, address to the organization's Global Forum on International Investment stated, "The size of these funds, and the fact that they are owned by governments have raised many questions regarding their operation and purpose. Potential host countries fear that SWF investment decisions could be motivated more by political objectives than by profit considerations, and that the funds could target security-sensitive and other 'strategic' assets." Remarks available at http://www.oecd.org/document/13/0,33 43,en_2649_34863_40336589_1_1_1_1,00.html.

4. Interview with the author, October 2009, Washington, DC.

5. With the introduction of the CIC, however, SAFE seemed to have become more attuned to the wishes of the state. As mentioned below, this was largely a result of the competitive dynamic that the presence of the CIC introduced.

6. See "FDI by Sovereign Wealth Funds," in *UN World Investment Report 2008*, chap. 1, sec C. Also see "Annex Table A.I.11" on 216. Available at http://www.unctad.org/en/docs/wir2008p1_en.pdf. The report was updated in September of 2009, but the 2009 edition (and subsequent editions) make no mention of the size of SAFE. For the relevant section see "FDI by Sovereign Wealth Funds on the Rise Despite the Crisis" in the UN World Investment Report 2009, chap. 1, sec. C, subsec. 2. Available at http://www.unctad.org/en/docs/wir2009_en.pdf.

7. Anonymous, "China's ForEx Reserves Growth Slows in Q2, Total Reaching $2.45 Trillion," *Xinhua News*, July 11, 2010. Available in English online at http://news.xinhuanet.com/english2010/business/2010-07/11/c_13394250.htm.

8. For China this would have been about $400–500 billion. Wang Xiangwei, "Fed's 'Printing Presses' Give Wen a Headache," *South China Morning Post*, March 23, 2009, China Briefing, 4.

9. Effectively, these excess reserves constitute a form of national savings.

10. This process will be discussed in greater detail in chapter 10.

11. Moreover, because foreign exchange conversion is mandatory, SAFE has a very low cost of capital. "Beijing Bulls," *Financial Times*, August 7, 2008, 12.

12. "SAFE once aimed to have as much as 5% of its portfolio in equities. That would be $90US billion, the amount of CIC's initial capital that it plans to invest abroad in equity and fixed income or more than the equity holdings of the Swiss National bank, the Hong Kong Monetary Authority, many pension funds, and probably the Saudi Arabian Monetary Agency." Rachel Ziemba, "My Say, Where Are the SWFs?" *The Edge* (Singapore), September 22, 2008.

13. "The State Administration of Foreign Exchange is believed to have moved 15 per cent of its US $1.8 trillion reserves into riskier assets in July last year, just when stock markets were beginning to fall." Grace Ng and China Correspondent, "Shifting Dynamic of US-China Relations," *Straits Times* (Singapore), March 18, 2009.

14. Wang, "Fed's 'Printing Presses' Give Wen a Headache." It should, however, be noted that not all these losses were necessarily realized. Had SAFE patiently held many of these investments, the ensuing market recovery would likely have restored respectable returns for SAFE.

15. "Beijing Bulls."

16. SAFE seems to have conducted most of its equity investing via its Hong Kong branch office (SAFE Investments Inc.). Wang, "Fed's 'Printing Presses' Give Wen a Headache."

17. For more on the SAFE-CIC competitive dynamic see Sarah Eaton and Zhang Ming, "A Principal-Agent Analysis of China's Sovereign Wealth System: Byzantine by Design," *Review of International Political Economy* 17, no. 3: 481–506.

18. Costa Rica established diplomatic relations with the People's Republic of China on June 1, 2007, after more than six decades of ties with Taiwan. "World Briefing Asia: Taiwan Loses another Friend to China," *New York Times*, June 7, 2007, A17; Daniel Zueras, "Central America: Costa Rica Discusses Free Trade with China," *Global Information Network* (2008): 1; and Kathrin Hille, "Island Sees Allies Dwindle," *Financial Times*, June 8, 2007, 12.

19. "China secretly agreed to use its foreign-exchange reserves to buy $300 million in bonds from Costa Rica as part of a deal that enticed the Latin American nation to switch diplomatic recognition to Beijing from Taiwan, newly published government documents show." Andrew Batson, "The Buzz: China Used Reserves to Sway Costa Rica," *Wall Street Journal*, September 13, 2008, B3.

20. Ibid.

21. Stephen Fidler and Adam Thomson, "Fierce Battle for Diplomatic Supremacy," *Financial Times*, September 12, 2008, 4; and Batson, "The Buzz: China Used Reserves to Sway Costa Rica."

22. Jamil Anderlini, "Beijing Uses Reserves Fund to Persuade Costa Rica Over Taipei," *Financial Times*, September 12, 2008.

23. "Costa Rican diplomats advised against keeping the terms secret, but the Chinese insisted, said people familiar with the matter." Anderlini, "Beijing Uses Reserves Fund to Persuade Costa Rica Over Taipei."

24. "SAFE doesn't publicly discuss its investments and took steps to ensure this deal would also be secret. In an English-language letter dated Jan. 2, 2008, a SAFE official named Fang Shangpu wrote to the Costa Rican finance ministry setting out terms of the bond deal, including a request that Costa Rica 'shall take necessary measures to prevent

the disclosure of the financial terms of this operation and of SAFE as a purchaser of the bonds.' On Jan. 7, finance minister Guillermo Zuniga replied in a letter saying 'It is a pleasure for me to confirm that these suggestions are acceptable to us.'" "Costa Rica also published a letter by foreign ministry official Edgar Ugalde, confirming that SAFE's first investment of $150 million took place on Jan. 23, [2008]." Batson, "The Buzz: China Used Reserves to Sway Costa Rica."

25. Batson, "The Buzz: China Used Reserves to Sway Costa Rica."

26. "In a statement Friday, China's foreign ministry did not contest the validity of the Costa Rican documents. 'China provides assistance to the Costa Rican government within its means. The goal is to help Costa Rica's economic and social development,' the statement said." Batson, "The Buzz: China Used Reserves to Sway Costa Rica."

27. Recipients of economic benefits have often changed their formal diplomatic recognition in what has been termed "checkbook diplomacy." For instance, in October of 2003 Liberia ceased recognizing Taiwan, and Dominica changed its recognition to the PRC in March of 2004. In late 2004, Vanuatu switched recognition from the PRC to the ROC before the prime minister was ousted and Vanuatu switched back. In January of 2005, Grenada changed its formal diplomatic recognition from ROC to PRC. In May of 2005, Nauru restored its relations with the ROC following its 2002 decision to suspend relations (it recognized the PRC in the interim). In October of 2005, Senegal changed its recognition from the ROC to the PRC, and in August of 2006, Chad established relations with the PRC and Taiwan ended relations with Chad. In April of 2007, Saint Lucia restored relations with the ROC. In January of 2008, Malawi switched diplomatic recognition from the ROC to the PRC.

28. For more on how Taiwan and China vie for diplomatic recognition using "checkbook diplomacy," see Graeme Dobell, "China and Taiwan in the South Pacific: Diplomatic Chess versus Pacific Political Rugby," *CSCSD Occasional Paper* no. 1 (May 2007), 10–22.

29. "China and Taiwan have for years used aid payments, infrastructure projects and the like as incentives for small countries like Costa Rica to take their side. But SAFE's international profile is relatively new. In the past year, it has used a Hong Kong subsidiary to buy small stakes in publicly listed companies including BP, Total of France and at least three Australian banks." Anderlini, "Beijing Uses Reserves Fund to Persuade Costa Rica Over Taipei," 1. "Purchase of US-denominated Costa Rican government bonds by China's State Administration of Foreign Exchange (Safe) is the clearest proof yet that Beijing regards its $1,800bn in foreign reserves—the world's biggest—as a tool to advance foreign policy, as well as a potential source of income. . . . 'This is the first smoking gun that proves China uses its foreign exchange reserves for political purposes,' said Kerry Brown, senior fellow with the Asia programme at Chatham House in London." Ibid.

30. This is a departure from the more generally accepted international norm of allocating developmental aid (which comes from national fiscal accounts) along political lines. China's typical instruments of preferential aid and loans are the China Export-Import Bank, China Development Bank, and the Ministry of Commerce, often in conjunction with the Ministry of Foreign Affairs. For an excellent treatment of China's aid in the African context see Deborah Brautigam, *The Dragon's Gift: The Real Story of China in Africa* (Oxford: Oxford University Press, 2009) esp. 107–17. Axel Dreher and Andreas Fuchs have also done an interesting empirical analysis of Chinese aid flows in which they find that China's "politicization" of its aid is not much different than other donor states' determinants of aid. See Axel Dreher and Andreas Fuchs, "Rogue Aid? The Determinants of China's Aid Allocation," Courant Research Centre Discussion Paper 93 (October 2011). The distinction between "fiscal" assets and "monetary" assets is helpful in understanding how this particular episode of China's economic statecraft breaks with previous rounds of the PRC-ROC "checkbook diplomacy" battle. Fiscal assets are those assets that *belong*

to the state, usually gained as a result of taxes that have been paid to the government. States are generally free to spend their fiscal assets in a political manner (such as foreign aid, domestic welfare, etc.). Monetary assets are those for which the state is merely acting as *custodian*, generally held by an independent central bank or trust. Strictly speaking, when a country has an independent central bank, these assets are not the government's to spend. Rather, the central bank is statutorily made independent of the political leadership. This arrangement allows the central bank to manage the macroeconomic levers of the economy relatively insulated from political pressures. In the case of China, what we observe is that the government is able to effectively direct the allocation of these foreign exchange reserves to pursue political objectives.

31. "Now, China is Costa Rica's strategic partner, and trade between them has climbed from $630 million in 2004 to $1.7 billion in 2006." Raul Gutierrez, "Central America: Taiwan's President Seeks to Strengthen Ties," *Global Information Network* (2007): 1. This figure grew again to $2.87 billion in 2007. For more on Costa Rica's growing trade ties see Zueras, "Central America: Costa Rica Discusses Free Trade with China"; "Costa Rica, China Launch Free Trade Talks," *World Trade* 22, no. 2 (2009): 14; and Vanessa I. Garnica, "China Proves Tough Negotiator for Costa Rica," *Tico Times* (San Jose, Costa Rica) April 20, 2009.

32. "Analysts say this region of the Americas has become a chessboard for the two Asian countries, which are battling for something more than trade partners: Diplomatic support and recognition is the ultimate aim." Gutierrez, "Central America: Taiwan's President Seeks to Strengthen Ties." Although both sides generally try to deny their use of economics to further their diplomatic goals, evidence suggests that both sides make economic benefits contingent on diplomatic recognition. Wang Baodong (spokesman for China's embassy in Washington) was quoted as saying, "There are still a few countries that have not established diplomatic relations with China. Even though the Chinese people and government hold friendly feelings toward these countries, the Taiwan question constitutes the main obstacle to the development of our relationships." Larry Luxner, "Two Chinas Battle for Influence," *LatinFinance* (2007): 1. For more on "checkbook diplomacy," Taiwan's response, and its efforts to shore up support among other Latin American allies, see "China/Taiwan: Costa Rica Switches Allegiance to PRC, More May Follow," *Asialaw* (2007): 1; and Fidler and Thomson, "Fierce Battle for Diplomatic Supremacy."

33. "Encouraging the handful of countries that still recognise Taipei as the legitimate representative of the Chinese people to switch allegiance is an important foreign policy goal for Beijing, which regards Taiwan as a renegade province." Anderlini, "Beijing Uses Reserves Fund to Persuade Costa Rica Over Taipei."

34. When asked to elaborate on the details of the donation, Marco Vinicio, Costa Rica's foreign trade minister, was only willing to say, "It is part of the co-operation." Fidler and Thomson, "Fierce Battle for Diplomatic Supremacy"; also see Patrick Fitzgerald, "China to Invest in New Technology Park in Costa Rica," *Tico Times* (San Jose, Costa Rica) March 20, 2009.

35. Estimated costs for the science and technology park were approximately $65 million, although the Costa Rican foreign trade minister is reported to have said, "We don't have an exact cost yet because (the project) will be divided into five phases. This first (phase) will have a cost of $20 million, and includes biotechnology, nanotechnology, information technology and mechatronics." Ibid.

36. The state in this case was unified, as demonstrated by the presence of Hu himself and the foreign policy coordination under China's Ministry of Foreign Affairs (MOFA). "The modernisation of Recope will involve the establishment of a partnership between the refinery and the China National Petroleum Corp (CNPC), with the aim of enlarging Costa Rica's oil-refining capacity and possibly building a new refinery for exporting end products to other Central American countries. Expansion of Recope's oil-refining capacity to a target of 60,000 barrels of oil per day—48,000 for domestic use and the remainder

for exporting to the rest of the region—will cost an estimated US$1bn." Economist Intelligence Unit, "Costa Rica Politics: Co-Operating with China," *ViewsWire* (December 22, 2008). Also see E. Watkins, "Costa Rica Nixes Exploration; Wants Chinese Refinery," *Oil & Gas Journal* 107, no. 18 (2009): 32.

37. Economist Intelligence Unit, "Costa Rica Politics: Co-Operating with China." The bank in question may have been the China Development Bank, although this could not be confirmed.

38. J. McTague, "China Makes a Mark in Trade," *Barron's* 88, no. 47 (2008): 26; and Watkins, "Costa Rica Nixes Exploration; Wants Chinese Refinery."

39. In January 2008, environment and energy minister Roberto Dobles announced plans by China National Oil & Gas Exploration & Development Corp. (now known as China Southern Petroleum Exploration & Development Corp., based in Guangzhou and a subsidiary of China National Petroleum Corp.) to explore Costa Rican territorial waters. Watkins, "Costa Rica Nixes Exploration; Wants Chinese Refinery."

40. "Huawei Chosen to Build First 3G Network in Costa Rica," *SinoCast China Business Daily News*, January 12, 2009.

41. Economist Intelligence Unit, "Costa Rica Politics: Co-Operating with China."

42. In the Costa Rica episode, there have been suggestions that "people close to the president may have benefited from the deal." Fidler and Thomson, "Fierce Battle for Diplomatic Supremacy."

43. This body also conducts the most senior appointments of fifty some managers of SASAC's largest corporations.

44. While SAFE is nominally a direct report to the PBoC, it has a reputation for operating largely independently of much oversight. Interview with the author, June 2008, Beijing.

45. Bear in mind that these events were unfolding in the midst of the discussions about the creation of the CIC in early to mid-2007.

46. For a good study of such competitive dynamics "with Chinese characteristics" see Yi-min Lin, *Between Politics and Markets: Firms, Competition, and Institutional Change in Post-Mao China* (Cambridge: Cambridge University Press, 2001). Alternative entities that could have served the purposes of the State Council may have been the China Development Bank or any of the state-owned banks (including ICBC, Bank of China, etc.) or possibly the Ex-Im Bank or the National Social Security Fund.

47. The SAFE–Costa Rica case provides a good example of such behavior. Unfortunately, in many episodes in Chinese foreign policy, the commercial and political aspects are often intertwined, making a perfectly disaggregated test of such dynamics difficult. Politically expedient activities may often carry some commercial merit. Likewise, commercially attractive behavior may often bolster political goals. Nonetheless, it is useful to specify the ideal types even if complex realities rarely accommodate neat, clean experimental testing of theoretical abstractions.

48. China's use of economics to achieve its foreign policy objectives was not limited to economic support. China's strategic engagement also included diplomatic and political support. The Costa Rican vice president noted that China promised support for Costa Rica in international forums like the UN. Batson, "The Buzz: China Used Reserves to Sway Costa Rica." China has also sent "high-ranking military delegations to many countries in Latin America." See Luxner, "Two Chinas Battle for Influence."

9. WHAT RIGHT LOOKS LIKE

1. NSSF 2008 Annual Report, published on May 9, 2009, available on their website, www.ssf.gov.cn (in Chinese only).

2. See Stuart Leckie and Ning Pan, "A Review of the National Social Security Fund in China," *Pensions* 12, no. 2 (2006): 88–97.

3. See NSSF's 2012 Annual Report, published in June 2013, available in Chinese at http://www.ssf.gov.cn/cwsj/ndbg/201309/t20130928_5909.html.

4. See Leckie and Pan, "A Review of the National Social Security Fund in China," 88–97; and Michael McCormack, *Chinese Sovereign Wealth Funds: 2008–2010 Opportunities for Foreign Asset Managers* (Shanghai: Z-Ben Advisors, 2008), 21–43.

5. According to Leckie and Pan, government outlays accounted for 100 percent of the increase in funds in 2000; by 2005 this source had dropped to only 25 percent of the increase in funds as investment returns grew. More recently, the NSSF has been given jurisdiction over the management of a number of provincial-level social security funds.

6. See "[NSSF's] Investment Concept," available in Chinese at http://www.ssf.gov.cn/tzln/.

7. McCormack, *Chinese Sovereign Wealth Funds*, 21.

8. "One of the earliest investments of this kind occurred in June 2004, when the Bank of Communications (BoCom), one of China's smaller yet more profitable state-owned banks, restructured in preparation for a Hong Kong listing. The NSSF invested RMB10bn (US $ 1.2bn) in BoCom as a strategic investor, and became the third largest owner of BoCom after the MoF and HSBC. In July 2005, BoCom shares were listed in Hong Kong at a price 42 per cent higher than that paid by the NSSF, netting it with a handsome (although unrealised) return of over RMB4.2bn (US $ 0.5bn)." Leckie and Pan, "A Review of the National Social Security Fund in China," 93. Leckie and Pan are referring to the Bank of Communications IPO prospectus and IPO Allotment Result, June 2005.

9. "The managers included Boshi (now re-named Bosera), Changsheng, Huaxia, Harvest, Penghua and Southern, all considered among the best in the Chinese fund management industry." Leckie and Pan, "A Review of the National Social Security Fund in China," 92.

10. The NCSSF's 2004 annual report, available in Chinese at http://www.ssf.gov.cn/xxgk/tzycb/cwbg/200904/t20090427_903.html.

11. See "Section Three 'Fund Key Financial Data,'" in NSSF's 2012 Annual Report in Chinese at http://www.ssf.gov.cn/cwsj/ndbg/201309/t20130928_5909.html.

12. 2012 Fund Annual Report, available in Chinese at http://www.ssf.gov.cn/cwsj/ndbg/201309/t20130928_5909.html.

13. From the point of view of security externalities, domestic investment flows are much less likely to generate international security concerns than cross-border investments ceteris paribus.

14. "Among various asset categories, the fixed income assets account for 50.67%, domestic stocks account for 26.22%, overseas stocks account for 6.17%, industrial investments account for 16.30%, cash and equivalent for 0.64%." "Size of the Fund and Assets Allocation of NSSF," on the NSSF website, available in English at http://www.ssf.gov.cn/Eng_Introduction/201206/t20120620_5603.html.

15. 2008 Fund Annual Report, available in Chinese at http://www.ssf.gov.cn/xxgk/tzycb/cwbg/200905/t20090507_918.html.

16. See NSSF website: http://www.ssf.gov.cn. "According to the NSSF website, 'the NSSF aims to be a solution to the problem of aging and serves as a strategic reserve fund accumulated by central government to support future social security needs.'" Leckie and Pan, "A Review of the National Social Security Fund in China," 95.

17. The most likely source of political pressure would arise when the NSSF would need to be tapped to bail out a failing provincial pension fund. Such a crisis would be likely to provoke the sort of politicization that has been relatively absent up to this point in the NSSF's history. It should be noted that even this noncommercial activity would be limited in its strategic security ramifications because it would be a domestically focused effort.

18. "The international fund managers have in general been impressed (and perhaps somewhat surprised) by the level of professionalism demonstrated in the selection pro-

cess. Many commented that the process appeared fair *and without political interference*. It seems that the NSSF, in its selection of overseas managers, has set a new higher standard of governance for other Chinese government agencies and for China's fund management industry generally." Leckie and Pan, "A Review of the National Social Security Fund in China," 94 (italics added).

19. In particular, it may be instructive to watch private equity placements like the CIC's placement of US$3.2 billion with J. C. Flowers. The placement reportedly constitutes 80 percent of the new fund. It would be instructive to assess the degree to which the firm coordinates with the CIC on its investment activities.

20. The National Social Security Fund is the only organization bureaucratically tasked in its mission, but it does face some commercial pressure to generate returns on its portfolio, as its performance is often compared to other long-term liability-oriented investors (such as life insurance companies). In addition, the NSSF was created against an implicit comparison with provincial and municipal social security funds. In the sense that its performance and activities can be compared against those of peers, the NSSF operates in a "competitive" market structure. This provides the state with some degree of supervisory benchmarking and thus leverage for controlling the NSSF, but the NSSF faces little genuine competition for its mission.

21. This dynamic is similar to what was observed among oil companies and their expertise vis-à-vis the state in chapter 5.

22. Of course, the size of the economic interaction seems large enough to matter given that China is Costa Rica's second largest trading partner. The economic interaction was also fairly inelastic given the generous, noncommercial 2 percent cost of capital extended to Costa Rica, something that was not widely available in the marketplace for sovereign debt. Finally, the goals China had for this episode of economic statecraft were commensurate with the tools being used. Taiwanese diplomatic recognition did not seem to be particularly important to Costa Rica's overall strategic interests.

10. THE CHINA INVESTMENT CORPORATION

1. Li Yang, director of the Finance Research Institute of the Chinese Academy of Social Sciences, traveled to Singapore on a fact-finding trip to study Temasek and the GIC (Singapore's two sovereign wealth funds) as part of the preparation to create the CIC. Apparently Korea's sovereign wealth fund was also studied although my research was not able to confirm this.

2. Xin Zhiming, "$200 Billion Investment Firm Starts Operation," *China Daily*, October 1, 2007.

3. According to a senior analyst, there was a contest between competing bureaucratic interests over the structure, organization, and control of the CIC. Interview with the author, June 2008, Beijing.

4. Zhang Ming and Sarah Eaton "Dragon on a Short Leash: An Inside-out Analysis of China Investment Corporation," Working Paper No. 0821 (Beijing: Chinese Academy of Social Sciences, November 26, 2008).

5. "[M]ost of these investment arms are staffed by government people, largely party cadres. Both their lack of experience and their independence are open to question." Henny Sender, "China Turns Risk Averse as Capital Outflows Rise," *Financial Times*, January 18, 2008, 21.

6. CICC was the first Chinese joint-venture investment bank. CICC was a joint venture between Morgan Stanley and CCB. Because of its early entry into the China market, CICC was well-positioned to dominate the early IPO business of China. CICC took several of the initial big Chinese SOEs public.

7. Morgan Stanley retained 34.3 percent, China National Investment & Guaranty Company owns 7.65 percent, Government of Singapore Investment Corporation owns 7.35 percent, and Mingly Corporation owns 7.35 percent.

8. "During the spring and summer [of 2005], China Jianyin bailed out several of the country's largest securities firms, including Galaxy Securities, China Southern Securities, Shenyin & Wanguo and Guotai Junan." Jamil Anderlini, "Firm Hand Steers Vehicle of Financial Reform; Banker Who Has Handed Out $60USb Is the Force Behind Restructuring," *South China Morning Post*, February 6, 2006.

9. The "Big Four" banks had accumulated significant amounts of bad debt as a result of loans made to failing state-owned enterprises in the 1990s. The "Big Four" banks are all state-controlled and largely state-owned with some publicly listed shares. They are Industrial and Commercial Bank of China (ICBC), Bank of China (BOC), Agricultural Bank of China (ABC), and China Construction Bank (CCB).

10. Although by the time of the ICBC recap, the MOF and Communist Party Organization Department had agitated against the PBoC's growing bureaucratic "empire" and the ICBC recapitalization was limited to $15 billion in exchange for 50 percent of the equity (MOF retained the other 50 percent). In contrast, Central Huijin received 85 percent of CCB's equity and 100 percent of BOC's equity. Anderlini, "Firm Hand Steers Vehicle of Financial Reform."

11. See Victor C. Shih, *Factions and Finance in China* (Cambridge: Cambridge University Press, 2008).

12. The CIC has made limited efforts to improve its transparency. These include a disclosure of the management team and the CIC's internal reporting structure. In particular, its involvement in the Santiago Protocols for sovereign wealth fund operating and reporting standards as well as its own website are both positive steps in this direction. In 2008, the CIC began publishing an Annual Report, which has greatly improved CIC's transparency.

13. "The CIC Board of Directors is mandated and authorized to oversee the company's operation and overall performance." CIC website: http://www.china-inv.cn/cicen/gover nance/governing_bod.html.

14. Traditionally, the State Council has had to approve all SOE investments abroad that are over $200 million, but the CIC enjoys a bit more latitude in its approval process. According to CIC sources and analysts, decisions on investments over $100 million up to $1 billion go to the CIC Investment Committee for approval, while those over $1 billion would need to have State Council approval. Decisions on investments below $10 million were reported to be discretionary. Presumably, investments between $10 and $100 million were handled in the normal course of internal reporting operations. See interviews with the author, June 2008, Beijing.

15. The fund's first chairman, Lou Jiwei, was promoted to minister of finance in 2013. The fund sat leaderless for four months, reflecting what many believe to have been factional and bureaucratic divisions among China's senior financial elites over the future leadership (and by implication, strategic direction) of the fund. See George Chen, "Power Struggle in Beijing Leaves CIC Leaderless," *South China Morning Post*, May 27, 2013.

16. On May 27, 2013, Jin Liqun was replaced by Li Xiaopeng, who has spent most of his career moving up through the ranks at ICBC.

17. See Anonymous, "China's Trillion-Dollar Kitty Is Ready," *Asia Times*, October 2, 2007.

18. That Li Keping was Gao's successor at NSSF as deputy chairman suggests that the CIO role was being transitioned to one of Gao's protégés rather than stripped from him.

19. See Xinhua News Agency, "China's Forex Investment Company to Debut Next Friday: Report," September 19, 2007. His departure along with Jin Liqun and Peng Chun

might signal bureaucratic horse trading as the new leadership of the CIC was being put into place.

20. These interbureaucratic struggles predated the CIC. Central Huijin's recapitalization of ICBC was a considerably smaller $15 billion and entitled Central Huijin to only 50 percent of the equity (as opposed to the $45 billion that had been splashed out for BOC and CCB). "[T]he smaller stake was a result of high-level opposition from competing regulatory agencies, which criticised the 'empire-building' of the People's Bank of China (PBOC) and its reformist governor, Zhou Xiaochuan, to whom Mr Xie and Huijin officials report." Anderlini, "Firm Hand Steers Vehicle of Financial Reform."

21. Perhaps most significantly, on September 28, 2011, Lou was successful in implementing a massive reorganization of the CIC that effectively saw the splitting of the CIC's domestic (primarily banking recapitalization and supervision) assets and workload from its international investment activities. The result is that the CIC's international investing activities are now likely to be done on an even more strictly commercial basis. At the same time, the CIC's Central Huijin work, which focuses on China's domestic banking sector, would likely remain opaque and highly politicized given the massive equities involved. For more on this reorganization see below.

22. For instance, fairly early on, Hu Huaibang was replaced as chairman of the Board of Supervisors by Jin Liqun. Hu was formerly secretary of the Disciplinary Board at the CBRC and a member of the Communist Party Discipline and Inspection Committee. He was an anticorruption, Communist Party representative on the board. Jin was a vice president of operations at the Asian Development Bank. Prior to that position he was vice minister of finance, director general of the World Bank Department at MOF. The current composition of the Board of Supervisors indicates a strong banking focus.

23. For example, the leadership transition from Lou Jiwei to Ding Xuedong ensured that the helm of the CIC would remain in the hands of a MOF loyalist rather than pass (as some expected) to Gao Xiqing. Ding majored in finance at the MOF's Financial Science Institute before obtaining both his master's and doctorate degrees from there. Although he began his career at SASAC, most of his rise to the top occurred in the Ministry of Finance. From 2008 to 2010, he was the vice minister of finance.

24. According to the 2012 Annual Report, the CIC employs 583 individuals as of June 2013 (up from 67 as of May 31, 2009). Of this total, the vast majority (443) work at CIC International, far out numbering the 140 employees of Central Huijin. Of these, 363 employees have postgraduate degrees, 250 have overseas educational experience, and another 174 have worked abroad. Forty-one employees even have foreign citizenship!

25. Additional evidence of MOF ascendancy within the CIC's leadership includes the valuation and sale of Central Huijin (discussed below); by valuing it at near book value, the MOF received a good price while the PBoC was not given full compensation for its valuable asset. This conforms with reports of an intense struggle between the MOF and PBoC over the PBoC's rapidly growing influence over the banking sector, an arena that MOF had traditionally dominated. The creation of the CIC can be interpreted as MOF's institutional effort to wrest back control over the banking sector.

26. It ought to be noted that the PBoC cannot directly buy bonds from the Ministry of Finance, so this transaction was conducted using the PBoC-owned Agricultural Bank of China (ABC) as an intermediary. For further details on the CIC's financing see Rachel Ziemba's helpful post from December 5, 2007, and the update on December 14, 2007, on *RGE Analysts' Economonitor* titled, "How Is China Funding the China Investment Corporation (CIC)?" available at http://www.economonitor.com/analysts/2007/12/05/how-is-china-funding-the-chinese-investment-corporation-cic/.

27. "The interest payments on all these bonds are below those of comparable bonds and current inflation. The main (only) audience for these bonds is thought to be the

commercial banks who are already the major purchasers of the frequently issued steriliza-tion bills and longer term bonds." Ibid.

28. Ibid.

29. China Investment Corporation, *2011 Annual Report*, 40.

30. China Investment Corporation, *2012 Annual Report*, 9.

31. "In addition, China's accumulation of U.S. debt in 2007 was not very profitable given the appreciation of the renminbi (RMB) against the U.S. dollar. The yield on 10-year U.S. treasury bills fluctuated between 4.5% and 5.0% throughout the year. However, since the beginning of 2007, the RMB has appreciated 6.0% relative to the U.S. dollar. As a result, the effective rate of return on U.S. treasury bills valued in Chinese currency was negative in 2007. For example, on January 1, 2007, the exchange rate was 1 yuan of RMB = 12.82 cents of U.S. dollars. If China had invested 100 billion yuan in one-year U.S. treasury bills on January 2, 2007, it would have been offered a return of 5.0%. After conversion into U.S. dollars, China would have invested $12.82 billion. At the end of the year, China would have been paid $13.461 billion by the U.S. Treasury for its investment. However, the exchange rate at the end of 2007 was 1 yuan = 13.59 cents. So, after converting the U.S. dollars back into RMB, China would have received the equivalent of 99.051 billion yuan for its investment—a loss of 949 million yuan, or a -0.9% return on its investment. When evaluated in its domestic currency, China lost money on its investments in U.S. govern-ment debt in 2007." (Michael F. Martin, "China's Sovereign Wealth Fund," Congressional Research Service Report for Congress, January 22, 2008, 16.)

32. According to Lou, the interest cost on the outstanding bonds is about 300 million yuan (more than $40 million) per day. See Xinhua, "China's Sovereignty [*sic*] Wealth Fund Seeks to Be a Stabilizing Presence in Global Markets," *People's Daily Online*, November 30, 2007, available at http://en.people.cn/90001/90778/6312612.html. Moreover, hopes of access to additional foreign exchange reserves depended on the CIC performance. Lou stated, "If I am making losses every day, how can I face asking the government for more money?" See "China Wealth Fund Aims for Stability, Openness," *China Daily*, October 16, 2007. It is also important to note that the annual dividends from the CIC's bank ownership were originally estimated to be in the neighborhood of US$7.8 billion. This would have helped to satisfy more than half of the CIC's interest obligation. See Katherine Ng, "CIC Dispels Fund Concerns," *The Standard*, March 10, 2008, available online at http://www.thestandard.com.hk/news_detail.asp?sid=17984607&art_id=62790&con_type=1&pp_cat=1. In fact, based on the CIC's reported financial statements' "Income from long-term equity investments," this annual dividend payout to CIC was closer to the $26 billion range in 2008. Moreover, these profits increased sharply each year, with the 2012 income topping $63 billion. If this assessment is correct, Central Huijin provided more than enough to cover the cost of servicing the CIC's debt payments.

33. "'Our purpose [at CIC] is to reduce the liquidity in China,' says one senior CIC staffer." Henny Sender, "China Turns Risk Averse as Capital Outflows Rise." In Chinese central banking such forced savings is a common method of directly adjusting the money supply because interest rate mechanisms (commonly used as the primary monetary tool in the West) are not really permitted to operate effectively. "Most of the newly-issued bonds ended up in the hands of the PBoC, effectively soaking up some of the perceived excess liquidity in China's money markets." Martin, "China's Sovereign Wealth Fund," 7.

34. "The RMB raised from these bond sales are not converted into foreign currency immediately. It seems like the 600b RMB bond was converted into foreign exchange in q3 [2007], the 200b RMB from the small bond issues in q4 [2007] and the last bond issue will be converted into foreign exchange in q1 2008. . . . Given the RMB's ongoing appre-ciation, the Ministry of Finance has every incentive to only buy foreign exchange when it actually needs the money." Brad Setser, "What to Do With Over a Half a Trillion a Year?

Understanding the Changes in the Management of China's Foreign Assets," *Council on Foreign Relations Working Paper*, January 15, 2008, 13. This sentiment was reiterated in subsequent conversations with the author.

35. It should be noted that as of 2012, the CIC continued to issue a single consolidated annual report that seemed to be almost exclusively oriented around the activities of CIC International, although the financial statements were reported for the whole of the CIC and thus still included Central Huijin figures.

36. The office in Hong Kong was originally called CIC International (Hong Kong) and was set up in November 2010. The office in Toronto was a "Representative Office" that was designed to facilitate the CIC's relationships with the North American investment community and portfolio companies. It was established in January 2011.

37. From the CIC's website, available at http://www.china-inv.cn/wps/portal/!ut/p/ a1/jZBRC4IwFIV_Uey6xrTHpaVTVw8q2V5ihNqgVMIk-vWZPTu9bwe-j8M9SKI cyVr1ulKdbmp1_2VJLwegYLkJhCDYHpgDO3FchzxKrQE4TwLYJ3iZ7_osIHYMAM TBwL1t4NkbAcDpMh8mjsGcH46AwR8K8FO4okKyVd1tpeuyQXnxLq6vTvc FOiFp7IiIGfBT2wj8RxwB00pzb7SPLMs_cZlwzb-yB5VV/dl5/d5/L2dBISEvZ0FBIS9nQS Eh/?tagid=capital.

38. Keith Bradsher, "$200 Billion to Invest, But in China," *New York Times*, November 29, 2007.

39. Ownership figures were as of April 2009 from the company websites.

40. "There are indications that the State Council, the PBoC and the NDRC insisted that the CIC provide help in the restructuring of these two state-owned banks as a condition of the CIC's establishment." Martin, "China's Sovereign Wealth Fund," 10. The CRS text references Professor Michael Pettis of Beijing University. He confirmed this sentiment in my conversations with him.

41. The $67 billion figure was reported in the press at the time, but in subsequent research I have only been able to confirm $19 billion that was used in ABC and $20 billion at CDB. "China Investment Co to Invest a Third of Its 200 Bln USD 'Cautiously'—Official," AFX News Limited, November 7, 2007. At the end of 2008, the CIC provided another RMB 146.1 billion (~$21 billion) to capitalize the newly formed joint stock company holding vehicle for CDB. At the same time, there were reports that the CIC now had additional funds that had originally been reserved for recapitalizing ABC and CDB but were no longer needed. These approximately $7 billion of newly freed up capital were to be added to the CIC's funds earmarked for foreign investment (primarily to be placed with third-party mandates).

42. It ought to be noted that as of December 31, 2012, the CIC reported that it owned 40.21 percent of ABC. This is most likely the result of IPO dilution. The NSSF generally would be allocated a fraction of ABC shares prior to the IPO. ABC enjoyed the world's largest IPO in August of 2010, raising $22.1 billion.

43. For more detail on the CDB see chapter 5.

44. See CDB's 2007 Annual Report section titled "Financial Review," available at http:// www.cdb.com.cn/english/Column.asp?ColumnId=91. "ABC and CDB are the two largest banks still in the process of this restructuring, which involves government recapitalisation— CDB received $20bn at the end of last year [2007] and ABC expects even more—and eventual stock market listings." From: Anderlini, "Illegal Lending Scandal Hits China Development Bank," *Financial Times*, August 30, 2008, available at http://www.ft.com/ cms/s/0/54aa86a4-762b-11dd-99ce-0000779fd18c.html#axzz3i3Had1Xu.

45. This figure has since been revised as less capital was needed that originally thought to recapitalize CDB and ABC. It is now thought that the CIC had between $80 and $90 billion earmarked for foreign investment. See the more detailed discussion of the revision below.

46. Drawing the line between the CIC and state banks is not easy. See Brad Setser, "The Implications of Sovereign Wealth Fund Investments for National Security," *Testimony before the US-China Economic and Security Review Commission*, February 7, 2007, 9.

47. Share ownership is sometimes difficult to keep up to date given the multiple reorganizations and historic lack of transparency with regard to government ownership. These figures are based on company reports of the publicly listed firms. The government generally holds its ownership stake in the holding company, a subsidiary of which is the publicly listed firm. The figures have also been confirmed by the CIC's own 2008 Annual Report, specifically, "Exhibit 7: Top Five portfolio holdings of Central Huijin," 35, available at http://www.china-inv.cn/cicen/include/resources/CIC_2008_annualreport_en.pdf.   The only significant point of disparity was in the CIC's share of China Construction Bank. Initially it was reported that CIC controlled 57 percent, but the CIC's 2008 annual report listed its ownership as 48.2 percent. The difference, I had assumed, was explained by the dilution stemming from CCB's stock offering, but in the 2009 annual report, the CIC's holdings were once again listed as 57 percent. Welcome to the world of Chinese accounting! By 2012, this figure was 57.21 percent, presumably the result of reinvested dividends or share buybacks.

48. Figures are taken from China Investment Corporation *2012 Annual Report*, 35, table 3, "Top Five Portfolio Holdings of Central Huijin."

49. Central Huijin also apparently recapitalized the much smaller China Everbright Bank for about $2.7 billion in preparation for its IPO. See "China Everbright Agrees to Capital Injection Plan," *China Daily*, November 28, 2007. Also see "SAFE Investments to Offer Bailouts to State-Owned Banks," *SinoCast China Business Daily News*, December 26, 2007, 1.

50. "World News: China Fund Plans to Steer More of its Money Overseas," *Wall Street Journal*, April 24, 2008, A8. Although according to my calculations (based on publicly available information), this $80–90 billion figure still does not add up. Even if the ABC and CDB recapitalizations only required $60 billion instead of the originally projected $67 billion, that only frees up an additional $7 billion, which when added to the original projection of $66 billion for foreign investment only amounts to $73 billion. I suspect that Gao's announced figure may have anticipated some of the additional capital infusions to the CIC that were not yet publicly announced or may have included funds from the CIC's bank dividends or other returns on investment in excess of the CIC's interest payments.

51. "'The initial Dollars 200bn was basically the first batch and if CIC gets their investment framework right and shows it is capable of earning decent returns there is no question they will be allowed to invest more,' said Qu Hongbin, chief China economist for HSBC." Jamil Anderlini, "CIC Gears Up for Dollars 30bn Drive," *Financial Times*, February 11, 2008, 24. See also Sender, "China Turns Risk Averse as Capital Outflows Rise."

52. China Investment Corporation, *2011 Annual Report*, 4, 8.

53. Note that this figure is a top-down estimate based on publicly available information and does not include any allowance for redeployed excess dividends from Central Huijin nor reinvested returns from the CIC's portfolio of investments.

54. "China Fund Grabs Big Stake in Morgan Stanley," *AFP*, December 19, 2007. Note that in the 2012 annual report, this was reported as the CIC having given $5.6 billion to Morgan Stanley. The discrepancy may be attributable to an initial investment of $5 billion plus a follow-on investment of $600 to $800 million as a coinvestment in a $5 billion global property fund Morgan Stanley was setting up in 2009.

55. Wang Xiangwei, "Fed's 'Printing Presses' Give Wen a Headache," *South China Morning Post*, March 23, 2009, China Briefing, 4.

56. In October 2008, Mitsubishi UFJ Financial Group, Inc. invested equity into the struggling Morgan Stanley, which was facing pressure as a result of the credit crunch

brought on by the subprime mortgage crisis. This infusion diluted the CIC's stake down to 7.68 percent. On June 2, 2009, the CIC bought another $1.2 billion of Morgan Stanley's stock, effectively returning the CIC to its previous ownership stake of 9.86 percent. See http://www.china-inv.cn/cicen/resources/resources_news01.html. When Morgan Stanley was reorganized into a bank holding company under the direct supervision of the Federal Reserve, the CIC converted its original stake (which was in mandatory convertible notes and mandatory convertible equity units) to common stock. See China Investment Corporation, *Annual Report 2010*, 35.

57. One example of the type of benefits the CIC hoped to gain from these acquisitions can be seen in Blackstone's provision of investment banking advisory services to CDB's failed $3 billion purchase of Barclays.

58. Henny Sender, "Sources of Needed Cash Scared Off," *Financial Times*, January 28, 2009, 4.

59. "World News: China Fund Plans to Steer More of its Money Overseas," *Wall Street Journal*, April 24, 2008, A8.

60. Jamil Anderlini, "CIC to Buy Stake in HK Rail Group Float," *Financial Times*, November 21, 2007; "CIC Invests in China Railway IPO," *China Economic Review*, November 21, 2007. I believe that China's initial investment in Blackstone was also partly colored by an intention to signal constructive Chinese government support for the IPO. Drawing on China's domestic IPO experience, if the government is a prominent investor or supporter of an IPO it is often taken as a mark of support and friendliness. I am not convinced that the China Jianyin leadership intended to signal a Chinese capital invasion of US public markets, although that was the response it seemed to generate.

61. By the time the CIC issued its first annual report, only a small portion of this internationally designated capital had been publicly committed. According the CIC's 2008 annual report (which was made public in August 2009), the CIC still held 87.4 percent of its "Global Investment Portfolio" (those funds not used for Central Huijin) in cash or cash equivalents. See China Investment Corporation, *2008 Annual Report*, 35, "Exhibit 6: Global Investment Portfolio Distribution," available at http://www.china-inv.cn/cicen/include/resources/CIC_2008_annualreport_en.pdf.

62. In 2012 this split was 63.5 percent externally managed versus 36.2 percent internally managed. China Investment Corporation, *2012 Annual Report*, 36.

63. In 2012, the CIC's global portfolio distribution consisted of 32.4 percent "Long-term Investments" (presumably primarily made up of the CIC's "direct investments"); 32 percent "Public Equities"; 19.1 percent "Fixed Income"; "Absolute Return Investments" (presumably hedge funds and private equity placements) accounted for 12.7 percent; and "Cash/Other" stood at 3.8 percent. The CIC's diversified equities exposure was highly concentrated in US equities (49.2 percent) with another 27.8 percent in non-US advanced economies (presumably the EU and Japan), and emerging markets making up the remaining 23 percent. Figures taken from China Investment Corporation, *Annual Report 2012*, 36–37.

64. Although, to its credit, the CIC has worked hard to demonstrate its passive and nonstrategic roles as minority investors in these companies.

65. China Investment Corporation, *Annual Report 2012*, 29.

66. Although the United States has some institutional foreign investment review mechanisms in place, whether or not these are adequate is outside the scope of this research.

67. See for example, the instances of state-sponsored financial support discussed in chapters 4 and 5.

68. Given the senior party leadership personnel policies, many of these individuals if successful at the CIC are likely to continue upward to higher positions of authority within the CCP, bringing with them whatever human capital and knowledge they have built during their time at the CIC.

69. To its credit, the CIC has thus far worked hard to minimize the possibility of such externality concerns by forgoing board seats in several instances, stressing its role as a passive investor, and explicitly steering clear of highly sensitive industries or investments.

70. Potentially indicative in this regard is the rise of Zhou Yuan through the ranks of the CIC. Zhou seems to have been the thought leader behind the CIC's strategic planning effort. He moved up to the Executive Committee from within the CIC's Department of Special Investments (the department in charge of the CIC's concentrated direct investments). In addition, the 2012–2016 Strategic Plan suggested more moves may be in the pipeline in the areas of energy, mining, infrastructure, and agriculture. To the degree that international investments provide access to strategically important assets, such activity would seem to warrant concerns from a strategic transfer security externality perspective.

71. "Such a concentration of the country's wealth in one entity has inevitably drawn intense interest . . . from powerful forces within the state bureaucracy. Each of these groups has its own ideas on how the money can best be spent." Jamil Anderlini, "China Wealth Fund's Early Coming of Age," *Financial Times*, December 21, 2007.

72. "There clearly isn't a consensus inside China on what the CIC should be doing." Brad Setser, "Does the China Investment Corporation (CIC) Have a Coherent Investment Strategy?" online blog #234551, available at http://www.rgemonitor.com/blog/setser/234551/. Setser is now a Treasury Department official at the National Economic Council.

73. To the degree that these state-owned banks are motivated by policy outcomes that support the government's objectives, they can be used as effective levers for realizing national interests. To the extent these banks are focused on maximizing shareholder value and risk-adjusted return, their malleability to serve commercially questionable foreign policy goals of the state will be limited.

74. "The establishment of the China Investment Corporation was an initiative sponsored by the State Council and the Finance Ministry to redistribute the balance of power between the ministry and the central bank, the PBOC." Paul Glasson, "Regional Focus to Global Push: The China Syndrome," *The Australian*, March 4, 2009, 22. See also interview with the author, June 2008, Beijing; and Ming and Eaton, "Dragon on a Short Leash."

75. I note that this purpose of the CIC seemed to be strongly resisted by the commercially oriented PBoC. Resistance could also be detected in the public statements of the CIC's senior management itself. In the course of my research in Beijing, however, several interlocutors confided that the vision to have the CIC support Chinese firms was championed by the NDRC and some elements within the Ministry of Finance and the Ministry of Commerce (interviews with the author, June 2008, Beijing). Since 2008, the CIC publicly sought to disavow itself of this goal. The trend seemed to be moving the CIC away from such activities, reflecting in part the consolidation of Lou Jiwei's power and the ascendancy of a commercially oriented leadership. One of the strongest pieces of evidence of the CIC's move toward operating on a commercial basis was its 2008 annual report, publicly available as of August 2009 at http://www.china-inv.cn/cicen/include/resources/CIC_2008_annualreport_en.pdf.

76. Jason Dean and Andrew Batson, "China Investment Fund May Tread Softly," *Wall Street Journal* September 10, 2007, A2.

77. "China's Trillion-Dollar Kitty Is Ready."

78. Xinhua, "CIC to Be Stable Force in Global Financial Market," *People's Daily Online*, December 11, 2007, available at http://en.people.cn/90001/90776/6318860.html.

79. Xinhua, "China's Sovereignty [*sic*] Wealth Fund Seeks to be a Stabilizing Presence in Global Markets," *People's Daily Online*, November 30, 2007, available at http://en.people.cn/90001/90778/6312612.html; Shenzen Daily, "Investment Fund Announces Strategic Plans," *Embassy of the People's Republic of China in the United States of America Website*,

ed. Yan Zhonghua, November 9, 2007, available at http://www.china-embassy.org/eng// xnyfgk/t379619.htm; and Xinhua, "China Investment Corporation Unveils Investment Plan," *Xinhua News Net*, November 7, 2007, available at http://news.xinhuanet.com/ english/2007-11/07/content_7029738.htm.

80. These dynamics were discussed in more detail in the SAFE case study of chapter 8.

81. "The way it [the CIC] made its investments was also highly dubious. It made its first investment in Blackstone in June 2007, three months before CIC was formally established, making one wonder how much due diligence it conducted before throwing away $3US billion." Wang, "Fed's 'Printing Presses' Give Wen a Headache."

82. Interviews with the author, June 2008, Beijing.

83. See Victor Shih, "Tools of Survival: Sovereign Wealth Funds in Singapore and China," *Geopolitics* iss. 14 (2009): 328–44, for more on how the leadership of the Ministry of Finance tended to be loyal to Wen Jiabao and Zhu Rongji, while the leadership of the NDRC tended to be associated with Jiang Zemin.

84. The State Council is the ultimate principal to which the CIC reports; at times this principal is divided by factional frictions or bureaucratic/institutional preferences. From 2008 to 2012, however, Wen Jiabao and his loyal subordinates at the Ministry of Finance consolidated the State Council's vision for the CIC as well as the key leadership positions over the CIC, thus creating a unified state that had established control. Interview with the author, September 2009, Washington, DC. It remains to be seen whether Li Keqiang's State Council changes direction in its vision for the CIC.

85. The theory suggests that this sort of a unified state will facilitate the state's ability to control the CIC in the future as well. So an alternative consensus regarding the vision for the CIC at the State Council could redirect the CIC's behavior away from its commercial orientation.

86. Jiang Zemin made effective use of the NDRC for political patronage during his tenure.

87. In addition, during the early days of the CIC, its personnel were augmented by foreign subject matter experts provided on-loan by international private-sector partners to help staff up the CIC. These resources further skewed the Relative Resources IV in the CIC's favor.

88. When there are a limited number of commercial actors available to the state, we might expect that these two dominant commercial actors might collude to resist the will of the state, in which case the Market Fragmentation IV would be coded as "concentrated." But the competitive dynamic and bureaucratic rivalry that existed between SAFE and the CIC precluded any collaboration, prompting a coding of "oligopolistc."

89. Interview with the author, June 2008, Beijing; See also Shih, "Tools of Survival: Sovereign Wealth Funds in Singapore and China."

90. Brad Setser, "The Implications of Sovereign Wealth Fund Investments for National Security," 7. See also Shih, "Tools of Survival: Sovereign Wealth Funds in Singapore and China"; and Michael McCormack, "Chinese Sovereign Wealth Funds: 2008–2010 Opportunities for Foreign Asset Managers" (Shanghai: Z-Ben Advisors, 2008).

91. For example, the CIC has been funded with its initial tranche of registered capital using the proceeds from special bonds that were effectively sold to the PBoC. This means CIC interest payments are directly payable to the state, often referred to in CIC publications as CIC's "shareholder." These features indicate a close reporting relationship between the state and the economic actor.

CONCLUDING IMPLICATIONS

1. Although some might contend that China is so complex and disjointed that it is really not a unified state actor, several of the cases in this book show that China is still, at the end of the day, a hierarchical, single-party, authoritarian regime. As a result, when

issues are important enough, state unity can be forged from the top down and China is able to exercise effective economic statecraft. The unity of the Chinese state can in fact vary overtime and by issue area.

2. "China's antitrust clampdown has already taken aim at scores of companies, both foreign and domestic, including recently against Microsoft, Qualcomm, Daimler, Volkswagen and a dozen Japanese manufacturers of auto parts and bearings." Neil Gough, "Western Companies Appear to Push Back against Chinese Crackdown," *New York Times*, September 4, 2014, B3; Also see "China Targeting Foreign Companies, American Chamber Says," *Bloomberg News*, September 2, 2014, available at http://www.businessweek.com/news/2014–09–01/u-dot-s-dot-companies-say-china-subjectively-enforcing-laws;   Neil Gough, "China's Antitrust Campaign Seen as Possible Breach of W.T.O. Rules," *New York Times*, September 9, 2014, B8. One of the most detailed studies on the discriminatory enforcement of China's Anti-Monopoly Law was conducted by the US-China Business Council. The complete report can be found at https://www.uschina.org/sites/default/files/AML%202014%20Report%20FINAL_0.pdf.

3. "With the economy slowing and foreign companies coming under increasing government scrutiny, the still-chilly investment environment is contributing to an increasing sense of pessimism among foreign multinational companies in China." American Chamber of Commerce in China, "AmCham China Supports Reform Agenda, Increasingly Concerned About Fairness," press release, September 2, 2014. Available at http://www.amchamchina.org/article/13239. Survey available at http://www.amchamchina.org/wp-investment2014.

4. US-China Business Council, "Competition Policy and Enforcement in China," available at https://www.uschina.org/reports/competition-policy-and-enforcement-china.

5. Gough, "China's Antitrust Campaign Seen as Possible Breach of W.T.O. Rules," B8.

6. Certainly, China (or any other state in its position) may not wish to reassure others, particularly if that would mean limiting its own potential to leverage economic power for noncommercial goals. But if China does not reform its domestic political economy, it will be difficult to reassure its region and the world about the strategic consequences of China's growing power.

7. In an international system dominated by the United States that largely plays by liberal, free-market rules, such a rising power can be a significant source of concern. For this reason, US-China policy must continue to impress upon China the importance of continuing its reform and liberalization efforts. Such efforts serve both American and Chinese long-term interests.

8. Such distortions tend to be disproportionately found in China's "strategic" sectors. Ironically, this suggests that the parts of the Chinese economy deemed to be most important are those that are most likely to underperform in the long run.

9. Some scholars (both in China and abroad) would argue that China's state capitalist model is more efficient over the long run. I would suggest that that position requires heroic assumptions about the wisdom and accuracy of state planners. Over the long run, such performance becomes even more difficult to sustain. While this is an important and interesting debate that warrants a robust discussion, it would be distracting to engage it here at the level of detail it deserves.

10. Such dynamics have the strong potential to be self-reinforcing and expansionary. Commercial actors will not want to give up market access; in fact the tendency would be for commercial actors to seek to expand economic links. "Indeed, as their business stakes increase enormously over time, it becomes increasingly difficult for politicians and officials to reverse and undermine ongoing commercial ties." Steve Chan, "The Politics of Economic Exchange: Carrots and Sticks in Taiwan-China-U.S. Relations," *Issues & Studies* 42, no. 2 (2006): 13. The self-reinforcing nature of the interest transformation security externality is that commercial actors act *in their own narrow interests* to promote greater

engagement and deeper ties. This trend will likely further undermine Taiwanese desires for de jure independence.

APPENDIX 1. CODING OF THE INDEPENDENT VARIABLES

1. Kenneth Lieberthal, *Governing China* (New York: Norton, 1995).

APPENDIX 2. CHINA INVESTMENT CORPORATION'S DIRECT INVESTMENTS IN THE AFTERMATH OF THE FINANCIAL CRISIS

1. China Investment Corporation, *Annual Report 2009*, 32. It appears that much of this figure was deployed into passive index funds and was placed with other external asset managers (hedge funds, private equity funds, etc.), but there were still some large direct acquisitions, as described below.

2. Company filings have shown that the value of this investment doubled in less than a year. Teck is also "a significant producer of gold, molybdenum and specialty metals, with interests in several oil sands development assets." See the company description found at http://www.teck.com/Generic.aspx?PAGE=About+Us&portalName=tc. One year earlier, in July 2008, Teck had purchased the Fording Canadian Coal Trust, one of the largest suppliers of high-grade coal for making steel. Teck's $14 billion acquisition was financed in part with a $9.8 billion bridge loan that Teck was unable to service once the bottom dropped out of the commodities markets as a result of the financial crisis. When Teck began to falter, the CIC was ready. The CIC began negotiating a $1.5 billion private placement in mid-April 2009. The private placement that closed in July 2009 garnered the CIC a 17.2 percent share of Teck and 6.7 percent of the voting rights as well as a seat on the board as Teck's largest single investor. China Investment Corporation, *Annual Report 2009*, 38; and China Investment Corporation, *Annual Report 2010*, 33. For more information about the CIC's purchase refer to the CIC's press release at http://www.china-inv.cn/cicen/resources/resources_news08.html.

3. China Investment Corporation, *Annual Report 2009*, 38.

4. China Investment Corporation, *Annual Report 2009*, 38.

5. This round of purchases involved the deployment of $35.7 billion. "Of the USD 200 billion in registered capital, slightly over 50% was allocated to global investment. . . . In 2010, CIC invested an additional USD 35.7 billion of its investment capital and became fully invested." China Investment Corporation, *Annual Report 2010*, 9. As was the case earlier, the majority of this deployment was into passive index funds and other third-party asset managers. The direct investments discussed here constitute the most concentrated holdings of the CIC and the most likely causes for strategic concern.

6. Incidentally, the CIC also invested 150 million Canadian dollars for a 7.43 percent stake in Sunshine Oilsands in February 2012. China Investment Corporation, *Annual Report 2011*, 21.

7. The majority of these direct investments were likely funded by the CIC's exited positions, realized gains, and the new $30 billion "injection" reported in December 2011. Given that this additional funding was provided to "enhance its role as a vehicle to diversify foreign exchange investments," it is not surprising to find that the asset mix has shifted to round out the CIC's direct investment holdings from a portfolio diversification perspective. See China Investment Corporation, *Annual Report 2011*, 8.

8. Although the CIC has shown a strong preference for English-speaking destinations, it seemed to be more active in Russia as well. The CIC's May 2012 purchase of just under 5 percent of Polyus Gold for $424.5 million was followed in June by the announcement that the CIC had set up the "Russia-China Investment Fund" in conjunction with the Rus-

sia Direct Investment Fund. In December 2012, the CIC spent $187 million to purchase a 4.58 percent stake in the Moscow Exchange.

9. To the CIC's diplomatic credit, it has gone to great lengths to maintain a passive role in most of its direct holdings. Without a voice in the management and direction of its portfolio companies, however, the CIC stakes are subject to the preferences of others and the CIC investor does not have as much control.

Index